Learning, Development and Education

In the **World Library of Educationalists series**, international experts compile career-long collections of what they judge to be their finest pieces – extracts from books, key articles, salient research findings, major theoretical and practical contributions – so the world can read them in a single manageable volume. Readers will be able to follow the themes and strands and see how their work contributes to the development of the field.

Leaving a promising business career at age 27 to begin his higher education, Knud Illeris exemplifies the true spirit of youth and adult education that has resulted in his work being published in almost 20 countries, including the UK, Germany, China, Korea and Brazil. Knud Illeris' work revolves around the way learning takes place and in some cases does not take place. Split into five parts:

- learning theory
- learning and life course
- special learning issues
- various learning approaches to education
- learning in working life.

Learning, Development and Education: From learning theory to education and practice is arranged thematically and examines learning in theory practice through Illeris' model based on three dimensions of learning and competence development – emotional, cognitive and social, and four types of learning.

In this collection, written over a period of almost twenty years and published in multiple languages, spanning Faroese to Chinese, some of his most important and influential works are chronicled. This compelling overview of Illeris' contribution to educational thinking and theory charts the challenges and obstacles faced by disciplination and selection, and offers a genuine impression and understanding of an almost lifelong engagement with a wide range of topics in the field of learning – an engagement which has been the central area of Illeris' academic life.

Knud Illeris has been Professor of educational research at Roskilde University and of lifelong learning at Aarhus University, Denmark.

World Library of Educationalists series

Other books in the series:

Landmarks in Literacy
The selected works of Frank Smith
Frank Smith

Multiculturalism in Education and Teaching
The selected works of Carl A. Grant
Carl A. Grant

Thinking and Rethinking the University
The selected works of Ronald Barnett
Ronald Barnett

China through the Lens of Comparative Education
The selected works of Ruth Hayhoe
Ruth Hayhoe

Educational Experience as Lived: Knowledge, History, Alterity
The selected works of William F. Pinar
William F. Pinar

Dysconscious Racism, Afrocentric Praxis, and Education for Human Freedom: Through the Years I Keep on Toiling
The selected works of Joyce E. King
Joyce E. King

A Developing Discourse in Music Education
The selected works of Keith Swanwick
Keith Swanwick

Struggles for Equity in Education
The selected works of Mel Ainscow
Mel Ainscow

Faith, Mission and Challenge in Catholic Education
The selected works of Gerald Grace
Gerald Grace

Learning, Development and Education

From learning theory to education and practice

Knud Illeris

LONDON AND NEW YORK

First published 2016
by Routledge
2 Park Square, Milton Park, Abingdon, Oxon OX14 4RN

and by Routledge
711 Third Avenue, New York, NY 10017

Routledge is an imprint of the Taylor & Francis Group, an informa business

© 2016 K. Illeris

The right of Knud Illeris to be identified as author of this work has been asserted by him in accordance with sections 77 and 78 of the Copyright, Designs and Patents Act 1988.

All rights reserved. No part of this book may be reprinted or reproduced or utilised in any form or by any electronic, mechanical, or other means, now known or hereafter invented, including photocopying and recording, or in any information storage or retrieval system, without permission in writing from the publishers.

Trademark notice: Product or corporate names may be trademarks or registered trademarks, and are used only for identification and explanation without intent to infringe.

British Library Cataloguing in Publication Data
A catalogue record for this book is available from the British Library

Library of Congress Cataloging in Publication Data
Names: Illeris, Knud, author.
Title: Learning, development and education : from learning theory to education and practice / Knud Illeris.
Description: New York, NY : Routledge, 2016. | Series: World library of educationalists series | Includes bibliographical references.
Identifiers: LCCN 2015048196| ISBN 9781138658691 (hbk) | ISBN 9781315620565 (ebk)
Subjects: LCSH: Learning. | Continuing education. | Adult learning. | Transformative learning. | Organizational learning.
Classification: LCC LB1060 .I445 2016 | DDC 370.15/23--dc23
LC record available at http://lccn.loc.gov/2015048196

ISBN: 978-1-138-65869-1 (hbk)
ISBN: 978-1-315-62056-5 (ebk)

Typeset in Sabon by
Servis Filmsetting Ltd, Stockport, Cheshire

Printed and bound in the United States of America by
Edwards Brothers Malloy on sustainably sourced paper

CONTENTS

Acknowledgements   vii

Introduction   1

PART I
Learning Theory   7

1. A Comprehensive Understanding of Human Learning   9
2. The Development of a Comprehensive and Coherent Theory of Learning   21
3. Learning in the Competition State: Problems and alternative perspectives   33

PART II
Learning and Life Course   45

4. Lifelong Learning as a Psychological Process   47
5. Learning, Identity and Self-Orientation in Youth   57
6. Adult Learning   74
7. Lifelong Learning and the Low-Skilled   84

PART III
Special Learning Issues   99

8. Learning and Cognition   101
9. Transfer of Learning in the Learning Society   112
10. Adult Learning and Responsibility   124

11.	Adult Education between Emancipation and Control *Annegrethe Ahrenkiel and Knud Illeris*	135
12.	Mislearning, Defence and Resistance	146

PART IV
Various Learning Approaches to Education — 153

13.	The Organisation of Studies at Roskilde University: The concept, practice and problems of project organisation	155
14.	Project Work in University Studies: Background and current issues	159
15.	Learning, Experience and Personal Development	165
16.	Transformative Learning	174
17.	Transformative Learning Re-defined: As changes in elements of the identity	185

PART V
Learning in Working Life — 199

18.	Workplaces and Learning	201
19.	Workplace Learning and Learning Theory	217
20.	The Workplace as a Framework for Learning	231
21.	Workplace Learning as Competence Development	243
	Index	258

ACKNOWLEDGEMENTS

The following articles have been reproduced with the kind permission of the respective journals.

Illeris, K. (2003) Learning, identity and self-orientation in youth. *Nordic Journal of Youth Research (SAGE)*, 11(4), 357–376.
Illeris, K. (2003) Workplace learning and learning theory. *Journal of Workplace Learning*, 15(4), 167–178.
Illeris, K. (2005) Lifelong learning and the low-skilled. *International Journal of Lifelong Education*, 25(1), 15–28.
Illeris, K. (2009) Transfer of learning in the learning society. *International Journal of Lifelong Education*, 28(2), 137–148.
Illeris, K. (2014) Transformative learning re-defined: as changes in elements of the identity. *International Journal of Lifelong Education*, 33(5), 573–586.
Illeris, K. (2015) The development of a comprehensive and coherent theory of learning. *European Journal of Education*, 50(1), 29–40, 2015.

The following chapters have been reproduced with the kind permission of the respective publishers.

Illeris, K. (1998) Adult learning and responsibility. In *Adult Education in a Transforming Society*, 107–125, Copenhagen: Roskilde University Press.
Illeris, K. (1999) Project work in university studies: background and current issues. In *Project Studies – A Late Modern University Reform?*, Copenhagen: Roskilde University Press, 25–32.
Illeris, K. and Ahrenkiel, A. (2000) Adult education between emancipation and control. In *Adult Education in the Perspective of the Learners*, 116–136, Copenhagen: Roskilde University Press.
Illeris, K. (2002) The organisation of studies at Roskilde University: the concept, practice and problems of project organisation. In *Principles of Education and Research*, 2nd edition, Copenhagen: Roskilde University Press.
Illeris, K. (2004) Mislearning, defence and resistance. In *Adult Education and Adult Learning*, 109–118, Copenhagen: Roskilde University Press.
Illeris, K. (2004) The workplace as a framework for learning, In *Learning in Working Life*, 77–89, Copenhagen: Roskilde University Press.
Illeris, K. (2007) Learning, experience and personal development. In *How We Learn*, 125–134, London: Routledge.

Illeris, K. (2009) A comprehensive understanding of human learning. In *Contemporary Theories of Learning*, 7–20, London: Routledge.

Illeris, K. (2009) Lifelong learning as a psychological process. In *The Routledge International Handbook of Lifelong Learning*, 401–410, London: Routledge.

Illeris, K. (2011) Workplaces and learning. In *The SAGE Handbook of Workplace Learning*, 32–45, London: SAGE.

Illeris, K. (2011) Workplace learning as competence development. In *The Fundamentals of Workplace Learning*, 48–63, London: Routledge.

Illeris, K. (2012) Learning and cognition. In *The Routledge International Handbook of Learning*, 18–27, London: Routledge.

Illeris, K. (2014) Learning in the Competition State (translated from Læring i konkurrencestaten, Copenhagen: Samfundslitteratur, 207–223).

Illeris, K. (2015) Adult learning. In *The Routledge Companion to Human Resource Development*, 21–29, London: Routledge.

Illeris, K. (2015) Transformative learning. In *The SAGE Handbook of Learning*, 331–341, London: SAGE.

INTRODUCTION

It is with great pleasure that I have received the invitation from Routledge to make a contribution to the World Library of Educationalists, not least because, as far as I can see, I shall be the first contributor who is not a native English speaker – native English speaking scholars hardly realize how big an advantage it is as a matter of course to master the totally dominating language of the international academic discourse. On the other hand, I have had the advantage of understanding the Scandanavian languages, especially German – and without an insight into German critical psychology and sociology, I would never have been able to develop my theoretical understanding of learning and, especially, barriers to learning.

So I have with enthusiasm thrown myself into the selection of a broad and comprehensive collection of articles and other writings which I think in a satisfactory way may give an impression of my academic work during the past almost 50 years. But also here the language question turns up: Even though my books on project studies and problem-oriented education became bestsellers in Scandinavia in the 1970s, I did not write anything in English until 1986 and my first book in English was published in 2002, after three years' intensive and expensive efforts on translation and finding a publisher, which was actually not a usual academic publisher but the NIACE (National Institute of Adult Continuing Education). Only after this book, *The Three Dimensions of Learning*, had obtained considerable international attention and sales did the doors of Routledge swing wide open for my next book, *How We Learn*, in 2007 – which has by now come out or is in production in languages, that span Chinese to Faroese – and various later books.

This history of my late international career is also part of the reason why my early special areas of academic interest are in the present collection only represented by two rather short texts, whereas all the other texts relate to my work during the latest years. Another reason for this is that my work during this period has increasingly concentrated on the broader and more general topics of youth and adult learning and education, especially on developing the general theory of learning, which as far as I can see is now the most widespread coherent existing learning theory, and the broadest, especially because it includes the topic of barriers to learning, i.e. what happens when intended learning does not come through – which in relation to practice is just as important as what happens when intended or unintended learning takes place.

Part 1 of the five parts of this book is simply called Learning Theory, and for this part I have selected three general, fundamental and relatively new chapters. The first of these, 'A comprehensive understanding of human learning', is an overview of my general learning theoretical understanding and was the opening chapter of a book presenting sixteen *Contemporary Theories of Learning: Learning theorists . . . in their own words* that I edited for Routledge in 2009. This chapter can also be seen as presenting the framework for an understanding of human learning, which is fully developed in my book *How We Learn* and to which all the other chapters can be related, including the figure 'the learning triangle' repeated in various versions in several later chapters.

The second chapter, 'The development of a comprehensive and coherent theory of learning', describes the personal background to my understanding of human learning and how this learning theory was developed, gradually and stepwise, over a period of almost 40 years, where I got the various different sources of inspiration and how I by and by managed to combine them into a coherent construction. This chapter was originally written on request for *The European Journal of Education* (No. 1, 2015) for their 50-volume Jubilee issue.

Finally, Chapter 3 presents a translation of the summary chapter of a Danish book *Learning in the Competition State* that was published in Danish in 2015. This chapter is not so much about learning theory but deals with how contemporary educational policy in many countries during the latest 10–15 years has reformed their educational systems in order to obtain optimal national competitiveness, and how this has proved to be very problematic, because education and learning have been treated as a kind of industrial production, and existing knowledge about how learning and non-learning take place has to a great extent been neglected. As a response to this an educational policy aiming at sustainability on different levels is suggested.

Part 2 of this book is called Learning and Life Course and contains four chapters. The first of these, Chapter 4, 'Lifelong learning as a psychological process', is taken from *The Routledge International Handbook of Lifelong Learning* (2010), and after a short introduction deals with how the character of human learning is changed over a lifetime from uncensored and confident learning in childhood to fundamentally directed by the process of identity building in youth and later, in adulthood becoming increasingly selective and goal oriented, and in mature adulthood even exclusive and conclusive.

In Chapter 5, 'Learning, identity and self-orientation in youth', which was published in the *Nordic Journal of Youth Research*, *Young*, No. 4, 2003, the characteristics of youth learning are further elaborated. Chapter 6, 'Adult learning', which originally was published in *The Routledge Companion to Human Resource Development* (2014), is a similar elaboration of what characterises learning in adulthood. Finally, Chapter 7, 'Lifelong learning and the low-skilled', taken from the *International Journal of Lifelong Education*, No. 1, 2005, deals with the special learning problems of this group of adults with whom I was especially concerned as a consultant to the Danish Ministry of Labour and under the authority of the Danish so-called labour market educational courses from the late 1980s to the end of 2004.

In Part 3, Special Learning Issues, I take up various more specific topics in relation to learning. The first of these, Chapter 8, 'Learning and cognition', explains why the usual identification of learning as a mainly or entirely cognitive matter, especially in connection with schooling and education, is insufficient and false, and all learning also includes emotional/motivational and social dimensions, which, whether they are given attention or not, are always active and of significant importance to learning quality and how learning outcome comes into play in new situations.

In connection with this the concept of 'transfer of learning' is a classic issue of learning psychology, dealing with the fact that sometimes, actually quite often, learning which has taken place in a specific context (e.g. school or educational learning), cannot be recalled or practiced in a different context (e.g. working life or everyday life). This issue is elaborated in Chapter 9, 'Transfer of learning in the learning society' originally published in the *International Journal of Lifelong Education*, No. 2, 2009, and claims that learning transferability is connected to and different in relation to the four different types of learning: cumulation, assimilation, accommodation and transformation.

The next two chapters are both taken from reports from The Adult Education Research Project, 1998–2000, of which I was the leader. Chapter 10 is 'Adult learning and responsibility', and Chapter 11, which I wrote together with Annegrethe Ahrenkiel, is 'Adult education between emancipation and control'. They are both rooted in the view that in democratic countries adults are fundamentally regarded as responsible for their own behaviour and decisions, which also includes their learning and education, and therefore it is both formally and practically important and results in better and deeper learning, when in educational activities they are not regarded and treated as pupils but as independent grown-ups able to control and take responsibility for their own learning. Actually it was probably the most important result of this research project that it demonstrated that in all the various kinds of adult education the most crucial and significant feature for the instructors and the adult learners was to give up traditional school expectations of pupil and teacher roles. Whenever this took place successfully, the learning became much more personal, intense and useful.

Finally, Chapter 12, the last chapter of Part 3, is on learning barriers, 'Mislearning, defence and resistance', and is a slightly changed version of a chapter in my book *Adult Education and Adult Learning*, published by Roskilde University Press in 2004. As already mentioned it is a rather special and very important feature of my theoretical learning understanding that these three kinds of non-learning are quite as important as the understanding of more or less positive learning events and courses.

Part 4 is called Various Learning Approaches to Education and includes five chapters. The first two are about project work or project studies, the type of practical organization of educational practice that was introduced in 1972 at the new university in Roskilde near Copenhagen, where I worked for the following 33 years, and which was partly inspired by an experiment at a teacher training college, which I had observed in previous years and described in detail in a report of more than 500 pages. Chapter 13, which is taken from an official introduction to the *Principles of Education and Research* at Roskilde University from 2002, is titled 'The organization of studies at Roskilde University: the concept, practice and problems of project organisation'. And Chapter 14, which was published in a report from the 25th anniversary conference of the university in 1997, titled Project Studies – a late modern university reform? is a general discussion titled 'Project work in university studies'. It is notable that both of these contributions were made after many years of experience with project education in practice, but the remarkable fact is that all of this was a more or less local and limited Danish endeavour, hardly known outside Scandinavia or described in other languages. Actually, when I talked about our 'project university' at a conference on 'Experiential Learning' in Cape Town in 1996 and later at a conference on 'Transformative Learning' in New York 2003 – in both cases by request and in addition to the official programme – people did not at all know the concept, and I attracted considerably bigger audiences for these presentations than the more traditional contributions.

In Chapter 15, 'Learning, experience and personal development', which is an excerpt from my aforementioned book *How We Learn* (Routledge, 2007), the connection between learning and the design and practice of educational activities is discussed on a much more general level, mainly stressing the importance of being in accordance with the learners' experiential backgrounds, interests and motivations, including what many learners themselves very often do not know or think much about as preconditions, because they – like many teachers and instructors – are used to being focussed on the prescribed learning content and not on what it means to themselves or what they can use it for.

Both of the two last chapters of Part 4 deal with the concept of transformative learning, in which I have taken much interest during the latest 10–15 years, when I had a close connection to Teachers College at Columbia University in New York and where this concept was coined by Jack Mezirow in 1978. Chapter 16, 'Transformative learning', is taken from *The SAGE Handbook of Learning* (2015) and is a general presentation and discussion of this by now rather popular concept – as I see it and understand it – which is necessary to add, because it gradually has become more of a trend than a precise academic concept and practice. And in Chapter 17, which is taken from *The International Journal of Lifelong Education*, No. 5, 2014, and called 'Transformative learning re-defined: as changes in elements of the identity', I go deeper into the relating of transformative learning to the concept of identity, which I find necessary in order to avoid the general popularization and sometimes almost religious celebration of this currently very important concept and kind of learning.

Part 5, the last part of the book, is Learning in Working Life. My interest in this area started some time in the middle of the 1980s due to an application from a group of progressive business people who had some ideas about project organization and were interested in some theoretical support. I found this very challenging, and it later lead to my engagement in the qualification of the low-skilled part of the workforce as mentioned before. I have here selected four contributions, the first of which, Chapter 18, is a general introduction, 'Workplaces and learning', taken from *The SAGE Handbook of Workplace Learning* (2011), and followed by another general introduction, 'Workplace learning and learning theory', Chapter 19, originally an article in the *Journal of Workplace Learning* (No. 4, 2003).

In Chapter 20, which is taken from the book on *Learning in Working Life* (Roskilde University Press, 2004), which I edited and wrote together with the 15 other participants of the Learning Lab Denmark 'Consortium on Workplace Learning', titled 'The workplace as a framework for learning'. Chapter 21, 'Workplace learning as competence development', is a more recent contribution from my book *The Fundamentals of Workplace Learning* (Routledge, 2011) in which I also discuss the concept of competencies, which has become so widespread in latter years but, as I see it, is somewhat problematic and is rather used to legitimate the educational policy of the 'competition states' than to qualify the learning and education of the workforce.

So I hope that this selection of contributions about human learning in theory and practice will provide the reader with a genuine impression and understanding of my almost lifelong engagement with a wide range of topics in the field of learning – an engagement which has been the central area of my academic life, activities and research ever since I, at the age of 27, dropped a promising business career and joined a course at upper secondary school level in order to be matriculated for university studies and experienced it as an awful waste of time, more oriented towards disciplining and selection than towards useful learning and personal development.

PART I

LEARNING THEORY

CHAPTER 1

A COMPREHENSIVE UNDERSTANDING OF HUMAN LEARNING

Already in the 1970s Knud Illeris was well known in Scandinavia for his developing work on project studies in theory and practice. In this work, learning theory was applied, mainly by a combination of Jean Piaget's approach to learning and the so-called 'critical theory' of the German–American Frankfurt School that basically connected Freudian psychology with Marxist sociology. In the 1990s, Illeris returned to his learning theoretical roots, now involving many other theoretical approaches in the general understanding of learning, which was first presented in The Three Dimensions of Learning *and later fully worked out in* How We Learn: Learning and Non-learning in School and Beyond. *The following chapter presents the main ideas of this understanding and is an elaborated version of the presentation Illeris made at a conference in Copenhagen in 2006 when the Danish version of* How We Learn *was launched. The article was published as the opening chapter in* Contemporary Theories of Learning, *Knud Illeris (ed.) 2009.*

Background and basic assumptions

Since the last decades of the nineteenth century, many theories and understandings of learning have been launched. They have had different angles, different epistemological platforms and a very different content. Some of them have been overtaken by new knowledge and new standards, but in general we have today a picture of a great variety of learning theoretical approaches and constructions, which are more-or-less compatible and more-or-less competitive on the global academic market. The basic idea of the approach to learning presented in this chapter is to build on a wide selection of the best of these constructions, add new insights and perspectives and in this way develop an overall understanding or framework, which can offer a general and up-to-date overview of the field.

Learning can broadly be defined as *any process that in living organisms leads to permanent capacity change and which is not solely due to biological maturation or ageing* (Illeris 2007, p. 3). I have deliberately chosen this very open formulation because the concept of learning includes a very extensive and complicated set of processes, and a comprehensive understanding is not only a matter of the nature of the learning process itself. It must also include all the conditions that influence and are influenced by this process. Figure 1.1 shows the main areas which are involved and the structure of their mutual connections.

On the top I have placed the basis of the learning theory, i.e. the areas of knowledge and understanding which, in my opinion, must underlie the development of a

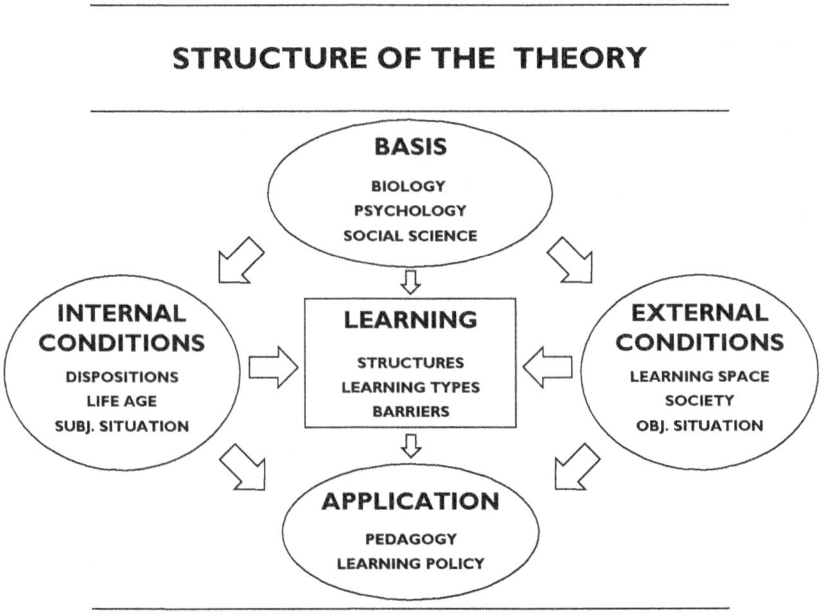

STRUCTURE OF THE THEORY

BASIS
BIOLOGY
PSYCHOLOGY
SOCIAL SCIENCE

INTERNAL CONDITIONS
DISPOSITIONS
LIFE AGE
SUBJ. SITUATION

LEARNING
STRUCTURES
LEARNING TYPES
BARRIERS

EXTERNAL CONDITIONS
LEARNING SPACE
SOCIETY
OBJ. SITUATION

APPLICATION
PEDAGOGY
LEARNING POLICY

Figure 1.1 The main areas of the understanding of learning.

comprehensive and coherent theory construction. These include all the psychological, biological and social conditions which are involved in any learning. Under this is the central box depicting learning itself, including its processes and dimensions, different learning types and learning barriers, which to me are the central elements of the understanding of learning. Further there are the specific internal and external conditions which are not only influencing but also directly involved in learning. And finally, the possible applications of learning are also involved. I shall now go through these five areas and emphasise some of the most important features of each of them.

The two basic processes and the three dimensions of learning

The first important condition to realise is that all learning implies the integration of two very different processes, namely an external interaction process between the learner and his or her social, cultural or material environment, and an internal psychological process of elaboration and acquisition.

Many learning theories deal only with one of these processes, which of course does not mean that they are wrong or worthless, as both processes can be studied separately. However, it does mean that they do not cover the whole field of learning. This may, for instance, be said of traditional behaviourist and cognitive learning theories focusing only on the internal psychological process. It can equally be said of certain modern social learning theories which – sometimes in explicit opposition to this – draw attention to the external interaction process alone. However, it seems evident that both processes must be actively involved if any learning is to take place.

When constructing my model of the field of learning (Figure 1.2), I started by depicting the external interaction process as a vertical double arrow between the

A comprehensive understanding of human learning 11

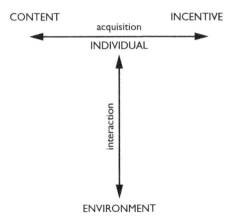

Figure 1.2 The fundamental processes of learning.

environment, which is the general basis and therefore placed at the bottom, and the individual, who is the specific learner and therefore placed at the top.

Next I added the psychological acquisition process as another double arrow. It is an internal process of the learner and must therefore be placed at the top pole of the interaction process. Further, it is a process of integrated interplay between two equal psychological functions involved in any learning, namely the function of managing the learning content and the incentive function of providing and directing the necessary mental energy that runs the process. Thus the double arrow of the acquisition process is placed horizontally at the top of the interaction process and between the poles of content and incentive – and it should be emphasised that the double arrow means that these two functions are always involved and usually in an integrated way.

As can be seen, the two double arrows can now span out a triangular field between three angles. These three angles depict three spheres or dimensions of learning, and it is the core claim of the understanding that all learning will always involve these three dimensions.

The content dimension concerns what is learned. This is usually described as knowledge and skills, but also many other things such as opinions, insight, meaning, attitudes, values, ways of behaviour, methods, strategies, etc. may be involved as learning content and contribute to building up the understanding and the capacity of the learner. The endeavour of the learner is to construct *meaning* and *ability* to deal with the challenges of practical life and thereby an overall personal *functionality* is developed.

The incentive dimension provides and directs the mental energy that is necessary for the learning process to take place. It comprises such elements as feelings, emotions, motivation and volition. Its ultimate function is to secure the continuous *mental balance* of the learner and thereby it simultaneously develops a personal *sensitivity*.

These two dimensions are always initiated by impulses from the interaction processes and integrated in the internal process of elaboration and acquisition. Therefore, the learning content is, so to speak, always 'obsessed' with the incentives at stake – e.g. whether the learning is driven by desire, interest, necessity or compulsion. Correspondingly, the incentives are always influenced by the content, e.g. new information can change the incentive condition. Many psychologists have

12 *A comprehensive understanding of human learning*

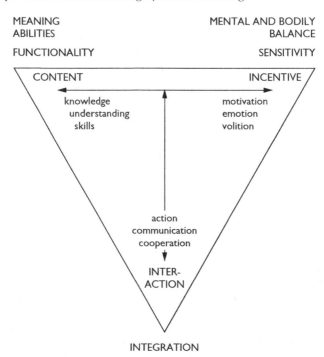

Figure 1.3 The three dimensions of learning and competence development.

been aware of this close connection between what has usually been termed the cognitive and the emotional (e.g. Vygotsky 1978; Furth 1987), and recently advanced neurology has proven that both areas are always involved in the learning process, unless in cases of very severe brain damage (Damasio 1994).

The interaction dimension provides the impulses that initiate the learning process. This may take place as perception, transmission, experience, imitation, activity, participation, etc. (Illeris 2007, pp. 100ff.). It serves the personal *integration* in communities and society and thereby also builds up the *sociality* of the learner. However, this building up necessarily takes place through the two other dimensions.

Thus the triangle depicts what may be described as the tension field of learning in general and of any specific learning event or learning process as stretched out between the development of functionality, sensibility and sociality – which are also the general components of what we term competencies.

It is also important to mention that each dimension includes a mental as well as a bodily side. Actually, learning begins with the body and takes place through the brain, which is also part of the body, and only gradually is the mental side separated out as a specific but never independent area or function (Piaget 1952).

An example from everyday school life

In order to illustrate how the model may be understood and used, I shall take an everyday example from ordinary school life (which does not mean that the model only deals with school learning).

During a chemistry lesson in the classroom, a teacher is explaining a chemical process. The students are supposed to be listening and perhaps asking questions to be sure that they have understood the explanation correctly. The students are thus involved in an interaction process. But at the same time, they are supposed to take in or to learn what the teacher is teaching, i.e. psychologically to relate what is taught to what they should already have learned. The result should be that they are able to remember what they have been taught and, under certain conditions, to reproduce it, apply it and involve it in further learning.

But sometimes, or for some students, the learning process does not take place as intended, and mistakes or derailing may occur in many different ways. Perhaps the interaction does not function because the teacher's explanation is not good enough or is even incoherent, or there may be disturbances in the situation. If so, the explanation will only be picked up partially or incorrectly, and the learning result will be insufficient. But the students' acquisition process may also be inadequate, for instance because of a lack of concentration, and this will also lead to deterioration in the learning result. Or there may be errors or insufficiencies in the prior learning of some students, making them unable to understand the teacher's explanation and thereby also to learn what is being taught. Much of this indicates that acquisition is not only a cognitive matter. There is also another area or function involved concerning the students' attitudes to the intended learning: their interests and mobilisation of mental energy, i.e. the incentive dimension.

In a school situation, focus is usually on the learning content; in the case described it is on the students' understanding of the nature of the chemical process concerned. However, the incentive function is also still crucial, i.e. how the situation is experienced, what sort of feelings and motivations are involved, and thus the nature and the strength of the mental energy that is mobilised. The value and durability of the learning result is closely related to the incentive dimension of the learning process.

Further, both the content and the incentive are crucially dependent on the interaction process between the learner and the social, societal, cultural and material environment. If the interaction in the chemistry lesson is not adequate and acceptable to the students, the learning will suffer, or something quite different may be learned, for instance a negative impression of the teacher, of some other students, of the subject or of the school situation in general.

The four types of learning

What has been outlined in the triangle model and the example above is a concept of learning which is basically constructivist in nature, i.e. it is assumed that the learner him- or herself actively builds up or construes his/her learning as mental structures. These structures exist in the brain as dispositions that are usually described by a psychological metaphor as *mental schemes*. This means that there must in the brain be some organisation of the learning outcomes since we, when becoming aware of something – a person, a problem, a topic, etc. – in fractions of a second are able to recall what we subjectively and usually unconsciously define as relevant knowledge, understanding, attitudes, reactions and the like. But this organisation is in no way a kind of archive, and it is not possible to find the different elements at specific positions in the brain. It has the nature of what brain researchers call 'engrams', which are traces of circuits between some of the billions of neurons that have been active at earlier occasions and therefore are likely to be revived, perhaps with slightly different courses because of the impact of new experiences or understandings.

However, in order to deal systematically with this, the concept of schemes is used for what we subjectively tend to classify as belonging to a specific topic or theme and therefore mentally connect and are inclined to recall in relation to situations that we relate to that topic or theme. This especially applies to the content dimension, whereas in the incentive and interaction dimensions we would rather speak of *mental patterns*. But the background is similar in that motivations, emotions or ways of communication tend to be organised so that they can be revived when we are oriented towards situations that 'remind' us of earlier situations when they have been active.

In relation to learning, the crucial thing is that new impulses can be included in the mental organisation in various ways, and on this basis it is possible to distinguish between four different types of learning which are activated in different contexts, imply different kinds of learning results and require more or less energy. (This is an elaboration of the concept of learning originally developed by Jean Piaget, e.g. Piaget 1952; Flavell 1963.)

When a scheme or pattern is established, it is a case of *cumulative* or mechanical learning. This type of learning is characterised by being an isolated formation, something new that is not a part of anything else. Therefore, cumulative learning is most frequent during the first years of life, but later occurs only in special situations where one must learn something with no context of meaning or personal significance, for example a PIN code. The learning result is characterised by a type of automation that means that it can only be recalled and applied in situations mentally similar to the learning context. It is mainly this type of learning which is involved in the training of animals and which is therefore also referred to as conditioning in behaviourist psychology.

By far the most common type of learning is termed *assimilative* or learning by addition, meaning that the new element is linked as an addition to a scheme or pattern that is already established. One typical example could be learning in school subjects that are usually built up by means of constant additions to what has already been learned, but assimilative learning also takes place in all contexts where one gradually develops one's capacities. The results of learning are characterised by being linked to the scheme or pattern in question in such a manner that it is relatively easy to recall and apply them when one is mentally oriented towards the field in question, for example a school subject, while they may be hard to access in other contexts. This is why problems are frequently experienced in applying knowledge from a school subject to other subjects or in contexts outside of school (Illeris 2009).

However, in some cases, situations occur where something takes place that is difficult to immediately relate to any existing scheme or pattern. This is experienced as something one cannot really understand or relate to. But if it seems important or interesting, if it is something one is determined to acquire, this can take place by means of *accommodative* or transcendent learning. This type of learning implies that one breaks down (parts of) an existing scheme and transforms it so that the new situation can be linked in. Thus one both relinquishes and reconstructs something, and this can be experienced as demanding or even painful, because it is something that requires a strong supply of mental energy. One must cross existing limitations and understand or accept something that is significantly new or different, and this is much more demanding than just adding a new element to an already existing scheme or pattern. In return, the results of such learning are characterised by the fact that they can be recalled and applied in many different, relevant contexts. It is typically experienced as having understood or got hold of something which one really has internalised.

Finally, over the last few decades it has been pointed out that in special situations there is also a far-reaching type of learning that has been variously described as significant (Rogers 1951, 1969), expansive (Engeström 1987), transitional (Alheit 1994) or transformative learning (Mezirow 1991). This learning implies what could be termed personality changes, or changes in the organisation of the self, and is characterised by simultaneous restructuring of a whole cluster of schemes and patterns in all of the three learning dimensions – a break of orientation that typically occurs as the result of a crisis-like situation caused by challenges experienced as urgent and unavoidable, making it necessary to change oneself in order to get any further. Transformative learning is thus both profound and extensive, it demands a lot of mental energy and when accomplished it can often be experienced physically, typically as a feeling of relief or relaxation.

As has been demonstrated, the four types of learning are widely different in scope and nature, and they also occur – or are activated by learners – in very different situations and connections. Whereas cumulative learning is most important in early childhood, and transformative learning is a very demanding process that changes the very personality or identity and occurs only in very special situations of profound significance for the learner, assimilation and accommodation are, as described by Piaget, the two types of learning that characterise general, sound and normal everyday learning. Many other learning theorists also point to two such types of learning; for example, Chris Argyris and Donald Schön have coined the well-known concepts of single and double loop learning (Argyris 1992; Argyris and Schön 1996), Per-Erik Ellström (2001) speaks about adaptation-oriented and development-oriented learning, and also Lev Vygotsky's idea (1978) of transition into the 'zone of proximal development' may be seen as a parallel to accommodative learning.

However, ordinary discussions of learning and the design of many educational and school activities are concentrated on and often only aimed at assimilative learning, as this is the sort of learning that the usual understanding of the concept of learning is about. But today this understanding is obviously insufficient, and the much-demanded generic competencies can only be built up by a combination of assimilative, accommodative and, eventually, transformative learning processes.

Barriers to learning

Another problem is that much intended learning does not take place or is incomplete or distorted. In schools, in education, at workplaces and in many other situations, very often people do not learn what they could learn or what they are supposed to learn. Therefore I find it important also to discuss briefly what happens in such cases.

Of course, it cannot be avoided that we all sometimes learn something that is wrong (cf. Mager 1961) or something that is inadequate for us in some way or another. In the first instance, this concerns matters such as mislearning, which can be due to misunderstandings, lack of concentration, insufficient prior learning and the like. This may be annoying and in some cases unlucky, but simple mislearning due to 'practical' reasons is not a matter of great interest to learning theory as such mislearning can usually be corrected rather easily, if necessary.

However, today much non-learning and mislearning are not so simple, but have a background in some general conditions that modern society creates, and in some respects the investigation and understanding of such processes are definitely as important as more traditional learning theory to understand what is happening and to cope with it in practice.

The central point is that in our complex late-modern society, what Freud called *defence mechanisms* – which are active in specific personal connections (cf. Anna Freud 1942) – must necessarily be generalised and take more systematised forms because nobody can manage to remain open to the gigantic volumes and impact of influences we are all constantly faced with.

This is why today people develop a kind of semi-automatic sorting mechanism vis-à-vis the many influences, or what the German social psychologist Thomas Leithäuser (1976) has analysed and described as an *everyday consciousness*. This functions in the way that one develops some general pre-understandings within certain thematic areas, and when one meets with influences within such an area, these pre-understandings are activated so that if elements in the influences do not correspond to the pre-understandings, they are either rejected or distorted to make them agree. In both cases, this results in no new learning but, on the contrary, often the cementing of the already-existing understanding.

Thus, through everyday consciousness we control our own learning and non-learning in a manner that seldom involves any direct positioning while simultaneously involving a massive defence of the already-acquired understandings and, in the final analysis, our very identity. (There are, of course, also areas and situations where our positioning takes place in a more target-oriented manner, consciously and flexibly.)

However, not only the volume but also the kind of influence can be overwhelming. Not least, on television we are faced every day with so much cruelty, wickedness and similar negative impact that it is absolutely impossible to really take it in – and people who cannot protect themselves from this are doomed to end up in some kind of psychological breakdown. Other new forms of similar overloading are caused by the endless changes and reorganisations many people experience at their workplaces, social institutions, etc. or by the helplessness that can be felt when consequences of the decisions of those in power encroach on one's life situation and possibilities.

In the most important cases, for instance when a change to a basically new situation in a certain life area must be overcome, most people react by mobilising a genuine *identity defence* which demands very hard work of a more-or-less therapeutic character to break through, usually by a transformative learning process. This happens typically in relation to a sudden situation of unemployment or other fundamental changes in the work situation, divorce, death of closely related persons or the like, and it is worth realising that such situations happen much more frequently in the modern globalised market society of today than just a generation ago.

Another very common form of defence is *ambivalence*, meaning that in a certain situation or connection one is both wanting and not wanting to learn or do something. A typical example is that people who unwillingly and without any personal fault have become unemployed on the one hand know very well that they must engage themselves in some retraining or re-education, and on the other hand strongly wish that this was not the case. So they go or are sent to some courses but it is difficult for them to concentrate on the learning and they use any possible excuse to escape, mentally or physically.

In all such defence situations, learning is obstructed, hindered, derailed or distorted if it is not possible for the learner to break through the defence, and the task of a teacher or instructor will often be to support and encourage such a breakthrough before more goal-directed and constructive training or education can take place. But teachers are usually not trained for such functions, although they quite frequently are necessary if the intended learning shall be promoted.

Another psychological mechanism which may block or distort relevant learning is *mental resistance*. This is not, in itself, so very time-specific, as all human beings in any society will experience situations where what they try to accomplish cannot be carried through, and if they cannot understand or accept the barriers they will naturally react with some sort of resistance.

In practice it is sometimes quite difficult to distinguish between non-learning caused by defence and non-learning caused by resistance. However, psychologically there is a great and important difference. Whereas the defence mechanisms exist prior to the learning situation and function reactively, resistance is caused by the learning situation itself as an active response. Thus resistance contains a strong mental mobilisation and therefore also a strong learning potential, especially for accommodative and even transformative learning. Often when one does not just accept something, the possibility of learning something significantly new emerges. And most great steps forward in the development of mankind and society have taken place when someone did not accept a given truth or way of doing or understanding things.

In everyday life, resistance is also a most important source of transcendent learning, although it may be both inconvenient and annoying, not least for teachers. In any event, today it should be a central qualification of teachers to be able to cope with and even inspire mental resistance, as precisely such personal competencies which are so much in demand – for example, independence, responsibility, flexibility and creativity – are likely to be developed in this way. This is why conflict or dilemma raising may be taken in as effective but demanding techniques in some particularly challenging educational situations.

Internal and external learning conditions

What has been discussed in the above – the processes, dimensions, types and barriers of learning – I regard as features which should be included in any learning theory that aims at covering the whole field of the concept. However, there are also other issues that influence learning without being directly involved in learning as such and thus can be termed the conditions of learning. These issues are also taken up in my book *How We Learn* (Illeris 2007), but in this article I shall only shortly indicate what they are about.

The internal conditions of learning are features of or in the learner that influence learning possibilities and are involved in the learning processes. *Intelligence* is supposed to be a measure of the general ability to learn, but it has always been disputed whether or not a general and measurable instance of this kind exists, and there is certainly not a general agreement about its definition. Since 1983, American psychologist Howard Gardner (1983, 1993, 1999) has claimed that there are several independent intelligences – a view which to some extent corresponds to the understanding of learning presented here because it includes not only cognitive but also emotional and social abilities. A somewhat similar concept is about individual *learning styles*, but the nature and existence of these still seem to be more an open question. In contrast to these general measures, it is obvious that the more specific individual features of gender and life age to some degree influence the learning possibilities.

The external conditions of learning are features outside the learner that influence learning possibilities and are involved in the learning processes. These can roughly be divided into features of the immediate learning situation and learning space and more general cultural and societal conditions. The kind of learning space makes up for differences between everyday learning, school learning, workplace learning, net-based learning, interest-based learning, etc. and for difficulties in applying learning outcomes across the borders of these spaces – the so-called 'transfer problem' of learning (Eraut 1994; Illeris et al. 2004; Illeris 2009). General societal conditions are dependent on time and place: obviously the learning possibilities are much more wide-ranging today than a century ago and they also differ between the countries and cultures of today.

Finally, some important questions about the use and applicability of learning theory, especially in the areas of educational practice and policy, are also briefly discussed in the book. Some very common misunderstandings in these areas are pointed out, as well as some typical connections between different understandings of learning, different schools of pedagogy and different fundamental assumptions of learning policy. In the last chapter, the book concludes by mapping the most important understandings and theorists of learning in relation to the learning triangle shown in Figure 1.3.

Conclusion

The general conclusion is that learning is a very complicated matter, and analyses, programmes and discussions of learning must consider the whole field if they are to be adequate and reliable. This implies, for instance, that all three learning dimensions must be taken into account, that the question of relevant learning types must be included, that possible defence or resistance must be considered and that internal as well as external learning conditions must also be dealt with. This is, of course, a very wide-ranging demand. To word it differently, it could be said that if for some reason it is not possible or appropriate to include all these areas, it must be clear that the situation or process has not been fully covered, and an open question will remain as to what happens in the areas that are not discussed.

I shall round off by illustrating this more concretely through two examples from my own research and practice.

The first example has to do with youth education. Many Western countries have a high ambition to the effect that all or the great majority of young people should complete some academically or practically qualifying post-16 education programme. The goal of the Danish government is for 95 per cent to receive such qualifications, but although 95 per cent commence a programme, less than 80 per cent complete it.

This, of course, has been the subject of a great deal of research, debate, reforms, etc. but with almost no or even negative effect. From a learning point of view, it would seem not to have been fully realised that today young people of this age are highly engaged in a process of personal identity development, which is an absolute necessity to be able to navigate in the late-modern, globalised market society. Therefore, young people fundamentally meet all learning initiatives – consciously or unconsciously – with such questions as: What does this mean *to me?* or What can *I* use this for? – implying that it is only worth paying attention to if it is subjectively accepted as a usable contribution to the present demands of the identity process. And the premises of this judgement lie equally in all three learning dimensions, i.e. the programme offered must not only have an acceptable, interesting and challenging content, it must also contribute to an acceptable positioning in relation to contemporary trends on the youth lifestyle market, and it must be organised in ways and by teachers or other persons who are in harmony with the personal needs of the young learners. One may think that such demands are not relevant or acceptable, and many people in the educational field are of this opinion, but the inevitable consequence will then be a continued high drop-out rate (see e.g. Illeris 2003, 2007).

The second example is about retraining of low-skilled workers who against their will have become unemployed – which is a very frequent state of affairs in today's society. These adults are very often referred to various practical courses to acquire a basis for employment in a new trade where it is possible to get a job. But the process leading to this has been experienced not as guidance (as it is officially called) but as placement. Furthermore, even when the person in question realises that the training may lead to a return to the labour market, which is usually a very strong wish, their identity is tied to their former trade and a strong defence blocks the engagement in new learning. If the guidance received had made time for personal reflection and participation in the decision, this defence could have been overcome. When asked, the great majority of people in this situation answer that they would probably have chosen the same course, but they had not been given the opportunity to make the mental switch before the course. Now they are forced to undergo a demanding transformative learning process at the same time as they are expected to acquire a great many new practical qualifications (see e.g. Illeris 2006).

In learning terms, in both of these examples a lot of resources are invested in endeavours that have little or no chance of success because the considerations of the 'system' or the authorities have not included an adequate and realistic analysis of the learning situation.

References

Alheit, Peter (1994): The 'Biographical Question' as a Challenge to Adult Education. *International Review of Education*, 40(3/5), pp. 283–98.
Argyris, Chris (1992): *On Organizational Learning*. Cambridge, MA: Blackwell.
Argyris, Chris and Schön, Donald A. (1996): *Organizational Learning II – Theory, Method, and Practice*. Reading, MA: Addison-Wesley.
Damasio, Antonio R. (1994): *Descartes' Error: Emotion, Reason and the Human Brain*. New York: Grosset/Putnam.
Ellström, Per-Erik (2001): Integrating Learning and Work: Conceptual Issues and Critical Conditions. *Human Resource Development Quarterly*, 12(4), pp. 421–35.
Engeström, Yrjö (1987): *Learning by Expanding: An Activity-Theoretical Approach to Developmental Research*. Helsinki: Orienta-Kunsultit.
Eraut, Michael (1994): *Developing Professional Knowledge and Competence*. London: Falmer.
Flavell, John H. (1963): *The Developmental Psychology of Jean Piaget*. New York: Van Nostrand.
Freud, Anna (1942): *The Ego and the Mechanisms of Defence*. London: Hogarth Press.
Furth, Hans G. (1987): *Knowledge As Desire: An Essay on Freud and Piaget*. New York: Columbia University Press.
Gardner, Howard (1983): *Frames of Mind: The Theory of Multiple Intelligences*. New York: Basic Books.
Gardner, Howard (1993): *Multiple Intelligences: The Theory in Practice*. New York: Basic Books.
Gardner, Howard (1999): *Intelligence Reframed: Multiple Intelligences for the 21st Century*. New York: Basic Books.
Illeris, Knud (2003): Learning, Identity and Self-Orientation in Youth. *Young – Nordic Journal of Youth Research*, 11(4), pp. 357–76.

Illeris, Knud (2006): Lifelong Learning and the Low-Skilled. *International Journal of Lifelong Education*, 25(1), pp. 15–28.

Illeris, Knud (2007): *How We Learn: Learning and Non-learning in School and Beyond*. London/New York: Routledge.

Illeris, Knud (2009): Transfer of Learning in the Learning Society. *International Journal of Lifelong Education*, 28(2), pp. 137–148.

Illeris, Knud et al. (2004): *Learning in Working Life*. Copenhagen: Roskilde University Press.

Leithäuser, Thomas (1976): *Formen des Alltagsbewusstseins* [The Forms of Everyday Consciousness]. Frankfurt a.M.: Campus.

Mager, Robert F. (1961): On the Sequencing of Instructional Content. *Psychological Reports*, 9, pp. 405–13.

Mezirow, Jack (1991): *Transformative Dimensions of Adult Learning*. San Francisco: Jossey-Bass.

Piaget, Jean (1952 [1936]): *The Origins of Intelligence in Children*. New York: International Universities Press.

Rogers, Carl R. (1951): *Client-Centered Therapy*. Boston: Houghton Mifflin.

Rogers, Carl R. (1969): *Freedom to Learn: A View of What Education Might Become*. Columbus, OH: Charles E. Merrill.

Vygotsky, Lev S. (1978): *Mind in Society: The Development of Higher Psychological Processes*. Cambridge, MA: Harvard University Press.

CHAPTER 2

THE DEVELOPMENT OF A COMPREHENSIVE AND COHERENT THEORY OF LEARNING

Introduction

How does human learning function? And what happens when intended learning fails or becomes distorted? I have been working intensively on these questions since the late 1960s. In 2007, I published 'How We Learn — Learning and non-learning in school and beyond' (Illeris, 2007 [2006]) which has now been published, fully or partly, in 17 languages and has sold over 100,000 copies. In this book, I outline the construction and main elements of a comprehensive and coherent learning theory, based on extensive studies of international literature on the topic and practical research and work on learning activities from childhood to adulthood in schooling, education and working life. In the following, I shall try to recall how this theory was gradually built up in various publications, but, first, I shall outline very briefly its main features.

The central element is the *learning triangle*, which depicts the superior *structure* of all human learning:

Figure 2.1 shows that all learning involves two kinds of processes, shown as double arrows. The vertical double arrow is the *interaction* between the learner and the environment, which initiates and supplies the learning input. The horizontal double arrow is the internal *acquisition* process, which includes the learning *content* and the learning *incentive*. The content may be any kind of human capacity, such as knowledge, skills, attitudes, understandings, beliefs, behaviour, competencies, etc. The incentive is the mobilisation of mental energy to drive the process, i.e. the motivations, emotions and volition involved (modern brain research has estimated that we spend on average about 20% of our energy on mental processes). It is a central understanding that the content and the incentive of the acquisition process always function in an integrated and inseparable way (as emphasised by modern brain research, e.g. Damasio 1994). So all learning includes three dimensions: the content, the incentive, and the interaction. No learning process can be fully understood without considering all three dimensions.

Furthermore, the learning theory distinguishes between two superior kinds of learning and four learning types. Learning as addition includes *cumulation*: starting a new mental scheme, and *assimilation*: adding new elements to existing schemes. Learning as reconstruction includes *accommodation*: changing elements of schemes, and *transformation*: changing elements of the identity (which involves a multitude of schemes). These learning types refer to the character of the acquisition process.

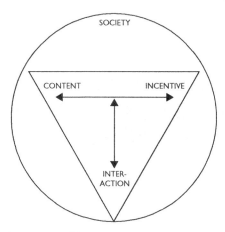

Figure 2.1 The three dimensions of learn.

The acquisition itself always involves new impulses being added to one or more existing schemes (or in the case of cumulation to existing dispositions) so that both the existing schemes and the new impulses are influenced or changed. This is why the same impulses in collective situations such as teaching may and usually do involve different learning outcomes for each of the learners. Or, as formulated by the American learning psychologist, David Ausuble: '*The most important single factor influencing learning is what the learner already knows*' (Ausuble, 1968, p. vi).

The third main area of the theory is learning barriers or what happens when intended learning is not understood or is understood in an insufficient or distorted way. In this area, there are three categories which are mainly related to each of the three learning dimensions, but with a strong tendency to merge: *Mislearning* is mainly related to the content dimension and includes misunderstandings, lack of concentration, lack of relevant conditions or prior learning, unclear communication, etc. *Learning defence* is mainly related to the incentive dimension and includes rejected or distorted learning, due to what Freud termed defence mechanisms, or conflicting learning, due to ambivalence or the like. Finally, *learning resistance* is mainly related to the interaction dimension and includes learning which is unwanted or contrary to the learner's values, preferences, understandings, etc. In addition, the theory involves various other areas, the most important of which are the learners' personal dispositions and preconditions, learning at different ages, the influence of different kinds of learning spaces, and the influence of the general conditions of society.

I shall try to explain how this theory was gradually developed over a period of almost 50 years.

As the enormous capacity to learn is a central feature of what makes human beings superior to all other species, the development of a theory of human learning is necessarily very complex and extensive. Therefore a review of how my theory was developed must include an unravelling of my various experiences, influences, ideas and considerations and may seem a little self-centred. However, it can also be read as an account of how combining many different contributions, finding their essential values, judging them and elaborating them critically in a general perspective and commitment — the so-called and often criticised eclectic type of approach — can produce a coherent whole, which is certainly not the one and only truth, but a structure and overview that can be used and can help to grasp and handle a rather confusing and complex field of reality.

How it all started

At the age of 27, I chose to break off a promising career in the travel business. I wanted to go to university, but first had to take a two-year course at secondary school level to pass the matriculation. I was extremely motivated because I expected to learn more about the basic reasons for topical cultural and social problems, but I was very quickly greatly disappointed. First, I experienced an awful waste of time. I was used to concentrated work all day, but now I had to sit passively in a classroom and be active for only a few minutes in each lesson. Then, I began to wonder who had decided what we should learn and why. Most of it seemed rather unimportant to me, there was very little about the functions of society and how they related to peoples' lives, and absolutely no connection to the more critical and theoretical ideas which emerged at that time. Only gradually, as many of the other students dropped out, did I realise that the purpose of the course was not so much about learning and an introduction to current societal issues as about adaptation and selection in relation to the dominating power structures and social order. This led to my idea that, by finding out how learning functions, one could obtain a useful tool to reorganise schooling and education in ways which could be less repressive and more appropriate for the learners.

From behaviourism to Piaget and Rogers

Having passed the matriculation, I started to study psychology at Copenhagen University in 1968. But this too was a great disappointment, apart from a very inspiring study environment after the student revolt in the spring term and a student-directed introductory course. The prescribed book on cognitive and learning psychology was an American whopper, totally dominated by a behaviourist approach which was so far away from learning in everyday life and education that I found it useless for my endeavour. A new Danish book on the subject was not much better, although it had a few pages on German Gestalt psychology, including learning by problem-solving, which made it clear to me that learning could not be investigated and understood independently of the mental state of the learner as an individual agent.

However, I soon discovered that other people dealing with learning had similar frustrations and had found different approaches. For example, many preschool and primary school teachers related to more progressive pedagogical sources such as John Dewey who was well-known in Danish educational circles. Furthermore, in a more direct relation to learning psychology, some of the older students were attracted by Carl Rogers' ideas of student-centred education and significant learning (Rogers, 1961; 1969) and a group of younger educational researchers at the Danish Pedagogical Institute focused on the work of Jean Piaget and had some of his publications translated into Danish (Piaget, 1952 [1936]; 1967 [1964]). One of these, Thomas Nissen, had even developed Piaget's understanding further on two important points: first, he had added a new learning type called cumulation to Piaget's concepts of assimilation and accommodation. This is the type of learning whereby a new learning scheme is launched and thus forms a kind of bridge to the simple kinds of learning studied by behaviourism. At the same time, it shows the limited corner of human learning of this approach. Second, Thomas Nissen found Piaget's concept of equilibrium between assimilation and accommodation too tight, and he demonstrated how children alternated between assimilatively- and accommodatively-dominated periods in their learning (Illeris, 2007, p. 150). I also discovered some rather striking similarities between Rogers' description of the course of significant learning events and Nissen's description of important accommodations. This was my very first step towards the development of a broader understanding of learning because Rogers' very open and visionary approach was linked to Piaget's very thorough and detailed work.

Problem orientation and participant direction

My first written work was a detailed draft of a new psychology curriculum at the university, based on learning theory, supplemented by some motivational considerations. This attracted a great deal of attention but never led to any changes.

The next step for me was to observe a one-year experimental course at a teacher training college in which the three subjects of psychology, didactics and pedagogy were merged and dealt with in group projects with the teachers acting as supervisors. In addition to a detailed report, this led to my dissertation on 'Problem Orientation and Participant Direction' as the fundamental principles of schooling and education (the participants being students, teachers and other directly involved persons), and to a 'junior lectureship' at the newly-created Roskilde University Centre, where the dominant study activities should be interdisciplinary project work in self-directing study groups.

In the dissertation, my approach to learning was combined with the contemporary German qualification theory, which claimed that, in late modernity, traditional qualifications such as knowledge, skills and adaptation had to be supplemented by innovative qualifications (the term 'qualifications' was used rather like the term 'competencies' today, and 'innovative qualifications' were flexibility, imagination, inventiveness, ingenuity, etc.). In continuation of this, my central idea was that such qualifications were mainly developed through accommodative learning, because this involves reconstructions and new ideas, and that such learning in educational practice is mainly supported and provided by problem-oriented and participant-directed learning activities. A revised version of this dissertation was published in 1974 and immediately became the 'Bible' of progressive schooling, education and teacher training in Denmark and also to some extent in Sweden and Norway.

The pedagogy of counter-qualification

In the following years, in addition to the supervision of study groups, I was engaged as the leader of a project in youth vocational training which was to support 'general' qualification and personal development, together with professional education. Concerning theory, I was attracted by the Frankfurt School which tried to combine Marxist understandings of society with Freudian understandings of the individual. A branch of this School at the University of Hannover, which included researchers such as Oskar Negt, Thomas Leithäuser and Thomas Ziehe, was engaged with schooling and education and was generally in line with my approach and thereby in many ways able to support my understanding. The central idea was that genuine learning implied a subjective and positive connection between the learner's objective interests and subjective motivation and the learning content, which always includes a cognitive, an emotional and a social dimension.

In 1981, I published a new book, 'The Pedagogy of Counter-Qualification'. A more precise title would have been about double-qualification, as the central claim was that people had to be educated to function appropriately in present society and also to lead this society in a more democratic and social direction. But I chose the term 'counter-qualification', probably because all kinds of 'counter-concepts' were very popular at that time. Apart from this, the most important difference with the previous book was an extension and clarification of the social and societal argumentation in relation to the basic structure and practice of capitalism.

The most important theoretical addition was my understanding of psychological barriers to learning, mainly inspired by the concept of everyday consciousness which Leithäuser had adopted from the French philosopher Henri Lefebvre (Leithäuser, 1976). The main cause for such barriers is that we all accumulate so much information that our brain is unable to process it all. But very often, and especially in relation to more or less enforced learning in schools and education, we also reject learning or only learn superficially because we do not see it as being of any use or importance to us. However, in the cases of active resistance to learning, there may often be a strong impulse towards alternative learning. When I asked my students when they had learned something which was really important to them, about 2/3 or 3/4 referred to cases of learning resistance: it was when someone tried to persuade me to do this or that that I realised I would not do it but, on the contrary, follow a quite different track!

New inspiration

After this, I was, for many years, inspired by practice experience in youth and adult education. This helped me to divide my understanding of non-learning into mislearning, learning defence and learning resistance. Mislearning concerns mistakes, lack of precondition or concentration, bad teaching, disturbances and the like, and can usually be corrected by new learning if necessary. Concerning learning defence, we must all develop comprehensive systems concerning the amount of information and often also the content of this. We can either reject certain kinds of information, or we can distort it so that it is in accordance with what we already know or mean. In contrast to this resistance is mobilised when we are in open conflict with what could or should be learned.

In 1994, I received some very inspiring and challenging input to my understanding by reading three newer American contributions which had as their basis the rejection and overruling of the behaviourism of the 1970s and 1980s.

The first of these books was 'Educating the Reflective Practitioner' by Donald Schön (Schön, 1987). It was much in line with my own attitudes and standpoints, but related more to working and business life than to schools and educational institutions and thereby contributed to a better understanding of the connections between educational learning and practice learning — or between formal and informal learning.

I was also challenged by David Kolb's 'Experiential Learning' (Kolb, 1984) which presented a comprehensive and well-structured understanding of learning and, within some aspects, went beyond earlier theories and my own understanding. But, in my view, it was also problematic in at least two fundamental ways: it claimed to include all kinds of learning in a rather simple and specific model and saw all learning as in some way experiential. And it proposed that learning always takes place in a particular sequence, from concrete experience to reflective observation, abstract conceptualisation and active experimentation back to new concrete experience. This was all very captivating, but I also found it somehow too streamlined and too simple. Human learning is not as uniform and cannot be described in such specific models and sequences.

Finally, I read a book called 'Learning As Desire' by Hans Furth who had been one of the central figures in the introduction of Piaget's work in America (Furth, 1987). This book was an attempt to combine the fundamental approaches of Piaget and Freud in a general platform and to understand learning as an integrated cognitive and emotional process. Obviously, Furth was very well acquainted with Piaget's work, and the book often referred to interviews in which Piaget in his later years and in a more straightforward language summed up what he regarded as the main points of his work (Bringuier, 1989 [1980]). But Furth's understanding of Freud was rather problematic. Whereas Freud describes personal development as a battlefield between the personal instances and a power struggle between the principles of pleasure and reality, Furth only refers to a rather practicable balance between the emotional and the rational. Furthermore, he had problems with the role of the death drive, which is a late and regarded by many as a problematic construction in Freud's work. But Furth's book was probably the first to really understand the emotional dimension as an integrated and inevitable part of any learning and to discuss the balance and interplay between the cognitive and the emotional dimensions in different kinds of learning courses.

Altogether, the three books left me with an urge to find out what was right and what was wrong in relation to the basic features of learning and how my own understanding could be extended to overcome the new challenges.

The decisive breakthrough

From 1988, I was research leader of a rather large project on development of the Danish national system of vocational training of mainly unskilled and unemployed adults. This, at that time, was regarded as an important element of the national competitiveness and was jointly directed and supported by the trade-unions, the employers' association and the Ministry of Labour. Several investigations had shown that, not only the professional qualifications, but perhaps even more so the personal qualities of the low-skilled workforce were central in this connection. The challenge was to find out how personal qualities such as flexibility, cooperativeness, self-esteem, etc. could be stimulated as an integrated part of professionally-targeted courses (as this part of the workforce would not engage in personality-targeted courses) by designing the courses as project work and by educating the instructors to deal with this side of the qualification. So, for about two years, I elaborated my new learning theoretical inspiration in relation to its possible consequences for these courses and, in 1996, produced a research report which included three substantial, critical and constructive chapters on the theories of Furth, Kolb and Leithäuser, respectively, and other chapters that discussed these issues in relation to the qualification theory and the design and practice of education and training courses.

Whereas the other reports from the project usually came out in 200 copies, this rather special, theoretical and not easily accessible report was sold in more than 10,000 copies in a couple of years. Obviously I had hit an issue which was central to many teachers and instructors in all parts of the educational system, and the feedback I received from many practitioners stressed two features: first, the introduction of the emotional (and not only motivational) dimension of learning, the integrated connection between the cognitive and the emotional — or the content learning and personal development — and the discussions on the relationship between the two in various situations, corresponded to the experience of the readers. Second, calling attention to learning defence and learning resistance was also an eye-opener in relation to the everyday experiences and problems of practice and led to more attention being given to explaining and discussing *why* specific knowledge, skills and ways of understanding and behaviour were important for learning and practice.

Retrospectively, I have no doubts that the very thorough and critical work behind this report was the decisive breakthrough which led me to grasp and expound my understanding of human learning as a whole in a new, deeper and more coherent perspective.

The three dimensions of learning

However, the report only dealt with some specific elements of learning and could only be a kind of jumping-off point for a more comprehensive theory on learning as a whole. So, in the following years, I took up other issues in different connections. In the autumn term of 1998, my colleagues granted me a leave from all teaching and supervision in order to concentrate on the compilation of a more complete presentation of my understanding of learning.

This was, as I remember it, an extremely satisfying term, alternating between periods of reading and consideration on the one hand and writing and formulating on the other hand. I later described this process as a kind of voyage of discovery. From the start, I had only some basic understandings of the area I wanted to explore and only vague ideas about many issues. However, as I worked my way through the landscape, it was gradually mapped and described in detail. My ambition was to cover all important concepts of and contributions to learning in relation to the general structural understanding I had developed over time. The main means to achieve this was the construction of the learning triangle, which can be briefly described as follows:

The interaction process between the learner and the environment provides the learner with some input, which may or may not be absorbed by the learner through an acquisition process. When absorbed, the input is connected to the results of subjectively-relevant prior learning and thereby forms the learning outcome, which is always individual, and influenced and sometimes distorted or misunderstood by the learner.

At that time, the three dimensions were called cognitive, psycho-dynamic and social and societal. It is essential that all learning involves all three dimensions, although many models and contributions to the learning theory may neglect one or two of these. The social and societal dimension is concerned with the interaction process and has (at least) the two mentioned levels, as there are always other persons involved directly or indirectly, and it is also somehow related to society or mankind. However, the most complex and difficult aspect to explain was the fundamentally integrated and at the same time independent situation of the cognitive and psycho-dynamic dimensions of the acquisition process. It took me a long time to fully understand that the cognitive content is always subjectively influenced by the learners and the individual emotional and motivational value ascribed to it, and that the emotional and motivational engagement is always influenced by the learning content in question.

My difficulties with this understanding was due to the fact that, in the first presentation of the learning triangle in Danish in 1999, there were three double arrows in the vertical dimension to show that the interaction process could meet the acquisition process in different positions between the cognitive and the emotional pole. But this version was quickly abandoned, and in the English translation of 2002 and ever since, there has only been one vertical double arrow because I found it essential to illustrate that the acquisition process had to be understood and treated as an integrated whole. In the English translation, I also changed the term psycho-dynamic to emotional, and in the second Danish and English edition of 2006/2007, the terms for all three dimensions were changed to the content dimension, the incentive dimension and the interaction dimension, respectively, because there had been some uncertainty about the exact meaning of the various terms.

Obviously, the learning triangle was an attempt to provide a clear and simple illustration of the most fundamental elements of the theory. However, at the same time, it was the general point of departure and structural anchoring of my dealing with a very broad selection of theoretical contributions, issues and concepts in relation to human learning. So this figure has been a kind of trade mark of my approach and understanding ever since it was launched in the 1999/2002 book. But the book also contained many other considerations, discussions, and perspectives.

I now included a very broad range of topics and issues, some of which were of minor importance, such as learning jumps (the sudden accommodative or transformative shift from one understanding to another) and different kinds of learning models. But some new and more important topics which I had not developed before were also included. One was the concept and issue of transformative learning as introduced by Jack Mezirow, which was very much in line with Rogers' concept of significant learning. Another important area was what characterised and was important for learning in different learning spaces, such as educational learning, everyday learning, practice learning, and workplace or organisational learning, and similarly what characterised learning in childhood, youth, adulthood and mature adulthood. Great attention was also given to experiential learning as originally introduced by John Dewey and taken up by David Kolb and many others, and which had been a key issue in discussions on adult and lifelong learning since the late 1980s.

The aim was to cover all relevant areas of the topic of learning in a coherent way and it was a great experience and satisfaction to me that the book was also received and treated as a valuable contribution to learning theory in general.

How we learn

I had now succeeded in providing a satisfying and usable answer to my original question about how human learning takes place. When published in English in 2002, the book together with some articles in relevant journals opened to me an international platform in the area of learning theories, and for some years I could concentrate on dessiminating my messages and understandings and enjoy the discussions on the various issues and ideas I had presented.

However, gradually I also experienced that although the book dealt with most of the important issues in relation to learning, it still had the nature of a draft. Many considerations were relevant and balanced in relation to a specific approach and understanding, but they did not really provide a coherent and well-structured presentation. So, after some years, I began to consider how I could make a presentation which did not resemble a voyage of discovery, but was a well-structured and rounded whole and, presenting the mutually connected topics and elements of human learning more clearly.

A transformation of this kind did not seem impossible or overwhelming, but it involved many considerations on how to fit everything into a simple and manageable structure. Many details had to be re-considered and re-formulated. I chose to leave out or shorten some topics, as they were too peripheral and stood in the way of a clear focus on more essential matters. As an example, I can mention the topic of reflection, which plays a central role in many contributions to the learning theory (e.g. in Dewey, Kolb, Schön and Mezirow), but, from a structural point of view, is basically a displacement or postponement of some learning from the input situation to a later time with better possibilities for elaboration and further consideration. The structure of this kind of learning does not involve any fundamental difference from what takes place in other connections. Therefore this topic, which in the 1999/2002 book had a rather prominent position, was now included in the chapter on the content dimension of learning, as it is a kind of further elaboration of the learning content. I also included a chapter on the importance of heredity, dispositions, environment, intelligence, gender, ethnicity, and learning styles, as these leave their unmistakable stamp on the kind and value of any learning.

In accordance with these various considerations, the new book developed three main theoretical areas following two introductory chapters. I shall briefly mention the main topics of each of these areas:

The structure of learning is the main area and includes the learning triangle, specific chapters on each of the three learning dimensions, and a transversal chapter on issues such as experiential learning, personal development, competence, identity and learning models.

The types of learning make a distinction between learning as addition and learning as change, each including two learning types so that altogether there are the four learning types: cumulative, assimilative, accommodative and transformative learning.

Learning barriers make a distinction between mislearning, learning defence and ambivalence, and resistance to learning.

Preconditions to learning include heredity, dispositions, environment, intelligence, gender, ethnicity, and learning styles.

Learning in different life ages includes the characteristics and differences between learning in childhood, youth, adulthood, and mature adulthood.

Learning spaces include everyday learning, school and educational learning, workplace and organisational learning, net-based learning, interest-based learning and grassroot activities, and transversal learning.

The book was published in Danish in 2006, in English in 2007, and was later translated into several other languages. Furthermore, the theory was also presented in various handbooks, including *The Routledge International Handbook of Lifelong Learning* (Jarvis, 2009) and *The Routledge International Handbook of Learning* (Jarvis & Watts, 2012). So this theoretical contribution gradually became part of the contemporary international discussion and understanding of human learning (see note at the end of this article).

New topics and additions

Following the publication of 'How We Learn', I edited and published 'Contemporary Theories of Learning', which includes chapters by 16 leading learning theorists, 'The Fundamentals of Workplace Learning', and 'Transformative Learning and Identity' (Illeris, 2009a; 2011; 2014). Especially the latter is of interest here because it re-defines the issue and concept of transformative learning as any learning involving change in elements of the individual identity. Hence, it proposes an up-to-date answer to the question of 'what form transforms', expressed by Robert Kegan in 2000 (Kegan, 2000) as a kind of summing up of the general notion that Mezirow's original definition of transformative learning in relation to meaning perspectives, frames of reference and habits of mind is now too restricted to the cognitive learning dimension.

I also published a book in Danish on the concept of competence, which has become central in relation to the aim and target of contemporary learning activities, but is misused by educational authorities because they do not or will not realise that the central idea behind using the term competencies instead of, for example, skills or qualifications, is that competencies cover what a person or a group of persons are able to do or achieve in all the predictable and unpredictable situations of the ever-changing globalised modernity.

So the original reason for using the term competencies — which was to stress what is important in today's complex and ever changing world of practice — is betrayed and replaced by a rattling off of competencies which claim to be the outcome of all the various educational courses and activities. This is a remarkable example of the confusion between what is taught and what is learned, which politicians and administrators have practised so often, and which tends to entail attempts to measure the various postulated competencies. This implies that unmeasurable qualities such as flexibility, creativity, empathy, and openness to change and innovation — the need for which was the original reason for the introduction of the term competencies — are left out and a new and stronger concentration on the measurable and insufficient 'hard' outcomes of reproductional knowledge and skills are reinforced.

My second new publication in Danish is an edited book 'Learning in the Competition State'. The term, concept and practice of the 'competition state' has been developed mainly by economists to charaterise the dominating trend of politics and administration in which financial competitiveness is taken as both the point of departure and the final objective of all important governmental endeavours and decisions at all levels.

To meet this objective and achieve maximal financial effectivity, many measurements and tests and positive and negative incentives are used to promote the authorities' various reforms and decisions which are forced on the institutions and their staff. At the same time, schools and educational institutions are merged into huge mass production centres with strong boards of mainly commercial managers and quasi autocratic leaders and the influence of teachers, instructors, and administrative staff, not to speak of the students, is strongly reduced.

The model for all this is modern commercial concerns and companies which compete on the market and develop maximal profits for owners and shareholders. But educational institutions are not managing industrial and commercial production of lifeless commodities. Their 'production' is human capacities and competencies and this is a quite different matter because there will always be reactions from the learners which are conditioned by human experience and preferences.

Furthermore, competition will always produce winners and losers. Whereas losers in commercial life can go bankrupt, losers of the educational competition are human beings who may find themselves in very vulnerable positions with poor life conditions, a need for social and financial support, and great distrust and lack of motivation in relation to new educational endeavours.

All kinds of national and international tests are used to control learning. The practice of institutions, teachers and instructors is regulated, and learning activities are increasingly directed towards what can reasonably or unreasonably be measured. The main outcomes of this seem to be a sweeping tendency to reduce learning to what is measured. Teachers and instructors are de-motivated and a stressed and dejected environment is developed. Thus, in relation to learning, the competition states and their educational policies make the fundamental error of assuming a kind of automatism between education and learning and an identity and between what is taught and what is learned. Hence, the many educational reforms of the competition states tend to produce insufficient learning, especially in the human and social dimensions, and an increasing number of drop-outs and students who do not meet the current needs of society.

As a conclusion, I can only maintain that, internationally, there is a fundamental and rapidly growing need for a better understanding of how learning functions and can be improved. But currently, the learning theory seems to be neglected or conceived as an exclusive domain of speculations with no practical implications, where a specific kind of economic understanding has become the final goal and yardstick of all arrangements and activities of the educational sector and its institutions and programmes.

However, there is also a growing interest in sober learning theoretical insight which can be used in relation to learning activities and is not governed by ideas of financial competitiveness, especially on the part of teachers, instructors, supervisors and mentors at floor level. The need to deal with the development and continuous adjustment of the learning theory seems to be greater than ever. But it must also be emphasised that the genuine learning theory is about how learning takes place and functions in various situations and conditions, and not about how it can be streamlined as an industrial production process — simply because learning is an entirely human and in no way industrial matter.

Note

The ideas of this article can be studied in detail in 'How We Learn', which has been published in Danish, Swedish, Norwegian, English, German, Polish and Chinese and in a shorter and more concentrated form also in Romanian, Greek, Korean and Brazilian/Portuguese (Illeris, 2009b). In addition, articles on more limited parts of the theory, mainly in relation to adult education and workplace learning, have been published in Dutch, Icelandic, Finnish, Lithuanian, Slovenian, and Italian.

References

AUSUBLE, D. P. (1968) *Educational Psychology: A Cognitive View* (New York, Holt, Rinehart and Winston).
BRINGUIER, J. -C. (1989 [1980]) *Conversations with Jean Piaget* (Chicago, University of Chicago Press).
DAMASIO, A. R. (1994) *Descartes' Error: emotion, reason and the human brain* (New York, Grosset/Putnam).
FURTH, H. G. (1987) *Knowledge As Desire* (New York, Columbia University Press).

ILLERIS, K. (2007 [2006]) *How We Learn: learning and non-learning in school and beyond* (London, Routledge).
ILLERIS, K. (Ed) (2009a) *Contemporary Theories of Learning. Learning Theorists... in their own Words* (London, Routledge).
ILLERIS, K. (2009b) A comprehensive understanding of human learning, in K. ILLERIS (2009a). *Contemporary Theories of Learning. Learning theorists... in their own words* (London, Routledge).
ILLERIS, K. (2011) *The Fundamentals of Workplace Learning* (London, Routledge).
ILLERIS, K. (2014) *Transformative Learning and Identity* (London, Routledge).
JARVIS, P. (Ed) (2009) *The Routledge International Handbook of Lifelong Learning* (London, Routledge).
JARVIS, P. & WATTS, M. (eds) (2012) *The Routledge International Handbook of Learning* (London, Routledge).
KEGAN, R. (2000) What form transforms? A constructive-developmental approach to transforming learning, in: J. MEZIROW and Associates (Eds) *Learning as Transformation: critical perspectives on a theory in progress* (San Francisco,CA, Jossey-Bass).
KOLB, D.A. (1984) *Experiential Learning: experience as the source of learning and development* (Englewood Cliffs, NJ, Prentice-Hall).
LEITHÄUSER, T. (1976) *Formen des Alltagsbewusstseins* [The forms of everyday consciousness] (Frankfurt a. Main, Campus).
PIAGET, J. (1952 [1936]) *The Origin of Intelligence in Children* (New York, International Universities Press).
PIAGET, J. (1967 [1964]) *Six Psychological Studies* (New York, Random House).
ROGERS, C. R. (1961) *On Becoming a Person* (Boston, MA, Houghton-Mifflin).
ROGERS, C. R. (1969) *Freedom to Learn* (Columbus, OH, Charles E. Merrill).
SCHÖN, D. A. (1987) *Educating the Reflective Practitioner* (San Francisco, CA, Jossey-Bass).

CHAPTER 3

LEARNING IN THE COMPETITION STATE

Problems and alternative perspectives

The approach to learning in the competition state

During the last half of the twentieth century in most Western countries and not least in the Scandinavian countries, the general political administrative concept called the welfare state was developed. The overriding objective of the welfare state was to frame a society that could create security, reasonable living conditions and a high degree of equality for the members of society. However, since the 1990s, the political ideal has been to develop a competition state where the overriding objective is that the nation should manage as well as possible in international economic competition and inner structures are also largely based on competition between businesses and institutions and among citizens (Cerny 1997, 2010, Pedersen 2011, 2013).

However, the 'competition state' is quite fundamentally a problematic concept, because everything and everyone is subject to unilateral financial management based on the argument that this is necessary. Which, of course, it is not. The world and the individual nations could be managed on the basis of many other rationales which, in other ways, can combine consideration for human existence and the sustainability of nature with economic forms that do not grant financial transactions and tax planning a haven to create a necessity that results in ruthless exploitation of natural resources and the everyday life and mental balance of ordinary people. Nevertheless, unfortunately today the competition state is the foundation for controlling the conditions for our existence, and we must relate to it and try to free ourselves from it. In this article I shall concentrate on the relation of the competition state to education and learning.

One of the most important means of promoting national competitiveness is that as many as possible are educated to the highest level possible. Basically, this is a matter of the exploitation by the competition state of people's fantastic possibilities for learning. This could be a key area in connection with efforts to develop the sustainability of the international community on all levels, but in competition states it is harnessed to the hopeless attempt to be ahead of all the other competition states by means of competence development with far-reaching consequences for those involved, and in particular for the most vulnerable among both learners and teachers.

It would seem to be a matter of course that the competition state has a vital need to optimize learning at all levels of society, because it needs a workforce with the best possible competences in order to be competitive, both to increase productivity and so that members of society can manage their situation in life in ways that entail the lowest possible public expenditure and keep taxes down. From the viewpoint of members of society, a high level of competence is also necessary to constantly be able to keep up and remain informed about all the changeable contexts of which we are part, to be able to make the right decisions, manage many challenges and have a good life.

Therefore, in and for the competition state it is a basic condition to invest in a high level of competence and thereby also a high level of education, which should actually be a cut above the other states in order to cope with competition. In 1997, when Tony Blair, one of the earliest standard-bearers of the competition state, as a newly-elected British prime minister was asked what the three most important points in the policies of the new government were, his famous answer was 'Education, education, education'. At around the same time, the Danish prime minister, Poul Nyrup Rasmussen, wanted to make Denmark one of the five best countries in the world with respect to education.

These are fine words, but they have also proved to be words that are not so easy to live up to. In practice, neither of the countries has had any great success with its education policy. In September 2012, Susan Harris replied thus to Tony Blair in the *Daily Mail*, 'Failed, failed, failed – Labour billions did nothing to raise standards, says report' – after Britain (again) had done rather badly by international comparison (Harris 2012). Nor have the many school and education reforms in Denmark throughout the 2000s met with any great success.

In my view, three interconnected and fundamental mistakes lie behind these depressing results, all of which are characteristic of the competition state's lack of understanding of how people function when it is not merely a matter of economic conditions. The first is that it has been difficult for the decision-makers to distinguish between education and learning; what they have regarded as improvements in education programmes have by no means always led to better learning. Second, measurements have had decisive significance for the programmes' design and operation with no consideration of the fact that what is measurable is improved at the expense of everything that cannot be measured, but which nevertheless is at least as important on economic and human levels. Third, and by extension, there is a lack of understanding of the importance of learning that has to do with personal development and the development of identity.

Educational problems

The decisive focal point of the efforts to improve study programmes has been that the majority should receive more education, and preferably without it costing more in relation to the number of those who are fully qualified. Therefore, the emphasis has been on creating larger schools and educational institutions with fewer administrative costs per pupil or student with strong, almost autocratic leaders who can make the institutions function efficiently and tests and measurements that show whether learning is proceeding well enough – preferably better than in the competing countries. There has also been focus on standards aimed at learning corresponding to prioritized learning needs and towards better and more effective teaching, even though it has been difficult to discover what this means.

However, this has not been so easy in practice and efforts to convert all this into better results have not really met with any success. There have been clear signs that the top-down systems have resulted in increased problems at the lower levels. Better results have been partly achieved in national and international tests at primary and lower secondary school level, but these have only covered a very small part though important of the intended learning. At the same time, however, at least in Denmark, an increasing share of the pupils have had to receive costly remedial instruction (Langager 2014). There has also been a significant increase in the number of pupils whose parents have moved them to private schools because they do not think that the children have learned enough or that public schools provide satisfactory well-being.

Dropout has been extensive in youth education programmes and efforts to remedy this have not been succesful. In addition, an increasing number of pupils in upper secondary school have scraped though with such poor results that they have virtually documented a completely inadequate academic level. The lack of internships in vocational education and training programmes has led to doubt about what many of those who have completed the programmes are really qualified to do. Overall and constantly, the programmes have been very far from achieving the Danish objective that 95% of young people should complete a youth education programme (Katznelson 2014). In higher education, there have also been problems around the academic level of some graduates in both professional education and academic programmes.

Thus, in general there are continued problems in achieving important educational targets. Even though it can be difficult to establish what has really taken place with respect to learning and standards, there are many signs that despite various reforms, restructuring and large-scale efforts on the floor, on the whole things have not gone particularly well.

Proceeding on to the labour market, where today learning in working life is regarded as a very important part of competence development, there has been a great increase in cases of stress, burnout and similar symptoms of the workload being too great or wrong. At any rate, there has not been any room for the kind of learning that should involve people keeping up and developing in step with the challenges presented by work (Prætorius 2013).

Learning problems and identity

A sharp line cannot, of course, be drawn between learning and educational problems. However, in the scope of this article the crucial criterion for such a distinction is the degree to which, and how the problems have been caused by problematic understanding and practice of education, or by erroneous understanding and practice of learning.

The understanding of learning has been erroneous in the sense that although general formulations have expressed a broad learning concept including both acquisition of knowledge and personal development, practice and, in particular, tests and measurements have largely emphasized standards. It is, naturally, important that pupils and students should acquire the academic content of various education programmes, at least to the extent that this content has been selected according to criteria that match the development of society and learners' needs and not merely some academic traditions.

Simultaneously, however, since the 1980s there has been a general societal development that is extremely well described in current psychology and sociology. This has to do with the quite paramount necessity of developing an identity with a quality that incorporates a personally embedded balance between stability and flexibility (Giddens 1991, Beck 1992, Bauman 2000, 2001, Illeris 2014a).

This concerns the mental structure that contains and sums up the criteria that the individuals have developed for managing their existence in relation to continually changing surroundings, and which, on one hand, are embedded in personal experience, interests and opinions and, on the other hand, are open to change when it is personally necessary and acceptable – also including changes in relation to the acquired knowledge.

It often seems that leading politicians, administrators, and representatives of both employers and employees have learned to say that one should be flexible, adaptable, creative and innovative without having more systematic and qualified notions of how to achieve all of this. This is not something that falls from the sky and such stringent demands have been made on previous generations to a very small extent only. It is something that has to be learned, and today it requires, especially throughout adolescence, a colossal effort to develop such a contemporary identity and to use it later in adult life in a balanced way, constantly being able to renew it.

It is not something that is usually taken into account in our education system, but there are, at least in Denmark, a few pockets where it can thrive, e.g. typically in so-called continuation schools, which also have been an attraction, more in spite of than because of the school policy that has been pursued. Another important example in Denmark is the famous 'goofing around' years, for which so many take time off. These typically occur after a youth education programme where identity development is linked more to breaks than to lessons, which have been completely geared towards academic content. In addition, smoking hashish has become a big problem (Simonsen 2014) in relation to identity development in youth education.

In this context, it is paradoxical that standards and identity development are by no means incompatible. On the contrary, they can inspire and enrich one another if there is understanding and room is made for it. As a general rule, academic learning is strengthened when it can contribute to identity development, and conversely where there is identity development, there is usually increased engagement that can also benefit academic standards.

However central all this is for learning and education today, it would seem to lie beyond the horizon that characterises the instruments of the competition state: it cannot be described as course material, it cannot be measured, and it has to do with human matters and not with production and economics. Nevertheless, the advocates of the competition state would like the workforce and citizens to be developed with precisely the qualities promoted by appropriate identity development.

Mental strain, separation and disabilities

The other central theme that learning problems in the competition state has actualized comprises different categories of mental strain, the learning problems that these strains entail, and the separation and dropout from education and on into working life that all too often are the result.

For as long as education has been compulsory in Denmark, there have also been some pupils who have not been able to 'keep up' for a variety of reasons. In other words, their learning has been so different or so inadequate that they have had to be taken out of ordinary teaching situations and/or they have been unable to complete courses of education on which they had started.

Ever since it became common for all children to enter family day care or the nursery, it has gradually become the case that the adults should draw attention to children who do not function age-appropriately intellectually, emotionally or socially so that they can receive special support and, if necessary, be referred for special help. In such cases in primary and lower secondary school, either support functions in connection with ordinary teaching are initiated or the child is removed from the class for remedial teaching.

In Denmark, Søren Langager (Langager 2014) among others, has investigated the tension between trends to try to keep as many of the vulnerable pupils as possible in normal teaching and trends to separate more of them out into remedial instruction and to make certain diagnoses. Langager also describes how in recent years there has been an almost explosive growth in the number of so-called ADHD (attention deficit/hyperactivity disorder) children and children with other diagnoses. On the other hand, the new Act on the Folkeskole (municipal primary and lower secondary school) aims to retain as many children as possible in normal teaching – inter alia if it is possible and affordable, which would seem rather problematic – by means of resource teachers and two-teacher systems, partly for social reasons but also because it is less expensive. At present, it is uncertain how these matters will develop. It is, however, quite clear that the children's institutions in the competition state have a strong tendency to function in such ways that create or make visible mental and behavioural problems in a growing number of children.

Other more or less similar problems seem to be in evidence in youth education programmes, i.e. upper secondary education and vocational education and training, which award a qualification, and basic vocational education and training and the so-called production schools, which do not award a qualification but aim to develop vulnerable young people in ways that enable them to carry on to earn qualifications. In this context, it should be noted that these youngsters are beyond the age of compulsory education. Simultaneously, however, for the last 30 years there has been broad political support for a policy that as many young people as possible should complete a youth education programme leading to a qualification. It has been a declared objective since the beginning of the 1990s that 95% of young people should complete a youth education programme, but in spite of various reforms and other measures, the level has been down around 80% up to now (Katznelson 2014).

To understand the huge fiasco of the competition state's education policy, it is fundamental to return to the question of identity development (Illeris 2014b). It is significant that youth education contributes far too little and in an inexpedient manner to identity development, which over the last decades has increasingly been shown to be central and necessary for the young, both individually and societally.

Today, youth education programmes treat young people like schoolchildren (perhaps with the exception of the few youngsters who are the winners in the struggle for all too few internships), and instead of courses that support and promote up-to-date identity development and adulthood, these programmes are a kind of mental confinement in fundamental dependence. This occurs primarily through enforced content that is largely determined on the basis of a quite inflexible and more and more obsolete perception of professionalism, with grading that turns the youngsters into objects of this professionalism. And although the most recent reform of the upper secondary school is a small step in the right direction in this context, and vocational education and training could develop identity and independence to a higher degree if all pupils could obtain an internship, it is, first and foremost, the completely dominant and out-of-date way of treating young people like children that determines the fiasco of youth education. In addition, in recent years the education policy of competition states has to a large degree continued the practice of delaying adulthood into further education.

This is something approaching a disaster because the policy of competition states aims to make everyone 'profitable' co-players in the struggle for economic competitiveness and growth. Or to put it bluntly: if we cannot manage to have more youngsters complete a youth education programme, and it should be added with a result that can be used in society and working life, then in the long term as a nation we risk – dare one formulate it so openly – ending up as *losers* in international economic competition.

There will, of course, always be a considerable number of young people with the capacity for managing both identity development and academic achievement almost irrespective of what they are faced with. The question, however, of the number that cannot manage this is of quite decisive importance, socially, economically and personally. For we are already well on the way to a situation where young people without adequate qualifications fall into unemployment, dissatisfaction, substance abuse, crime etc. and more or less permanently must be provided for and paid for by the rest of the population. This is untenable and expensive.

All this leads to the next problem. The more the competition state fails in this area and the more people who are unfit for work and must be supported financially and behaviourally, the greater becomes the pressure on the rest of the population and especially on their efficiency in economic terms. Maintaining this efficiency, which already plays a large role in the public and the private labour market, creates new problems and losers, typically through the development of stress, disillusionment, burnout, and physical disabilities (Prætorius 2013).

Things come back to bite one and the competition state is leading us effortlessly into a downward spiral; in Denmark we are already well on the way down statistically and are not as high up as we once were – even if we sometimes manage to drag ourselves up a few levels in some areas.

On top of that, somewhere in the not-too-distant future various breakdowns are lurking in our expected standard of living due to the over-exploitation of resources to which all the competing competition states contribute, even though there is much talk of the opposite.

What can be done?

It seems quite obvious, in fact imperative, when one stops to think about the state of affairs described above, or about other more or less similar societal issues in other sectors, that we cannot continue as we are. Fundamental, radical changes are necessary.

This can, of course, be discussed from many different angles and at many different levels. In the following, I shall first examine what our target should be in general terms – because as stated, it is clear that the competition state is untenable as a concept. On the one hand, competition always produces both winners and losers, and in a globalized world, the winners very quickly will have to take care of the losers. This is already happening when northern European EU countries feel compelled to 'save' the economies of some of the countries in southern Europe not out of the goodness of their hearts, but out of necessity, because we are all becoming increasingly dependent on each other in the world as a whole. On the other hand, competition leads to exploitation of the natural resources of the Earth, which very soon will result in breakdown in a number of areas. Therefore, in the first instance the question must be what can be done here and now in relation to the competition state in which we find ourselves but which cannot possibly carry on for much longer. At the same time, we must have some very clear ideas of where we should be heading in the slightly longer term in order to move in the right direction in our current efforts.

Next, I shall discuss the form of learning that we must aim for and how we can do that. First and foremost this is connected with the fact that the competition state's rising utilization of measurements in relation to learning almost automatically means upgrading the types of learning that can be measured. This indirectly leads to giving lower priority to other types of learning that are difficult or impossible to measure, but which everybody knows are increasingly central to keep in step with the growing complexity and pace of change that globalization inevitably brings with it.

Finally, I shall briefly examine the present situation in the Danish education system and present some deliberations that concern where and how improvements can be made in the short and the long term.

Learning and sustainability

As many others have done, I shall use the concept of sustainability as the keyword for an alternative aim, and I should like to emphasize that this concept cannot be limited to climate and ecosystems (Prætorius 2013). It may be clear that in these areas the competition state is well on the way to leading the world into a completely chaotic breakdown. But if the Earth is to accommodate as many as 10 billion, and we are to live in an even somewhat civilized and peaceful co-existence, then a more far-reaching sustainability must be developed. This can be broken down into the following five levels.

First, there is the quite general level of the viability of the planet itself as fit for human habitation and our ability to obtain food, water, clothing, housing, fresh air and other necessities for all. Up to now, the concept of sustainability has largely been talked of in relation to this level.

Second, one can speak of the sustainability of individual continents, areas and countries. This can most easily be seen as sustainability under the auspices of individual nations or unions of nations, for instance, the EU. If peace and cooperation are to be achieved, economic, social and cultural sustainability must prevail within each of these areas, and the standard of living must be more or less uniform.

Third, there is an institutional level where one can speak of, for instance, the Danish education system with underlying areas such as primary and lower secondary school and individual schools. In this area, sustainability will increasingly be a matter of forms of administration and relations that ensure that the institutions function reasonably expediently, smoothly and satisfactorily for staff and users.

Fourth, is an inter-personal level that has to do with relations between people, the way we interact, cooperate and solve conflicts – mutual respect and flexibility.

Fifth and finally, there is individual sustainability, where one is in harmony with oneself, lives a life which one is satisfied with and can vouch for and has the opportunity to realise one's potential – if one masters the balance between mental stability and flexibility.

These divisions could have been made in different ways, but what is important is to illustrate that this concept of sustainability has to do with the very basis of our individual and joint existence. We all have the right to a good life, and in a globalized world we are all in the same boat; we are mutually dependent in a number of different areas and at different levels.

It is, therefore, an inescapably general objective for our learning, whether inside or outside the education system, that it should be in accord with and aim at the sustainability that is needed on all levels. This is a great challenge and, naturally, it can be met in many different ways and differently weighted, but the listing and actualization of the whole of this broad spectrum can in particular be used to identify fields, habits and traditions that are inconsistent with sustainability in one or more areas or levels.

For example, there would seem to be considerable disagreement in parts of the Danish education system on the relation between what learners experience as what they need and what the system emphasizes. A lack of sustainability can result if this cannot and is not justified and discussed in a manner that learners can accept. Why is it necessary for a certain subject and certain academic content to form part of a certain study programme? Why work with the content in a certain way? Why is the learning measured and valued as it is? Moreover, could all or some of it not be done better in another way?

Like other social conditions, the education system has a long history and has been regularly adjusted and reformed when important changes occurred. However, this also is why there is always tension between past, present and future. If the tension becomes too great, it can effect sustainability in such a way that some of those involved no longer feel that what is taking place is relevant, legitimate and expedient, thus reducing and making a mess of the scope, pace and quality of learning. There is really nothing new about this, but it is the result brought about when conditions at the various levels change all the time and at an increasingly faster pace. In the following section, I shall more closely examine how these matters interact in learning contexts at present.

Learning quality

We are here faced with a problem concerning what kind of learning is required and how this learning is to be created. This problem forms part of a larger context where the competition state falls short because the economic concepts are based on a false view of human nature.

Economic theories and calculations cannot accommodate the fact that it is only to a limited extent and in limited areas that human beings behave rationally in relation to economics. In principle, they presuppose that humans will always pursue the greatest possible financial benefit. However, this is not what happens in reality. Like other living creatures, humans are governed by the wish to survive, have a good life and ensure the continuation of the species through reproduction and care for new generations. While a certain amount of money is necessary for this, very many practical, emotional and inter-personal matters are more important, and most people prioritize these rather than financial gain (perhaps with the exception of what one might regard as a group of 'economically dazzled' fellow citizens). In general, we prioritize what we experience as 'a good life', and this also applies in the area of learning.

Previously, the focus of learning research was a quite limited process of acquisition that at best could be related to professional qualification in the school and education systems of industrial society. However, in the perception of learning in recent years it has become unavoidable to understand that academic learning forms only part of the building blocks needed for the broader dimensions that include rational, emotional and social learning development and are embedded in outer contexts that range from the school environment to global development (Illeris 2007, 2014b, Jarvis & Watts 2012). It is this, inter alia, that has been expressed by the focus of modern psychology and, in particular, sociology, on the identity concept. One cannot comprehend what is taking place in the learning processes of people today without considering their identities, which overlay and hold modernity's diversity of learning elements together in an individual whole. From the viewpoint of the competition state, this has typically been expressed by great interest in the concepts of competence and competence development but in a completely mistaken way, where competences are seen as isolated building blocks of 'skills' enumerated in long lists, instead of being viewed from a holistic perspective of identity, where the single competence elements are linked and expressed in very complex patterns of behaviour and personality that drive an individual's capabilities (Illeris 2012).

Qualifications are necessary, of course, no one would dispute that, but it is also clear that today professional competency is not enough without the ability to make use of it and carry it through into new and changing content and social contexts, which is largely absent in all parts of the school and education system that do not include real-life practice – including in primary and lower secondary school, upper secondary education, vocational education with school-based practical training, and large parts of study programmes at university level, etc.

What is important in this context, and something that the politicians and administrators responsible for education in the competition state tend to overlook – perhaps because these matters were not so acute in the industrial society in which many of them gained their educational experience – is that education and learning are not the same and that the education programmes that are developed today do not automatically lead to the learning we're aiming for. Once upon a time, perhaps up to about the 1970s, the Danish school and education system was regarded as one of the best in the world, because – maybe due to an idiosyncratic interaction between Grundvigian and cultural-radical ideas about the school – to a higher degree than most other countries it managed to initiate more holistic learning processes. But in the competition state, subsequent governments have increasingly followed the ruling trends from the EU, the OECD and others who have put forward economic and administratively based perceptions of education with an emphasis on adjustments, evaluations, tests, league tables, incentives and the like, which have overshadowed and distorted the possibility of teachers adapting their teaching to their abilities and the qualifications and situations of their students (Pedersen 2011).

In the name of efficiency, attempts have been made to standardize education programmes and teaching to what is regarded as the most correct and powerful in economic-administrative thinking. The result is that a great part of the engagement that is quite central to the type of holistic learning that is needed in a modern, complex and changeable society has come under pressure.

Numerous studies have been conducted of how to practise the best possible teaching, but there has been a general tendency to focus far too much on specific courses and teaching practise. More generally, it is now well documented that school and educational learning is something that takes place in learners by virtue of their interaction with the teaching situation and that the most decisive and fundamental element in this context is the learners' engagement. This basically is linked to whether the learners' experience makes use of the learning for something relevant to them. As far as the teaching itself is concerned, it is by now also clear that the most decisive factor is the engagement projected by teachers and their ability to initiate and maintain meaningful challenges as experienced by the learners in relation to the content of the teaching and the learners as different individuals. Even the new, extremely measured and technically oriented approach related to 'visible learning', particularly emphasizes that learning initiatives should be substantiated, explained, evaluated and made visible in other ways, because it increases the engagement of both teachers and learners. However, it is at the same time precisely this engagement on two levels that is stifled by all the measures employed by the competition state's 'streamlining' approach to education programmes (cf. e.g. Meyer 2004, Hattie 2008, 2012).

There was lively discussion about teaching quality at the beginning of the 2000s, of which, among others, the then Danish minister for education spoke a great deal in relation to PISA and other similar tests that were introduced around that time. But these only concern quality at a very limited and low level in relation to what is required of humans today. If one wishes to speak about quality in learning, it is quite inadequate to emphasize a largely reproductive level. To a far greater degree, learning concerns issues such as what one can use it for in practice, when one thinks about it at all, how one can connect it to other areas of content, and how one can develop and continue it in the many new contexts that constantly arise. On such an analytical basis, one can, for example, present an overview like the following of what meets the requirements of teaching quality on a number of different levels that in contrast to the well-known learning target models such as Bloom's taxonomy (Bloom et al. 1956) are deliberately designed as a more universal and general overview with a view to insight and understanding, and not as a technical instrument.

1. On the absolutely elementary level, something can be said to have been learned when it has been acquired such that it can be repeated or reproduced more or less adequately and coherently. For example, one typically starts a new subject like this, and as a rule, tests and elementary examinations and the like are conducted at this level.
2. At a higher level, something has been learned if it can be used in standardized situations such as problem solving. This level is well known, for example, from arithmetical problems and translations from foreign languages, and it is also a level that usually is possible to measure.
3. The next level can be where something has been learned so that it can be applied in routine situations in practice, for example, how one most appropriately can serve a new customer in a shop. In such contexts, measurement is complicated by the fact that to be reasonably reliable it must take place in practice. If the practice situation is isolated and, for example, within a school situation, this means standardization, which means going back to the previous level.
4. The next level is that something has been learned if it can be used in a relevant manner across the many different practice situations that normally are part of certain jobs or fields of practice. Measurements as such would be very complicated and incomplete here, but more experienced practitioners in the field in question would be able to obtain a qualified estimate of a practitioner's functional capability by following the person over a period of time. However, this is not just an estimation of the level of learning alone, but far more of an element in a more complicated totality.
5. Finally, a level of learning can be outlined where what has been learned can be used freely and appropriately in all known and new, unpredictable practice situations. At this level, learning can in principle not be measured because

new, unknown situations can always occur. In some contexts, one can try to measure results such as a firm or unit's financial results. However, there is naturally much more here than what has been learned during prior education and subsequent practice, and the measurement is only a snapshot that is unable to take new situations and demands into account that may be different in relation to what formed the basis of the measurement.

In general, the aim today is that as many as possible are educated to the highest level possible, which means up to level 4 or 5 for most people, while measurements largely only affect levels 1 and 2. Nevertheless, far-reaching individual and system-oriented consequences are drawn from these measurements, which are not justified but are assumed to be useful indications of how the individual can perform in the future. In general, this is relevant to the extent that these indications prove to be predictive for practice, for the great majority at any rate. But flexibility is necessary in the systems in order to allow for the individuality seen in single cases.

However, by far the greatest and most important problems regarding measurements are that they inevitably come to be learning targets, i.e. that one learns with a view to achieving a good result in the measurements instead of for personal development and enrichment. The more measurements are carried out, the more focus on measuring levels 1 and 2, the greater the consequences are for the learners, and the more problematic the measurements become – for the learners, for the teachers and the institutions and for society as a whole. This is because much time and resources are wasted on efforts that only to a small extent lead to better and more flexible practice.

In the final analysis, the whole situation can be summed up in the paradox that by using measurements as a decisive instrument of regulation *we are developing a school and education system where consideration for national competitiveness takes precedence over consideration for learning and the learner. This tends to lead to learning as a whole becoming more insufficient, thus weakening national competitiveness!*

References

Bauman, Zygmunt (2000): *Liquid Modernity*. Cambridge, UK: Polity Press.
Bauman, Zygmunt (2001): *The Individualized Society*. Cambridge, UK: Polity Press.
Beck, Ulrich (1992 [1986]): *Risk Society: Towards a new modernity*. London: Sage.
Bloom, Benjamin S. – Kratwohl, David R. – Masia, Bertarm B. (1956): *Taxonomy of Educational Objectives*. New York: David McKay Company.
Cerny, Philip G. (1997): Paradoxes of the Dynamics of Political Globalization. *Government and Opposition*, 32/2, p. 251–274.
Cerny, Philip G. (2010): *Rethinking World Politics: A theory of transnational neopluralism*. Oxford: Oxford University Press.
Giddens, Anthony (1991): *Modernity and Self-Identity*. Cambridge, UK: Polity Press.
Harris, Susan (2012): Failed, failed, failed. *Daily Mail Online*, September 11.
Hattie, John (2008): *Visible Learning: A Synthesis of over 800 meta-analyses relating achievement*. London: Routledge.
Hattie, John (2012): *Visible Learning for Teachers: Maximizing impact on learning*. London: Rouledge.
Illeris, Knud (2007): *How We Learn: Learning and non-learning in school and beyond*. London: Routledge.
Illeris, Knud (2012): *Kompetence – Hvad, hvorfor, hvordan?* Copenhagen: Samfundslitteratur, 2. edition. [Competence – what, why, how?].
Illeris, Knud (2014a): *Transformative Learning and Identity*. London: Routledge.
Illeris, Knud (ed.) (2014b): *Læring i konkurrencestaten – Kapløb eller bæredygtighed*.

Copenhagen: Samfundslitteratur. [Learning in the Competition State: Competition or sustainability?].

Jarvis, Peter and Watts, Mary (eds) 2012: *The Routledge International Handbook of Learning*. London: Routledge.

Katznelson, Noemi (2014): Unges identitetsudvikling – uddannelse og tilknytning til arbejdsmarkedet. In Knud Illeris (ed.): *Læring i konkurrencestaten – Kapløb eller bæredygtighed*. Copenhagen: Samfundslitteratur. [Identity development in youth: education and attachment to the labour market].

Langager, Søren (2014): Specialpædagogikkens børn – inklusionspolitik, diagnosekultur og læringsmiljøer. In Knud Illeris (ed.): *Læring i konkurrencestaten – Kapløb eller bæredygtighed*. Copenhagen: Samfundslitteratur. [The children of remedial instruction].

Meyer, Hilbert (2004): *Was ist guter Unterricht?* Berlin: Cornelsen Scriptor. [What is good teaching?].

Pedersen, Ove Kaj: (2011): *Konkurrencestaten*. Copenhagen: Reitzel. [The Competition State].

Pedersen, Ove Kaj (2013): *Political Globalization and the Competence State*. In Benedikte Brincker (ed.): Introduction to Political Sociology. Copenhagen: Reitzel.

Prætorius, Nadja (2013): *Den etiske udfordring i en global tid*. København: Dansk Psykologisk Forlag. [The ethical challenge in a global time].

Simonsen, Birgitte (2014): *Unges forbrug af rusmidler – set i et uddannelsesperspektiv*. In Knud Illeris (ed.): Læring i konkurrencestaten – kapløb eller bæredygtighed. København: Samfundslitteratur. [The use of drugs – seen in an educational perspective].

PART II

LEARNING AND LIFE COURSE

CHAPTER 4

LIFELONG LEARNING AS A PSYCHOLOGICAL PROCESS

From a psychological point of view learning can be defined as 'any process that for living beings leads to a durable change of capacity and is not caused by oblivion, biological maturing or ageing' (Illeris, 2007). For humans this process is ongoing throughout life, whether it be intentional or incidental. In order to examine what this means in relation to the slogan of lifelong learning it will be useful to start by observing some of the most important characteristics of the very complex process of human learning. After this the question will be how human learning potential can be used and what is specific and important in different phases of the life course.

Some basic features of human learning

First of all, it is important to observe that human learning always consists of two very different processes, which are usually going on simultaneously and in an integrated way and therefore also are experienced as one and the same thing. On the one hand, learning is an external interaction process between the individual and his or her social and material environment. On the other hand, the impressions and influences that the individual receives from this interaction must be elaborated and internalised by an internal process of acquisition. Only if both of these processes are active will there be any learning (Illeris, 2007).

However, the criteria of the two processes are very different. The interaction process, on the one hand, is by nature social, cultural and societal; it is dependent on when and where it is taking place: what can be learned today is, for instance, to a great extent marked by modern technology that did not exist just a few decades ago. The acquisition process, on the other hand, is by nature individual and psychological; it is dependent on the immense and highly differentiated capacities of the human brain as developed over millions of years as part of our species' adaptation to environmental conditions: the human capacity for learning is characterised by the processes of language, thinking and consciousness, whereas other species may have sharper senses or better physical resources of strength and suppleness (see, for example, Solms and Turnbull, 2002).

Another important aspect of learning is that the acquisition process always includes both an incentive and a content dimension. The incentive is the mobilisation of the necessary mental energy for the process to take place – it is what we usually talk about as motivation. The content is about what is learned – it is impossible to speak about learning without speaking about something that is learned.

In schooling and education, learning content is usually conceived as knowledge and skills, but it can also be such properties as understanding, insight, meaning, attitudes, methods, viewpoints, culture, qualifications, competencies, etc. It is, however, important to realise that the incentives – emotion, motivation and volition – are not only driving forces, but also an integrated part of the learning processes and outcomes. If something is learned in an active and positive mode the learning will be easier to recall and apply in a broad range of different situations. But if the learning process has been reluctant or disengaged the learning result is obsessed with negative feelings and needs some kind of surmounting to be reactivated.

It is also important to be aware that the acquisition is always an integration of new impact into structures that have been developed by prior learning processes (this is the Piagetian view, which was strongly emphasised by Ausuble, 1968). This is in direct opposition to the traditional understanding of learning as a transfer of knowledge and skills. There is no such simple transfer, but a joining together in which the existing mental schemata are just as important as the new impact. And as the existing schemata are always individual structures – no two individuals have learned exactly the same during their life course – the learning result is also always a specific individual creation.

In addition, there are many different types of learning. Learning typologies can be set up from many perspectives, but it is significant that all the more advanced typologies in some way make a main distinction between what may be termed as additive and restructuring learning (e.g. Piaget, 1952 [1936]; Flavell, 1963; Rogers, 1969; Bateson, 1972; Engeström, 1987; Argyris, 1992). By additive learning is meant the usual everyday event of adding new elements to the already developed mental structures. This is generally easy, not very demanding, and we are doing it all the time, whenever we meet something new that is worth remembering. Restructuring learning, on the other hand, is demanding, because we have to break down and reorganise our patterns of behaviour or understanding in order to include some new elements that cannot fit into the existing structures. It is a way of learning that we can use when we meet impressions or situations that we cannot immediately grasp or cope with. But we only make the effort if the new is something that we experience as important or interesting to us. If not, we rather tend to reject it or distort it so that it is in accordance with the already established patterns or notions.

This leads us to the last general point on learning that will be mentioned here: that human beings in the overwhelmingly complex existence of today are not equipped to take in all the learning possibilities they are faced with. Our mental capacity, however magnificent it may seem, is not able to match the versatile and ever changing cultural and societal developments of the latest centuries. So we all have to develop ways of defence and resistance in order to avoid a lot of possible learning. Just think of how much you generally remember from half an hour's TV news! (Illeris, 2007).

Learning through the life course

Seen from the point of view of learning, it seems to be adequate to operate using four main phases of life (Illeris, 2003a, 2007):

- *Childhood* lasts from birth to the onset of puberty, which occurs these days around the age of 11–13 (previously it was at a later point).
- *Youth* lasts from puberty until the preconditions for a more or less stable

identity are established, typically through relatively permanent relationships with partners and work, or perhaps a consciousness of not wanting to enter into such relationships. It is a characteristic of present-day society that the period of youth is longer than it has ever previously been, and has a very fluid transition to adulthood.

- *Adulthood* lasts from the end of the youth period until the 'life turn' – a concept that implies that the end of life has been perceived on the distant horizon, and the person is beginning to accept this and relate to it.
- *Mature adulthood* lasts until death or, in terms of learning, perhaps only until mental weakness begins to take hold to a considerable extent.

In the following, the main characteristics of learning motivation in each of these four life ages will be examined and described in more detail.

Learning in childhood is uncensored and confident

The overall characteristic of children's learning is that, in line with their development, they are absorbed in capturing the world by which they see themselves surrounded and of which they are a part. In child psychology there are comprehensive descriptions of the many different facets and stages in this capturing process, including, for example, Freud's division into phases, Erikson's development ages and Piaget's stages theory. Here only certain overriding factors that determine some of the general conditions for the process will be pointed out.

In learning terms, it is naturally important that cognitive learning capacity develops gradually throughout childhood. It is also important that children basically expect to be guided by adults as to what and how they should learn. As babies their only connection with the surrounding world is through the mother and other adults, and the first 'capture' involves establishing the separation between themselves and the surrounding world (e.g. Stern, 1985). The child is from the start subject to the control of adults and can only gradually free itself from it.

In childcare institutions and in the early years at school, children are still obliged to unfold and develop within a framework set by adults. They must of necessity accept this as a basic condition, even though naturally they can resist when they feel that they are being restricted or they are unable to understand what is going on – and this resistance is also a highly significant factor in development and learning. However, children are typically ready to accept explanations that tell them that learning something may be good or important for them later even if they cannot grasp it right now.

Nevertheless, the development of our late-modern society has brought about certain trends for change that apply to some of these basic factors affecting learning in childhood. In general, cultural liberation gives children plenty of opportunities for activities, relations and impulses that previously lay beyond their reach, while at the same time, the disintegration of traditions and norms weakens or removes a number of fixed points and structures from which children could previously take their bearings. Like young people and adults, children today perceive a number of potential choices from an early age – of which some are real and many others are only apparent – while previously there was a much higher degree of certainty (e.g. Giddens, 1991).

The mass media play a special role here. More than parents or other adults, they give children the opportunity to experience – or often almost force on to them – a mass of impulses, including such things as catastrophes, violence and sex; experiences to which they have not previously had access, and which can have strong emotional influences on them. Also, introducing these things in advance of the formation of personal experience makes it more complicated for children to later acquire their own experiences in these spheres.

Another important factor is that developments in some spheres of society can happen so fast that adults have difficulty keeping up, while children can leap, so to speak, straight into the development at its present stage, which in some areas such as information technology makes some of them able to overtake adults.

From a learning perspective, it is generally important to remember that childhood as a life age is basically influenced by the huge acquisition process of integrating and relating to the whole of the complex material, social and societal environment. This requires a broad spectrum of protracted constructive processes that the child is disposed to carry out, trusting in adults and being supported by them. Childhood is typically a period of primarily gentle, gradual and stable additive learning processes, even though these processes have tended to become more complex and contradictory. Examples of the processes that are gone through are motor and linguistic development, acquisition of symbol management (including reading, writing and arithmetic), and knowledge of the surrounding world and its rules, structures and means of function.

In connection with these processes, there also occur a number of reconstructions, mainly directed towards getting the acquisition process back on track again when it has gone astray, but also more complex in the spheres connected to identity development, including the development of gender roles (Illeris, 2007).

Learning in youth is searching and identity building

Youth has not always been perceived as a life age in its own right. Historically, the concept of youth developed together with capitalism and industrialisation. In the beginning, the concept of youth was limited to a few years, but gradually it became a longer period and the notion of youth increasingly spread beyond the middle classes. The period of youth has from the start been linked with a particular need for socially necessary learning and personal development. With Erik Erikson's book, *Identity, Youth and Crises* (1968), the conception of youth took the direction typical for the interpretation today, which is that youth is primarily a period for a more or less crisis-determined development of a personal identity or self-comprehension.

However, with the development of late modernity, recent decades have seen a further expansion of the youthful period, so today it may often extend far into the twenties. In addition, youth has become very much idealised – and commercialised – as the age of freedom and happiness with no responsibilities, while at the same time, the personal and societal problems that attach to youth seem to be steadily increasing. The essence of this development, particularly as seen from a learning perspective, is that the demands on the formation of identity have undergone an explosive growth in line with cultural liberation – there is a lot of 'identity work' that young people have to do, as well as getting through their education, forming relationships with a partner, finding their place in society and so on.

Previously there was family affiliation, a gender role, class attachment and usually also an attachment to a particular profession, as well as a mass of given values and norms that the young person was expected to take on, perhaps through a somewhat rebellious process. Now all this is disintegrating or becoming redundant, and the young person must find his or her own way through personal choices. It is not only about education, career, partner and home; also lifestyle, personal identity and a lot of preferences and attitudes must be chosen. Development in these areas has been overwhelming, and young people currently have to struggle with new, untried processes, the conditions of which change almost from day to day – new educational opportunities, new consumer opportunities, new communication systems and new lifestyle offers make themselves felt in an almost chaotic confusion; everything seems possible, and yet young people perceive countless limitations, for many opportunities are completely inaccessible for the vast majority – only very few can become actors, TV hosts, designers or sporting heroes (see Simonsen, 2000).

Earlier it was generally accepted that human beings were cognitively fully developed from about the onset of puberty. But today it seems clear that, throughout the period of youth, new possibilities can be developed for thinking dialectically, making use of practical logic, recognizing what one knows (meta-cognition) and mastering critical reflection. Modern brain research has most recently shown that the working memory – the brain centre that precisely stands for such advanced cognitive functions – is only fully developed at the end of the teenage years. It is thus only during the period of youth that, together with all the other changes that take place during these years, we acquire our full cognitive capacity (Brookfield, 2000).

In terms of learning, the first part of the youth period is in the more developed countries still subject to compulsory education, and later one should go through some youth education and, as a rule, also some further education of a more vocational nature. However, all learning in the youth period is very much oriented towards the formation of identity and can only be understood in this light. This leads to a contradictory relationship with a lot of problems. Often young people react more or less reluctantly to academic subject requirements, which for the most part are forced upon them, and which they may find outdated, while the representatives of the system attempt to keep their concentration on academic work, which they themselves are trained in, are committed to and are under an obligation to uphold.

The most important things for young people to learn today are to be able to orient themselves, to be able to make choices that can be answered for, to keep up with everything, not to waste their lives on the wrong thing, and to be able to decline in the many situations where a choice has to be made. Society and employers also demand maturity, independence, responsibility and so on. The best security for the future seems not to be learning a subject on what are perceived as traditional premises, but to be ready to change and take hold of what is relevant in many different situations. Uncertainty cannot be countered by stability, but only by being open, flexible and constantly oriented to learning.

Youth is also the period in which to learn how to deal with gender and sexual relations. For both genders this is closely linked with the personal identity process – and here as in education it is most often the formation of identity that is given priority: young people today are often more absorbed in reflecting themselves in their partners than they are in the partners themselves.

There is so much to be learned in the period of youth: academically, emotionally, socially, societally and, most of all, in terms of identity. Whereas childhood is a time for constructive additive learning, youth is a period for major reconstructions and transformations in which, one by one, profound changes are made to the knowledge structures and the emotional patterns. And the reflexivity that is so characteristic of late modernity, where it is always the individual's relationship to him- or herself that is the focal point of learning, unfolds without doubt most dramatically in the years of youth as an essential yet enormously taxing tool for the identity process (Illeris, 2003b).

Learning in adulthood is selective and goal oriented

The beginning of the adult period may typically be marked by external events such as starting a family or finishing education. There are no decisively new cognitive opportunities; what happens in terms of learning and consciousness is that the person fully takes on the management of, and responsibility for, his or her own life, with this normally occurring gradually as a long process throughout the years of youth and into adulthood.

In general adulthood has traditionally been marked by a kind of ambition that implies a striving to realise more or less clear life aims relating to family, career, interests or something else – but in late modernity this representation is also on its way to being overlaid by the continual societal changes, the unpredictability of the future, the conditioning of the market mechanism and the unending succession of apparent choices.

Many factors that were in earlier times already marked out for the individual have now become things to be decided on again and again. It is no longer possible to make your choice of life course once and for all when young, and then expect to spend the rest of your life accomplishing it. Whereas, once a large number of factors were given, based on gender or class affiliations, for example, all now appears to be redundant (Giddens, 1991). The fact that this is only how it appears can be seen from statistics showing that the large majority of people, now just as previously, live their lives in the way that their gender and social background has prepared them for. However, this does not influence the perception that now this is something people choose themselves, something for which they are responsible, and thus for which they have only themselves to blame if it turns out to be unsatisfactory.

With the earlier, firmer structures, the individual could use his or her years of youth to develop an identity, or at least a sort of draft identity, that would be of help in governing future learning. In career terms, school and education would have provided for the acquisition of a groundwork that was regarded as feasible for the rest of that person's life, so that whatever was needed later could generally be gained through practice learning at work and maybe a few additional courses. In life also, it was necessary to keep up with any developments, but this did not go too fast for people to manage to acquire the requisite learning as they went along. Thus, for the vast majority of people, learning in adulthood was fairly manageable and predominantly additive in nature, with its most characteristic aspect probably being the development of a system of defence mechanisms that could screen out any new impulses that were too insistent, thus ensuring stability and self-respect.

Becoming an adult formally in our society means coming of age and so taking responsibility for one's own life and actions. This happens legally by the age of 18, but from a psychological perspective it is actually a process, and it is characteristic that this process has become longer and longer, to such an extent that today it is most often accomplished well into a person's twenties or perhaps never. Late-modern society's promotion of youth also makes it difficult to let it go.

In the field of learning this goes hand in hand with the continual extension of the average time spent in education. Today, after the compulsory school years, a majority go on to further courses for many years before the end of the preliminary period of education. In addition to this, adult education programmes have been greatly developed, and correspondingly young people's expectations today are for recurrent or lifelong education; they can hardly imagine that they could 'stick' in the same job all their lives.

However, it is basically characteristic that adults learn what they want to learn, and have very little inclination to acquire something they do not want, that is, something they do not perceive as meaningful for their own life goals, of which they are aware in varying degrees of clarity (Illeris, 2006). As a consequence of this, rather than having various more or less unconnected learning motives, adults have more coherent strategies relating to goals that are normally fairly clear and known to the individual.

This approach to education is, however, far from always in accordance with the way adult education is organised. In principle, adult education is nearly always voluntary. Nevertheless, very many participants in adult education today have been indirectly forced to take part in programmes, and many even feel they have been 'placed' there by different counselling bodies. It is experienced as particularly contradictory when one feels that one is an adult and would like to manage one's own life. Adult education is at present a strange mixture of old ideals concerning public enlightenment and modern vocational orientation and economically oriented targeting (Illeris, 2003c).

With the pace of change and need for reorganisation in the late-modern period, the phrase 'lifelong learning' primarily implies a need to be constantly prepared for reorganisation. This can be hard enough for young people, but for those who first became caught up in this development as adults, the challenge of reorganisation is even harder. The stability, self-assurance and professional pride that were crucial qualifications for many a few years ago now seem like burdensome encumbrances. Where before there was stability, there now has to be flexibility, and if there is to be any hope of survival in the job market, the defence mechanisms of stability must very quickly be replaced with service-mindedness and readiness for change.

Societal demands that adults must learn on a far greater scale and in a totally different way than previously are inescapable on every level. It is primarily a demand for a mental reorganisation and personal development, but there may also be technical or academic demands, for example, typically in connection with information technology developments. All these demands are for profound restructuring processes of a reflexive nature – and that is something many adults will not spontaneously accept.

At the same time, however, there are still many participants in adult education who are there of their own free will because they wish to or need to learn something specific – and in some cases also for more social reasons. On this basis it might be expected that these adults would themselves take responsibility for the learning that the course is providing. However, ordinary conceptions and experiences of education often get in the way of this. Even though the institutions, the teachers and the participants might say and believe otherwise, everyone in the education situation obstinately expects that the responsibility will lie with the teacher. It is, after all, the teacher who knows what has got to be learned.

The situation is paradoxical, for while these adult participants have a tendency to behave like pupils, they have a very hard time accepting the lack of authority the traditional pupil role entails. They get bored and become resistant in a more or less conscious way – but nevertheless they will not themselves take on the responsibility, for that is actually far more demanding. The conflict can only be resolved by effectively making a conscious break with the prevailing roles as pupils and teachers at school. And as a rule it is the teacher who has to take the initiative and insist on it. It is normally only when the participants realise that they truly can take responsibility and use the teacher as a support for their own learning that the picture alters, and after that the way is clear for the learning to become goal-directed, effective, transcendent and libidinal, as is characteristic of adult learning outside, which is not institutionalised (Illeris, 2004).

However, there is much to suggest that the conditions described here stand in the way of complete changes. The 'new youth' of late modernity, who have in recent years turned youth education upside down, are well on their way to making their entry into adult education as the 'new adults' (Simonsen, 2000).

Learning in mature adulthood is exclusive and conclusive

'The age of maturity', 'the third age' or 'second adulthood' are all terms for the phase of life that for most people in modern society lies between the so-called 'life turn' and actual old age, and can well last a period of 20 years or more.

The life turn is a psychological phenomenon concerning the perception and acknowledgement that the remaining time in your life is not unlimited. It is, however, most often external events that bring about and mark the life turn – typical examples are the children leaving home, losing a job, taking early retirement or being given reduced hours; it can also be a divorce or the death of a loved one, and for women the menopause may play a part in the situation.

In contrast to the first age of adulthood, the mature age is characteristically not dominated by the same form of purposefulness – the goals being reached for do not have the same existential nature as having a family, raising children, or work and career. As far as they are able – and the mature age is for many today a period with certain personal and financial abilities – people spend their time on things they perceive as quality activities, such as cultural or social activities, or helping others, their partner, if they have one, their children, their grandchildren or disadvantaged groups that they are involved with.

In this context there may often be important elements of learning, both formal education and less formal processes of development and change, characterised by being something absolutely personally chosen, because it is experienced as important or interesting, or perhaps has the nature of something one needs to prove to oneself and to others that one is well capable of but simply has not had the opportunity to do previously (Jarvis, 2001).

However, it must be remembered that this only applies to relatively privileged mature adults. Many people have more than enough to do just getting by practically and financially, and have neither the opportunity nor the reserves to look towards the self-actualisation or learning in which those in more favourable positions increasingly get involved. The new wave of learning and education for mature adults is for the time being mainly a middle-class phenomenon.

Cognitively there may be a trend towards learning beginning to happen more slowly if it concerns new areas the person is not very committed to, but this does not normally apply when it concerns things he or she is interested in, and for which he or she has good presuppositions and experiences. The usual popular notion that elderly people are worse at learning things can thus be seen to relate only to the fact that they can be slower in learning something new – which people are often not particularly interested in acquiring. People are satisfied with their own interests and experiences, and if the new matter is not connected to that it can make it more difficult to mobilise mental energy.

It is something else, of course, if it is a case of dementia or other diseases – but it is still worth noting that, even when such disability occurs, there would seem to be a tendency for it not to directly affect the areas where one has special competence and which one has maintained, and where the brain therefore has been 'kept in good condition' (Goldberg, 2005).

Three general lines of development in lifelong learning

It is important to stress that the described typical background attitudes to learning in various life ages are current attitudes, for the details of life ages are to a great extent determined by history, culture and society, and can alter rapidly. It has become clear, for example, how late modernity has influenced learning today, particularly in childhood and youth, but also increasingly in adulthood.

Nevertheless, there are also a number of important common links running through the life ages that are more general and that, to a certain extent, run across changing circumstances. From the descriptions previously given, three closely linked long lines of development of this kind can be pointed out:

- First, a gradual liberation occurs throughout the life ages for the individual in relation to the external determination of learning. Whereas learning in childhood is framed in an interaction between biological maturing and external influences, in youth it is characterised to a great extent by young people's fight to have a say in things and, partly through this, construct their identity. In first adulthood, people move towards learning what they themselves think is important, but to a great extent this is determined by their external conditions. It is only in mature adulthood that external determinations move into the background for those people who have the opportunities and the resources to liberate themselves.
- In close interaction with this gradual liberation of learning from its external bondage, there also typically occurs an individuation, that is, learning increasingly directs itself towards the development of an individual person and is determined by personal needs and interests. Again it is a development that first takes off properly in the period of youth, but which only has a full impact in mature adulthood.
- Finally, there also occurs a gradual development of responsibility for learning that is closely connected with the two other developments and so follows the same pattern.

In modern society, it seems very clear that it should be both a condition and a goal for society to strive to organise itself along the lines of these developments and to support them. However, learning is not only an individual process and education can also have perspectives other than supporting personal development and the provision of qualifications for individuals, which the late modern individualisation trend so clearly puts in central position. Society wants something from us, and individualisation goes hand in hand with equally strong measures that seek to control our learning.

References

Argyris, Chris (1992) *On Organizational Learning*, Cambridge, MA: Blackwell.
Ausuble, David P. (1968) *Educational Psychology: A cognitive view*, New York: Holt, Rinehart and Winston.

Bateson, Gregory (1972) *Steps to an Ecology of Mind*, San Francisco, CA: Chandler.
Brookfield, Stephen D. (2000) 'Adult cognition as a dimension of lifelong learning', in John Field and Mal Leicester (eds) *Lifelong Learning: Education across the lifespan*, London: RoutledgeFalmer, pp. 89–101.
Engeström, Yrjö (1987) *Learning by Expanding: An activity-theoretical approach to developmental research*, Helsinki: Orienta-Kunsultit.
Erikson, Erik H. (1968) *Identity, Youth and Crises*, New York: Norton.
Flavell, John H. (1963) *The Developmental Psychology of Jean Piaget*, New York: Van Nostrand.
Giddens, Anthony (1991) *Modernity and Self-identity*, Cambridge: Polity Press.
Goldberg, Elkhonon (2005) *The Wisdom Paradox*, New York: Simon and Schuster.
Illeris, Knud (2003a) 'Learning changes through life', *Lifelong Learning in Europe* 8(1): 51–60.
—— (2003b) 'Learning, identity and self orientation in youth', *Young – Nordic Journal of Youth Research* 11(4): 357–76.
—— (2003c) 'Adult education as experienced by the learner', *International Journal of lifelong Education* 22(1): 13–23.
—— (2004) *Adult Education and Adult Learning*, Malabar, FL: Krieger Publishing.
—— (2006) 'What is special about adult learning?', in Peter Sutherland and Jim Crowther (eds) *Lifelong Learning: Concepts and contexts*, London: Routledge, pp. 15–23.
—— (2007) *How We Learn: An introduction to learning and non-learning in school and beyond*, London: Routledge.
Jarvis, Peter (2001) *Learning in Later Life*, London: Kogan Page.
Piaget, Jean (1952 [1936]) *The Origins of Intelligence in Children*, New York: International Universities Press.
Rogers, Carl R. (1969) *Freedom to Learn*, Columbus, OH: Charles E. Merrill.
Simonsen, Birgitte (2000) 'New young people, new forms of consciousness, new educational methods', in Knud Illeris (ed.) *Adult Education in the Perspective of the Learners*, Copenhagen: Roskilde University Press, pp. 137–56.
Solms, Mark and Turnbull, Oliver (2002) *The Brain and the Inner World*, New York: Other Press.
Stern, Daniel N. (1985) *The Interpersonal World of the Infant*, New York: Basic Books.

CHAPTER 5

LEARNING, IDENTITY AND SELF-ORIENTATION IN YOUTH

> The identity development process nowadays is interesting for us because we ourselves experience having to select our own identity and lifestyle. We think a lot about who we want to be, the viewpoints we want to represent, the food we want to eat, the work we want to do, and if we want to join a religion.
>
> We are very much the main characters in our own lives because we must constantly reflect and make conscious decisions. We have to spend a lot of time considering personal interests, the possibility for personal development, and other topics that can be related to ourselves.
>
> Not least do we experience confusion concerning choices in life, because there is nobody to tell us what is right. We have to listen to our inner voice, knowing that we risk making the wrong or merely incompetent choices which we ourselves will be responsible for. (Klyvø et al., 2000: 3–4)

This quotation is from the concluding report in a project entitled 'The development of identity in reflexive modernity', written by a group of first-semester students at Roskilde University (RUC). The content is not unusual, but a remarkably clear formulation of something that practically all young people are struggling with today and which has a far-reaching influence on their learning processes. Today all young people are very preoccupied with who they want to be, because they experience that there are some crucial choices to be made, that they will have to make them themselves, and that they will also have to bear the consequences on their own. For good or for bad, they inevitably experience that they are the main characters in their own lives in a way that is completely different from what was at all possible previously. Even though a huge amount of advice and guidance is available, in the final analysis they have only themselves to rely on. They must always 'listen to their inner voice' because there are innumerable possibilities that can be full of tensions and contradictions and they themselves are often very ambivalent, balancing as they do between the demand that everything must be sensational and the fear of not being able to manage.

However, to understand what this implies for learning, we need a learning concept encompassing more than merely acquiring knowledge and skills and thus corresponding to the modern understanding of competence, which comprises the totality of capacities that can be mobilized, including personal ability and willingness to undertake such mobilization. Therefore, in this article I start by exploring learning in general and the most important differences between learning in childhood, youth and adulthood. From this angle I then focus on

The concept of learning

The theoretical basis of the reflections on learning in the following is the comprehensive and contemporary learning concept developed in my recent book *The Three Dimensions of Learning* (Illeris, 2002). This concept – which has received much interest in relation to adult education research (Illeris, 2003) – brings together central points from a wide range of different non-behaviourist American, British, European Continental, Nordic and Russian learning theories in a common general understanding. In doing so it differs from mainstream learning theory by taking in emotional, motivational, social and societal angles as being equally as important as the cognitive side of learning, and by including such issues as mis-learning, defence and resistance as important elements of the conception. This also makes the theory well suited as a point of departure for exploring the issues of contemporary learning and identity development in youth.

Learning in general is understood as all the processes leading to permanent capacity change, whether it be physical, cognitive, emotional or social in nature, and which do not exclusively have to do with biological maturation. This means that the learning concept also spans such functions as personal development, socialization and qualification, as the differences between these terms mainly concern the perspective that is adopted. Thus when I deal with learning in youth, I refer to the whole register of mental and capacity development and readjustment. One of the central points of this concept is that these functions can only be separated analytically and not in reality.

Simultaneously, the concept also implies that all learning is part of a certain structure covering two very diverse types of processes and three dimensions. The two types of process are closely integrated and both must be active before learning can take place. On the one hand, there are interaction processes between the learner and the surroundings and, on the other hand, there are the inner mental acquisition and elaboration processes, by means of which impulses from the interaction are united with the results of earlier learning. The interaction processes are social and cultural in nature and in general follow a historical-societal logic, i.e. they are fundamentally dependent on how and when they take place, as the interaction possibilities are different in different societies and different historical epochs. Conversely, the acquisition processes are psychological in nature and in general follow a biological-structural logic, i.e. they follow the patterns that have been genetically developed through the ages as part of the development process of the species.

In addition, the acquisition processes always include two integrated sides: the cognitive or knowledge and skills side, and the emotional or psychodynamic side. During the pre-school years the two sides of the acquisition processes gradually split away from each other, but they are never totally separated (cf. Damasio, 1994; Furth, 1987). All cognitive learning always has an emotional component which is marked or 'obsessed' by the emotional situation prevalent during learning, for example whether the motivation was pleasure, necessity or even compulsion. All emotional learning also contains rational elements; a knowledge or understanding of the matters in question.

In this manner, learning will always include three integrated dimensions, which may be termed cognitive, emotional and social-societal. Through the cognitive dimension, knowledge, skills, understandings and, ultimately, meaning and

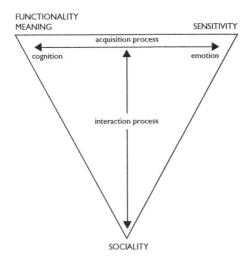

Figure 5.1 The processes and dimensions of learning.

functionality are developed. Patterns of emotion and motivation, attitudes and, ultimately, sensitivity are developed through the emotional dimension. Through the social-societal dimension, potentials for empathy, communication and cooperation and, ultimately, sociality are developed. Figure 5.1 illustrates the connection between the two types of process and the three dimensions that are active in any learning and which must always be included if one wishes to form a complete picture of a learning situation or process.

The results of learning are stored in the central nervous system as dispositions that can be described as schemes or mental patterns. With respect to the cognitive dimension of learning, one typically speaks of schemes or, more popularly, of memory. In the emotional and the social-societal dimensions, one would employ terms such as patterns or, more popularly, inclinations. Under all circumstances, it is decisive that the results of learning are structured before they can be retained. This structuring can be established in various ways, and on this basis it is possible to distinguish between four different levels of learning that are activated in different contexts, imply different types of learning results, and require more or less energy. (This is an elaboration of the concept of learning originally developed by Jean Piaget, cf. Illeris, 2002.)

When a scheme or pattern is established, it is a case of *cumulative* or mechanical learning, characterized by being an isolated formation, something new that is not a part of anything else. Therefore, cumulative learning is most frequent during the first years of life, but later occurs only in special situations where one must learn something with no context of meaning, for example a telephone or pin code number. The learning result is characterized by a type of automation that means that it can only be recalled and applied in situations mentally similar to the learning context.

By far the most common form of learning is termed *assimilative* or learning by addition, meaning that the new element is linked to a scheme or pattern that is already established. One typical example could be learning in school subjects that are precisely built up by means of constant additions to what has already been learned, but assimilative learning also takes place in all contexts where one gradually develops one's capacities of a cognitive, emotional or social-societal nature. The results of learning are characterized by being linked to the scheme or pattern in question in such a manner that it is relatively easy to recall and apply them when one is mentally oriented towards the field in question.

However, in some cases, situations occur where something takes place that is difficult immediately to relate to any existing scheme or pattern; this is experienced as something one cannot really understand. But if it is something one is determined to acquire, this can take place by means of *accommodative* or transcendent learning. This type of learning implies that one breaks down (parts of) an existing scheme and transforms it so that the new situation can be linked in. Thus one both relinquishes and reconstructs something, and this can be experienced as painful and something requiring energy. The result of the learning is characterized by the fact that it can be recalled and applied in many different, relevant contexts. It is typically experienced as having got hold of something which one really has internalized.

Finally, in special situations there is also a far-reaching type of learning that has been described as *transformative* learning (Mezirow, 1991). This learning implies what could be termed personality changes and is characterized by simultaneous restructuring in the cognitive, the emotional and the social-societal dimensions, a break of orientation that typically occurs as the result of a crisis-like situation caused by challenges experienced as urgent and unavoidable, making it necessary to change oneself in order to get any further. Transformative learning is thus both profound and extensive and can often be experienced physically, typically as a feeling of relief.

In relation to these four types of learning, it is important to note that together they characterize what happens when somebody actually learns something. But an adequate learning concept must also relate to what takes place in the frequent situations where somebody could learn something but does not, or perhaps learns something quite other than what had been intended. This concerns matters such as mislearning and mental defence, distortion or resistance, which, naturally, can be due to miscommunication, but in our complex late-modern information society must necessarily also be generalized and take more systematized forms, because nobody can remain open to the gigantic volumes of impulses we are faced with. I shall not deal in a general manner with these matters here but shall return to them in a later more definite context.

To sum up: what has been outlined is a concept of learning which basically is constructive in nature, i.e. it is assumed that the learner him or herself actively builds up his/her learning as mental structures that can be termed, for example, meaning, functionality, sensitivity and sociality. But in contrast to classical constructivist and social-constructivist concepts, it is pointed out here that the mental structures are built up in interaction with different types of processes and in the three different, but always interconnected dimensions.

This more complex concept of learning is of great importance when one specifically wishes to deal with certain learning processes, for example, those that mark learning during youth. It establishes that there are different types of learning which are widely different in scope and that the whole field must always be in the picture, and that, for example, one cannot understand cognitive learning without also considering what happens in the emotional and social-societal dimensions.

Learning and the phases of life

On a general level, there are considerable differences between the nature of learning in different phases of life. Life-span theory usually distinguishes between the four main phases in the human life course: childhood, youth, adulthood and mature adulthood (cf. Illeris, 2003; Jensen, 1993). This means that they operate with a youth phase that is usually understood as a transition between childhood and adulthood. For a broad understanding of the special nature of learning in this youth phase it is therefore adequate to look at the differences between learning in childhood and in adulthood and subsequently regard the youth phase as a transition period between these two.

Learning in childhood could be described as a campaign to conquer the world. The child is born into an unknown world and learning is about acquiring this world and learning to deal with it, in parallel with this being made possible by biological maturation. When viewed in relation to later phases of life, two learning-related features are most prominent, especially in the small child. In the first place, learning is *comprehensive* and *uncensored*. The child throws itself into everything possible, and is limited only by its biological development and the nature of its surroundings. Second, the child places utmost *confidence* in the adults around it. So to speak, it has only those adults to refer to, without any possibility of evaluating or choosing what the adults present it with – and must, for example, learn the language they speak, the culture of which they are a part, etc.

This is basically the case throughout the whole period of childhood and until puberty. In principle the child's capturing of its surroundings is uncensored and trusting; its endeavour is to make use of the opportunities that present themselves in an unlimited and indiscriminate fashion. But in the complex world of today, apart from the immediate surroundings, the child inevitably meets with a great diversity of mediated or secondary possibilities for experience or patterns of meaning, not least from the mass media or from its friends. This complicates the situation and marks the later period of childhood today, makes learning far more unclear and contradictory, and provokes defence, selection and mistrust and thus erases the uncensored, trusting approach, which, however, must still be maintained as the basis of learning in childhood.

Learning in adulthood is the other side of this picture. Being an adult essentially means that one is capable of and willing to take responsibility for oneself and one's actions. In our society this formally happens at the age of 18, but in reality this takes place gradually in the course of the increasingly lengthy period of youth. From the point of view of learning, in principle being an adult also means that one takes responsibility for oneself, i.e. that consciously or less consciously one selects and decides what one wants to learn and not to learn. For in our complicated modern society the amount of what one can learn far outstrips what any person can manage to learn, and this applies not only to the content of learning but also to attitudes, modes of understanding, communication possibilities, patterns of action, lifestyle, etc. Selection becomes a necessity.

In principle, adults themselves would carry out and take responsibility for this selection. But even this would be completely impossible. This is why today people have to develop a kind of automatic selection mechanism. The German social psychologist, Thomas Leithäuser, has described this selection mechanism as 'everyday consciousness' (Leithäuser, 1976, cf. Illeris, 2002), which functions in the way that one develops some general pre-understandings within certain thematic areas. When one meets with influences within such an area, these pre-understandings are activated so that if elements in the influences do not correspond to the pre-understandings, they are either rejected or distorted to make them agree. In both cases, this results in no new learning but, on the contrary, often the cementing of the already-existing understanding. Through everyday consciousness, to a high degree adults take responsibility for their own learning and non-learning in a manner that seldom involves any direct positioning. On a more general level, learning in adulthood is fundamentally characterized by the following:

- adults learn what they want and what is meaningful for them to learn;
- adults draw on the resources they already have in their learning; and
- adults take as much responsibility for their learning as they want to take (if they are allowed to).

(Illeris, 2002: 219)

However, just as children's basic learning patterns are often erased by the increasing and complex secondary learning possibilities, adults' learning, especially in educational contexts, can be strongly marked by the forms of institutionalized learning in school that they experienced and accustomed themselves to in childhood and youth. When adults enter an institutionalized education programme, there is a distinct tendency for them to slip into the well-known pupil role where the control and responsibility are left up to the teacher. This is the easiest way, on the face of it, and often the teacher is also inclined to take on the traditional and secure controlling teacher role.

On the basis of these brief descriptions of important features of learning in childhood and adulthood, learning in youth can basically be described as a gradual transition from the uncensored, trusting learning of childhood to the selective and self-controlled learning of adulthood. Even though this picture on both sides is extremely complicated by the communication and information forms of late modernity, it is nevertheless precisely this transition that fundamentally lays down the conditions for learning during the youth phase.

It typically begins with 11–13-year-old children becoming more restless and sceptical in school and other learning situations controlled by others. At the beginning their resistance to adult-controlled learning is unsure and diffuse. It gradually becomes stronger and more conscious, and reaches its peak at the age of 14–15, typically in the form of rebellion and a struggle for power. Finally, in youth education programmes and sometimes also far into higher education study programmes, the situation takes on yet another character. Now, to a certain extent, the study programmes are self-chosen, and in principle the possibility exists of changing or dropping out at the same time as the young people gradually start to target their learning. In this way rebellion and resistance become mixed with the possibility of making one's own choice, and the power battle is mixed with or takes on the character of argumentation and negotiation.

But, simultaneously with this development in the emotional and social dimensions, a crucial development also takes place in the cognitive area: the transition from the concrete operational to the formal operational stage, which, according to Piaget, concludes the cognitive development on the structural level. Around the onset of puberty one acquires a new possibility for thinking and learning abstractly and logically-deductively.

However, this assumption has subsequently received much criticism. On the one hand, far from all adults are capable of thinking formal-operationally in the mathematical-logical sense implied by Piaget's definition. Empirical studies show that this is the case for fewer than 30 percent in Great Britain, but simultaneously confirm that at the start of puberty a crucial development occurs in the possibilities for abstract thinking and learning, justifying the mention of a new cognitive phase (Shayer and Adey, 1981). On the other hand, it has been claimed that at later periods important new cognitive possibilities can be developed, extending far beyond the formal-operative. Stephen Brookfield, has summed up this critique by pointing to four possibilities for learning which, in his opinion, are first developed during adulthood: the capacity to think dialectically, the capacity to make use of practical logic, the capacity to realize how one can know what one knows (meta-cognition), and the capacity for critical reflection (Brookfield, 2000).

The conclusion to all this must be that in puberty, physiological maturation takes place in the central nervous system which makes a new type of abstract and stringent thinking and learning possible, enabling one to operate context-independently with coherent systems of concepts, and that through youth and adulthood this ability can be further developed in the direction of, inter alia, formal-logical, practical-logical, dialectical, meta-cognitive and critically reflexive thinking and learning. Thus, in the case of learning in youth a new cognitive capacity is present to understand and acquire large-scale conceptual contexts, that to a high degree characterizes learning motivation during the years of youth. One is determined to discover how things are connected and this applies to personal as well as social, natural-scientific, societal, political and religious matters.

Thus, the growing urge for independence and the increasing need to understand how the young and their surroundings function and why this is the case are the basic features of learning during youth. Young people increasingly want to take on the responsibility for their own learning and non-learning, they want to select and reject for themselves, and in this connection they want to understand what they are dealing with and their own roles and possibilities. However, the situation is extremely complicated by the duality of late modernity: on the one side, the apparently boundless degrees of freedom and volumes of information; and, on the other side, a far-reaching, indirect controlling process on the part of parents, teachers, youth cultures, mass media and formal conditions for options. In the area of learning, the transition from child to adult has also become a lengthy, complex and ambiguous process with floating contours and unclear conditions and targets.

Youth, responsibility and identity

From a psychological perspective, as clearly illustrated in the opening quotation, what is primarily central in learning by young people is identity development, and it makes itself felt in all possible contexts and in many different ways that can be both ambivalent and unclear – also for the young people themselves. The question of responsibility has a central position and may be regarded as a good example of the complexity of the situation.

On the face of it, it is very simple. On the one hand it is part of young people's development that they gradually both can and want to take over responsibility for their own learning. On the other hand, it is the declared aim of society, the school and the parents that they should gradually assume this responsibility. Why, then, is it so complicated?

Viewed from the perspective of the young, there is an almost interminable range of choices to be made, and from the time they were very small they have been told repeatedly in all possible direct and indirect ways, that they must choose what they really want to do – what feels exactly right for them. In late modernity, the range of situations and possibilities for choice have increased to the practically limitless. From early childhood this is manifested, in particular, in options for consumption – toys, videos, candy, clothes, etc. – but also in activities and social relations, and children constantly see and hear adults in numerous choice situations. In addition, the choices almost always appear to be and are presented as being free. You can choose what you want and the only thing you must take into account is what you really want. Therefore, you must constantly listen to your inner voice which is actually something that often requires a great deal of sensitivity and self-understanding that can only be developed gradually by means of the unending range of choices, rejections and new choices.

At one time, identity was something one developed and, to a great extent, inherited – something that was largely framed by one's gender, class, family, ethnicity and where one lived. Now one can apparently choose everything oneself. While matters such as gender and ethnicity are given, it is energetically denied – not least by young people themselves – that this makes any difference, or it is something that is applied, interpreted and modelled in the identity process parallel with other matters. The possibilities are, in principle, endless. One can always make a new choice and continue to do so – but it is one's own responsibility and equally one's own fault if the choice is not right. It is not strange that the young are virtually identified with this endless and absolutely decisive process of choice and identification and that there is a tendency for everything to be seen and experienced in this perspective. There is no way around it; it is a matter of one's life and happiness.

All this is different from the perspective of the school, the parents and society. While it is certainly very crucial that young people make the right choices, what is right can only be decided by the individual to the same extent as the sum of the choices fits in with the needs of the society. This concerns not only educational level and occupational choice, but just as much choices of consumption and lifestyle in the widest sense, of maintaining and continuing what is presented as the free market society. If too many people do not consume enough, and if too many do not choose the stressed, globalized lifestyle of late modernity, we cannot maintain economic growth and we will lag behind in the international competition.

The choice is not nearly as free as young people think. The individual has a number of internal dispositions and unconscious experiences that set a limit, and there also exist numerous mechanisms that serve the purpose of all of us making the right choice, at the same time as we maintain the notion of free choices and believe in them as the best thing in the world. While it is, of course, correct that there are far more possibilities for choice than previously, much is established as unconscious pre-structuring in the individual, or they are patterns and notions that have been adopted insensibly and are fertilized every day in the mass media, advertisements, etc.

Youth is a transition phase but it is fundamentally, now as earlier, a transition and a pass to a certain type of society; a society that has already set the framework and influenced the individual up through childhood, and a society that is so diverse, opaque, and in many ways disjointed and self-destructive that it must of necessity be a transition that is insecure, ambivalent, searching, floating and changing with an unclear course towards an unclear goal.

In this way, the processes of choice and identity are woven into a fundamental and unclear contradictory relationship, which in its very essence has to do with young people having to learn what society needs while experiencing it as their own free choice. They must construct themselves; they must know and experience that they are completely their own construction, but this must be done within a framework with limited room for manoeuvre. They must all individually and voluntarily learn to choose (almost) the same.

The concept of identity

There is nothing new in the development of identity being perceived as a process that, first and foremost, takes place in the phase of youth and, conversely, that

Learning, identity and self-orientation in youth 65

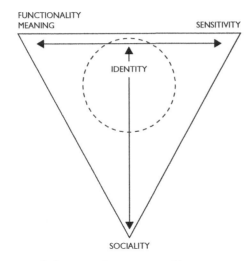

Figure 5.2 The position of identity in the structure of learning.

youth is perceived as a stage of life psychologically focused on the formation of an identity that one can build on for the rest of one's life. The classical identity concept was primarily drawn up by Erik H. Erikson, especially in his book *Identity, Youth and Crisis* (Erikson, 1968). The word 'identity' itself derives from the Latin *idem*, which means 'the same' and has to do with the experience of being the same or recognizable both to oneself and others in changing situations. This also points to the duality in the identity, so central to Erikson's concept, namely that one is an individual creation, a biological life, while simultaneously being a social and societal being. Therefore, identity is always an individual biographical identity, an experience of a coherent individuality and life course, at the same time as being a social, societal identity, an experience of a certain position in the social community.

In this way there is a striking parallel between Erikson's concept of identity and the concept of learning outlined earlier. In both cases, there are two linked characteristics that always coexist and work together. Corresponding to Erikson's personal side of identity is the individual acquisition process in learning; corresponding to Erikson's social side of identity is the social interaction process of learning. Thus, from the point of view of learning, identity development can be understood as the individually specific essence of total learning, i.e. as the coherent development of meaning, functionality, sensitivity and sociality. As shown in Figure 5.2, its core area can be placed around the meeting between the two basic processes of learning.

However, if we return to the youth phase in our present post-modern society, it is clear that both Erikson's notion of a more or less fixed identity as the goal, and identity confusion as the frightening counter picture, must be relativized today. When one of society's most central and direct requirements of its members is that we must always be flexible and ready for change, a fixed, stable identity becomes problematic. When older people are often criticized and rejected by the labour market because they are inflexible, this has precisely to do with the fact that over the years they have built up stable identities and self-understandings, which they cannot or will not change.

Simultaneously, the demand for such a targeted identity process implied a great challenge to be met with rebellion and resistance, and these could also be important elements in building up identity. But today it can be difficult to see what a rebellion should be targeted at, because parents, teachers and other counsellors are usually well-meaning, understanding people, there is great scope for personal choice on the intimate level, and on the large societal and global levels everything is mixed into an impenetrable, unclear confusion of power, manipulation, experts and propaganda, making it difficult to canalize any rebellion. Confusion is almost a matter of course, and the requirement is to be able to live with this confusion, to be able to manage and handle the incoherent, changing and always risky world of which one is a part.

In spite of its being criticized and to some extent outdated, Erikson's theory is still extremely interesting, partly because it is the fundament to which direct or indirect reference is most often made in the discussions, and partly because it so unambiguously positions identity as something which one acquires oneself, develops, builds up, constructs – or learns. One has, naturally, some genetic dispositions. Identity cannot be just anything at all – but is nonetheless strongly marked by the learning possibilities offered by the life of the individual and the way in which the individual relates to them. The theory also provides a clear picture of identity as a stable formation, which at the same time is susceptible to influence, fundamentally developed through a crisis-laden process that is transformative in nature and the central development process during the period of youth.

In relation to the learning concept outlined at the beginning of this article, on the basis of Erikson's theory identity formation can therefore in general be described as a holistic learning process that in a significant manner includes and influences the whole field of learning. Even though there have been clear general changes in the nature of the identity – so far-reaching that some researchers today are of the opinion that the very term is misleading – it is still a process of this comprehensive nature that is the central rationale of learning in the period of youth.

Identity problems and narcissism

However, it is clear that Erikson's identity theory and the entire classical conception of identity development can only form a point of departure today. It has become increasingly visible that these concepts presuppose a society with a degree of stability and common norms and forms of consciousness that no longer exist.

The first important signs of this development were registered by American psychoanalysts as early as the 1960s. They were described in more detail first and foremost by Heinz Kohut (1977) and Otto Kernberg (1975) as 'narcissistic personality disturbances' and 'pathological narcissism', respectively, and in Europe by Thomas Ziehe in his work on puberty and narcissism (Ziehe, 1975). This formed the theoretical foundation of the narcissism debate that, well into the 1980s, played a dominant role in the conception of 'the new youth'.

The starting point of all this was that new types of psychological problems were becoming dominant in the clinical picture emerging in psychoanalytical practice. In contrast to the classical anxiety neuroses, these symptoms were more diffuse and typically were, for example, a lack of self-esteem, feelings of emptiness, a feeling of not really existing, a lack of pleasure in work and of initiative, and an increased tendency towards routine behaviour. In relation to more classical neuroses and psychotic states, it was characteristic that by and large the patients had maintained a coherent self. They were not threatened by self-dissolution, regression or mental fragmentation, but primarily by lacking ego stability, a need to reflect themselves and to gain self-esteem through others, and a fear of losing contact with themselves psychologically. Therefore their existence was dominated by an urge to avoid getting into situations where the unstable self could be threatened.

At that stage, the concept of identity was included in the narcissism debate to a limited extent only. Nevertheless, it must be viewed as the beginning of a steadily more extensive interest in identity formation. Today these changes apply to most young people up to the age of 25–30 in western capitalist countries, and the discussion about identity formation has developed in many directions. In the following I shall attempt to capture some main trends in this discussion from a perspective concerning the significance of identity for learning and education during youth.

Dissolution trends in identity

The most consistent and extreme challenge to the traditional perception of identity was developed during the 1990s within the psychological mode of social constructionism as represented typically by social psychologists such as Kenneth Gergen (1991, 1994) and John Shotter (1993). This mode is fundamentally based on the premise that mental processes and phenomena are developed in social interaction. Thus it is obviously in opposition to the perception of learning outlined here as it only addresses one of the two integrated processes of learning, namely the process of social interaction, while the individual process of mental acquisition is not addressed or, in the most radical formulations, is directly disallowed (corresponding to classical cognitive and behaviourist modes of perception, which only deal with the cognitive dimension of learning).

In the view of social constructionism, identity and the self are also perceived as social constructions that are formed through social interaction and relations, and it is questionable whether one can speak at all of a fixed identity or an authentic self, because when the social situations and contexts change, identity and the self must also do so. Identity takes on an incoherent, situation-determined form with the character of a number of different social roles that the individual assumes or slides into, as a worker, parent, road-user, etc., and the roles do not have to have any inner cohesion. The late-modern person is just as split as the world in which he or she lives.

In his most widely read book, Gergen uses the term 'the saturated self' (Gergen, 1991). This is a self or an identity that is constantly exposed to influences that are so many and varied that the self or identity cannot contain them, at any rate not in any coherent or holistic understanding. It is rather reminiscent of the above-mentioned concept about everyday consciousness, but whereas Leithäuser describes this as a defence system that precisely tries to hold together an identity across the lines of the incoherent influences, in Gergen's perception the defence has definitively broken down and thus a liberation has taken place. Gergen sees no contradictions in this while Leithäuser would probably view it as a fragmentation bordering on the pathological. The question, however, is whether such an extreme dissolution of identity is a reasonable description. At any rate, other current ways of perceiving the situation are also to be found, which, while being aware of the dissolution trends, also note that there still exists a type of inner mental coherence in the individual.

One of these perceptions focuses on the life story or the individual biography as that which holds the individual together mentally and which thus can be said to form a type of identity (Alheit, 1994; Antikainen et al., 1996; Dominicé, 2000). The self-understanding of the late-modern person is held together by his/her perception or narration of his/her life story. The narration is neither a precise nor a truthful account of the actual life course, but a history developed through the constant interpretation and attribution of significance assigned to events and contexts which one subjectively finds important – in the same way as the identity is a more or less coherent entity which, however, constantly develops and is reinterpreted.

The English sociologist, Anthony Giddens (1991) has a somewhat different perception. While Giddens also refers to the life story as an important element in self-understanding, he places the major emphasis on what he calls 'self-identity', which he defines as 'a reflexively organized endeavour' that includes the maintenance and revision of a coherent life story and of reflexively structured life planning and lifestyle 'in terms of flows of social and psychological information about possible ways of life'. What is most important in Giddens is thus that the identity is the result of constant reflexive processes where one constructs and reconstructs one's self-perception in the light of impulses from one's surroundings.

In contrast to social constructionism, the life story and the reflexivity-oriented perceptions are characterized by the fact that individuals seek to counter the late-modern trends towards dissolution and fragmentation of the identity by different means that can create a certain inner coherence and continuity. This implies that somewhere 'deep inside' there must be a mental instance, a self or a core identity, from which this resistance or counter-move can derive. Child psychologist Daniel Stern (1985) is of the opinion that even during the first years of life, the child normally develops a 'core self' with crucial significance for further personality development.

From the point of view of learning there is every reason to pay attention to the necessity of such a core identity. This is so, in the first place, because total identity fragmentation or situation identity appears to be an impossible and exaggerated consequence of the dissolution trends of late modernity. In the second place, this is so because it implies that what must be learned and maintained is precisely the duality of both a core identity and extreme flexibility, which must not have the nature of identity confusion but rather that of constant reconstruction.

In the introductory quotation, the students used the phrase that they must constantly listen to their inner voice. Metaphorically, this phrase presupposes the existence of a mental instance within the individual that one can consult and from which one can get an answer that is precisely an expression of oneself or one's identity. The phrase also suggests that today it may be difficult to get into contact with this identity, that it can be hidden under other layers that one must penetrate.

A picture emerges of the tendency for the late-modern person to react by trying to maintain a fairly stable core identity in the face of dissolution trends and demands for flexibility and readiness to change. However, it is also clear that maintaining this core costs willpower; it is under constant external pressure and must be surrounded by layers or structures of a more flexible nature. If the core is really threatened, if the defence cannot withstand the pressure, then symptoms such as those described in connection with narcissism appear and the feeling of losing oneself emerges.

A perception of a core identity surrounded by a layer of more flexible structures also harmonizes with the concept of learning described in this paper, partly because it acknowledges both the social and the individual sides of the mental processes, and partly because it allows room for both stable patterns and structures and on-going changes through influences and learning, cognitively, emotionally and socially.

On the other hand, it seems unrealistic to imagine total fragmentation or a lack of a stable identity All the experience that the individual has had throughout childhood and youth with respect to the way in which she or he functions and is regarded in a wide range of different contexts cannot but leave generalized traces about who one is and how one is regarded by others. Even if one feels uncertain and unstable, these can also be elements of an identity. Total emptiness or the lack of authenticity also involve total incapacity and, in the last instance, mental breakdown.

But what do these complicated matters concerning the identity process imply for young people and their behaviour, for example in education programmes?

Identity development and self-orientation

Classical identity formation can, as in Erikson (1968) for example, be described as a gradual forward-moving process with many sub-processes and side-tracks, but nevertheless leading step by step to a more or less stable identity that not only involves self-esteem and self-knowledge but also the laying out of guidelines and preferences with respect to working life, family life, conception of society and interests, which basically should function as the foundation of the future existence.

All of this is as such still present and functions as a type of ideal or guideline for young people. At any rate, this is the way they would like to experience it. Most of them, for example, would like to aim towards a permanent job and a stable relationship with children and family life in good surroundings with good friends and interests that engage them. But at the same time young people fully realize that the world is not like that any more, society is changing from one day to the next, an education is always merely provisional, and, as a rule, relationships are only permanent for a time (Simonsen, 2000). It is therefore absolutely necessary also to be prepared for the changeable and unpredictable – the only thing one can predict is unpredictability.

This situation is reflected in the development task typically facing a young person today. Young people must at one and the same time develop a reasonably stable and sustainable core identity and simultaneously be able, practically and mentally, to handle an enormous variability, a risk society in which one can never be sure of anything (compare again with the introductory quotation).

This is a huge and completely incalculable task which earlier generations find difficult to fully understand. The way in which young people approach this task has probably been formulated most precisely by Ziehe in the term 'search processes' (Ziehe and Stubenrauch, 1982). Young people typically become involved in a continuous, limitless search within the varied fields of opportunity that face them. They try out one thing after another with respect to absolutely everything such as friendships, relationships, sexuality, alcohol, drugs, interests, activities, competitions, sports, music, education, and ways of living, and they move around globally either on the internet and through the media, or directly by travelling. Everything is of interest and a great deal is rejected, but the field of opportunity is still huge – at any rate as it is experienced by the individual – and every choice one makes is only temporary, because another choice can always be made, and very often is made.

Instead of identity development, a concept that refers back to a context that no longer exists, there is reason to find a new term for this comprehensive process. Here I will use the term *self-orientation* which is suitable for capturing the fact that this is a very wide-ranging process where one orients oneself with a view to finding oneself, one's options, ways of functioning and preferences, gradually building up a certain core identity and some rationales for all the choices with which one is constantly presented. On the basis of this concept of self-orientation, in conclusion

I will attempt to sum up the way in which young people today typically function in relation to learning and qualification through education and other activities.

Identity development and education

It is clear that today education is very central to the lives and consciousness of young people, and studies also show that young people are very prepared and basically positive about the need to educate and qualify themselves (Simonsen, 2000). But the old question, 'What are you going to be when you grow up?', has now taken on dimensions that are quite boundless, partly because it has become more a question of 'Who can I be?' than 'What can I be?', and partly because young people are presented with lists of thousands of educational and occupational choices at the same time as, from earliest childhood, they have learned that it is a matter of choosing what is absolutely right for one personally, what they really want, what can help to realize their personal talents and preferences. The opportunities are there and all you have to do is to make your very own choice, find precisely what you are enthusiastic about, and what can make you happy.

This is where the search processes get underway, and must do so, because the apparently free choice situation is essentially both impossible and untrue. In the first place, freedom of choice is an illusion. A great number of personal and social prerequisites are demanded, there is competition for places, there are things that the individual cannot manage, situations that are unbearable, and it is anything but certain that happiness lies at the end of the path one has entered.

In more traditional sociological terminology, it would be said that 'in reality' and 'behind the backs' of the young an extensive, widely diversified sorting process takes place. But young people do not look at it in this way. Their point of departure is more subjective and they experience it precisely as a search. 'What am I really enthusiastic about?', is the most fundamental question to which very few can give an even vaguely grounded answer. However, since one must choose something or other, one embarks on a course that may prove good. It may turn out that it is not particularly interesting or profitable, it may be boring – and this is often the most negative experience of all – or there may be practical difficulties, or one does not like the teacher or foreman, or one's friends are not fantastic. There can be many reasons as to why the choice made does not live up to one's expectations, and then it is a matter of stopping, the sooner the better, because it is not about finding something that is just bearable or acceptable. It is always about finding what is exactly right, what one can really be enthusiastic about. In addition, one must always consult oneself because in the final analysis it is only within oneself that the yardstick is to be found.

These search processes obviously demand a great deal from young people. They must constantly have their antennae spread to capture and decode the signals according to which they can navigate. Naturally, the content of an education or activity is important because under no circumstances may this be experienced as boring. But just as important are the people involved: the teachers, co-workers, friends, the group. One has to get on with them really well, and they must be stimulating and positive, at the same time as one must count for something among them – one must be visible and be confirmed. And then there are all the circumstances from the physical and social environment to the practical rules and regulations, work hours, etc. All of these things count and they must be assessed and weighted. The chosen activity must be re-chosen every day.

This, of course, also demands a great deal of the surroundings, of teachers, managers and institutions, because they are constantly being judged, in fact being judged twice over, as they have to meet the expectations of participants who will otherwise drop out, and they must simultaneously live up to the outer demands, which are typically expressed in endless different kinds of evaluations. Not very long ago a study programme was adequate if the teaching was academically accountable and the other conditions were regulated – and in many cases this yardstick is still at work in the minds of managers and teachers in the area. In this case, the study programme is the yardstick and those who cannot accept or meet the challenges must find something else.

But for young people today, the yardstick is quite different – it is the needs and feelings of the individual. This cannot be changed; our whole society would have to go back 30 years or more. One can support and help and provide guidance, and this can be a good thing and save a lot of difficult situations if it is done sensitively and with understanding. But one cannot shift the yardstick, the rationale of what is right or wrong. Ever since our children were small, we adults have repeatedly told them that the most important thing is to choose whatever feels exactly right – the red soda and not the green one, the activities that are exciting and not boring.

For good and for bad, we live in a society that is fundamentally designed as a market society. In such a society in the final analysis it is the consumers' choices that are decisive, and this also applies to study programmes and, within the individual programmes, for the choices between subjects, activities, teachers and supervisors. On the other hand, this independence is intolerable for society. We cannot have thousands of superfluous designers, actors, pop stars and studio hosts while we lack home helps, cleaners and engineers.

This is why regulation and sorting must take place as a counter weight to the free search processes, and in a market society consumer patterns are influenced by making commodities more attractive. This can take place by means of product development, i.e. by making study programmes and occupations more attractive to the young. It can also take place through marketing and through better sales personnel. We might just as well face up to the fact that any job in the education sector today carries with it extensive involvement in these types of activities, even though we use other words that fit in better with the self-perception that is dominant in the education systems.

But seen from the perspective of young people, these counter moves only make the situation even more complicated and incalculable. The education sections of the newspapers contain not only long lists of possible study programmes but also more and more advertisements in which schools and systems try to make themselves as attractive as possible. This increases the need for search processes and it also increases the risk of making choices that prove to be wrong. But there is no denying the fact that the basis of existence for the study programmes is the intake of participants.

The processes that I have chosen to call self-orientation are thus unavoidable for young people, and fundamentally it is on this basis that they make their choices, and experience and assess the study programmes, the subjects and all other activities that can contribute to their development and qualification. If one deals with youth education and other activities for young people today, it is vital to understand that the young continuously assess them and relate to them on the basis of their contribution and value with respect to self-orientation. Young people meet every activity with the questions: 'What does this mean for me? What part does it play in my self-orientation? What use can I make of it in my current self-development project?'

In addition, even if academic content can be of central importance in relation to a desired qualification or education, it is not relevant if the young cannot themselves see and experience its relevance in relation to self-orientation. For this reason, teachers, supervisors and other representatives of the study programmes are forced into the roles of product developers, marketers and salesmen. If, in their opinion, the content in question is to retain the status they attribute to it, they must be able to convince the young people that this is the case. They must be able to do even more than that, because young people do not only want to be convinced, they want to be filled with enthusiasm. Some may call this popular pedagogics or show pedagogics. But this is not actually the case. The appeal would quickly disappear if personal engagement, the feeling of an enthusiastic self, could not be felt in the background, just as young people themselves want to be fired up and be enthusiastic about what they do.

Self-orientation has become the unavoidable condition for youth education. This self-orientation can be extremely exhausting and almost create dependency for the individual; one must go on, one cannot escape from it because new opportunities always arise. It is very difficult to say that one has come through it, and from this point of view the young are really geared to 'lifelong learning'. Some of them manage – those who are equipped to deal with the conditions of late-modern society. They could also be identified as precisely those who develop a core identity that is sufficiently stable and consistent to be able to deal with constant changes and new developments. They have a central core that can provide useful answers when one 'listens to one's inner voice'. Others find it difficult to get to this point. Their search movements continue to be diffuse. They perhaps correspond more to the social constructionists' descriptions of the fragmented self. Their core identity is too disjointed and unstable to be able to handle the tempting offers and unpredictability of their surroundings. It is they whom the English sociologist Scott Lash terms the 'reflexive losers' of late modernity (Lash, 1994: 130). They are unable to handle the reflexivity and self-understanding necessary to manage self-orientation.

And many, perhaps the majority, are probably somewhere in between. Their self-orientation takes them far enough for them to be able to manage, but there is also an underlying feeling of things not being quite as good as they should be. They manage but they have not captured the happiness they have been promised and to which they think they have a right. They have never found 'perfection' and they still do not know what this is. Under all circumstances, it is self-orientation that lays down the fundamental human conditions for the education and qualification activities of young people today.

Acknowledgement

This article is an abridged and adapted translation of Chapters 3 and 4 in K. Illeris, N. Katznelson, B. Simonsen and L. Ulriksen: *Ungdom, identitet og uddannelse* (Youth, identity and education), Copenhagen: Roskilde University Press, 2002.

References

Alheit, Peter (1994) 'The Biographical Question as a Challenge to Adult Education', *International Review of Education* 40: 283–98.
Antikainen, Ari, Houtsonen, Jarmo, Kauppila, Juha and Turunen, A. (1996) *Living in a Learning Society: Life-Histories, Identity and Education*. London: Falmer.
Brookfield, Stephen (2000) 'Adult Cognition as a Dimension of Lifelong Learning', in John

Field and Mal Leicester (eds) *Lifelong Learning – Education Across the Lifespan*. London: Routledge-Falmer.
Damasio, Antonio R. (1994) *Descartes' Error: Emotion, Reason and the Human Brain*. New York: Grosset/Putnam.
Dominicé, Pierre (2000) *Learning from Our Lives*. San Francisco: Jossey-Bass.
Erikson, Erik H. (1968) *Identity, Youth and Crisis*. New York: Norton.
Furth, Hans G. (1987) *Knowledge As Desire*. New York: Columbia University Press.
Gergen, Kenneth J. (1991) *The Saturated Self: Dilemmas of Identity in Contemporary Life*. New York: Basic Books.
Gergen, Kenneth J. (1994) *Realities and Relationships*. Cambridge, MA: Harvard University Press.
Giddens, Anthony (1991) *Modernity and Self-Identity*. Cambridge: Polity Press.
Illeris, Knud (2002) *The Three Dimensions of Learning*. Copenhagen: Roskilde University Press.
Illeris, Knud (2003) 'Towards a Contemporary and Comprehensive Theory of Learning', *International Journal of Lifelong Education* 22(4): 411–21.
Jensen, Johan Fjord (1993) *Livsbuen – Voksenpsykologi og livsaldre* (The life arch: adult psychology and life ages). Copenhagen: Gyldendal.
Kernberg, Otto (1975) *Borderline Conditions and Pathological Narcissism*. New York: Jason Aronson.
Klyvø, Line, Hey, Anne Sophie, Jensen, Line Weltz, Willumsen, Pernille and Kerrn-Jespersen, Helga Morell (2000) 'Identitetsdannelse i den refleksive modernisering' (Identity formation in reflective modernity), Roskilde University, student project report.
Kohut, Heinz (1977) *The Restoration of the Self*. New York: International Universities Press.
Lash, Scott (1994) 'Reflexivity and Its Doubles: Structure, Aesthetics, Community', in Ulrich Beck, Anthony Giddens and Scott Lash (eds) *Reflexive Modernization*. Cambridge: Polity.
Leithäuser, Thomas (1976) *Formen des Alltagsbewusstseins* (The forms of everyday consciousness). Frankfurt: Campus.
Mezirow, Jack (1991) *Transformative Dimensions of Adult Learning*. San Francisco: Jossey-Bass.
Shayer, Michael and Aday, Philip (1981) *Towards a Science of Science Teaching*. London: Heinemann.
Shotter, John (1993) *Cultural Politics of Everyday Life*. Buckingham: Open University Press.
Simonsen, Birgitte (2000) 'New Young People, New Forms of Consciousness, New Educational Methods', in Knud Illeris (ed.) *Adult Education in the Perspective of the Learners*. Copenhagen: Roskilde University Press.
Stern, Daniel (1985) *The Interpersonal World of the Infant*. New York: Basic Books.
Ziehe, Thomas (1975) *Pubertät und Narzissmus* (Puberty and narcissism). Frankfurt: Europäische Verlagsanstalt.
Ziehe, Thomas and Stubenrauch, Herbert (1982) *Plädoyer für ungewöhnliches Lernen* (Pleading for unusual learning). Reinbek: Rowohlt.

CHAPTER 6

ADULT LEARNING

The purpose of this chapter is to give a short up-to-date account on adult learning in relation to learning in general and to children's learning. Adult learning has been part of my focus for over forty years. My research and developmental work has been on what characterizes human learning, especially learning in youth and adulthood with a specific interest in less educated learners (e.g. Illeris 2004, 2006a, 2007, 2009).

Adult learning did not emerge as a special area of interest before about 1970. Prior to 1970 there was, in the industrialized countries, a kind of general understanding that studies of learning should be related mainly to children and youth. Of course there would also be some learning in adulthood, but this would either be for updating, minor issues, or new matters. The age of important and organized learning was considered with few exceptions to be over when one had finished an education and/or got a permanent job. For example, the great names in personality psychology in the 1950s and 1960s launched the ideals and concepts of "the mature personality" (Allport 1961) and "the fully functioning person" (Rogers 1961), i.e. the adult person who had reached a level of integrity and needed no further learning or development, and Erikson saw youth as the age of identity development, whereas adulthood was the age of stabilization of what had already been learned (Erikson 1968). For adults stability was both the norm and the ideal, and changes were related to disruptions and weakness.

Around the 1970s changes in the world were more frequent and the ideal of stability was supplemented by an ideal of flexibility. Adults needed to be able to change, which implies a need to reject earlier learning and engage in new learning. Gradually adult learning became a very important issue. These new tendencies followed two main courses, learning for work and learning for social change.

In the trades and industries interest in adult learning was mainly related to the movement of human resource development (see e.g. Swanson and Holton 2001), and in practice seemed to be realized according to the so-called "Matthew effect" that "for whoever has to him shall be given and he shall be caused to be in abundance" (Matthew 13:12), i.e. that those who already have learned most also get the best opportunities to learn more, both in practice at work and by further educational activities – which as a side-effect inevitably will lead to an increased social imbalance.

But adult learning also became a focal point in social movements which involved the uneducated, poor, and oppressed people in a combination of basic education and personal consciousness raising, often related to political objectives. The most famous and widespread of these movements was, no doubt, initiated by Brazilian Paulo Freire, who combined the teaching of reading and writing with so-called "generative themes," and whose book *Pedagogy of the Oppressed* has been translated into a great number of languages and sold more than 700,000 copies (Freire 1970). Another similar, but in the English speaking world not so well-known example, was started by German trade union courses, in which the sociologist Oskar Negt introduced exemplary learning, similar to Freire's generative themes (Negt 1968). The idea of transformative learning, introduced in the USA by Jack Mezirow (and to which I shall return later in this chapter), was similarly inspired by the women's liberation movement (Mezirow 1978).

Somewhere between these two trends the United Nations published the book *Learning to Be* (Faure *et al.* 1972) which introduced the catchphrase or slogan of "lifelong learning." Lifelong learning gained a central position in international politics and was adopted by many countries although it has often had a stronger impact as a slogan than in consequent learning arrangements for ordinary people.

Adult learning versus children's learning

American Malcolm Knowles claimed that adults' and children's ways of learning differ and that an increasing focus on adult education should be accompanied by an increased interest in researching and understanding of what characterized adult learning to inform adult education. He proposed the term of "andragogy" in relation to adult education and as a counter play to "pedagogy" for children (e.g. Knowles 1970), but this raised a veritable storm of protest and rejection from learning theorists and educational scholars, who claimed that learning is the same for all people and would certainly not let the up and coming adult education field be overtaken by the "andragogy morass" (Davenport 1987, see also Hartree 1984). More recently, British Alan Rogers has deliberately maintained "that there is nothing distinctive about the kind of learning undertaken by adults" (Rogers 2003: 7).

This question, however, needs a closer elucidation to avoid such unprofitable discussion covering an underlying power struggle. For the traditional psychology of learning, there are no age-conditioned differences, because learning has been studied as a common phenomenon of which researchers endeavored to discover the basic and decisive characteristics. Therefore research often involved animals and humans in constructed and simple laboratory situations. And in relation to adult education the researchers claimed that adults' learning as a psychological function is basically of the same kind as children's learning.

This depends, however, on which definition of learning is used. If learning is defined as only the internal psychological function of acquisition of new knowledge, skills and attitudes, as traditional learning psychology tends to do, it is to some extent possible to claim that, independent of the concrete conditions such as age differences or social background, learning processes are fundamentally the same.

But if the emotional dimension and social interaction processes are also seen as necessary and integrated elements of learning, the picture changes. The majority of modern learning theorists have accepted this, and some have even considered learning as mainly or only a social process (e.g. Lave and Wenger 1991, Gergen 1994). In relation to age it is obvious that the nature of our relationships to the social and societal environment changes during the life course from the newborn child's total dependence to a striving for independence in youth and adulthood and, eventually, a new sort of dependence at old age. These changes strongly influence the character of the social and emotional dimensions of learning. In order to see what is characteristic of adult learning, I shall therefore start by pointing out some basic features of children's learning.

In general, learning in childhood could be described as a continuous campaign to capture the world. The child is born into an unknown world and learning is about acquiring this world and finding out how to deal with it. In this connection, two learning-related features are prominent, especially for the small child. First, children's learning is comprehensive and uncensored. The child learns everything within its grasp, throws itself into everything, and is limited only by its biological development and the nature of its surroundings. Second, the child places utter confidence in the adults around it because it has no criteria to evaluate their behavior. Children must, for example, learn the language these adults speak and practice the culture they practice.

Throughout childhood, the child's capturing of its surroundings is fundamentally uncensored and trusting as it endeavors, in an unlimited and indiscriminate way, to make use of the opportunities that present themselves. Of course, late modern society has led to growing complexity and even confusion of this situation as older children receive impressions from their pals and especially from the mass media, which go far beyond the borders of their own environment. But still the open and confident approach must be recognized as the starting point.

Opposite childhood learning stands learning during adulthood. Being an adult essentially means that an individual is able and willing to assume responsibility for his/her own life and actions. Formally, our society ascribes such "adulthood" to individuals when they attain the age of 18. In reality, it is a gradual process that takes place throughout the period of youth, may last well into the twenties or be entirely incomplete if the formation of a relatively stable identity is chosen as the criterion for its completion (which is the classical description of this transition provided by Erik Erikson, 1968).

As concerns learning, however, being an adult also means, in principle, that the individual accepts responsibility for his/her own learning, i.e. more or less consciously sorts information and decides what he/she wants and does not want to learn. The situation in today's complicated modern society is that the volume of what may be learned by far exceeds the ability of any single individual. This is immediately true concerning content in a narrow sense, but it also applies to views and attitudes, perceptions, communications options, behavioral patterns, lifestyle, etc. So input must always be sorted.

As a general conclusion, however, children's uncensored and confident learning is in contrast to adults' selective and self-directed learning, or to put it in more concrete terms:

- adults learn what they want to learn and what is meaningful for them to learn;
- adults draw on the resources they already have in their learning;
- adults take as much responsibility for their learning as they want to take (if they are allowed to); and
- adults are not very inclined to learn something they are not interested in, or in which they cannot see the meaning or importance. At any rate, typically, they only learn it partially, in a distorted way or with a lack of motivation that makes what is learned extremely vulnerable to oblivion and difficult to apply in situations not subjectively related to the learning context (Illeris 2006a: 17).

These conditions imply that learning incentives or adult education options, consciously or subconsciously are met by skeptical questions and considerations such as: Why do "they" want me to learn this? What can I use it for? How does it fit into my personal life perspectives?

Finally learning in youth in this connection can be seen as a transition in which the uncensored learning of children is gradually replaced by the selective learning of adults, and the identity is developed as a kind of scale or yardstick of the selectivity.

Common adults' attitudes to learning

It is not only researchers, administrators and teachers who traditionally have had the idea that learning is mainly related to childhood and youth. Also among adult learners this understanding is widespread. When adults have to involve themselves in ordinary learning courses, they will often talk about it as "having to go back to school" and this is certainly not meant positively. On the contrary adults experience the situation as if they are forced to return to an artificial kind of childhood, something that is degrading or even humiliating – because returning to school indirectly means not being good enough for the tasks in which one is involved.

In what we call free and democratic societies adults are in principle regarded as people of majority who can and must take responsibility for themselves and what they do and say. But at the same time they are subject to risks and situations which they cannot control. In relation to learning and education, anyone can suddenly and without having any responsibility for it themselves realize that their qualifications have become worthless and no longer can be sold on the (labor) market. This may happen, for example, if the owners and stakeholders of their workplace decide to move it to a country far away in which labor is cheaper, or if a new management undertakes a reorganization which makes certain departments and persons unnecessary. But there may also be other and more personal reasons as for example, a bad relationship to a leader, low concentration because of too many problems at home, too many days lost through illness, etc.

A considerable number of adult learners do not participate in adult education because they want to do so, but because for some reason outside their control they have to do so. The central condition is that these adult learners are not in control of the situation. Therefore they are ambivalent – and the slogan of lifelong learning may in such situations become very ambiguous. Reality seems quite different from the 'maybe' good intentions of powerful organizations like UNESCO, OECD, the EU or the World Bank. Adult education today is usually far from the emancipating projects of the folk high schools or public enlightenment – in relation to which the idea of lifelong learning was originally launched.

Therefore not only the concrete learning content, but also the general learning situation and the messages and influence it contains, will often be met with skeptical attitudes, and will be seen and dealt with in the light of the individual's own experience and perspectives, whether it is communicated in the form of conversation, guidance, persuasion, pressure or compulsion. If the possibilities for learning shall be turned in a positive direction, the adults must accept them psychologically, they must be able to understand the meaning of the learning activities in relation to themselves and their life situations (see e.g. Illeris 1998, 2003, 2006b).

Adult learning possibilities

Whereas questions of the specific character of adult learning were neglected by traditional learning psychology and also by most adult educational research, there has been some often indirect discussion concerning adults' possibilities for learning.

The cognitive learning theory put forward by Jean Piaget in the 1930s on the basis of extensive empirical studies, focused on the development of learning possibilities in childhood through a number of cognitive stages and sub-stages and thus maintained that there is a highly specific developmental course. This development ends between the ages of 11–13 when the "formal operational" level is reached. The formal operational level makes logical-deductive thinking possible as a supplement to the forms of thinking and learning acquired at earlier stages (see e.g. Flavell 1963).

However, Piaget's perception of this process has been questioned from several quarters. On the one hand, it has been pointed out that far from all adults are actually able to think at a formal operational level. Empirical research indicates that in England in about 1980 actually less than 30 per cent of adults could think at this level, even though at the beginning of puberty a decisive development occurs in the possibilities for learning and thinking in abstract terms, so that distinguishing a new cognitive phase extending beyond the formal operational level is justified (Shayer and Adey 1981, Commons et al. 1984). American adult education researcher Stephen Brookfield has pointed to four possibilities for learning which, in his opinion, may only be developed in the course of adulthood: the capacity for dialectical thinking, the capacity for applying practical logic, the capacity for realizing how one may know what one knows, and the capacity for critical reflection (Brookfield 2000).

Recent brain research seems indirectly to support Brookfield's claims. A well-established understanding today, psychologically as well as neurologically, is that the brain matures for formal logical thinking in early puberty. But evidence has been found that the brain centres of the frontal lobe that conduct such functions as rational planning, prioritization and making well-founded choices, do not mature until the late teenage years (Gogtay et al. 2004) or perhaps even later. This finding seems to provide some clarification of the differences between the capacity of formal logical and practical logical thinking and learning as well as between ordinary cognition and meta-cognition in adolescence and early adulthood.

The general conclusion must be that during puberty and youth a physiological and neurological maturing process takes place that makes possible new forms of abstract and strictly logical thinking and learning. An individual acquires the potential to operate context-independently with coherent concept systems and manage balanced and goal-directed behavior (whether or not this potential is actually applied is, as mentioned, a different question). Teenagers' determination to find out how things are structured and to use such understanding in relation to their own situation could be seen as a cognitive developmental bridge signifying the difference between children's and adults' ways of learning.

The longing for independence and the longing for coherent understanding of how they themselves and their environment function and why things are the way they are, in a decisive way, separates adult learning from the learning of childhood. Up through the period of youth, individuals will increasingly assume responsibility for their own learning and non-learning, make choices and rejections, and in this context understand what they are dealing with and their own roles and possibilities.

However, all this has been enormously complicated by the duality of late modernity between the apparently limitless degrees of freedom and reams of information, and the far-reaching and often indirect pressure for control from parents, teachers, youth cultures, mass media, and authorities. The transition from child to adult has thus, in the area of learning, become an extended, ambiguous and complicated process, with blurred outlines and unclear conditions and goals.

Barriers towards learning

In our complicated modern society the amount one can learn far outstrips what any person can manage, and this applies to the content of learning as well as the options for attitudes, modes of understanding, communication possibilities, patterns of action, lifestyles etc. Selection becomes a necessity, and in principle adults would like to carry out and take responsibility for this selection themselves.

Thus, adults' basic desire to learn and to direct and take responsibility for their own learning are strongly modified, first by the impact of their school experiences, and second by the inevitable selection which is necessarily developed into the kind of semi-automatic defense system which has been described as "everyday consciousness" (Illeris 2004: 113ff., 2007: 160ff.).

The way this works is that one develops some general pre-understandings within certain thematic areas. When one meets with influences within such an area, these pre-understandings are activated so that if elements in the influences do not correspond to the pre-understandings, they are either rejected or distorted to make them agree. In both cases, the result is not new learning but, on the contrary, the cementing of already existing understanding.

This is also part of the reason why adults are skeptical and often reluctant vis-à-vis everything that others want them to learn and they themselves do not feel an urge to learn. Consciously or unconsciously, they want to decide for themselves. But, at the same time, it is easier to leave the decisions to others, to see what happens, and retain the right to protest, resist or drop out if one is not satisfied. In sum, the attitude is thus very often ambiguous and contradictory.

However, the very widespread and important mechanisms of learning defense should not be confused with learning resistance, which is a much more active and usually also conscious kind of general learning barrier. Whereas the system of learning defense is gradually built up during youth and exists in advance of the situations in which it works, resistance is provoked by elements in the learning situation and content which are unacceptable to the learner. There may be many reasons for learning resistance, of which some are unconscious and may be anchored in traumatic experiences in childhood, whereas others are conscious and may, for instance, have to do with political, moral, or religious convictions.

Teachers and educators need to realize that learners are excited and sensitive in situations of learning resistance. Often, when adults are asked when they have really learned something of personal importance, they refer to situations of learning resistance. Therefore, in such situations learners should not just be turned down or neglected, but the teacher should try to find an opportunity for a personal talk, so the learner can be helped to find the reason for the reaction, determine what was at stake, and the consequences for different actions.

Identity, life projects and transformative learning

The main thread here is that adult learning may be subjectively meaningful or not and this outcome is determined by the learner's life course and life projects.

The essence of the life course has resulted in the building up of an identity, i.e. a central mental instance containing the understanding of who one is, who one wants to be, and how one experiences oneself and is experienced by others. While the concept of identity was originally a psychological construction, mainly elaborated by Erikson (1968), it has been further explained by modern sociologists, such as German Ulrich Beck (1997) [1986]), British Anthony Giddens (1991) and Polish-British Zygmunt Bauman (2000). The central understanding which has been developed, at least as I see it (Illeris 2014), is what Bauman has termed the age of "liquid modernity" (Bauman 2000). In order to cope with the ever-changing world we have to develop identities which are so stable that we have a coherent experience of ourselves, and at the same time so flexible that we can transform ourselves in accordance with changes in our life situations. In this regard Jack Mezirow's concept of transformative learning gains new meaning and importance, because it can be seen as the kind of adult learning which deals with the necessary transformations of the identity.

In relation to identity, the role of life projects in relation to adult learning has relevance. Adults usually have life projects that are relatively stable and long-term, for example, a family project that concerns creating and being part of a family, a work project that concerns a personally and financially satisfying job, perhaps a leisure-time project concerning a hobby, a life project to do with fulfillment, or a conviction project that may be religious or political in nature.

These life projects are embedded in the life history, present situation and possible future perspectives of the individual and are closely related to identity. We design our defenses on this basis so that we usually let what is relevant for our projects come through and reject the rest. Also on this basis, as the central core of our defenses, we develop defense mechanisms to counter influences that could threaten the experience of who we are and would like to be.

These matters typically comprise the fundamental premises for school-based or course-based adult learning seen from the perspective of the learners. These premises make the learners' initial motivation quite crucial and influence how they regard the study course in relation to their life projects.

In some cases, adult learning can lead to extensive, enriching development for the participants if they arrive with positive motivation and the study programs live up to or exceed their expectations. But in many adult education activities a considerable proportion of the participants only become positively engaged if they meet a challenge that "turns them on" at the beginning or along the way. Quite often, in current adult education situations, participants are only engaged superficially and do not learn very much, leading to the waste of human and financial resources.

What we all must realize is that the adult's way of learning is very different from the child's and that adult education must, therefore, be based on fundamentally different premises. The basic requirement is that the adult must take, and must be allowed to take, responsibility for his or her own learning. Adult learning activities should be designed out of respect, support and even demand for this basic requirement. We all have a great deal to learn in order to fully understand these fundamental conditions of adult learning.

Current adult learning theory

Efforts to work out a theoretical basis for adult learning came late and have been rather sparse until the 1980s. However, since then quite a few important contributions have been launched of which the most important shall be taken up here.

I have already mentioned Jack Mezirow's contribution on transformative learning, which was launched in 1978 and has been further developed (e.g. Mezirow 1991, 2000, 2006, 2009). Seen from a theoretical point of view the most important innovation in Mezirow's approach has been his attention to adults' possibilities of involving themselves in a type of learning that implies changes of a broader and further-reaching kind than what is comprised in Piaget's concept of accommodation (cf. Illeris 2007, 2014).

American Robert Kegan's constructive-developmental theory of human development refers to broad personal learning at different levels and can be understood as partly a support and partly a critique of Mezirow's approach as being too narrowly cognitively oriented (Kegan 1982, 1994, 2000).

The most comprehensive contribution has, however, been delivered by the British sociologist Peter Jarvis, who since the middle of the 1980s has published books and articles on adult and lifelong learning and at the same time has edited the *International Journal of Lifelong Education* and a number of international handbooks. His first important book was *Adult Education and Lifelong Learning* (Jarvis 1983), which has later been revised twice. Then came two more exceptional books which strongly introduced the social dimension of adult learning (Jarvis 1987, 1992). After many other publications in 2006–2008 he published a trilogy on *Lifelong Learning and the Learning Society*, covering his full theoretical understanding (Jarvis 2006, 2007, 2008) and finally he has edited two important international handbooks (Jarvis 2009, Jarvis and Watts 2012). In general his theory can be said to be founded in the philosophical and social dimensions, whereas the psychological dimension is less comprehensive. Jarvis' contribution has supplied a comprehensive and coherent theoretical understanding of adult learning.

Other theories from later years have helped to complete the picture. Some of the most specific contributions have been made by the Finnish psychologist Yrjö Engeström (e.g. Engeström 1987, 2009 [2001]) building on the Russian activity-theoretical approach from the mid-war period (Lev Vygotsky, Aleksei Leontjev), the American organizational theorists Chris Argyris and Donald Schön's contributions on organizational learning (e.g. Argyris and Schön 1996), the German sociologist Peter Alheit (e.g. Alheit 2009) who has been a driving force of the so-called biographical approach, seeing adult learning in the perspective of the life course in interaction with important external events – and, finally, I hope it will not be too presumptuous to mention my own contribution in this connection (e.g. Illeris 2004, 2007, 2011, 2014).

Seen in relation to the concept and issue of human resource development I hope that this chapter has contributed to making it clear that such development is not just a practical matter of following various more or less detailed recommendations or prescriptions. The human mind is not an automatically functioning construction following certain rules or directions but an extremely complex, unpredictable and personal creation following its own ways or ideas and sometimes also unconscious patterns – and that all of this has become particularly distinct in the present ever-changing world. In relation to adult learning the point of HRD must therefore be to encourage and make space for the manifold potentials offered by the available human resources.

References

Alheit, P. (2009) Biographical learning – within the new lifelong learning discourse, in K. Illeris (ed.) *Contemporary Theories of Learning*, London: Routledge.

Allport, G.W. (1961) *Pattern and Growth in Personality*, New York: Holt, Rineholt and Winston.
Argyris, C. and Schön, D. (1996) *Organizational Learning II – Theory, Method, Practice*, Reading, MA: Addison-Wesley.
Bauman, Z. (2000) *Liquid Modernity*, Cambridge, UK: Polity Press.
Beck, U. (1997 [1986]) *Risk Society: Towards a New Modernity*, London: SAGE.
Brookfield, S.D. (2000) Adult cognition as a dimension of lifelong learning, in J. Field and M. Leicester (eds) *Lifelong Learning – Education Across the Lifespan*, London: Routledge-Falmer.
Commons, M.L., Richards, F.A. and Armon, C. (eds) (1984) *Beyond Formal Operations: Late Adolescent and Adult Cognitive Development*, New York: Praeger.
Davenport, J. (1987) Is there any way out of the andragogy morass?, *Lifelong Learning: An Omnibus of Practice and Research* 11(3): 17–20.
Engeström, Y. (1987) *Learning by Expanding: An Activity-Theoretical Approach to Developmental Research*, Helsinki: Orienta-Kunsultit.
—— (2009 [2001]) Expansive learning: toward an activity-theoretical reconceptualization, in K. Illeris (ed.) *Contemporary Theories of Learning*, London: Routledge.
Erikson, E.H. (1968) *Identity, Youth and Crisis*, New York: Norton.
Faure, E., Herrera, F., Kaddoura, A.R., Lopes, H., Petrovsky, A.V., Rhanema, M., and Ward, F.C. (1972) *Learning to Be: The World of Education Today and Tomorrow*, Paris: UNESCO.
Flavell, J.H. (1963) *The Developmental Psychology of Jean Piaget*, New York: Van Nostrand.
Freire, P. (1970) *Pedagogy of the Oppressed*, New York: Seabury.
Gergen, K.J. (1994) *Realities and Relationships*, Cambridge, MA: Harvard University Press.
Giddens, A. (1991) *Modernity and Self-Identity*, Cambridge, UK: Polity Press.
Gogtay, N., Giedd, J.N., Lusk, L., Hayashi, K.M., Greenstein, D., Vaituzis, A.C., Nugent, T. F. III, Herman, D.H., Clasen, L.S., Toga, A.W., Rapoport, J.L. and Thompson, P.M. (2004) Dynamic mapping of human cortical development during childhood through early adulthood, *Proceedings of the National Academy of Sciences of the USA* 101(21): 8174–9.
Hartree, A. (1984) Malcolm Knowles' theory of andragogy: a critique, *International Journal of Lifelong Education* 3: 203–10.
Illeris, K. (1998) Adult learning and responsibility, in K. Illeris (ed.) *Adult Education in a Transforming Society*, Copenhagen: Roskilde University Press.
—— (2003) Adult education as experienced by the learners, *International Journal of Lifelong Education* 22: 13–23.
—— (2004) *Adult Education and Adult Learning*, Malabar, FL: Krieger.
—— (2006a) What is special about adult learning, in P. Sutherland and J. Crowther (eds) *Lifelong Learning – Concepts and Contexts*, London: Routledge.
—— (2006b) Lifelong learning and the low-skilled, *International Journal of Lifelong Education* 25: 15–28.
—— (2007) *How We Learn: Learning and Non-Learning in School and Beyond*, London: Routledge.
—— (ed.) (2009) *Contemporary Theories of Learning: Learning Theorists . . . In Their Own Words*, London: Routledge.
—— (2011) *The Fundamentals of Workplace Learning: Understanding How People Learn in Working Life*, London: Routledge.
—— (2014) *Transformative Learning and Identity*, London: Routledge.
Jarvis, P. (1983) *Adult Education and Lifelong Learning: Theory and Practice*, New York: Croom Helm.
—— (1987) *Adult Learning in the Social Context*, New York: Croom Helm.
—— (1992) *Paradoxes of Learning: On Becoming an Individual in Society*, San Francisco: Jossey-Bass.
—— (2006) *Towards a Comprehensive Theory of Human Learning*, London: Routledge.
—— (2007) *Globalisation, Lifelong Learning and the Learning Society: Sociological Perspectives*, London: Routledge.
—— (2008) *Democracy, Lifelong Learning and the Learning Society: Active Citizenship in a Late Modern Age*, London: Routledge.

—— (ed.) (2009) *The Routledge International Handbook of Lifelong Learning*, London: Routledge.
Jarvis, P. and Watts, M. (eds) (2012) *The Routledge International Handbook of Learning*, London: Routledge.
Kegan, R. (1982) *The Evolving Self: Problem and Process in Human Development*, Cambridge, MA: Harvard University Press.
—— (1994) *In Over Our Heads: The Mental Demands of Ordinary Life*, Cambridge, MA: Harvard University Press.
—— (2000) Which "form" transforms? A constructive-developmental approach to transformative learning, in J. Mezirow and Associates (ed.) *Learning as Transformation: Critical Perspectives on a Theory in Progress*, San Francisco: Jossey-Bass.
Knowles, M.S. (1970) *The Modern Practice of Adult Education – Andragogy Versus Pedagogy*, New York: Association Press.
Lave, J. and Wenger, E. (1991) *Situated Learning: Legitimate Peripheral Participation*, New York: Cambridge University Press.
Mezirow, J. (1978) *Education for Perspective Transformation: Women's Reentry Programs in Community Colleges*, New York: Teachers College, Columbia University.
—— (1991) *Transformative Dimensions of Adult Learning*, San Francisco: Jossey-Bass.
—— (2000) Learning to think like an adult: core conceptions of transformative theory, in J. Mezirow and Associates (ed.) *Learning as Transformation: Critical Perspectives on a Theory in Progress*, San Francisco: Jossey-Bass.
—— (2006) An overview on transformative learning, in P. Sutherland and J. Crowther (eds) *Lifelong Learning – Concepts and Contexts*, London: Routledge.
—— (2009) Transformative learning theory, in J. Mezirow, E.W. Taylor and Associates (ed.) *Transformative Learning in Practice: Insights from Community, Workplace and Higher Education*, San Francisco: Jossey-Bass.
Negt, O. (1968) *Sociologische Phantasie und Exemplarisches Lernen* [Sociological imagination and exemplary learning], Frankfurt: Europäische Verlagsanstalt.
Rogers, A. (2003) *What is the Difference? A New Critique of Adult Learning and Teaching*, Leicester, UK: NIACE.
Rogers, C.R. (1961) *On Becoming a Person*, Boston: Haughton Mifflin.
Shayer, M. and Adey, P. (1981) *Towards a Science of Science Teaching*, London: Heinemann Educational.
Swanson, R.A. and Holton, E.F. (2001) *Foundations of Human Resource Development*, San Francisco: Berrett-Koehler.

CHAPTER 7

LIFELONG LEARNING AND THE LOW-SKILLED

This article is a combined result of a three-year research project on low-skilled learners' experiences as participants of various kinds of adult training and education in Denmark, and the findings of a three-year research consortium on workplace learning, summing up and generalizing our various findings as to how low-skilled adults function in relation to participation in training and education activities, how they feel about it, what is important to them, and consequently what works in practice in relation to this very important but often neglected group of adult learners.

The problem of the low-skilled

This article is not the result of a specific study but draws on four equally important sources:

1. Since 1987 I have been a consultant to the Danish adult vocational training system, which mainly trains unskilled, semi-skilled and unemployed workers during 2–4 week courses that consist of practical content and some general elements. Among other things over the years, I have conducted considerable developmental work, been in direct personal contact with hundreds of participants and carried out more than 200 structured interviews of various kinds. This has given me a broad general insight into the participants' problems, thoughts and opinions in relation to training and education.
2. From 1998 to 2000 I was the leader of the Danish Adult Education Research Project, which included observations and interviews in both the vocational and the general adult education systems and the day high schools (which mainly offer half-year full-time courses for adults who are unable to follow more goal directed training, that is, they are often in a personal crisis in relation to work and training). The main purpose of this project was to find out how adult education is perceived and experienced by ordinary participants with no training or only limited training beyond compulsory schooling. This project gave me a deep insight into the psychological structures directing low-skilled adults' relations to adult education and training (Illeris 2003b, 2004a).
3. Between 2001 and 2004 I was the research director of the Research Consortium on Workplace Learning, which was run by Learning Lab Denmark and involved 11 senior researchers and five graduate students in theoretical and developmental work (Illeris 2003a). This work included 16 empirical projects

and many observations and interviews with participants in workplace learning of all sorts, with special emphasis on low-skilled employees and workers. In addition to the project reports, the Consortium published four edited books, several articles, a special issue of the *Journal of Workplace Learning* (Ellström and Illeris 2004), and a final book on the topic of 'Learning in working life', which was also published as an English edition (Illeris *et al.* 2004). This work added insight concerning how ordinary adults think and feel about learning at work.

4. Finally, I also count as important background my many years of work on learning theory and adult learning in a broad and comprehensive perspective and with special attention to the learners' perspective (e.g. Illeris 2002, 2003d, 2004a, 2004b).

Against this background, in the following I shall try to illustrate the well known fact that those who already have the weakest educational background also participate in all kinds of adult learning activities to a lesser extent than other groups. This is one of the most urgent problems in relation to the current endeavour of lifelong learning. I shall try to approach this problem from the perspective of low-skilled adults' feelings and opinions in relation to education and training, to uncover the psychological processes that tend to keep them away and, finally, I shall try to point to some practical measures that could help to overcome these barriers, that is, what to do and what not to do if the low-skilled are to be attracted to joining lifelong learning activities to a greater extent. Thus the main purpose of the article is to point to the psychological processes and barriers behind low participation by the low-skilled in learning activities, which are in general not very well understood by the authorities and therefore not fundamentally respected in the many well-meaning projects and measures that are set up in order to cope with this very important issue.

Who are the low-skilled?

In recent years, 'low-skilled' has been used by authorities as a general designation for those who are in a vulnerable situation in relation to the competence demands of modern society and economy. However, as these demands are growing in extent and complexity it is also becoming more and more difficult to find out who actually belongs to this group. Thus a first demand seems to be to delimit and define who the low-skilled actually are. They have traditionally been understood or defined as all whose formal education consists only of primary and lower secondary education and perhaps some short training courses. But if the issue is approached from the angle of who is vulnerable and at risk of being marginalized in society and in the labour market, three rather different main groups emerge besides, of course, a lot of more or less individual and random cases.

First, there is the 'classic' group of adult early school leavers who have not participated in or completed any formal qualifying education or training. Some of them manage very well on the labour market, but the majority are in more or less uncertain labour positions, often with alternating periods of employment and unemployment; some are really on the edge of the labour market, and some have lost their labour-market connection and are either in some kind of more or less compulsory retraining or have obtained some permanent benefit and are definitely marginalized. An important feature of many in this group is poor literacy and/or numeracy, which make their possibilities in today's labour market very limited.

But there are also many adults with a solid and recognized education that are in a vulnerable situation, because the vocational area for which they have been trained has been forced to radically reduce its workforce. This applies to the banking sector, for example, but to very many other sectors also, and there are also occupations that have ceased to exist. So, while strictly speaking, these people cannot be termed 'low-skilled', nevertheless they are in the same vulnerable position because the skills they have are not in demand.

Finally, a growing group of young adults has emerged who have never obtained a lasting job, although they may have developed considerable and often untraditional qualifications through their own winding routes. In the young generation direct, coherent and targeted qualification processes have for many been replaced by strongly individualized searching and interrupted trajectories in and out of education programmes, short time jobs, journeys and other non-work oriented activities, periods on social welfare or unemployment benefit, workfare and different types of projects in an unclear complexity that is very difficult to capture in fixed categories and statistics (cf. Weil *et al.* 2005). Some of these young adults are definitely not low-skilled in the traditional sense, but many seem to lack the stability and perhaps other social competences that are necessary for a lasting occupation today.

Naturally, in addition to the main groups outlined here there are also others who must be regarded as vulnerable in the present context. These are, for example, those who have completely given up getting into the official labour market and muddle through with a mixture of cash benefit, a low level of consumption, mutual services, and perhaps some petty crime at times – or those with health problems or a handicap.

Thus the problems traditionally related to the low-skilled have developed in scope and content, and the field has become more complicated and varied, requiring particularly differentiated, flexible and sensitive openings and services. This implies far-reaching demands for innovative thinking, engagement and flexibility, politically, administratively and from the top to shop-floor level in the business sector.

Under all circumstances, there can hardly be any doubt of the existence of a large group of adults with a considerable individual and social need for personal and/ or collective support for completing relevant work-related training or education programmes. This group of 'vulnerable' adults is only partially resembles the group that can be identified as the 'low-skilled'. However, I shall continue to use this term in the following, because it is a term in general use and there is still a significant group to whom it applies. But this is with the clear reservation that the term is on the way to becoming obsolete, and that while my deliberations do not cover all low-skilled learners, on the other hand they apply to a great number of people who are skilled, educated and/or trained but, nevertheless, are not in demand on the labour market.

The subjective feeling of ambivalence

In relation to any kind of formal education or training it is characteristic of most of this group that they are subjectively deeply ambivalent. They want and do not want to participate at one and the same time. When my colleagues and I have been interviewing such people, whether it has been at workplaces or in educational settings, we have observed that generally they know very well that what they need in order to obtain a stable job situation is formal education or training. But at the same time they strongly wish that this was not the case (Illeris 2003b, 2003c).

Those in this group who are formally low-skilled, are usually so because they did not do very well at school. They have nine or more years of everyday experience of not being good enough, they have been humiliated and marginalized, and they have wished to leave school as soon as they possibly could. Very few of them feel any desire to return to a situation that would remind them of all their failures and humiliations – and probably also repeat them. On the other hand, it becomes more and more obvious that this is the only way out of their vulnerable situation.

For those who are actually skilled or trained, but in unmarketable areas, the situation is a bit different. The reason why they are often reluctant to be retrained or re-educated has to do with their strong need to maintain their self-respect. Typically, they have for many years held a decent and respectable job through which they have earned their living and social position, and they have built up an identity as a valuable employee and a useful citizen who has contributed his or her share to society. They are therefore concerned to defend this identity, and they feel it somehow misplaced, unfair and infantilizing to have to go back to school and to the subordinate position of a pupil. But they also know that this is their only chance to find a way back to a life on the level they used to have.

For the young unemployed adults (roughly, those under 30 years of age) the kind of ambivalence is also slightly different. They do not find it humiliating to go back to school because they have grown up in a society that was already devoted to lifelong learning, and thus they have always known that it would somehow be their fate. But this does not mean that more schooling is an attractive prospect to them. They typically see it as something boring and restricting, which places them in an unwanted subordinate position. However, they also know that it is their only chance (Simonsen 2000).

The need for obliging outreach and opportunities

There is no doubt that the various groups of low-skilled or vulnerable people on the labour market nearly always have a rather clear awareness of their need for more education, not least in general areas such as reading, written skills, arithmetic and mathematics, foreign languages, computer skills and general social and cultural orientation. But the forces pulling in the opposite direction – the lack of self-confidence in terms of education and the unpleasantness of going back to school again – are usually the strongest. For this reason there must be a special incentive, a relevant opening that links up with the needs they have experienced and implying some circumstances that reduce social, practical and financial barriers. And at the same time it is of decisive importance that initiatives deliberately avoid all such arrangements, acts, formulations or references that can in any way be experienced as humiliating, disrespectful, infantilizing or the like, as this is not only offensive but may easily be taken as a most welcome excuse, in relation to oneself and others, to withdraw.

For adults who already have a vocational or other qualifying education, but who have become victims of structural unemployment and therefore must readjust and be retrained to get back on the labour market again, the main psychological problem is identity defence. In this situation it is very understandable that they have a more or less unconscious urge to cling to the professional identity that has hitherto been the basis of their self-respect and dignity, although it is now irrelevant and worthless. Therefore the challenge, for themselves and for those who are trying to help them out, is how to overcome or circumvent these defensive tendencies. Thus continuing education or retraining must be offered and conducted in ways that respect the wounded work identity at the same time as a new identity is gradually built up. The present counselling and educational systems do not seem to be geared to this or to adequately understand it (cf. Illeris 2003b, 2004a).

The young unemployed adults are strongly marked by the widespread individualization of late modern market society (Beck and Beck-Gernsheim 2002). They have usually been presented constantly with personal choices in all possible areas from earliest childhood, they think that free choices in all areas exist and should exist and that it is important, the very core of life itself, that they always make the right choice and thereby create themselves as what they want to be. Therefore, when they start an education or training course, it is typically to see if this might be something that 'turns them on' and could be a way to fulfil their often sky-high expectations. So what they need is support for holding on to a goal, not to give up at the first hint of problems, and the support must sometimes also include a function of 'dream crushing', which carefully and surely can help the young adults to realize what is outside of their reach. Not everyone can become a rock star or a designer, or host a TV show.

For others in this group the problem is to find anything that 'turns them on' or be enthusiastic about. They cannot live up to the eternal expectations of society and educators to 'feel' their own innermost motivation, and at the same time they cannot bring themselves to go for the jobs with least status, for example in the health or shop sectors. For the boys, not least for those with an ethnic background in less industrialized societies, there is most frequently a wish to enter an unskilled manual job as quickly as possible so that they can get good wages and avoid the endless choices that they cannot handle.

Contacts and the way in

The low-skilled who are in the labour market already often have, as mentioned, a sceptical approach to anything that reminds them of teaching and school, and at the same time workplaces are also often reluctant to involve them in special learning initiatives. There is therefore a need to create special initiatives, both to make workplaces involve this group in, for example, projects, action learning, learning oriented networks, job exchange and job rotation schemes that offer learning opportunities of another nature than teaching (Illeris et al. 2004), and to initiate and provide funding for relevant contacts and outreach activities from schools and training centres.

Simultaneously, it is of crucial importance to introduce openings and incentives that directly relate to the scepticism and blocks of the low-skilled in relation to general learning and upgrading, not least in such areas as reading, written formulation, arithmetic and computer skills, and likewise concerning general information about work-relevant and social subjects.

In workplaces it is in the first place a matter of establishing contacts with the sceptical workers and employees that can contribute to thematizing the needs for learning that most of them actually express in the studies conducted in the area. There would seem to be a need for personal contacts that can be experienced as loyal and respectful, whereas contacts experienced as coming from above, from management or public authorities, do not usually have the best chance of being successful. Experience has shown that outreach activity by interested co-workers, union representatives, health and safety representatives or people who themselves work with continuing education at shop-floor level stand the best chances of getting a relevant dialogue going (Illeris et al. 2004). But this requires time, engagement and a certain amount of experience of how it can be done. Therefore the resources must be present to upgrade such contact persons and for the necessary time and the practical opportunities needed.

In one of our projects we had remarkably good experience and results with adult educators contacting unskilled workers in local industrial enterprises. But we also learned that this requires that the educators have time for individual talks with the workers, have prepared relevant offers in advance and are willing to adjust them in accordance with the needs expressed by the workers and, consequently, that there is special earmarked funding available for such contact activities (Illeris et al. 2004). If the funding must be provided by the general operating costs of the institution, it seems to be almost a law of nature that this is not sufficient for the task to be successful.

Supportive counselling and not placement

However, many of the low-skilled that need training are not employed. Actually, the majority of adult education participants in Denmark have been placed, referred or sent to attend the education programme in question by public authorities or agencies, and this has usually not been a positive experience. In the course of my research I have been rather shocked to observe the proportion of participants in adult education programmes who felt they had been 'placed' there and who had no reasonable prior knowledge of what the course aimed to achieve (Illeris 2003b).

Part of the background for this is without doubt that the referring instances work under considerable time pressure and are subject to very tight limits as to the amount of time they are allowed to allocate to each client. The outcome is that these instances are forced to consider their task completed as soon as a client has been admitted into an education programme.

This situation is, however, doubly disempowering for the participants: first, they feel that they are under compulsion or pressure when they approach these authorities, and second, they feel that then they are not even shown reasonable individual concern. Even though in most cases they are objectively in a situation where they need education, they experience subjectively that they have been subjected to compulsion and placement, and they find this humiliating and frustrating.

It is immediately clear that in such a context it is rather incidental and uncertain if appropriate learning in the education course will even start, and it becomes even more paradoxical if one relates it to modern requirements for competence development. On top of this comes the fact that their frustrations can be a strong force for disintegration in the education programme, causing it to also fall apart for other participants who started with a more positive and focused approach.

This is also inappropriate from the perspective of society and national economy. In such cases it is actually only on paper (and in the statistics) that activation takes place. The motivation and personal 'acceptance of the education' that are the preconditions for suitable and focused learning and competence development are entirely absent, and instead there is insecurity, confusion, frustration, anger and other negative feelings. A waste of resources in the education institution, which may be much larger and possibly even affect teachers and perhaps other participants, thus counters the time saved in the referring instance. To the extent counselling takes place in such a way, we are looking at not merely what is ethically highly criticizable administration, but also a major error in economic terms.

For counselling in this context to be ethically defensible and practical as well as economically appropriate, it is of decisive importance that it is provided until the individual in question psychologically 'accepts the result', that is, has subjectively realized and accepted that the chosen education course is suitable and will therefore be prepared to achieve the best possible result. Only then is it humanly and economically reasonable to begin the education programme (Illeris 2004a).

Such an aim, let it be said, is by no means unrealistic. The precondition is, of course, first, that it is possible to find a realistic opportunity in the individual cases, but second, and equally important, that there is also time and support for the deep and personal adaptation process that is necessary. There is a need for a dialogue that takes its point of departure in the individual's own premises, there is a need for time for the individual to ponder the issues, discuss it with others with whom they feel confident, get used to the idea, find the subjectively positive aspects of the situation, and first and foremost accept entering into the project actively and wholeheartedly.

In our research we have observed that even though many were very dissatisfied with the process and certainly did not perceive it as something that had anything to do with counselling, they usually thought that the placement in which it had resulted was reasonable enough in spite of everything. However, they still experienced it as placement, and this implied humiliation and a negative attitude, which they felt very deeply (Illeris 2003b). All this 'counselling' could obviously have been carried through to a positive choice with relative ease, thereby leading to mental acceptance, which psychologically would have given an entirely different entry situation to the education and thus also to the learning.

The decisive importance of division of responsibility

It is also of decisive importance that the point of departure of planning is that the participants are *adults*, that is, humans who both formally and in reality are responsible for their own actions and decisions. Of course, this applies also to their learning and education. Actually, the element of adult education programmes and activities that participants react most strongly against is that their responsibility is not respected. Perhaps they do not even respect it themselves. But all this disrespect seems mainly to stem from the fact that we have all acquired some notions of learning from our school days in which the distribution of responsibility is different precisely because the students are children.

The question of division of responsibility is fundamental when we are concerned with adult education and workplace learning. Once we have realized this we have also received the key to understanding many apparently irrational matters that make their impact felt in many adult education and training programmes, ranging from general planning to all sorts of minor and major practical details at floor level. Part of this is that it is not just the teachers or instructors who 'by default' relate to the participants in a way that imposes a child's role on them by assuming a great deal of responsibility which, considered from an ethical, legal, practical and learning angle, ought to lie with the participants. It is also the case that the participants themselves basically perceive this as natural and legitimate even though, at the same time, they more or less consciously react against it.

Therefore the whole thing is not so simple that we can just decide that adult education and training within a certain given framework is the participants' responsibility. Those who manage the activities must make an active effort not to assume the responsibility, an action which rather paradoxically also involves them having to accept responsibility for 'returning' responsibility to the participants. This is not as uncomplicated as it may immediately sound. In practice, it has proved to be a highly difficult process, which very often involves surmounting deeply rooted resistance, and it therefore requires perseverance and determination on the part of instructors and participants alike (cf. Illeris 1998, 2004a).

First, it is always difficult for leaders and teachers to surrender their position of power voluntarily and even actively. In addition, assuming responsibility for not assuming responsibility appears both paradoxical and contradictory. However, this *is* exactly what is required. It is the situation in which adult educators very often find themselves, and it is a decisive criterion for a professional adult educator to be able to handle this. Furthermore, the situation may in practice be highly sensitive and emotional, and there is a very fine line between the participants' responsibility for their own learning and education and teachers' responsibility for providing the optimal conditions and input for this learning and education.

In the existing activities and systems, the participants may easily be perceived as irresponsible just because they hesitate to assume responsibility for what they ultimately experience that others have decided for them. It may well be that in many cases they would have decided the same thing or something similar themselves, but they have seldom had the opportunity for this because the culture dictates that most important decisions are made by others on their behalf. It may also well be that they find it difficult to make decisions themselves when they have the opportunity, but it is, after all, exactly what development of competence to a large extent is meant to produce. Therefore the 'systems' must not react to such problems by merely assuming responsibility, but on the contrary hold the participants to the fact that it is their responsibility.

What I am calling for is by no means an easy task. First, it is important to structure a system from the ground up so there is a clear and well-reasoned framework to relate to and wide opportunities for the participants themselves to navigate, individually or collectively, within this framework. Second, it is important to be constantly aware of not taking over the responsibility that ought to be the participants', even though, and especially at the beginning, they are often inclined to try to avoid the responsibility and manoeuvre the teacher or instructor back into the usual responsible teacher role. Third, it is important to contribute, in a considered and focused way, to having the participants both take on the responsibility for their own learning and understand that this is what they are doing, and that it is important that they actually do so.

Finally, participants taking responsibility for their own learning in no way means that there will be less responsibility for the leaders and teachers of the adult education programmes. On the contrary, it may be even more demanding in terms of responsibility when, in the many everyday situations and details, leaders and teachers must constantly decide what may reasonably be considered the participants' own responsibility and what the system and the teacher may and must assume responsibility for, instead of just fulfilling the traditional, responsible teacher role that everybody is so familiar with from their own school days.

The time, place and context of education and training activities

When planning the learning activities it is also important to constantly incorporate and respect the strained relation that many of the low-skilled have to school and education activities. At the start especially, both physically and from the point of view of content, everything must take place as close as possible to the daily work, and it also creates security if it can take place together with co-workers whom one knows well and trusts.

For those who are employed in larger enterprises, it will often be possible to place education activities in locations at the workplace, sometimes even combined with training directly connected to production or other work activities. Other courses with unemployed participants or a mixed composition of participants may circulate between locations at school and various relevant workplaces, which will allow the participants to experience various work environments.

In general it is always important to take into account the fact that for participants who may often be fundamentally ambivalent, such practical features as time and place may easily be decisive for their attitude. It is so very easy just to use practical problems or inconveniencies as an excuse for not participating, and it is much easier to accept a lot of transport and waste of time when attending a course that one has chosen voluntarily and perhaps even with enthusiasm.

In Denmark we have quite a few examples of vocational training courses that take place at or close to the workplace at the end of the workday and with a fifty-fifty share of work time paid by the employer and leisure time relinquished by the workers. This is experienced as a 'fair deal' and thus provides a good starting point and climate for the learning.

In programmes for the unemployed it is a really good investment to ensure that the practical circumstances include no details that potential participants can use as excuses for not attending. For many it is a threshold just to get started in a positive way, and providing the psychological conditions that can help them cross this threshold is often one of the most crucial challenges of the planning.

Learning content and methods

With respect to the content and methods of the learning activities, it is important to range widely. Part of the problem for low-skilled workers is often to see and understand the work in a larger context, to experience that it is performed in other ways at other places, to gain insight into what triggers and determines the changes that take place, to have the opportunity of asking questions and expressing doubt and resistance, to themselves try – for example through projects or the like – to be active in relation to their own work situation and work function, and to see that the experience and qualifications they have can be important and used as a starting point for learning more. It can be an almost euphoric experience for this group to realize that learning initiatives can also be something where one can make active use of one's experience, where one can play a part in deciding, and where what one contributes is not irrelevant.

One Danish example is a teaching programme at a large sugar factory where the participants prioritized teaching in the 'soft' subjects like communication, active listening and coaching. At the same time the participants typically emphasized being allowed to deal with subjects and problems from their own everyday work life as something positive and different from what they previously had experienced during their time at school. That anyone 'could be bothered doing something just for us' was quite a different and surprising experience that strengthened the self-confidence and self-awareness of many.

Very often workers' educational needs are not formulated clearly and unambiguously. Neither the enterprises' nor the employees' needs are something that can merely be 'uncovered'. Valuable teaching options rather emerge from a process in which the wishes of management, the needs of the employees and what the educational institution can offer must be developed and adjusted to each other. This is often experienced as time consuming, but it gives the processes a solid anchorage for all parties involved and is also of importance for the implementation and subsequent follow up (Jørgensen 2004).

For the unemployed it is in general not possible to establish direct links to work place conditions. It is therefore of decisive importance in other ways to make the relations to the labour market visible whenever it is possible. The great majority of the unemployed have the admission to the labour market as their all dominating reason for participating in educational and training activities, and they must be able constantly to see how the training activities relate to work openings which they can experience as realistic.

However, today this does not just mean training in practical knowledge and skills. In one of the surveys in which I have been involved, it was a remarkably clear conclusion that the unemployed experience personal qualities as more important for getting a job than practical skills. Courses and teachers are usually primarily focused on the practical content of training activities. Of course this is also important, but the participants often feel that it must somehow be related to the personal qualities that are so important today, so it should be an obligation that teachers and instructors find ways to include these essential issues. This is not so easy to do in ways that are neither superficial nor offending; it often implies techniques such as role play, and most teachers have only incidental qualifications for this, but nevertheless there is a strong need for training and discussions in this area.

But it must also be remembered that the most important qualification needs of the low-skilled are generally basic subjects such as writing, reading, languages and computer skills. This is usually also recognized by the learners themselves. But the more school-like teaching that is a necessary part of these subjects is precisely what they more or less consciously try to avoid. It was therefore a remarkable feature of the example mentioned above that when the participants had 'broken the ice' by projects closely connected to their work situation, it was easier for them later to come to terms with a more traditional teaching situation and take up the more school-like subjects.

On the pedagogical level, it is important that the division of responsibility discussed above is in practice translated into real participant direction, i.e. it is the participants who control the process in interaction with the teachers' qualified and loyal assistance and support. Another important pedagogical principle is problem orientation, that is, that the point of departure for the learning activities is taken in broadly defined thematic areas and problem fields that the participants find it important to work with in relation to the targets of their education programmes. This increases the possibilities for active, relevant learning. In general, participant direction and problem orientation are best practised through such pedagogical forms as action learning (Yorks *et al.* 1999) and project work (Illeris 1999, 2004a).

Monitoring, evaluation and implementation

Parallel with and at the end of education courses there are, as a rule, one or more forms of monitoring and evaluation of the participants' activities and qualifications. Such monitoring and evaluation is in its source and essence a societal necessity; society must ensure that persons have specific skills to handle specific functions or to be accepted into further education. At the same time, it can be of great significance for the individual that he or she can get her/his qualifications formally approved, practically as concerns status and psychologically as an acknowledgement that can provide identity and generate self-confidence.

However, it is also well known that monitoring and evaluation may have a very forceful and controlling influence on the education course and on the behaviour and consciousness of both participants and teachers in even the smallest details. It is therefore important that ways and means of practice in these areas are chosen carefully and in accordance with the participants' attitudes and preferences.

Generally, it is the common attitude among adult education participants in Denmark today that they would like to have documentation for completed education programmes, which not only testifies to satisfactory participation but also includes a certification of the qualifications they have acquired. With this, they also show willingness to accept that as a participant one must have one's qualifications tested, but there is widespread scepticism towards having this take place through an examination in the traditional sense. Many low-skilled participants have painful experiences with taking exams, and indicate, among other things, that it involves heavy and irrelevant psychological pressure, that the evaluation is unfair, that too much depends on luck and coincidence, etc.

In addition to this, there is generally very great dissatisfaction with any kind of attendance record, at least if there also are exams or another form of qualitative evaluation. Attendance monitoring is typically perceived as the most obvious expression of the imposed child-role and disempowerment inherent in 'returning to school'. They claim that adults are well able themselves to figure out what they must participate in and what they can do without, they are themselves able to take responsibility for prioritizing their activities, and what is important must be that they acquire the competences they are expected to acquire.

It is, on the other hand, not easy for the participants to give clear expression to possible alternative ways of monitoring and evaluating, as must be done in order to make it possible to document the competences acquired. However, it is a widely held view that evaluation must be carried out by the teachers with whom the students have daily contact, because regardless of the fact that there are both good and less good teachers, it is only they who have a background for knowing what the student actually knows and is able to do and understand. Furthermore, it is claimed that only in exceptional cases where the focus is on highly specific practical skills is a test or exam relevant. In most cases by far, the participants want the evaluation to be performed on the basis of the daily work and the minor and major assignments and projects that form part of the course.

Based on the assumption that participants are responsible adults and that the aim of the education programmes is generally concerned with the development of competences, there is every reason to respect the attitudes here expressed. In terms of learning, the concern is to find monitoring and evaluation forms that support, rather than inhibit, the participants' independence, responsibility, cooperation, etc., and thereby also their competence development.

The traditional forms of monitoring and evaluation must be considered an obsolete reflection of industrial society. With attendance monitoring and exams, the participants are placed in opposition to the 'system' as a powerful adversary in the same way as in the labour conditions seen in industrial employment. The concern here is conformity and submission to external power-based demands and not the joint promotion of personal development and having it realistically evaluated.

Naturally, the power aspect cannot be eliminated, but it is not impossible to find forms in which it assumes a less dominant character and to a higher degree respects the adult participants' experience, even though they also experience a certain duality between the wish for self-direction and the wish for obtaining formal approval.

The tasks of the teachers

In adult education and training of the type outlined here, the teachers and instructors must be professionally and pedagogically competent and loyal persons facilitating and supporting the participants' learning processes. There is no particular teacher role that fulfils this function best, and the most important thing is for the teachers themselves to develop a professional, authentic manner of functioning with which they feel comfortable.

As already mentioned, participant direction by no means implies that teachers have less work or responsibility. First and foremost, one key task is to establish the division of responsibility and participant direction described. Over and above this, among other things a secure and challenging learning environment must be created, relevant types of activities must be found, and relevant input must be provided in accordance with the needs of the participants and adjusted to other sides of the programme.

In addition a fruitful community must be created at the same time as the individual participant is supported in suitable ways, and space and routines must be created for reflection and reflexivity that ensure that the learning interacts with the interests and qualifications of the individual participant. All this must take place in ongoing interaction with the participants themselves controlling their own learning processes.

Especially when dealing with low-skilled and other vulnerable learners, the functions of the teacher go far beyond the traditional conception of teaching. I shall not go further into these considerations here as many of them have already been touched on indirectly. One important reference can be given to the concept of the 'interpretive professional' (Wildemeersch 2000).

The need for subjective anchorage

In general, educational initiatives for the low-skilled and other vulnerable groups seem to be becoming more varied and unclear than before. If this is to be handled seriously, that is as something other than making the statistics look good and perhaps dealing with the situation for a few of those with the strongest resources in the different groups, there is a need for radical initiatives that consistently take their starting point in and respect the situation as it is experienced by those whom it concerns. Nothing much happens if those who are to learn are not met with something that is meaningful for them on the basis of their own premises (Illeris 2004a).

For these groups it is this subjective anchorage that is the key to activities and measures that can provide a broader breakthrough. The various groups mentioned are in different ways in situations where they are not directly open to traditional educational initiatives. They do not really believe in them, they have bad experiences of not being able to live up to what is expected, and they usually have experienced repeatedly what it means to be rejected, not feel respected etc. An anchorage or a point of departure in this psychological experience and interpretation of the situation is an unavoidable necessity in these contexts.

But, simultaneously, relevant initiatives are also about coming further, because it is precisely the current situation and the way in which the individual relates to it that is the problem. A sustainable solution thus presupposes some type of breakthrough, an educational angst that must be overcome, an identity defence that must be opened, some unrealistic dreams that must be brought down to a realistic level, or perhaps some dreams and goals that must be found somewhere in what is experienced as a great unstructured vacuum.

These are processes that psychologically go deeper than what is generally understood as education (Illeris 2004b). Nevertheless, competence developing initiatives in the great majority of cases are the best way forward, because the development of better and more practically relevant competences are an important part of what is necessary to escape from the situation. However, it must be accepted on the political, administrative and practical levels that relevant competence development for these groups is directly connected to some deep and demanding psychological processes that cannot be disregarded if progress is to be made.

This does not merely require respectful understanding of the situation as the person in question experiences it. It also requires an accepting firmness that holds on to the social realities in the face of justified insecurity and unrealistic wishful thinking. Being educated for places for which they are not needed helps nobody, but if they are to go for something where they are needed, they must want it themselves. The psychologically liberating and the socially relevant qualifying processes must be united in one practical process.

Therefore people who can manage this duality must undertake these functions. These people can be difficult to find and it may be necessary to take action in this area from the point of view of both education and salary. In addition, time and relevant opportunities in relation to the labour market must be available, and overall it must be accepted that such processes cannot be successful over a broad area if there is not willingness to accept the subjective needs of those concerned and to invest the necessary resources. After all, there is a lot of money to be saved at the other end each time the process succeeds, and what was a painful and costly problem becomes a qualified workforce.

If we want to tackle the problems of the low-skilled and other vulnerable groups in the breadth and complexity they have today, we must realize that it does not help to invest in minimum solutions. We have to go into depth and take the psychological level seriously. Highly qualified people are needed to undertake the key functions. It must be ensured that the labour market parties involve themselves actively and disregard narrow interests. Relevant workplaces must also be involved, even though in some cases this might mean financial compensation or other similar incentives.

This is a large and serious human and social problem field. It is a matter of descending spirals that must be reversed. Half-baked solutions will only result in new problems with even greater human and economic costs. Recent Canadian statistics indicate that investing in the low-skilled is the category of educational expenses that pays the highest returns (Statistics Canada 2004). This should be sufficient motivation for those who pay attention mainly to economic features. For those who also take interest in human welfare, there are many other reasons to invest in this area. But at any rate, serious investments cannot neglect the problematic psychological conditions of the low-skilled and other vulnerable groups. Without their positive engagement, no sustainable and durable changes are possible.

References

BECK, U. and BECK-GERNSHEIM, E. (2002) *Individualization: Institutionalized individualism and its social and political consequences* (London: SAGE).

ELLSTRÖM, P.-E. and ILLERIS, K. (eds) (2004) Workplace learning – Scandinavian perspectives. *Journal of Workplace Learning*, 16(8).

ILLERIS, K. (1998) Adult learning and responsibility. In K. ILLERIS (ed.) *Adult Education in a Transforming Society* (Copenhagen: Roskilde University Press).
ILLERIS, K. (1999) Project work in university studies: background and current issues. In H. SALLING OLESEN and J. HØJGAARD JENSEN (eds) *Project Studies* (Copenhagen: Roskilde University Press).
ILLERIS, K. (2002) *The Three Dimensions of Learning* (Leicester: NIACE and Malabar, FL: Krieger Publishing, 2004).
ILLERIS, K. (2003a) Workplace learning and learning theory. *Journal of Workplace Learning*, 15(4), 167–178.
ILLERIS, K. (2003b) Adult education as experienced by the learners. *International Journal of Lifelong Education*, 22(1), 13–23.
ILLERIS, K. (2003c) Low skilled adults' motivation for learning. Paper presented at the CEDEFOP Conference on Lifelong Learning (Thessaloniki, 2–3 June).
ILLERIS, K. (2003d) Towards a contemporary and comprehensive theory of learning. *International Journal of Lifelong Education*, 22(4), 411–421.
ILLERIS, K. (2004a) *Adult Education and Adult Learning* (Malabar, FL: Krieger Publishing).
ILLERIS, K. (2004b) Transformative learning in the perspective of a comprehensive learning theory. *Journal of Transformative Education*, 2(2), 79–89.
ILLERIS, K. et al. (2004) *Learning in Working Life* (Copenhagen: Roskilde University Press).
JØRGENSEN, C. H. (2004) Connecting work and education: Should learning be useful, correct or meaningful? *Journal of Workplace Learning*, 16(8), 455–465.
SIMONSEN, B. (2000) New young people, new forms of consciousness, new educational methods. In K. ILLERIS (ed.) *Adult Education in the Perspective of the Learners* (Copenhagen: Roskilde University Press).
STATISTICS CANADA (2004) *International Adult Literacy Survey: Literacy scores, human capital and growth across fourteen OECD countries* (Ottawa: Statistics Canada).
WEIL, S., WILDEMEERSCH, D. and JANSEN, T. (2005) *Unemployed Youth and Social Exclusion in Europe: Learning from inclusion?* (Aldershot: Ashgate).
WILDEMEERSCH, D. (2000) Lifelong learning and the significance of the interpretive professional. In K. ILLERIS (ed.) *Adult Education in the Perspective of the Learners* (Copenhagen: Roskilde University Press).
YORKS, L., O'NEILL, J. and MARSICK, V. J. (1999) *Action Learning – Successful Strategies for Individual, Team and Organizational Development* (Baton Rouge, L. A: Academy of Human Resource Development).

PART III

SPECIAL LEARNING ISSUES

CHAPTER 8

LEARNING AND COGNITION

The concepts of cognition and learning

The concept of cognition has always had a central position in psychology and not least in relation to the psychology of learning. Cognition is a broad term including everything that has to do with knowledge, thinking, reason and understanding, and is traditionally placed in opposition to the other elements of the mind: the affective, which has to do with feelings and emotions, and the conative, which has to do with volition (e.g. Hilgard, 1980).

Linguistically the word comes from the Latin, *cognitus*, which means knowledge in a broad sense. Thus, the famous statement by the French philosopher René Descartes (1596–1660), *cogito, ergo sum* (1967 [1637]), is usually translated into 'I think, therefore I am'. But this translation has often been disputed and, according to the well-known Norwegian historian of philosophy Arne Næss (1912–2009), *cogito* in this connection rather means 'I experience' or 'I am somewhat aware' (Næss, 1963 [1962]: 143). This is not unimportant in the present connection, partly because it indicates that cognition in relation to learning can be much more than just the acquisition of knowledge – in modern terms it is ultimately about making meaning of what we experience (Bruner, 1990; Mezirow, 2000), and partly because the statement of Descartes is often regarded as the foundation of the separation between the mental and the bodily, which for centuries has been so significant in Western philosophy and mentality and has, among many other things, derailed and confused the basic understanding of human learning by also separating the cognitive from the social and the emotional. I shall return to this in the following.

As to the understanding of 'learning', there are also many and widely differing understandings. I shall here stick to the very comprehensive definition that learning is 'any process that in living organisms leads to permanent capacity change and which is not solely due to biological maturation or ageing' (Illeris, 2007: 3). This implies, among other things, that such processes as socialization, qualification, competence development and therapy are regarded as special types of learning processes or as special angles for perceiving learning.

Early learning research and behaviourism

Originally, learning research and learning theory were concentrated on very simple learning processes, and there was an underlying idea that a kind of learning mechanism could be discovered which would be the basic unit or 'atom' of all learning (Madsen, 1967: 64ff). The conception of learning was also limited to the cognitive field, including simple processes that can hardly be called anything but basic, especially when the learning of animals was studied. Two early examples, in brief, are as follows:

- First, at the end of the nineteenth century the German learning researcher Hermann Ebbinghaus (1850–1909) studied the learning of meaningless syllables such as nug, mok, ket, rop, etc., because such learning could be measured exactly and any distorting influence from the meaning of the learning content could be avoided (Ebbinghaus, 1964 [1885]). Today, this must be regarded as a derailment, as precisely the meaning of what is learnt is seen as a crucial quality.
- Second, during the early years of the twentieth century the Russian physiologist and Nobel Prize winner Ivan Pavlov (1849–1936) studied how a dog could learn by conditioning: he let a bell ring immediately before the dog was fed, and soon he could observe that it started to produce saliva whenever the bell rang. Later he performed a lot of experiments about the effects of various conditions in this connection (Pavlov, 1927).

Then, in 1913 the American John Watson (1878–1958) introduced the approach of behaviourism (Watson, 1930), which became dominant, especially in American and British learning psychology, right up to the 1980s. This implied that the study of learning was concentrated very much on cognitive and rather simple learning processes. Most important were probably the contributions of Edward Lee Thorndike (1874–1949) about trial-and-error learning, which led to the 'law-of-effect', stating that reactions implying a satisfying effect will be learned (Thorndike, 1931), and of B.F. Skinner (1904–90), who exceeded the cognitive domain by claiming that all learning is conditioned, including the learning of capacities such as independence and creativity, and that education should therefore be practised as teaching technology (Skinner, 1968: 1971).

Other classical cognitive learning approaches

However, parallel to the behaviourist dominance in the English-speaking countries, other and much broader approaches to cognitive learning were developed elsewhere. In Germany the Gestalt psychology, claiming that the mind is an indivisible whole, focused on learning as the acquisition of insight and pointed to problem solving as the way to do so (Köhler, 1925 [1917]; Duncker, 1945 [1935]) – the approach that Kurt Lewin (1890–1947) later developed into his 'field theory', experimental social psychology and the 'T-groups' (training groups) as a method to promote social learning (Lewin, 1976).

Of the greatest importance were, however, the two approaches that were made respectively by the Swiss biologist and epistemologist Jean Piaget (1896–1980) and the Russian psychologist Lev Vygotsky (1896–1934) and others of the so-called cultural historical school. Both these approaches are in their essence truly cognitive, although they also both clearly indicate that emotional and motivational factors play an important role in learning, and a collection of lectures by Piaget on this topic has been published in English since his death (Piaget, 1981).

Piaget is best known for his work on the development through several stages of intelligence in the child, but, in relation to learning, his understanding of assimilation and accommodation as two collaborating and equilibrating ways of learning (Piaget, 1952 [1936]) has been a very fruitful contribution to which I shall return later. Another important insight by Piaget was that all learning happens by new impulses being related to the results of prior learning in a way that changes both (which has later been further elaborated by the American David Ausuble: 'The most important single factor influencing learning is what the learner already knows' – Ausuble, 1968: vi).

The Russian cultural historical approach emphasizes that mankind's fundamental psychological structures have developed in interaction with the development of culture, and that the human capacity of learning and 'higher psychological functions' can only be understood in this perspective. The most important kinds of cultural activity are play, learning and labour and they are all dependent on our abilities to think and to speak (Leontjev, 1981 [1959]).

Vygotsky's conception of learning is mainly related to children's learning in school and problem solving guided by adults or more capable peers. In this connection, special attention is given to what he called learning in 'the zone of proximal development', indicating that teachers lead their activities into the zone where such developmental learning can take place (Vygotsky, 1978, 1986 [1934]). This approach has later been further elaborated by American researchers such as Michael Cole (1996): who has emphasized that this kind of learning should be 'a dialogue between the child and his future [. . .] not between the child and an adult's past' (Griffin and Cole, 1984: 62) – and not least by Finnish Yrjö Engeström, who has transferred the ideas into adult and workplace learning (Engeström, 1987, 2009).

Both Piaget's and the cultural historical approaches referred to learning in general, but were certainly predominantly thought and used in relation to the cognitive dimension of learning and may still be said to be the two most important contributions to the understanding of cognitive learning.

Newer cognitive approaches

During the 1960s and 1970s the above-mentioned approaches, and especially those of Piaget and Vygotsky, began to achieve influence in the USA and, together with influence from the new computer technology, this led to what has been called 'the cognitive revolution', which gradually reduced the influence of behaviourism. On the one hand, this resulted in the emergence of 'cognitive science', which treated learning and thinking as information processing and celebrated artificial intelligence (e.g. Calvo and Gomila, 2008) – but this trend has by and large disappeared because of its inability to include such human capabilities as intention and meaning making (Dreyfus and Dreyfus, 1986). On the other hand, it released a new wave of approaches to cognitive learning.

A first name to mention in this connection is that of the American psychologist Jerome Bruner. Right back in the 1940s he started his long career with cognitive studies that increasingly challenged traditional behaviourism. Later he was a central figure in relation to the so-called science-centred curriculum, which was a response to the 'sputnik-shock' in 1957 when the Russians sent the first satellite into space. In 1990 he published the book *Acts of Meaning*, which, in open opposition to behaviourism, introduced meaning as a central element of human learning and understanding. And in 1996 his publication of *The Culture of Education* was a clear dissociation from both behaviourism and cognitive science and a devoted pleading for the understanding of learning as a human and cultural process reaching far beyond the cognitive area (Bruner, 1990, 1996).

Another American psychologist to mention here is David Kolb. In his *Experiential Learning* from 1984 he takes his point of departure from the 'founding fathers', John Dewey, Piaget and Lewin, and comes to the conclusion that all learning is experiential and follows a specific circular pattern from concrete experience via reflective observation and abstract conceptualization to active experimentation and then back to new concrete experience (Kolb, 1984). Although this learning cycle is rather rigid in relation to the diversity of human learning, and once again predominantly is thought and used in relation to the cognitive area, Kolb's thinking was, no doubt, an important contribution to the establishment of a more differentiated understanding of learning.

The organizational learning theory of the American psychologists Chris Argyris and Donald Schön (1930–97) is also relevant in this connection, especially because of the distinction between single-loop learning, which remains within, and double-loop learning, which exceeds the existing frames of understanding (Argyris and Schön, 1978, 1996), and further for Schön's exploration of 'the reflective practitioner' and 'reflection-in-action' (Schön, 1983, 1987). These are all contributions that help to understand cognitive learning in working life.

Finally, the work of the American psychologist Jack Mezirow on transformative learning is mainly cognitive as it is about changes in meaning structures, meaning perspectives and habits of mind (Mezirow, 1978, 1991, 2000).

Personal development – crossing the boundaries of cognitive learning

Whereas all the approaches mentioned up till now have been totally or predominantly cognitive in their content and perspectives, the most important development in the understanding of human learning since about 1990 has been that learning is never and by no means only a cognitive matter – which implies that pure cognitive learning does not take place in normal human beings and that cognitive learning theories deal only with a special side of human learning. This has, since the middle of the twentieth century, been claimed by a few learning theorists, but during the last two decades this understanding has rapidly gained ground and has also been clearly confirmed by modern brain research (especially Damasio, 1994). Thus, the concept of cognitive learning is a kind of illusion – as it must also somehow have appeared to the famous German philosopher Immanuel Kant (1724–1804), as he wrote his *Critique of Pure Reason* in 1781 (Kant, 2002 [1781]).

Actually, the first reseacher who discovered this in practice can be said to be Sigmund Freud (1856–1939), who as early as 1895 described the phenomenon of 'catharsis', which is the mental breakthrough that can take place in psychoanalysis and psychotherapy (Freud and Breuer, 1956 [1895]). But Freud and his age did not think of this as learning and certainly not cognition – although it is firmly within the definition of learning that is used in this chapter.

However, half a century later another psychotherapist, the American Carl Rogers (1902–87), realized this connection and developed the concept of 'significant learning' for such learning that involves a change in the organization of the self (Rogers, 1951, 1969). Rogers also launched the issue of 'encounter groups', a special shaping of Lewin's 'T-groups', to promote significant learning and personal development (Rogers 1970). This strongly helped to see personal development as a kind of learning, which of course includes the cognitive dimension, but only as a part of a much wider totality.

Another contribution in this direction was delivered at the same time by the German-American psychoanalyst Erik H. Erikson (1902–94), who described the life course as a succession of stages connected by crises-like transitions, which can also be interpreted as periods of intensive personal learning (Erikson, 1968, 1994).

The social dimension of learning

However, seeing personal development as a kind of learning did not at this time really affect the conception of learning as a cognitive matter, probably because these ideas were so different; the serious challenge came when learning began also to be considered to have important and specific social and emotional dimensions.

The concept of social learning was first established in earnest by the American social psychologist Albert Bandura in the 1960s. It primarily concerned model learning and learning through imitation – phenomena that had often been dealt with before, not least by Piaget (1951 [1945]) – which Bandura and his work associates studied in a traditional behaviouristic fashion (Bandura and Walters, 1963; Bandura, 1977), which implied certain limitations.

A quite different approach at the same time was the sociological theories of socialization, which is the process through which the individual acquires current societal norms and structures, thus becoming part of the society in question. This was primarily taken up by the German-American 'Frankfurt School' which combined a Freudian and a Marxist approach into what was called 'Critical Theory'. Important names from this school are Max Horkheimer (1895–1973), Theodor Adorno (1903–69), Herbert Marcuse (1898–1979) and Jürgen Habermas, but, in relation to socialization learning, the later branch-off in Hanover became more important, especially through the works of Peter Brückner (1922–82), Alfred Lorenzer (1922–2002), Oskar Negt, Thomas Leithäuser and Thomas Ziehe. The central issue in all this is that the young generation mainly unconsciously comes to learn the culture and forms of consciousness and also cognition of its society, but at the same time develops defence and resistance towards societal elements which it dislikes (Brückner, 1972; Lorenzer, 1972; Negt, 1971; Leithäuser, 1976, 1998; Ziehe, 2009).

However, the real breakthrough of the understanding of all learning having a social dimension was not established until the early 1990s. Most significant was the claim in 1991 by the American anthropologist Jean Lave and the Swiss-American computer scientist Etienne Wenger that all learning is 'situated': it takes place in a specific situation and this situation does not only influence the learning but actually is part of it (Lave and Wenger, 1991), and later the book by Wenger on *Communities of Practice* (Wenger, 1998).

The broader movement of 'social constructionism' also strongly advocated the social inbeddedness of psychological processes, sometimes so strongly that the individual nature of the processes was denied (Gergen, 1991, 1994; Burr 1995). Also the biographical approach, seeing learning in the perspective of the personal life story, should be mentioned in this connection (Alheit, 1994, 2009).

The emotional dimension of learning

To some extent the emotional dimension was included in the personal development approach to learning, but this was not in any way emphasized or set out explicitly. It has also already been mentioned that both Piaget and Vygotsky pointed to this dimension without really integrating it in their predominantly cognitive theories. So when the Briton John Heron in 1992 launched this approach in his *Feeling and Personhood* it was certainly received as *Psychology in Another Key* as it was termed in the subtitle of his book (Heron 1992).

However, a more widespread acceptance of viewing the emotional as part of learning in general was in the following years probably promoted to a higher extent by the American Daniel Goleman's more popular book on *Emotional Intelligence* (Goleman, 1995) and, as already mentioned, new discoveries and understandings from the rapidly expanding area of brain research (Damasio, 1994).

Finally, it should be mentioned here that the first publication to give the social and the emotional a position that is fully equal to the cognitive was my own, *The Three Dimensions of Learning* (Illeris, 2002 [1999]). Other contemporary authors who, more indirectly, include the non-cognitive dimensions as general features of human learning are the American Robert Kegan (1994, 2009 [2000]) and the Briton Peter Jarvis (2006, 2009).

Cognitive learning as an integrated learning dimension

Thus, the development of the understanding of human learning has during the latest decades gradually led to an overall conception that all learning includes three dimensions – the cognitive or content dimension, the emotional or incentive dimension, and the social or interaction dimension – which are equal in the sense that each of them always play a role and no full understanding, analysis or planning of learning processes can omit any of these dimensions (Illeris, 2002, 2007, 2009). This can be illustrated by the 'learning triangle' (Figure 8.1).

The two double arrows inside the triangle depict the two different processes that are involved in any learning. The vertical double arrow shows the interaction process between the individual and what is exposed or happening in his or her environment. This process is going on all the time when we are awake, and whenever something that is new to the individual turns up there is a possibility of learning.

However, learning only takes place if there is also an active process of acquisition going on, as in the figure depicted by the horizontal double arrow. This acquisition takes place in the individual's brain and central nervous system and includes two poles or elements: the content and the incentive. The content may be identical with the cognitive, but may also include skills and personality qualities. It is obvious

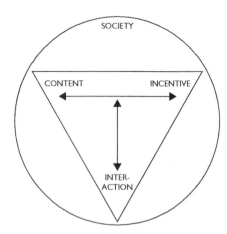

Figure 8.1 The three dimensions of learning. Source: Illeris 2007, p. 26.

that any learning must have a content, as to learn without learning something is nonsense. But neither can it be imagined that there can be any learning without an incentive in the form of a mobilization of mental energy. All mental processes demand energy, and modern brain research has estimated that we spend about 20 per cent of our energy supply on such processes (Andreasen, 2005). This mobilization is fundamentally emotional and, in relation to learning, usually referred to as motivation.

These fundamental features constitute the three learning dimensions as in the figure depicted by the learning triangle, and learning always takes place in a specific place and situation, which are finally societally constituted and in the figure depicted by the outer circle.

Seen in relation to cognition, the figure indicates that the cognitive element or dimension of learning is always part of a more complex structure, which also includes the emotional and the social, or, to be more precise, that the acquisition of cognitive learning content, such as knowledge, recognition, understanding or insight, is always integrated with and dependent on the learner's active interaction with the environment and mobilization of an incentive to drive the process. So both the learning process and the result or outcome always include all these three dimensions. For example, an unclear interaction and/or an ambivalent or unengaged incentive will tend to lead to an imprecise or weak learning outcome which can only be recalled in situations that are strongly resembling the learning situation, and if it is not reinforced it will soon be blurred or forgotten.

The types of learning

As illustrated above, it is ultimately not possible or appropriate to speak in isolation of cognitive, emotional or social learning, as all learning to some extent includes all of these. This insight is especially important in relation to schools and education, as learning in these institutions is very often thought and spoken of only in terms of the cognitive, academic or professional content. This then leads in the direction of a one-sided focus on what is or should be learnt at the expense of how it is learnt and of which engagement or motivation is involved, and thereby of the learning quality, which may be seen in relation to when the learning can be recalled, what it can be used for and how soon it will be forgotten.

However, a quite different and more relevant kind of learning can be established by taking as the point of departure how the new elements are connected to what has already been acquired, i.e. to the mental schemes that are the results of prior learning and always include all three learning dimensions. This was actually the approach that was introduced by Jean Piaget who, as already mentioned, was the first to realize that new learning is always acquired or taken in by relating it to what has already been learnt, in which process both the old and the new are changed (e.g. Piaget, 1952 [1936]). Piaget distinguished between assimilative and accommodative learning, but later contributions have made it possible to divide each of these into two, which makes four learning types, of which the first two may be understood as learning by addition and the last two as learning by reconstruction (Illeris, 2007).

The first learning type in this typology was pointed out by the Danish psychologist Thomas Nissen, who named it 'cumulation' (Nissen, 1970). This is learning that starts up a new mental scheme because the content cannot be related to any existing scheme. This happens quite often in our first years, but already by the age of two it becomes more scarce and after the age of about six years it is used only when we have to learn something by heart, e.g. a pin code. Cumulation is the kind of learning that we use for training animals and which was in the early days of behaviourism studied as simple conditioning. The main character of what is learnt in this way is that it can only be recalled in situations that subjectively are experienced as identical with the original learning situation.

After this comes 'assimilation' as the learning type that we use in usual everyday learning and also in most school learning and training. This takes place simply by adding a new element to an already existing mental scheme; it is not very demanding, and we all do it again and again by noticing what is new in a situation, finding a subjectively relevant existing scheme and elaborating the new element into this scheme.

The learning type that Piaget termed 'accommodation' is only commanded by humans and in very limited forms by the most developed animals. We use it whenever we are confronted with information or come into situations in which we cannot subjectively immediately relate or add what we experience to any existing scheme. In such cases we have the possibility to break down (part of) one or more schemes and reconstruct them such that the new impulses can fit in. This results in qualitatively new learning; we so to speak exceed our own boundaries and acquire a new understanding or way of behaving or experiencing. In traditional German psychology this was termed an 'aha-experience', and it often implies a feeling of relief. But it also demands much more mental energy than assimilation, and we therefore tend to only mobilize for this type of learning when we are really engaged. If not, we have the possibility of just avoiding learning or make a 'distorted assimilation' by reducing the new into something that is already known or familiar, a matter of course or a prejudice.

Finally, we can learn by 'transformation', which is actually precisely what Carl Rogers described as significant learning. This implies the reconstruction of several schemes, including the scheme of our self or identity. It has also been termed by Yrjö Engeström expansive learning (Engeström, 1987) and by Alheit transitory learning (Alheit, 1994) – whereas Mezirow's term of transformative learning is not always transformational in this sense, because it need not involve the self. Anyway, it is a very demanding kind of learning that we only resort to when we can find no other way out of a locked situation or position. But it is worth noticing that, as society becomes ever more complex and its changes ever more widespread, transformative learning is no longer a field that professionally is reserved for psychotherapy, but it is also quite often required in relation to youth and adult education and training, for example when people are referred to reschooling because they are unemployed and their qualifications are no longer marketable.

It should here be emphasized that this typology has been developed from Piaget's concepts, which are mainly related to the cognitive field, but can be fully applied to all of the three dimensions of the learning triangle.

Learning barriers

As a last point, barriers to learning shall be taken up as a topic that is of rapidly growing importance as societies and existence become more and more complex and changes become more and more frequent. So the traditional cognitively oriented types of barriers such as misunderstandings, insufficient prior learning, lack of concentration, or inappropriate communication have to a growing extent been surpassed by barriers related mainly to the two other learning dimensions (Illeris, 2007).

Learning defence in particluar has since the middle of the twentieth century expanded into something that we all have to develop to counter the enormous growth in the amount of information and influence that we constantly meet, and which often is of a manipulative or persuasive character. According to Thomas Leithäuser (1976) this has forced all of us to necessarily develop what he has called an 'everyday consciousness' that blocks or distorts possible learning, usually unconsciously, because we cannot even manage to consciously administrate which of the many influences to take in and which to reject. And gradually the defence against the amount of influences has been supplemented by defence against certain kinds of influence and also often by a genuine defence of one's identity.

Finally, an older but not so common barrier is that of learning resistance towards what the individual finds truly unacceptable. This involves a very strong mobilization of mental energy and therefore opens the individual for profound accommodative and transformative learning, often in opposition to what has been intended. If people are asked when they have learnt something that has really been of importance to them they will very often refer to situations of learning resistance (Illeris, 2007).

In today's 'learning society' it is obvious that learning barriers are a very important issue that contribute strongly to emphasizing that the cognitive side of learning is heavily and inseparably influenced by and integrated with non-cognitive processes.

References

Alheit, P. (1994): The Biographical Question as a Challenge to Adult Education. *International Review of Education*, 40.
—— (2009): Biographical Learning – Within the New Lifelong Learning Discourse. In K. Illeris (ed.): *Contemporary Theories of Learning: Learning Theorists . . . In Their Own Words*. London: Routledge.
Andreasen, N. C. (2005): *The Creating Brain: The Neuroscience of Genius*. New York: Dana Press.
Argyris, C. and Schön, D. (1978): *Organizational Learning: A Theory of Action Perspective*. Reading, MA: Addison-Wesley.
—— (1996): *Organizational Learning II: Theory, Method, Practice*. Reading, MA: Addison-Wesley.
Ausuble, D. P. (1968): *Educational Psychology: A Cognitive View*. New York: Holt, Rinehart and Winston.
Bandura, A. (1977): *Social Learning Theory*. Englewood Cliffs, NJ: Prentice-Hall.
Bandura, A. and Walters, R. H. (1963): *Social Learning and Personality Development*. New York: Holt, Rinehart and Winston.
Brückner, P. (1972): *Zur Sozialpsychologie des Kapitalismus* [The Social Psychology of Capitalism]. Frankfurt a.M.: Europäische Verlagsanstalt.
Bruner, J. (1990): *Acts of Meaning*. Cambridge, MA: Harvard University Press.
—— (1996): *The Culture of Education*. Cambridge, MA: Harvard University Press.
Burr, V. (1995): *An Introduction to Social Constructionism*. London: Routledge.
Calvo, P. and Gomila, Antoni (eds) (2008): *Handbook of Cognitive Science: An Embodied Approach*. Oxford: Elsevier.
Cole, M. (1996): *Cultural Psychology: A Once and Future Discipline*. Cambridge, MA: Harvard University Press.
Damasio, A. R. (1994): *Descartes' Error: Emotion, Reason and the Human Brain*. New York: Grosset/Putnam.
Descartes, R. (1967 [1637]): *The Philosophical Works of Descartes*. Cambridge: Cambridge University Press, 3rd reprint.
Dreyfus, H. and Dreyfus, S. (1986): *Mind over Machine*. New York: Free Press.
Duncker, K. (1945 [1935]): *On Problem-Solving*. The American Psychological Association, Psychological Monographs, 5.

Ebbinghaus, H. (1964 [1885]): *Memory: A Contribution to Experimental Psychology*. New York: Dover.
Engeström, Y. (1987): *Learning by Expanding: An Activity-Theoretical Approach to Developmental Research*. Helsinki: Orienta-Konsultit.
—— (2009): Expansive Learning: Toward an Activity-theoretical Reconceptualization. In K. Illeris (ed.): *Contemporary Theories of Learning: Learning Theorists ... In Their Own Words*. London: Routledge.
Erikson, E. H. (1968): *Identity, Youth and Crisis*. New York: Norton.
—— (1994): *Identity and the Life Cycle*. New York: Norton.
Freud, S. and Breuer, J. (1956 [1895]): *Studies of Hysteria*. London: Pelican Freud Library.
Gergen, K.J. (1991): *The Saturated Self: Dilemmas of Identity in Contemporary Life*. New York: Basic Books.
—— (1994): *Realities and Relationships*. Cambridge, MA: Harvard University Press.
Goleman, D. (1995): *Emotional Intelligence: Why it can Matter More than IQ*. London: Bloomsbury.
Griffin, P. and Cole, M. (1984): Current Activity for the Future: The Zo-Ped. In Barbara Rogoff and James W. Wertsch (eds): *Children's Learning in the 'Zone of Proximal Development'*. San Francisco, CA: Jossey-Bass.
Heron, J. (1992): *Feeling and Personhood: Psychology in Another Key*. London: Sage.
Hilgard, E. R. (1980): The Trilogy of Mind: Cognition, Conation and Emotion. *Journal of the History of the Behavioral Sciences*, 16: 107–17.
Illeris, K. (2002 [1999]): *The Three Dimensions of Learning: Contemporary Learning Theory in the Tension Field Between the Cognitive, the Emotional and the Social*. Copenhagen: Roskilde University Press and Leicester: NIACE.
—— (2007): *How We Learn: Learning and Non-learning in School and Beyond*. London: Routledge.
—— (2009): A Comprehensive Understanding of Human Learning. In K. Illeris (ed.): *Contemporary Theories of Learning: Learning Theorists ... In Their Own Words*. London: Routledge.
Jarvis, P. (2006): *Towards a Comprehensive Understanding of Human Learning*. London: Routledge.
—— (2009): Learning To Be a Person in Society: Learning To Be Me. In K. Illeris (ed.): *Contemporary Theories of Learning: Learning Theorists ... In Their Own Words*. London: Routledge.
Kant, I. (2002 [1781]): *The Critique of Pure Reason*. Cambridge: Cambridge University Press.
Kegan, R. (1994): *In Over Our Heads: The Mental Demands of Modern Life*. Cambridge, MA: Harvard University Press.
—— (2009 [2000]): What 'form' transforms?: A Constructive-developmental Approach to Transformative Learning. In K. Illeris (ed.): *Contemporary Theories of Learning: Learning Theorists ... In Their Own Words*. London: Routledge.
Köhler, W. (1925 [1917]): *The Mentality of Apes*. Harmondsworth: Penguin.
Kolb, D. A. (1984): *Experiential Learning: Experience as a Source of Learning and Development*. Englewood Cliffs, NJ: Prentice-Hall.
Lave, J. and Wenger, E. (1991): *Situated Learning: Legitimate Peripheral Participation*. New York: Cambridge University Press.
Leithäuser, T. (1976): *Formen des Alltagsbewusstseins* [The Forms of Everyday Consciousness]. Frankfurt a.M.: Campus.
—— (1998): The Problem of Authoritarianism: Approaches to a Further Development of a Traditional Concept. In K. Illeris (ed.): *Adult Education in a Transforming Society*. Copenhagen: Roskilde University Press.
Leontjev, A. N. (1981 [1959]): *Problems of the Development of the Mind*. Moscow: Progress. [Collected manuscripts from the 1930s].
Lewin, K. (1976): *Field Theory in Social Science: Selected Theoretical Papers*. Chicago, IL: Chicago University Press.
Lorenzer, A. (1972): *Zur Begründung einer Materialistischen Sozialisationstheorie* [Foundations of a Materialistic Theory of Socialization]. Frankfurt a.M.: Suhrkamp.
Madsen, K. B. (1967): *Almen Psykologi I* [General Psychology]. Copenhagen: Gyldendal.

Mezirow, J. (1978): *Education for Perspective Transformation: Women's Re-entry Programs in Community Colleges.* New York: Teachers College, Columbia University.
—— (1991): *Transformative Dimensions of Adult Learning.* San Francisco, CA: Jossey-Bass.
—— (2000): Learning to Think Like an Adult: Core Conceptions of Transformation Theory. In Jack Mezirow and Associates: *Learning as Transformation: Critical Perspectives on a Theory of Progress.* San Francisco, CA: Jossey-Bass.
Næss, A. (1963 [1962]): *Filosofiens Historie II* [The History of Philosophy]. Copenhagen: Vintens Forlag.
Negt, O. (1971): *Soziologische Phantasie und Exemplarisches Lernen* [Sociological Imagination and Exemplary Learning]. Frankfurt a.M.: Europäische Verlagsanstalt.
Nissen, T. (1970): *Indlæring og pædagogik* [Learning and Pedagogy]. Copenhagen: Munksgaard.
Pavlov, I. P. (1927): *Conditional Reflexes: An Investigation of the Physiological Activity of the Cerebral Cortex.* Oxford: Oxford University Press.
Piaget, J. (1951 [1945]): *Plays, Dreams and Imitation in Childhood.* New York: Norton.
—— (1952 [1936]): *The Origin of Intelligence in Children.* New York: International Universities Press.
—— (1981): *Intelligence and Affectivity: Their Relationship During Child Development.* Palo Alto, CA: Annual Reviews Inc.
Rogers, C. R. (1951): *Client-Centred Therapy.* Boston, MA: Houghton-Mifflin.
—— (1969): *Freedom to Learn.* Columbus, OH: Charles E. Merrill.
—— (1970): *Carl Rogers on Encounter Groups.* New York: Harper & Row.
Schön, D. A. (1983): *The Reflective Practitioner: How Professionals Think in Action.* New York: Basic Books.
—— (1987): *Educating the Reflective Practitioner.* San Francisco, CA: Jossey-Bass.
Skinner, B. F. (1968): *The Technology of Teaching.* New York: Appleton-Century-Croft.
—— (1971): *Beyond Freedom and Dignity.* New York: Knopf.
Thorndike, E. L. (1931): *Human Learning: The Messenger Lectures.* New York: Cornell University.
Vygotsy, L. S. (1978): *Mind in Society: The Development of Higher Psychological Processes.* Cambridge, MA: Harvard University Press.
—— (1986 [1934]): *Thought and Language.* Cambridge, MA: MIT Press.
Watson, J. B. (1930): *Behaviorism.* London: Kegan Paul.
Wenger, E. (1998): *Communities of Practice: Learning, Meaning and Identity.* Cambridge, MA: Cambridge University Press.
Ziehe, T. (2009): 'Normal Learning Problems' in Youth: In the Context of Underlying Cultural Convictions. In K. Illeris (ed.): *Contemporary Theories of Learning: Learning Theorists . . . In Their Own Words.* London: Routledge.

CHAPTER 9

TRANSFER OF LEARNING IN THE LEARNING SOCIETY

For more than a century learning psychology has dealt with the so-called transfer problem: that what has been learned in one context often can be difficult to recall and apply in a different context. This article, building on many years' theoretical and practical work in the field, starts by defining five main learning spaces in contemporary society, arguing that transfer problems usually turn up in relation to the transition of the boundaries between these spaces, and especially between the school and education space and the spaces of everyday life and working life. Focus is then turned to contemporary theories of learning and knowledge and four different learning and knowledge types are described, which are activated in different situations and imply different transfer possibilities. Finally, two ways of dealing with the problem in school and educational practice are outlined and discussed.

This article deals with the classical problem of transfer of learning as it presents itself in the modern context of issues like lifelong learning and the learning society. About a century ago, progressive learning researchers in North America observed that the results of learning in one type of setting were often not accessible when the learner moved to another setting. School learning, in particular, could often not be recalled and/or applied in everyday life or working life. For this reason, for almost as long as learning psychology has existed, it has been imperative to discover what it would take for learning to obtain utility value across transitions to new situations or learning spaces.

Two main understandings were proposed as answers to the problem. In 1901 Edward Lee Thorndike, often considered to be the founder of educational psychology, together with his colleague Robert Woodworth suggested that 'identical elements' must be present in the learning and application situation for transfer to occur (Thorndike and Woodworth 1901). And in 1908 another American psychologist, Charles Judd, put forward the more open and optimistic idea that general principles, rules and theories could form the basis for transfer of learning (Judd 1908).

Ever since, these two fundamental positions seem to have been opposites at the same time as other explanations have been sought relating to the nature of the learning content, features of the learner, or the nature of how what is learned is to be used (Illeris et al. 2004). And in the meantime the fundamental problem, in theory as well as in practice, has remained unsolved and its range has increased immensely in step with the general need for learning and the growth and importance of institutionalised learning in schools and education. For society this indicates a waste of resources. For learners it is also about reduced motivation and confidence in school learning.

In order to get to a contemporary understanding of how this problem can be handled in societies where most people more or less regularly participate in learning courses or recurrent education, I shall refer to three different fields of learning theory (for a coherent presentation of this topic, see Illeris 2007): the field of various learning spaces, the field of different types of learning, and the field of different kinds of knowledge application. Finally, I shall return to the topic of transfer and draw the outlines of a more general understanding and its consequences for human development and education.

Although my considerations refer to the transfer issue in general, my practical experience is mainly on how learning and training in schools and other educational institutions can be brought to cooperate with workplace learning. This well-known problem in connection with youth and adult vocational training has been addressed in three major empirical and analytical research projects that I have directed over a period of 15 years.

Background

In what was entitled the General Qualification Project, 1992–1997, six researchers worked together with many teachers and trainers in the Danish state adult vocational training system on a very broad and open development project. The main idea of the project was to find ways in which the practical upgrading of unskilled and low-skilled workers could be combined with strengthening relevant general knowledge and so-called generic skills such as flexibility, independence, responsibility, creativity, cooperation, etc. By re-educating trainers and organising a major part of the training courses in projects that were planned and evaluated in the training centres and carried out in relation to specific tasks at work, we gradually contributed to a new orientation of this nationwide training system. At the same time we developed a new theoretical framework of practical and general qualification (Andersen *et al.* 1994, 1996). Today, it is unfortunately necessary to add that since the training centres were redefined politically as economically independent units, participation has declined considerably and the new educational trends have almost disappeared.

In 1998–2000 in the Adult Education Research Project two senior researchers and three research assistants observed and interviewed participants from across the three main adult education and training systems in Denmark (the adult vocational training system, the adult general education system and the day high schools). The general aim of this project was to investigate the learning processes and the subjective experience of participants in the education, training and retraining of low-skilled adults, and the main output was a deeper and better structured understanding of the learning ambivalences and barriers of these adult learners (Illeris 2003, 2005, 2006a).

Finally, in 2001–2004 I headed a research consortium that functioned as an umbrella for 16 very different workplace learning development projects. The most important general output of all this was, on the one hand, an overview of the vast and very differentiated possibilities of workplace learning, including cooperation with programmes in schools, and on the other hand, important contributions to workplace learning and general adult learning theory (Illeris *et al.* 2004, Illeris 2004, 2006b).

During and after these three projects, I have worked with a more general understanding of learning theory, and it is in this connection that a new perspective on the issue of learning transfer has emerged (Illeris 2007).

The concept of learning spaces

Today in the official language the external conditions in connection with different environments of learning are usually referred to by the concepts of formal, informal and non-formal learning. The lack of expediency and exactness of these terms has, however, often been emphasised by researchers, most thoroughly and basically by Colley *et al.* (2003). In addition, these terms are very abstract, and in my opinion a set of much more descriptive concepts would be preferable.

In my book, *The Three Dimensions of Learning* (Illeris 2002: 175ff.), I introduced the concept of different 'learning spaces', and I elaborated it further in various later publications (Illeris 2004: 145ff., Illeris 2007, Illeris *et al.* 2004: 29ff.). The central idea behind the concept is that since all learning is situated (Lave and Wenger 1991), and the specific learning situation becomes an integrated part of the learning process and outcome, different types of learning situations or learning spaces imply different categories of learning with significantly different qualities. In today's society five main types of general learning spaces can be identified:

- *Everyday learning* takes place in daily life as we move around and do not participate in any specifically defined activities. This kind of learning is therefore mainly informal, multifarious, personal and related to the cultures and subcultures in which the person is integrated.
- *School and educational learning* is the intended learning that takes place inside the educational system (whereas unintended learning in this setting will have the character of everyday learning, often with some relation to the educational activities). This kind of learning is formal, rational and externally directed. Although it is officially aimed at goals outside the system, precisely because it takes place inside the system, it is usually experienced as directed by internal goals and standards such as the school subjects, exams or just pleasing the teacher in order to obtain a favourable personal situation with a minimum of discomfort and problems. Today quite a lot of evidence for this has been collected, e.g., in Scandinavia under the heading of 'the hidden curriculum' (Jackson 1990, Illeris 2002, 2007).
- *Workplace learning* (or learning in working life) is mainly the incidental learning which inevitably takes place as part of work (Marsick and Watkins 1990), but also includes more formalised learning related to work and taking place inside or outside the workplace. This learning is usually experienced as an integrated part of people's working life and is therefore usually immediately accepted as relevant and meaningful (if the person in question has any positive identification with the job or task). However, in a wider perspective workplace learning is often limited by the immediate needs of the production or service and influenced by power relations and financial interests, and it therefore tends to lack theoretical understanding and overview (Illeris *et al.* 2004).
- *Interest-based learning* takes place, e.g., in community activities, associations, grassroot activities and the like, or is simply related to a personal interest, conviction or hobby. It may be seen as a consciously goal-directed type of everyday learning in which incidental and informal features are replaced by a clear motivation and resolution, which generally makes this type of learning space very effective.

- *Net-based learning* has, finally, opened a new learning space of rapidly growing importance and with its own characteristics, advantages and disadvantages. In relation to school and workplace learning, it is very flexible because it can be practised independently of time and, to some extent, also of place. It also seems to be an advantage that it forces the learner to express him or herself in writing and thereby to make points, understandings and opinions clearer than generally needed in face-to-face conversation. The disadvantage is the lack of direct social contact, but frequent classes or meetings can to some extent eliminate this during a net-based course of some duration. Yet, so far we know very little about possible transfer problems in connection with this kind of learning.

As most people today are involved in all or most of these main types of learning spaces, the transitions between them become increasingly essential and complex, and it is my experience that important transfer problems usually occur in connection with transitions between these five main learning spaces.

However, the five learning spaces have a very different nature and history and this also influences transitions and transfer possibilities. Before the breakthrough of early industrialisation and capitalism, for the great majority there was only the learning space of everyday life in which working life, general socialisation and religious commitment were integrated. But for more and more people the introduction of wage labour created a sharp boundary between working life and private life. At the same time institutional and society-directed upbringing and learning in schools had to be introduced, partly to assure a minimal level of general skills for everybody, and partly to prepare for the acceptance of the position as a wage worker, subordinated to the whims of the employer.

In this way three life spaces with fundamentally different conditions were established, the ground was laid for the transfer problem, and it is still these three spaces that are fundamental. Only gradually has the growing complexity of society to a certain extent also separated the interest-based learning space from everyday learning, but the strength of this separation, and thereby also of transfer problems in this connection, is still a question of the subjective experience of the learner. And the new space of net-based learning is in many cases subjectively so closely connected to one of the other learning spaces that no transition is experienced and, consequently, no transfer problems occur. Perhaps it is only for people who have grown up before the computer age that net-based learning is experienced as something separated, and for later generations the use of computers may be so well integrated in all aspects of their lives that no separation and no boundaries are experienced.

Nevertheless, it is important to observe the general point that it is the subjectively experienced and often unconscious boundaries that constitute the transfer problems since learning as acquisition is always a personal matter. So to come closer to an understanding of how the transfer problems work it is necessary to look at the nature of this acquisition process—i.e., at the subjective side of learning (cf. Illeris 2007).

Four different types of learning

The first thing to observe in this connection is that transfer problems do not turn up every time one needs to or tries to use the results of learning processes across the boundaries of the learning spaces. It is therefore a crucial issue to find out when and under which conditions these problems occur. As I see it, the key to dealing with this question is to realise that there exist some fundamentally different types of human learning that occur in different kinds of situations, have a basically different nature, and also lead to learning results of a fundamentally different character and range.

In learning psychology several and very different learning typologies have been proposed ever since the classical behaviouristic differentiating between simple and operant conditioning. However, after having worked with this issue for decades, in my book *How We Learn* (Illeris 2007), on the basis of Jean Piaget's understanding of learning and some later elaborations, I have set up a typology of four basic learning types, which has appeared to be of basic significance and among other things has also paved the way for a new understanding of the transfer problem.

The point of departure for this typology is the understanding established by Piaget that to learn something actually means for the learner to include and organise it in his or her mental structures, which exist in the brain as dispositions that can be described by the metaphor of *mental schemes* (see Piaget 1952 [1936], Flavell 1963). This structuring can be established in various ways, and on this basis it is possible to distinguish between the following four different types of learning:

- When a new scheme is established, it is a case of *cumulative* or mechanical learning. This form of learning is characterised by being an isolated formation, something new that is not a part of anything else. Therefore, cumulative learning is most frequent during the first years of life and later occurs only in special situations where one has to learn something with no context of meaning or personal importance, for example a pin code number. Conditioning is also a case of cumulative learning. The learning result is characterised by a type of automation that means that it can only be recalled and applied in situations mentally similar to the learning context.
- By far the most common form of learning is termed *assimilative* or learning by addition, meaning that the new element is linked as an addition to a scheme that is already established. One typical example could be learning in school subjects that are precisely built up by means of constant additions to what has already been learned, but assimilative learning also takes place in all contexts where one gradually develops one's capacities. The results of this type of learning are characterised by being linked to the scheme in question in such a manner that it is relatively easy to recall and apply them when one is mentally oriented towards the field in question, for example a school subject, while they may be hard to access in other contexts. This is the main reason for the classical problems of learning transfer between school and other learning spaces, and sometimes also between different school subjects.
- However, in some cases, situations occur where something takes place that is difficult immediately to relate to any existing scheme; this is experienced as something one cannot really understand or relate to. But if it seems important or interesting, if it is something one is determined to acquire, this can take place by means of *accommodative* or transcendent learning, which implies that one breaks down (parts of) an existing scheme and reconstructs it in a way that allow the new situation to be linked in. Thus one both relinquishes and constructs something and this can be experienced as painful and something that requires a special effort. One must cross existing limitations and understand or accept something that is significantly new or different. The result of the learning is characterised by the fact that it can be recalled and applied in

many different, relevant contexts. It is typically experienced as having got hold of something which one really has internalised.
- Finally, over the last decades it has been pointed out that in special situations there is also a far-reaching type of learning that has, inter alia, been described as expansive (Engeström 1987) or *transformative* learning (Mezirow 1991). This learning implies what could be termed personality changes or changes in the organisation of the self. The outcome is therefore not something to be remembered and recalled, but something that has become part of the person. It is characterised by simultaneous restructuring of several schemes, including emotional and social patterns—a break of orientation that typically occurs as the result of a crisis-like situation caused by challenges experienced as urgent and unavoidable. Transformative learning is thus both profound and extensive and can often be experienced physically, typically as a feeling of relief or relaxation.

As has been demonstrated, the four types of learning are widely different in scope and nature, and they also occur—or are activated by learners—in very different situations and connections. Whereas cumulative learning is most important in early childhood, and transformative learning is a very demanding process that changes the very personality or identity and occurs only in special situations of deep-going significance for the learner, assimilation and accommodation are, as described by Piaget, the two types of learning that would characterise general, sound and normal everyday learning.

The parallel types of knowledge use

In relation to the issue of transfer, it is obvious that there are significant differences in the transfer potential of the four learning types. But before I go further with this, I shall briefly refer to a parallel typology of different kinds of knowledge use, originally set up by American educational philosopher Harry S. Broudy (Broudy *et al.* 1964) and later elaborated further by British educational researcher Michael Eraut (1994), who has also worked with the transfer issue and the application dimension of learning.

Eraut uses the concept of knowledge in a very broad or open sense, coming close to a general conception of capacity or competence, and at the same time he emphasises that one can acquire and possess knowledge in different ways with different qualities. As to the application of knowledge, both Broudy and Eraut point to four different modes of how knowledge is used, each referring back to the qualities of the knowledge in question and how it has been acquired:

- *Replication* of knowledge is about repetition and according to Eraut 'the replicative mode of knowledge use dominates a large proportion of schooling and a significant part of higher education' (Eraut 1994: 48). It is characterised by close similarity between the context in which it is acquired and that in which it can be used, and there is no reorganisation in between.
- *Application* of knowledge is about using acquired knowledge under new circumstances, but still follows the rules and procedures related to this knowledge when acquired, i.e., it respects the given ideas of what is considered right or wrong.
- *Interpretation* of knowledge is more demanding as it implies 'understanding', which involves personal perspectives or 'ways of seeing' and thus requires a

professional insight and an intellectual effort—for example 'the meaning of a new idea has to be rediscovered in the practical situation, and the implication for action thought through' (49).
- *Association* of knowledge, finally, involves 'a sense of purpose, appropriateness and feasibility; and its acquisition depends, among other things, on a wealth of professional experience', which in practice takes on the character of an 'intuitive capacity' (49). In other words, for knowledge to be associative in this sense it must be an integrated part of the personality or the self.

The parallelism of these modes of knowledge use and the four learning types described above is striking, and the fact that the two typologies have reached such similar conclusions in different ways and from different theoretical angles indicates that they have come close to some central understanding of a field which has challenged both practitioners and theoreticians of education for a long time.

Learning, knowledge and transfer levels

In relation to the issue of transfer it is remarkable that this parallelism makes it possible to set up a succession of four levels of learning and knowledge use which at the same time imply four different levels of transfer possibilities:

- Through cumulative learning, delimited, repetition-oriented knowledge is developed that can be used in situations that are subjectively the same as the learning situation in a decisive way.
- Through assimilative learning, knowledge oriented towards application to a certain subject (or scheme) is developed, which can be used in situations that bring the subject in question to the fore (cf. the theory of identical elements).
- Through accommodative learning, understanding- or interpretation-oriented knowledge is developed, which can be flexibly applied within a broad range of relevant contexts (cf. the theory of general principles).
- Through transformative learning, personality-integrated knowledge is developed on the basis of which associations can be freely made in all subjectively relevant contexts.

Although these four levels of transfer in practice are not so sharply separated as this schematic outline may indicate, they indicate a differentiated understanding of the concept of transfer with important implications for the connections between the acquisition and use of knowledge in the broadest sense, including skills, understandings, attitudes, values, ways of thinking and doing, ways of communication, ways of acquiring new knowledge, etc. The transferability of different kinds of learning processes and learning outcomes appears as directly dependent on the type of learning and the resulting type of knowledge.

However, in stating this it is very important to realise that even though the learning and knowledge types are ranked in a clear succession referring to the complexity and range of the different levels, one cannot and should not draw any conclusions implying that one type is 'better' than another. On the contrary, all of the four levels are necessary to build up the capacities and competences of an individual; everything starts with cumulation (in some areas already before birth), and the levels build on and presuppose each other in complicated individual patterns. None of us would have reached our present level of mental capacity without having practised all four learning and knowledge types—an ability which is a specific human privilege far from being equated by any other species. The challenge, to the individual as well as to the education systems, is to find ways to practise a balanced interaction between the four levels. The more complex levels are also the most demanding; nobody can manage to undertake accommodative and transformative learning all the time. These types of learning presuppose that cumulative and assimilative processes have established a basis of fundamental knowledge, something to be further developed and transformed, and we also need stability and time for cementing new capacities.

In daily learning, in schools as well as in everyday life and working life, it is especially the balance and variation between assimilation and accommodation that is challenging. Cumulation belongs, as stated earlier, mainly to the first years of life. Transformation is a very demanding type of learning to which we resort only when we cannot find any other way out of a crisis or a dilemma. And even a balanced combination of assimilation and accommodation seems to be a very demanding task, since it is obviously easier and less demanding just to stick to assimilation, i.e., to stand by our habitual understandings and ways of thinking and doing.

Theory and practice

Thus, returning to the original central issue of the transfer problem about how school and educational learning can be made more applicable outside the learning institutions, the key conclusion to all the considerations above seems to point towards the balance between assimilative and accommodative learning. This is, of course, just a new way of formulating the often repeated view that teaching in school and other educational institutions is too much oriented towards reproduction of subject-matter and the like. However, formulating the problem in a way that directly refers to learning theoretical understandings may lead to a clarification of and thereby also to a basic key for how to deal with the issue in practice.

Why, then, has this not been done before?, one might ask. The answer is, as I see it, that available learning theories have not been suitable for this purpose as they have generally been too narrow in their scope. Up to the 1980s learning theory was, at least in the English speaking countries, dominated by the behaviourist approach, which mainly dealt with cumulative and very simple assimilative learning processes and therefore, as appears from the considerations above, is unable to catch the core of the transfer issue. In contrast to this, in the approach of the American humanistic psychology of the 1950s, the main contribution to learning theory was Carl Rogers' concept of 'significant learning', which explicitly limited itself to the learning that involves 'a change in the organisation of the self' (Rogers 1951: 390), i.e., transformative learning, which is not very relevant in relation to transfer either, because it, so to speak, goes to the opposite extreme of the learning spectrum.

Actually, the German Gestalt psychology of the inter-war period came quite a bit closer to what is relevant in relation to transfer by concentrating on learning by problem solving (see Duncker 1945 [1935]), which is closely related to accommodative learning. But it did not really examine the nature of the difference between what has here been described as accommodative and assimilative learning, and this is probably why it did not consider the transfer issue either. Nor did the Russian Activity Theoretical approach of Lev Vygotsky *et al.* include this topic, although their concept of 'the zone of proximal development' (Vygotsky 1978, 1986 [1934]) could have been a relevant entry point for taking up this issue.

Finally, the constructivist approach of Jean Piaget and the 'Geneva School' was also launched in the inter-war period. It was here the learning concepts of assimilation and accommodation were formulated, but Piaget concentrated on the actual development of human intellectual abilities and the stages of this development, and this is probably why the transfer issue did not come into his scope. However, it is by taking this approach further, including the incentive and social dimensions of learning, and not least by also taking up the pertinent issue of practice learning and non-learning, that I have returned to the transfer problem from a much broader perspective and thus been able to see the close connection between the learning types and the transfer possibilities (Illeris 2007).

Obviously, it is in relation to everyday and workplace practice that the transfer issue is most urgent, and it is when different kinds of barriers to learning are considered in this connection that the question of barriers to transfer processes also becomes visible. So I shall finish my theoretical considerations by giving as an illustrative example a short account of how they have actually grown out of the practical developmental work in relation to vocational training and the education of youth and adults, in which I have been involved together with colleagues and teachers for more than 30 years (see Andersen *et al.* 1994, 1996; Illeris *et al.* 2004).

Project work

Our developmental work has been concentrated on two educational approaches that can be practised independently or in combination: project work and school–workplace interaction.

Project work is an educational design that can be traced back to the American educator William Kilpatrick, who in his efforts to transform John Dewey's educational thought into practical directions almost a century ago, developed the so-called 'project method' (Kilpatrick 1918; Dewey 1934). However, this was a method for individual studies, whereas the educational practice of project work developed in the Scandinavian countries since the 1970s is mainly a procedure for group work (see Illeris 1991, 1999, 2004; Nielsen and Webb 1999).

This Scandinavian version rests on the three fundamental principles of *participant direction, problem orientation* and *exemplarity* (the latter implying that the problem chosen must be a valid example of a more general and relevant scholarly, professional or societal issue). The typical procedure is that a group of students, supported by a counselling teacher, select a relevant problem, work out a detailed problem formulation and work plan, investigate and elaborate the problem, draw up a detailed report, suggest possible solutions if they can, or indicate what can be done, the whole procedure ending up in a presentation which, together with the report, may form the basis for a grade or approval.

In Denmark this approach has by now been introduced in a broad range of vocational and academic education programmes and, with some modifications, also in the upper and lower secondary school. In relation to the transfer issue it is central that such project work should increase the probability of a close combination of assimilative acquisition of relevant and useful knowledge and accommodative action, reflection and understanding, which—as already stated—are precisely the most important conditions for transfer of learning. This is also the reason why both the labour market organisations and private as well as public employers in general have been in favour of the approach.

In connection with our developmental work we have been educating various categories of teachers in applying the method and functioning as project counsellors.

School–workplace interaction

However, although project work in the form outlined above is a radical alternative to traditional institutional teaching and often includes quite extensive activities outside school, it does not usually bridge the gap between learning inside and outside schools. Thus there will still be a transition, and although transfer problems can be considerably reduced this way, they cannot be eliminated without direct interaction between two learning spaces.

We have therefore also made efforts to improve the direct interaction between school learning and workplace learning in connection with vocational training and education of youth and adults, and thus we have also been confronted with both the advantages and the problems of the issue of apprenticeship—which during the latest 15–20 years has come into the focus of learning and educational theory, especially through the work of American Jean Lave and Etienne Wenger (1991).

The advantage of the apprenticeship model is obviously that practical learning and socialisation at workplaces are directly combined with more theoretical learning and development of generic skills at school. However, countless reports, especially from the youth vocational training system and from adult education in areas where school courses alternate with trainee periods, have shown that in all such alternating courses there is an omnipresent learning problem which learners usually express as experiencing no or insufficient connection between school learning and learning in practice. This complaint has constantly recurred, at least since the 1960s, and in spite of all efforts to eliminate it, it seems that it has rather been growing than declining.

To deal with this problem we have tried to strengthen the connections between schoolteachers and workplace supervisors by mutual visits, common meetings, joint planning activities etc. But it has actually been very difficult to establish any kind of truly integrated courses, because school teachers are inclined to think and act in terms of curriculum and syllabus, whereas workplace supervisors think and act in terms of work processes and production. Even though they are dealing with the same trade or services, the two groups have great problems in really accepting and understanding each others' approaches.

Thus, in order to overcome this obstacle we have tried to combine the school–workplace interaction with the project work issue by introducing student projects in which problems are formulated at school to be dealt with at work, so that practical experience can be reported and elaborated in the following school period. In this way it is actually possible to force through some kind of integrated and experienced understanding by the students—but it has certainly not been without a lot of practical problems and obstacles. The following points can serve as an illustration of a typical project of this kind:

- A project, or a series of connected projects, is spread over two to four shorter school periods with work periods in between.
- The time in school periods is shared between ordinary teaching time and project time, the proportion of the two depending on specific considerations.
- The first school period starts with an introduction and discussion about learner activity, influence, responsibility and project work.
- On one of the first days, project groups are formed and problems, tasks and assignment of the projects are chosen and formulated by the groups.
- The rest of the project time at school is spent on planning, preparing and

developing knowledge of relevance to the project. The teacher serves as a counsellor or supervisor.
- The practical part of the project takes place in accordance with the workplace during the following work period. This may consist of individual or group tasks.
- During the next school period, the first part of the project time is spent on reporting and evaluating the projects. The second half is used to prepare a new project or the next step of a longer project.
- If the course includes an exam, it can take the form of a presentation of the project, if possible as a group discussion with individual grading (in practice all group members are given the same grade if there is no obvious reason for differentiation).

Conclusions

On the theoretical level, it is the main conclusion of this re-examination of the issue of transfer of learning that the possibilities of transfer between different learning spaces depend on the type of learning that has taken place and thereby also on the qualities of the learning outcome. Four different types of learning with corresponding qualities of outcome have been presented as a general overview of the field.

In practice it is, therefore, important to develop learning activities that encourage different types of learning, and in particular the importance of a balanced promotion of assimilative (additive) and accommodative (transcending) processes has been emphasised. Project work has been accentuated as a design of school activities that is, in general, well suited to establishing this balance.

In relation to the transfer of learning between school and working life, it has been stressed that close school–workplace integration is important, and integrated school–workplace projects have been recommended as the most appropriate way of establishing this interaction.

References

ANDERSEN, V., ILLERIS, K., KJÆRSGAARD, C., LARSEN, K., OLESEN, H. S. and ULRIKSEN, L. (1994) *Qualifications and Living People* (Roskilde: Roskilde University, The Adult Education Research Group).
ANDERSEN, V., ILLERIS, K., KJÆRSGAARD, C., LARSEN, K., OLESEN, H. S. and ULRIKSEN, L. (1996) *General Qualification* (Roskilde: Roskilde University, The Adult Education Research Group).
BROUDY, H. S., SMITH, B. O. and BURNETT, J. (1964) *Democracy and Excellence in American Secondary Education* (Chicago: Rand McNally).
COLLEY, H., HODKINSON, P. and MALCOLM, J. (2003) *Informality and Formality in Learning* (London: Learning and Skills Research Centre).
DEWEY, J. (1934) The way out of educational confusion. In R. D. ARCHAMBAULT (Ed.), *John Dewey on Education: Selected writing* (Chicago: University of Chicago Press).
DUNCKER, K. (1945 [1935]) *On Problem-Solving*. The American Psychological Association, Psychological Monographs, 5.
ENGESTRÖM, Y. (1987) *Learning by Expanding: An activity-theoretical approach to developmental research* (Helsinki: Orienta-Kunsultit).
ERAUT, M. (1994) *Developing Professional Learning and Competence* (London: Falmer).
FLAVELL, J. H. (1963) *The Developmental Psychology of Jean Piaget* (New York: Van Nostrand).
ILLERIS, K. (1991) Project education in Denmark. *International Journal of Project Management*, 1, 45–48.
ILLERIS, K. (1999) Project work in university studies: background and current issues. In

H. S. OLESEN and J. H. JENSEN (Eds.), *Project Studies* (Copenhagen: Roskilde University Press).
ILLERIS, K. (2002) *The Three Dimensions of Learning* (Leicester: NIACE).
ILLERIS, K. (2003) Adult education as experienced by the learners. *International Journal of Lifelong Education*, 22(1), 13–23.
ILLERIS, K. (2004) *Adult Education and Adult Learning* (Copenhagen: Roskilde University Press).
ILLERIS, K. (2005) Low-skilled learners learn at the workplace. *Lifelong Learning in Europe*, 10(3), 172–177.
ILLERIS, K. (2006a) Lifelong learning and the low-skilled. *International Journal of Lifelong Education*, 25(1), 15–28.
ILLERIS, K. (2006b) What is special about adult learning? In P. SUTHERLAND and J. CROWTHER (Eds.), *Lifelong Learning: Concepts and contexts* (London: Routledge).
ILLERIS, K. (2007) *How We Learn: An introduction to human learning in schools and beyond* (London: Routledge).
ILLERIS, K. & Associates (2004) *Learning in Working Life* (Copenhagen: Roskilde University Press).
JACKSON, P. W. (1990 [1968]) *Life in Classrooms* (New York: Teachers College, Columbia University).
JUDD, C. H. (1908) The relation of special training to general intelligence. *Educational Review*, 36, 28–42.
KILPATRICK, W. H. (1918) The project method: The use of purposeful act in the educative process. *Teachers College Record*, 19, 319–335.
LAVE, J. and WENGER, E. (1991) *Situated Learning* (Cambridge, MA: Cambridge University Press).
MARSICK, V. J. and WATKINS, K. E. (1990) *Informal and Incidental Learning in the Workplace* (London: Routledge).
MEZIROW, J. (1991) *Transformative Dimensions of Adult Learning* (San Francisco: Jossey-Bass).
NIELSEN, J. L. and WEBB, T. W. (1999) Project work at the new reform University of Roskilde: different interpretations. In H. S. OLESEN and J. H. JENSEN (Eds.), *Project Studies* (Copenhagen: Roskilde University Press).
PIAGET, J. (1952 [1936]) *The Origin of Intelligence in Children* (New York: International Universities Press).
ROGERS, C. R. (1951) *Client-Centered Therapy* (Boston: Houghton-Mifflin).
THORNDIKE, E. L. and WOODWORTH, R. S. (1901) The influence on improvement in one mental function upon the efficiency of other functions. *The Psychological Review*, 3, 247–261.
VYGOTSKY, L. S. (1978) *Mind in Society: The development of higher psychological processes* (Cambridge, MA: Harvard University Press).
VYGOTSKY, L. S. (1986 [1934]) *Thought and Language* (Cambridge, MA: MIT Press).

CHAPTER 10

ADULT LEARNING AND RESPONSIBILITY

A challenge from the everyday life of adult education

Recently I was invited by a technical school with which my university department has been cooperating off and on for the last 20 years to tell the staff something about teaching adults vis-à-vis teaching children or adolescents. The reason was that in the course of a very few years the proportion of adults had risen from almost none to more than half the student population of the school.

I have usually answered this question by referring to the differences in life situation between children, adolescents, and adults. I have stressed that while, in relation to school and education, children and adolescents are naturally preoccupied with their personal learning, development, understanding and conquest of the world around them, adults generally experience their educational activities in a broader context, first and foremost their working life and family situation, but also cultural, political and other societal preferences and issues.

As the educational consequences of this, I have pointed out that as a general rule adult education should relate very much to the experiential background, actual situation and future perspectives of the students. In addition, decisions about content and process should as far as possible be made by students and teachers in community. I regard this position as being quite parallel to that of Malcolm Knowles (1973, 1980), although the concept of andragogy has never had any influence in Denmark, and I agree with the criticism that has been levelled at it (e.g. Jarvis 1984, Tennant 1986, Davenport 1993). My own position is in general closer to that of the critical pedagogy (Wildemeersch 1992, Usher et al 1997, p. 98f), inspired mainly by the type of heritage of the Frankfurter school carried by scholars such as Oskar Negt (1971, 1989), Peter Brückner (1972), Thomas Leithäuser (1976, 1977), and Thomas Ziehe (Ziehe & Stubenrauch 1982).

However, I had a feeling that the teachers in question were already familiar with my position. Actually, I think that I know quite well, both from my connections with the school in question and from ten years' intensive work inside the Danish labour market education system (Illeris 1992, Illeris & Andersen 1994, Andersen et al 1996), what it is all about in practice.

The core of the problem is that, at least in vocational adult education courses, even when the teachers do their best to be in accordance with all the principles of adult experiential learning theory (e.g. Kolb 1984, Henry 1989, Boud 1989) it only works in situations where the teaching deals with very practical or technical issues and the efforts of the teacher may be characterised as instruction.

As soon as it comes to anything like teaching it seems that some other mechanisms are activated. In the teaching setting both students and teachers inevitably seem to regress to the classic roles of pupils and schoolteachers so familiar to everybody from their own school years. And the central features of this regression seem to be the lack of responsibility of the students and the direction and over-responsibility of the teacher (cf. Knowles 1980, p. 56).

Even when the students are skilled workers who exercise a high degree of independence and responsibility in their daily work, who are politically schooled in the labour movement, and who would never dream of abandoning their right to self-determination under other circumstances, entering a classroom in an educational institution seems to make them feel like school-children right to the core of their consciousness. They immediately lose all independence and dignity, they leave all initiatives and responsibility to the teacher, and they often start to behave like naughty boys and girls trying to challenge the teacher's authority. And for that matter, the same sort of transformation may also very often be observed even when the 'pupils' are highly educated academics like engineers, doctors, or lawyers.

Moreover, in spite of their pedagogical training and their explicit will to break with this locked division of roles, the teachers very often appear to be trapped in the same sort of regressive pattern, but in the opposite direction. Either they feel obliged to create a proper teaching-learning situation, or they are simply unable to resist the pressure on the part of the 'pupils' to undertake the much too familiar role of the traditional schoolteacher.

In my opinion the key to dissolving this seemingly inevitable setting which is unfortunate, unworthy and inappropriate in relation to adult education, is to be found in the concept of *responsibility* combined with deliberate, goal-oriented efforts to find out who should be responsible for what, and how to practice this division of responsibility consistently. Knowles (1975, 1980) also pays some attention to the important role of responsibility in adult learning and education, although he does not assign to it the same crucial position as I do here – whereas more topical writers such as Usher et al (1997) and Tennant (1997) with whom I generally feel more in line do not stress this feature).

Responsibility as a qualification or personal quality

So the invitation to talk about adult learning and education turned my attention towards the concept of responsibility. And, thinking it over, I realized that responsibility in this connection not only is a key concept in relation to the practical accomplishment of adult education, but also is one of the most predominant key words in current qualification theory and educational thinking.

The main issue in qualification theory throughout the last decade has been the necessity to develop 'general qualifications', 'core qualifications' or 'key competences' that, in opposition to traditional professional qualifications, mean personal qualities. And one of the qualities which is always mentioned in this connection is precisely the qualification of responsibility (e.g. Andersen et al 1996, p. 11).

Responsibility seems today to be one of the most sought after and therefore also one of the most attractive qualities of the labour force at all levels from unskilled workers to bosses, because everybody's responsibility is necessary in up-to-date production and business that rely heavily on quality, service and just-in-time delivery.

But responsibility is also an important qualification for social life in general. Modern society is so complex and things change so rapidly that everybody's responsibility is needed to make everyday life function in families, supermarkets, traffic and everywhere else where people meet and have to find their direction without too much trouble and waste of time.

In the Danish school system the Ministry of Education has run a minor campaign to support the development of the pupils' 'competence to choose'. The immediate background is the great number of choices a pupil has to make on his or her way through the educational system – choices of educational lines, courses, subjects, projects, topics, groups, books etc. Naturally, this competence should also enable them to do better in all the other situations of modern life where a choice must be made, ranging from essential issues like work, partner, or a place to live to all the everyday choices concerning consumption, TV channels and the like.

In some current writing on the role of education today, however, the concept of responsibility has quite another connotation. Here one can see responsibility presented as the necessary counterbalance to the economically oriented rationale of efficiency which is becoming ever more dominant in education as well as in most other societal sectors.

For example, in 1991 Danny Wildemeersch argued that the concept and thrust of experiential learning would be missing its goal if it is not *"primarily concerned with social commitment or with 'learning from responsibility', on a personal, institutional, and structural level"* (Wildemeersch 1991, p. 158). In 1992 he spoke about *"radical responsibility"* and concluded that pedagogy *"is currently learning to come to terms with ambiguity, difference and uncertainty, while loosing the naivety that it will produce the 'ultimate' correct answers. In doing so it radicalises the necessity to take a personal responsible stance. Taking both the learner and the dialogue seriously means that we can no longer hide behind abstract principles and projects, but that we are confronted with the concrete task to do justice to the Other, who challenges our responsibilities with regard to the present and the future generations"* (Wildemeersch 1992, p. 31–32). And in 1997 Wildemeersch generalizes: *"In processes of social learning issues of social responsibility are always interwoven with problem solving and learning activities"* (Wildemeersch 1997, p. 11).

The progress of these quotations shows how responsibility at an existential level has increasingly moved into focus in educational thinking at the same time as the disintegration and instrumentalisation of postmodernism has spread in society and its way of organising educational processes.

But, indirectly, Wildemeersch's formulations also include another point viewed in relation to the formulations of the qualification-demand of responsibility: as a general qualification, responsibility is not defined in relation to what or who you should be responsible towards. It seems to be implied either that responsibility could be a general personal quality without any direction, or that, as a matter of course, it must be responsibility towards the employer and the goals of the company. However, with Wildemeersch's formulations it becomes clear that the sort of responsibility which should be developed educationally both for ethical and societal reasons must be personal responsibility which includes the will and ability to also take responsibility for the direction of your responsibility.

Responsibility, direction and influence

But when responsibility is so obviously important whether seen from the perspective of qualification or in a more comprehensive societal view, why then do adults behave so irresponsibly in educational situations, even when teachers honestly offer them a lot of influence and, consequently, also responsibility for the process?

As already suggested, the most immediate answer to this question relates back to school experience. In primary school it is of necessity the teachers who, as the representatives of society, exercise day-to-day responsibility for the educational process. At least in Denmark, they are rather free to share this responsibility with their pupils, to delegate parts of it in various situations, but as school is compulsory this responsibility fundamentally rests with the societal system which by law makes its children go to school. And, as agents of the system, the teachers' role in this connection is to implement and abide by this compulsion. So they have the right and the obligation to determine when and to what extent they will delegate some of the power they are charged with exercising on behalf of the system.

Today, even though this power is exercised in ways that make the element of compulsion recede into the background as much as possible, nobody is in doubt about the fundamental positions which teachers, parents and children know instinctively. When it comes down to it, there is no doubt that all power is with the teachers. Therefore the great majority of children adjust and try to make the best of the situation, and the minority that seriously resist obtain nothing but a lot of trouble and personal failure.

Today most pupils continue to upper secondary school or vocational schools which, in principle, are voluntary. But only in principle as students have to choose one of these lines if they want to have what our culture generally accepts as a good life. As a matter of fact the schools at this level are usually experienced by the pupils as more coercive than primary school even though this compulsion is more indirect and informal. This is because students would appear to have chosen it themselves although the invisible structural compulsion is solid and practically unavoidable and its rationale is often impenetrable: why do I have to study maths when I hate it, don't understand a bit of it, and will never use it as I want to do something that has to do with human beings and not with sterile figures and abstract concepts. . .?

These conditions are fundamentally different in adult education. Compulsion is only ever directly involved as an exception (e.g. as a requirement from an employer); where there exists some sort of structural or indirect compulsion such as obtaining a specific grade or a certificate to get a job or a position, adults have the possibility to weigh the pros and cons themselves and to make a (responsible) choice in quite another way than at secondary school level. Most adult education is based on interest, and when the acquisition of some formal competence is required adults are usually in a position to make a regular and conscious choice to take a course in order to attain a personal goal or to decline if the conditions are not acceptable.

But in spite of all these conditions and considerations irresponsibility is the usual reaction in practice, as described above and experienced by the teachers. Furthermore, in addition to the regressive tendencies, there are also obvious reasons for this as what can responsibly be chosen is the course but not the way it is designed and conducted.

In general, it is the case in adult education that while the student has the responsibility for choosing a certain educational programme or course, the school or institution has the responsibility for its design; that is, so to speak, the tacit contract. And when the teacher as the agent of the institution offers the students a share in and responsibility for the construction or the didactics of the course, they are naturally inclined to react with suspicion. They have been offered this before and have seen that the premises were false. Moreover, the experience of this falseness seems to be very deeply embedded. It is difficult for them to believe that anything else could be the case.

But in adult education the situation can, in fact, be different — at least in most cases and to a certain degree. Even though the distribution of power is almost always uneven, and even though at the symbolic level the power of the system can be experienced as overwhelming, at the same time adult education is an exchange situation between two independent parties. If the student does not feel directly or indirectly forced to take the course in question, it is possible to set a limit for what can be accepted. At present this possibility is widening at the same pace as adult education is being made a commodity to be sold in the market-place of educational supply, even if it is a public authority or institution which is the supplier.

But the buyer, the student, has no experience of setting a price. On the contrary, the dominating experience is that one must accept what is being offered and it is no use protesting. At the same time, today the seller, the provider of the course, is usually aware that the commodity is better – and thus also more competitive in the long term – if the students are active and take responsibility. This results in the paradoxical situation that the seller has an interest in taking care of what on the face of it should be the buyer's interest, while the buyer spontaneously rejects it and goes for a less valuable commodity.

Responsibility in adult education

However, education is not only a commodity. Society has also a fundamental interest in its members being educated as much and as well as possible. At present this is indeed a widely supported political issue even if there is not much agreement about how to tackle it.

It is also widely accepted that a necessary qualification demand is the responsibility of everyone. The majority also agree on responsibility as a cultural and democratic aim and, ultimately, as a condition for the survival of mankind in line with Wildemeersch, whom I have quoted above.

Furthermore, at least the more educationally oriented representatives of society are about to realise that the development of responsibility of necessity implies that students must have and exercise substantial influence on their own studies. There is actually much talk about "responsibility for one's own learning" and the like.

This makes the distribution and practice of responsibility a *pedagogical* key issue of central importance in relation to the way in which educational activities function and the kind of learning that takes place. These matters naturally affect all forms and levels of education from primary school to adult education and regardless of subjects and aims. But as there are fundamental differences between the education of children, adolescents and adults in the distribution of responsibility, there are also fundamental differences at the pedagogical level.

In child and youth schooling and education it is obvious that activities should contribute to the gradual development of the pupils' sense of responsibility, mainly by handing over more and more responsibility for well-defined and limited tasks and duties, while teachers and administration have general responsibility for the educational processes.

In adult education, however, there is a difference. When the students are adults they are, in principle, responsible not only for the choice of an education or a course but also for their own learning and qualification, and the educational system and thus the teachers must provide them with the possibility to exercise this responsibility by giving it up and even insisting on not taking it.

Precisely where the boundary between youth and adulthood should be drawn is not so important. In Denmark when you are 18 you are legally entitled to manage your own affairs; you have the right to vote at general and national elections etc., to marry without the consent of your parents, and so on. So at this age you are formally considered a full and responsible member of society, and it would be reasonable also in educational practice to talk about adult education from about this age. But on the other hand, in our educational system we also have special programmes for young adults between 18 and 25, one of the main aims of which is to develop the students' ability to take responsibility for themselves, which implies that this capacity is not yet at hand and therefore must be supported. So in this respect you cannot speak of a borderline between adolescents and adults at a fixed age, and teachers will have to decide for themselves how to regard the young adult students they are dealing with.

What is essential, in my opinion, is that *when your students can be regarded as adults it means that they should also take over full responsibility for their own learning and education and, not least, that teachers and educational systems should not only give them the possibility to take over, but also insist that they do so and refuse to undertake this responsibility.*

Immediately this sounds very obvious and simple, and in a debate or discussion everybody can agree. But in practice, as I have already stated, it is not at all so obvious and simple, but a matter of great difficulty which requires overcoming deeply-rooted resistance, as well as great determination and hard work on the part of both teacher and students.

The job of the teacher in particular is very demanding in such processes. Immediately, because it is always difficult voluntarily to give up power and influence, but also because it is a paradoxical and seemingly contradictory task to accomplish taking responsibility for not taking responsibility. However, this is precisely what the teacher of adults must do: it is the very mark of his or her professionalism to accomplish this. It was also the recognition of this that made my technical school teachers so obviously and frankly experience that here was the threshold they had to cross in order to move from adolescent to adult education.

But the issue is, as some of my formulations may already have revealed, still more complex or contorted, because there is a very fine borderline to be drawn between the students' responsibility for their own learning and education and the responsibility of the teachers to provide the optimal conditions and input for this learning and education, and also often even to have to evaluate the results in a way that may be of crucial importance for the very life course of the student.

However, these are the conditions of our profession as adult educators, and it is important that they are faced and accepted so that we can responsibly decide our attitudes and the consequences for our practice. Very often the most difficult point is to avoid undertaking some of the responsibility that should be left to the students, and when we do not accomplish this we are doubly inadequate. At the ethical and social level we are not respecting our students as independent adults, and at the practical educational level we are not contributing optimally to establishing the conditions for an up-to-date learning and qualification process.

I am quite sure that my technical school teachers realized this, and they experienced it as a relief to better understand what the challenge actually is about and also as an almost overwhelming demand. Therefore they were also very eager to squeeze out of me every bit of practical advice that I could give them about methods and techniques to fulfil these challenging demands inside the framework of their quite traditional school.

And even though much of this may seem very simple and banal, in my experience, both from my own practice and from tutoring many other adult teachers, it is very challenging, and you very easily fall or are pressed back into the position of the over-responsible and all-directing teacher who knows everything and does not hesitate to demonstrate his/her knowledge and tell everybody else how things are to be understood or managed.

I shall, therefore, try briefly to make explicit some of the practical measures I was discussing with the teachers because I sometimes have the feeling that it is only at the practical level that educators really understand what all this is about. And I should like to stress once more that I am referring to what can be done by teachers in ordinary adult education with average students, traditional programmes, and no special conditions.

Project work and decision making

When as a teacher of adults you want to take the challenge of students' responsibility seriously it is not enough, or not even most important, to tell the students about the necessity for them to take over responsibility for their own learning and education. Of course it is a good idea to do so at an early point, but the crucial thing is to practice firmly and from the very first moment unwillingness to undertake any part of the responsibility that should be the students' and to reject any attempt to be pressed into the all-responsible teacher role that the students usually expect you to play.

It is also necessary that responsibility on the part of the students is not only something that is demanded and supported as a new form of practice within the traditional structures of teaching and studying. It must be built into the structures themselves as an unavoidable feature, so that it does not appear to the students as merely a demand or an idea forced upon them by the teacher personally, but occurs as a natural consequence of the social setting.

The most fundamental measure in this respect seems to be the introduction of project studies or project work as practised in Denmark for the last 25 years, first in the university studies in Roskilde and Aalborg, later at all levels and in most sectors of the educational system, including compulsory project work in the primary school (cf. Nielsen & Webb 1991, 1996).

I shall not here go into detail about project work as an educational method as I have described this thoroughly in other publications (Illeris 1986, 1997a, 1997b, 1997c). But I should like to draw attention to the features of project work which are crucial in placing responsibility with the students.

The key concept in this respect is 'participant direction' which basically implies that projects are directed by a group of students and their teacher or supervisor in common. But the roles of the students and the supervisor in relation to the direction of the project are different. First of all, of course, it is the students who carry out the project, whereas the supervisor generally should function precisely as an adviser who is willing and qualified to discuss the content, methods and process of the projects with students, to advise them, suggest suitable literature and persons or institutions to contact and so on. In this way the process usually takes the form of cooperation, with a natural and problem-free distribution of roles and tasks. But where there is conflict it is important to be aware of and to maintain that the students' responsibility is anchored in their own interest in the project, i.e. mainly that they find it meaningful and worth dealing with, whereas the supervisor's responsibility is anchored in his or her function as the representative of the educational system.

Another important area in which responsibility is at stake concerns decision-making within the given framework of any educational programme or course. Usually a lot of decisions are made by the teachers or the administration, often more or less routine, but in most of this decision-making it could be both reasonable and fair to involve adult students. Teachers often experience that such involvement will take time from the teaching, but the aim of the activities is not teaching, but learning. Especially when the development of personal qualities such as responsibility is an important part of the educational aims, involvement in decision-making processes is obviously a suitable measure from the perspectives of ethics and efficient learning.

In practice there are many ways to establish this involvement and, again, what is most important is to do so by routine or structural means, so that it is not a matter of the teacher personally forcing the students to participate but rather an unavoidable part of the curriculum. Two fundamental principles in particular are essential. First, that everybody should contribute, and decisions should be made against the background of a general view of the suggestions and attitudes of the whole group. Second, that decisions are made by consensus and voting is abandoned, at least when dealing with important decisions.

The immediate reaction is often a great deal of uncertainty and resistance as to the principle of consensus because it implies that everybody has the right to veto. The consequences seem quite unpredictable. But in practice it will usually prove to imply more responsibility and the will to consider all arguments seriously as everybody is aware that all interests must be taken into consideration in order to find a solution. In this way decision by consensus will contribute to processes of learning and experience, which may very well be of great importance for the development of responsibility.

Responsibility and postmodernism

Having discussed with the teachers for a couple of hours, in detail and with mutual enthusiasm, such techniques of distributing responsibility and participation we had to break up, but I feel quite sure that most of them will make a sincere effort to change their teaching radically in the directions we spoke about.

However, to be honest, I must also admit that I am quite sure that they will encounter much difficulty, and even if they are very keen on changing things they will have trouble and will experience resistance that will make many of them return to old and tried practices. And they will find this necessary because, although they may feel inadequate, the old ways do function in a way that they can manage and overview, and for some of them the changes will lead to unbearable uncertainty and never-ending problems.

The essence of these problems is, in addition to the more fundamental conditions that I have already been dealing with, that responsibility today is a most ambiguous affair. On the one hand the responsibility of all members of society is demanded more than ever before, but on the other hand it presupposes steady values and a coherent pattern of orientation, and a central feature of our post-modern society is exactly the dissolution and relativisation of such values and patterns.

As quoted above, Wildemeersch relates responsibility to doing justice to the Other and to present and future generations. This is a responsibility that extends as far as to the survival of man and the earth, and that is maybe all we can agree about. But between such ultimate perspectives and the problems of daily life there seems to be an endless area in which all structures have become relative. You can relate your responsibility to very faraway and superior values, or you can relate it to yourself and your immediate situation and needs, but very many, especially young adults, find it difficult to find any steady anchorage for their responsibility in the vast and ever-changing sea where common values, tradition and religion previously formed anchorages of general agreement.

Returning to the daily practice of adult education, the situation is that when you demand responsibility on the part of the students and even insist on their responsibility as a condition and basis of valuable and sustainable learning, it is a very demanding and sometimes confusing challenge for them and many of them will try to escape it, for instance by not taking a stand or by sticking to an extreme and impossible position.

But if you are able to survive such uncertainty and confusion, you will very often find that when the students try to and succeed in making their own decisions and planning, and when they experience that they are taken seriously that their decisions come through, and that they are supported in their efforts, the picture usually changes.

Actually, most adults do prefer to direct their own affairs, and inside the educational system there should really be a space of sheltered security where experience can be built up, mistakes can be accepted, you can learn from them, different opinions can be confronted and agreements can be hammered out. These can all be very important contributions to a learning process in line with current demands and developmental needs, and also with the attitudes and orientations of most students today.

When such processes are carried through it also means that little bits of the sea of uncertainty are conquered and structures are established to make orientation possible. So the process of responsibility goes hand in hand with the process of reflection and reflectivity which has been so much in focus as the necessity and core of post-modern society (e.g. Schön 1983, Giddens 1991). You might even say that reflectivity and responsibility become two sides of the same process.

One important condition for getting past the insecurity and resistance of the students is gentle but insistent urging by the teacher. In different kinds of adult education you will find different mixes of students, and as a teacher you will always have to find your own way of overcoming the barriers in relation to the students and areas of education you are dealing with. Sometimes and for some teachers facing up to conflict right at the beginning of a course may be the key. In other situations and for other teachers the risk of failure in the first step will make a much more slow and cautious procedure preferable.

Another important condition, of course, is the experience and attitudes that the students carry with them from school and other previous education. And this connection can constitute a bridge back to the challenge about the difference between teaching children and adolescents and teaching adults, which was the jumping-off point for all these considerations.

Conclusion

In child and adolescent schooling responsibility is fundamentally something which has to be gradually developed, and many contemporary ideas and programmes deal with this in different ways, identifying it as a key issue of modern school development. I have already mentioned the idea of developing 'competence to choose' in the Danish primary school. A couple of other and internationally more well-known examples are the Early Childhood Education and Primary School Curriculum Framework of New Zealand and the PEEL Project (The Project for

Enhancing Effective Learning) at secondary school level in Australia (Baird & Mitchell 1986, Baird & Northfield 1992). Many other examples of great diversity might be pointed to, but however different all these projects are, the orientation towards supporting the pupils' ability to take responsibility for their own learning seems to be a common and central feature.

In adult education, in my opinion, this issue should be seen and handled in a way that in practice may not be so very different from more advanced projects in adolescent education but nevertheless is fundamentally different in its basic way of understanding and attacking the problems.

The main point of difference is that adults should basically be understood and treated as responsible. And, if they do not immediately behave responsibly in relation to their own learning and education, it should be understood as an error developed by the circumstances which should be comprehended and overcome.

Of course the teacher may be supportive in this process, but this is not the support of an adult helping the child or adolescent to move towards adult standards. It is rather support to see and deal with conditions and obstacles that prevent adult students from exercising the responsibility which you expect them to have already developed and which will have the best conditions for developing precisely when confronted with this expectation. For this reason, the conditions in the curriculum and the physical and mental environment must also be geared to meet and relate to responsible behaviour.

References

Andersen, V., Illeris, K., Kjærsgaard, C., Larsen, K., Olesen, H.S. & Ulriksen, L. (1996): *General Qualification*. Roskilde: Adult Education Research Group, Roskilde University.

Baird, J.R. & Mitchell, I.J. (1986): *Improving the Quality of Teaching and Learning: An Australian Case Study – The PEEL Project*. Melbourne: Monash University.

Baird, J.R. & Northfield, J.R. (1992): *Learning from the PEEL Experience*. Melbourne: Monash University.

Boud, D. (1989): Some Competing Traditions in Experiential Learning. In Weil, S.W. & McGill, I. (eds.): *Making Sense of Experiential Learning*. Buckingham: Open University Press.

Brückner, P. (1972): *Zur Sozialpsychologie des Kapitalismus*. Frankfurt a.M.: Europäische Verlagsanstalt.

Davenport, J. (1993): Is there any way out of the andragogy morass? In Thorpe, M., Edwards, R. & Hanson, A. (eds.): *Culture and Processes of Adult Learning*. London: Routledge.

Giddens, A. (1991): *Modernity and Self-Identity – Self and Society in the Late Modern Age*. Cambridge: Polity Press.

Henry, J. (1989): Meaning and Practice in Experiential Learning. In Weil, S.W. & McGill, I. (eds.). *Making Sense of Experiential Learning*. Buckingham: Open University Press.

Illeris, K. (1986): The Use of Projects in University Education as Inspiration for Project Management. In Gabriel, E. (ed): *New Approaches in Project Management*. Zürich: Internet.

Illeris, K. (1992): General Qualification of Unskilled and Semi-skilled Workers. In Gam, P. et al (eds.): *Social Change and Adult Education Research*. Linköping: Linköping University.

Illeris, K. (1997a): The organisation of studies at Roskilde University. In Illeris, K. (ed.): *Roskilde University: Principles of Education and Research*.

Illeris, K. (1997b): Project Studies at Roskilde University. In Wassenburg, M. & Philipsen, H. (eds.): *Placing the Student at the Centre*. Maastricht: Maastricht University.

Illeris, K. (1997c): *Project Work in University Studies – Background and Current Issues*. Keynote speech at the conference on Project Work in University Studies, Roskilde University.

Illeris, K. & Andersen, V. (1994): General Qualification in Danish Adult Training Programmes. In Klenovsek, T. & Olesen, H.S. (eds.): *Adult Education and the Labour market*. Ljubljana: Slovene Adult Education Centre.
Jarvis, P. (1984): Andragogy: a sign of the times. *Studies in the Education of Adults*. No. 16, p. 32–38.
Knowles, M. (1973): *The Adult Learner: A Neglected Species*. Houston, Texas: Gulf Publishing Company.
Knowles, M. (1975): *Self-Directed Learning – A Guide for Learners and Teachers*. Englewood Cliffs: Prentice Hall.
Knowles, M. (1980): *The Modern Practice of Adult Education – From Pedagogy to Andragogy*. Englewood Cliffs: Prentice Hall, revised and updated edition.
Kolb, D.A. (1984): *Experiential Learning*. Englewood Cliffs: Prentice Hall.
Leithäuser, T. (1976): *Formen des Alltagsbewußtseins*. Frankfurt a.M.: Campus.
Leithäuser, T. (1977): Vergesellschaftung und Sozialisation des Bewußtseins. In Leithäuser, T. et al (eds.): *Entwurf zu einer Empirie des Alltagsbewußtseins*. Frankfurt a.M.: Suhrkamp.
Negt, O. (1971): *Soziologische Phantasie und exemplarisches Lernen*. Frankfurt a.M.: Europäische Verlagsanstalt. Überarbeitete Neuausgabe.
Negt, O. (1989): *Die Herausforderung der Gewerkschaften*. Frankfurt a.M.: Campus.
Nielsen, J.L. & Webb, T.W. (1991): *An Emerging Critical Pedagogy*. Roskilde: Roskilde University.
Nielsen, J.L. & Webb, T.W. (1996): Experiential Pedagogy. In Olesen, H.S. & Rasmussen, P. (eds.): *Theoretical Issues in Adult Education – Danish Research and Experiences*. Copenhagen: Roskilde University Press.
Schön, D.A. (1983): *The Reflective Practitioner*. New York: Basic Books.
Tennant, M. (1986): An evaluation of Knowles' theory of adult learning. *International Journal of Lifelong Education*. No.2, p. 113–122.
Tennant, M. (1997): *Psychology and Adult Learning*. London: Routledge, second edition.
Usher, R., Bryant, I. & Johnston, R. (1997): *Adult education and the postmodern challenge*. London: Routledge.
Wildemeersch, D. (1991): Learning from regularity, irregularity and responsibility. *International Journal of Lifelong Education*. Vol.10, no.2, p. 151–158.
Wildemeersch, D. (1992): Ambiguities of experiential learning and critical pedagogy. In Wildemeersch, D. & Jansen, T. (eds.): *Adult education, experiential learning and social change – the postmodern challenge*. The Hague: VUGA Uitgeverij.
Wildemeersch, D. (1997): *Paradoxes of Social Learning – Towards a model for project oriented group work*. Keynote speech at the conference on Project Work in University Studies, Roskilde University.
Ziehe, T. & Stubenrauch, H. (1982): *Plädoyer für ungewöhnliches Lernen*. Hamburg: Rowohlt.

CHAPTER 11

ADULT EDUCATION BETWEEN EMANCIPATION AND CONTROL

Annegrethe Ahrenkiel & Knud Illeris

Adult education is generally dominated by discourses of emancipation. This is often so when adult education is conceived from the view of the planners or teachers, and it is fundamental to such key concepts in theories of adult learning as self-direction (e.g. Knowles 1975, Brookfield 1985, 1986, Tennant 1997), transformative learning (Mezirow 1991), critical thinking (Brookfield 1987, Mezirow et al 1990), and social responsibility (Wildemeersch et al 1998).

In addition research using a biographical approach to adult education tends to focus on how people in their (late) adulthood realise an old dream when they return to educational institutions. We often see life histories where adult education of various kinds is said to be a turning point in people's lives. This phenomenon is often interpreted as the realisation of "unlived lives" as expressed in a popular phrase from biographical research (e.g. Alheit 1995, Dausien 1998).

But does adult education always play such an important role for the participants, also for the majority of people with a brief or no educational background after their basic schooling? Or could it be that researchers with a middle-class background and deeply rooted in the educational system as such interpret the empirical material from their own cultural perspective, and thus focus on emancipatory perspectives, neglecting elements of repression and control?

The Adult Education Research Project

In the "Adult Education Research Project" (Illeris et al 1998, Illeris 1998, Ahrenkiel et al 1998, 1999), which is financed by the Danish Ministry of Education and labour market authorities in cooperation with Roskilde University, we are dealing with the broad adult education systems which mainly serve adults with brief schooling and unemployed adults. These systems have expanded rapidly during the last eight years, partly as a consequence of the government's active labour market policy, but to some extent also because a growing number of adults are attracted by or feel it necessary to take an interest in adult education.

In Denmark there are three educational systems that are mainly oriented towards this group of participants.

The oldest system, launched in 1960, is the "Adult Vocational Training" (AMU) system, which traditionally offers short, mainly 1–4 week, courses of practical, labour oriented skills. These courses have gradually also come to include more general and personal qualification, and longer courses have been added in recent years.

During the 1970s another system emerged and later developed: Adult Education Centres (VUC), offering compensatory education and examinations for adults who want to improve their basic educational level. The subjects and exams are in principle equal to those of the lower and upper secondary school, but they have gradually developed their own interpretations of the syllabuses, and it is possible to take as few or many subjects as one wants and to combine subjects freely.

Finally, from the late 1970s the Day High Schools developed as a new branch of the Danish Folk High School and the public enlightenment movement, serving mainly unemployed adults who need to start a new life and career, and operating as high schools with general, cultural, creative and productive subjects, no examinations and not awarding any formal competence.

In the project we have followed selected courses in these three systems, observed the teaching and daily life, and interviewed participants in single and group interviews. In doing so we have consistently sought to look at adult education from the perspective of the participants.

Ambivalence and strategies

What we have found is basically that most of these adults approach education in very ambivalent ways. As already mentioned, adult education in Denmark has become a major concern of labour market policy. This means that the majority of the participants enter the adult education institutions because they are more or less forced to do so. They may be unemployed persons who have to be active in some kind of formal job or training course in order to continue receiving unemployment benefit (the government activating programme), or they may be workers who take courses because it is more or less directly demanded of them in order to keep their jobs.

Thus the concept of "lifelong learning" is no longer merely an ideological phrase or a political intention which mainly applies to middle-class women, as was formerly the case in Denmark. It is now a reality for a much larger group including both genders and all classes, and also to a great extent people with a working-class background. The majority of these participants are not just attending adult education because of an inner drive, but mainly out of necessity or because of direct requirements or being forced to do so.

From our observations and interviews it can be derived that more or less everybody who today is 30 years old or more has a deeply embedded notion that education, apart from necessary supplementary training when, for instance, new technology is introduced, is something that is related to childhood and adolescence. Adult education of a more prolonged and profound character is consequently somehow experienced as degrading and a threat to the status of adulthood. To be an adult means being able to conduct one's own life and make one's own living, and not being pushed back to school and to the status of a pupil.

But at the same time most people do want to keep their jobs or improve their possibilities of getting one and, at least up to their late 40s and usually up to their mid 50s, they are generally open to learning if this does not require rejecting what they have already committed themselves to. So very often when adults enter longer and/or re-qualifying courses they are very sceptical and very expectant at one and the same time. They hope for and demand enrichment and involvement but also fear being humiliated or challenged above the level of their personal thresholds. They are sensitive and vulnerable. While they hope for help and support in a critical life situation, they doubt that it is possible. They are ambivalent in a way that splits them apart.

These circumstances lead to participants telling about their reasons for being involved in adult education in most contradictory ways. On the one hand they emphasise that they have chosen to start an educational programme because they want to learn (e.g. about computers); on the other hand they are only attending the courses because they have to do something. In some stories the social motives are dominant (e.g. they want to meet new friends), but they are always mixed with other motives for qualification or personal development and with elements of passive resistance and perplexity.

Motivations are rarely straightforwardly positive or negative but seem to be a mixture of social, personal and/or technical elements with a focus on the concrete skills that the adults expect to gain from the programmes they participate in. At the same time there is a great deal of desperation or resignation in their statements. And when we ask them more about their everyday lives and their life histories (especially about the values that they have been orienting their lives towards so far), it becomes evident that their actual approach to adult education is very ambivalent and even confused.

This is also the reason why we prefer to use the phrase "educational strategies" rather than motives. In employing this terminology we want to emphasise that adults approach educational programmes under very contradictory circumstances and that these circumstances produce particular attitudes and ways of handling their participation which make it possible for them to cope with the current situation.

The educational strategies are not just visible to us as researchers when we interview people about their reasons for participating in adult education. They are also active in the classrooms, influencing the ways in which participants interact when they meet in the institutions. The strategies are formed as a result of the meeting and collision of the participants' approaches with the norms, traditions, culture and demands of the different institutions.

In this paper we will give some examples of the ambivalent approaches and of the different kinds of strategies the participants develop when involved in adult education. But first we will briefly describe a theoretical approach to understanding the identity problems that adults face in a (late) modern society. Finally, after the examples of strategies, we will discuss the limits and possibilities for adult education to be part of an emancipatory project for the subjects involved – and also for developing necessary qualifications in a modernised society.

Adults and identity

The mixed attitudes towards adult education are not just produced by the outward elements of economic power and control that compel our research subjects to participate in adult education. The broader social and economic conditions these participants are currently facing have consequences for their very identities.

For children and young people it is an integral part of their lives that they are developing and therefore have to learn new things all the time. But adults face the consequences of modernity from a different point. The adults that enter the educational institutions have typically had stable jobs and family lives, but some or all of this has changed. This means that the identities they have developed during a long life are also challenged. What they conceived of as stable factors in their lives no longer exist. They have to find new life orientations, but in contrast to younger people they have to develop these new orientations on top of some they have already established. Thus for them the development of a new identity simultaneously means discarding parts of the old identity, and the latter is often a process that is far more difficult and causes much more pain than the former.

In our research project we see many adults who try to use elements of their old identity under circumstances where it no longer fits. They talk about their old trade and the qualifications needed there, about the time when the children were still living at home, etc. In adult education today it is something else that matters, but what?

The problems of identity are part of the baggage participants bring with them into the adult education institutions. The breakdown of biographical continuity – the loss of a job, of family relations, and maybe of political, cultural, moral or religious orientations – means that they are very uncertain of the future and of their social identity. Their former experience does not seem to be relevant. At the same time the discourse of the possibility of modernity also dominates the educational institutions. When they were young they did not expect everything to be possible – they just got married, got a job and generally did as they were expected to do. Now they are suddenly told that everything is possible and that it is their own responsibility to succeed. But everything is not possible and they are not sure what the purpose of education is when the prospects of getting a new job are extremely doubtful. Are they just being kept busy at the educational institutions because they are not needed in the labour market or are they actually qualifying themselves for a steady job?

In the institutions they are talked to as responsible adults who are able to make their own decisions about what is relevant for them to do at the same time as being placed in the position of vulnerable children who have to be taken care of and not over-challenged.

On their way the participants learn to play the role of interested learners but they are still very uncertain about the rationality and sense of the educational project. What happens in the adult educational institutions cannot be understood without realising that questioning the fundamental meaning of the project is always present. Adult education can very often be characterised as the compulsion to develop without a clear perspective. (At this point we once more must stress that the situation is very different for young adults in their early 20s – cf. Simonsen, later in this book).

The ambivalent approaches

As already stated adults approach education in very ambivalent ways. A 50 year-old woman participating in a day high school course on the theme of "computers, people and society", describes her reasons for attending the course:

> "That is how it is today...The employment office does not ask: 'Do you want to stay at home or do you want to go to a day high school?' They ask [...] with the implicit intention that you must do something. The reason why I am here is that I have known many people who have attended day high schools, and they have told me nice things about it, and that there is a good deal of solidarity among the participants. And that they are not so strict and authoritarian in their ways out here [...] Actually it is compulsory – you are forced to choose something, really [...] So that is pretty much my motivation for being here, right. It is that I have to do something, and then I have to choose what

that is [...] you have to know what you want to do, because otherwise you will have something forced on you."

Later in the interview the same woman says that she also chose this course because she knew two of the other participants from another course they had attended together. She also says that she has been out of work for the last five years and that she has given up the hope of getting a new job. She has already taken other computer courses but she wants to learn more about IT. But what she really likes is the discussions about subjects such as the unions etc.

Even though this woman has given up the hope of getting a job, her choice of course is still oriented towards the labour market. She says that she wants to learn more about computers because "IT skills" are a requirement in every job advertisement today. But at the same time she does not really think that she can qualify for a job, so she wants to attend a school with a good social life. Her choice of course seems to be random or she wants to avoid something worse.

Other participants have much greater expectations as to what they can gain from the computer course. One of them remarks:

"There will probably be 50 companies waiting to employ me when I finish here."

Even though this remark is ironic, it reflects some of the elements of hope that all participants direct, and have to direct, towards the outcome of their adult education. Participants who are currently employed also feel some kind of pressure from their surroundings to learn and develop. A man in his mid 50s attending a general course at the vocational (AMU) school tells about the demands from his workplace:

"...we are actually forced to participate in different courses because we have to educate ourselves in order to perform our tasks in a better way..... I am at a workplace where there is a great need for it, so am I here voluntarily? We have to be at these courses, right, we have to be better at things, also because we have to do more and more of the work ourselves...If I refused to attend this course, then my career would be fairly short."

A lot of the participants find this general and not practical course very unsatisfactory, but feel compelled to go through with it. The elements of compulsion produce very sceptical attitudes towards the course, but these attitudes are also enforced by the actual content of the course.

The ambivalent attitudes towards adult education do not just apply to people with a brief educational background. In another project we compared how women with different educational backgrounds approach adult education. The more highly-educated women are also very ambivalent, even though they formulate their ambivalence differently, e.g. that they want to develop personally – but they also feel the pressure of demands on the part of their employers (Ahrenkiel & Eriksen, 1995).

What happens in the institutions?

The first days the participants spend at the adult educational institutions some of the fundamental conflicts show up very clearly. At the vocational course they eat breakfast together and one of the participants suddenly says aloud:

140   *Adult education between emancipation and control*

> *"I don't know how we're going to pass the time here if we are to sit down all the time."*

In answer to this another participant remarks that he knows someone who has been at the course before who has told him that they are also going to go for some walks outside. The situation illustrates that the participants are very sceptical about the course. The participant clearly expects the others to share his critical view of the course, otherwise he would not have made this statement in public at a time when he did not yet know the others. It connotes sitting down, passive listening and no practical work.

The teacher also expects the participants to be sceptical. The first topic he takes up when they are all gathered in the classroom is meeting and break times. They will not be allowed to leave early because the course must match the conditions on the labour market. Next, the teacher informs the participants about the formal rules they have to comply with in order to get their certificates. Thus from the beginning the participants are in the position of pupils who are expected to focus on the time they have to spend in school and to be indifferent to the content of the course.

Also at the day high school the teacher focuses on practical information and regulations to begin with. The participants are very uncertain about whether they can learn to use a computer at all. But instead of demystifying what a computer is by letting the participants work with one, they spend the first two days going through the course programme. The participants are told about how much time they will spend on word-processing, the Internet, e-mail etc. but they are very confused because they do not know many of the concepts and this just mystifies them even more. The course prepares the participants to take tests in each element (the PC driver's licence), but the school has not yet arranged how this is to take place. The day high schools have a tradition of being very sensitive to the participants and one way of practising this sensitivity is by advancing slowly and assuring the participants that they can learn things at their own pace. The following is a typical situation from a morning session before starting to perform different tasks individually (as quoted from the diary of the observer):

> *"The teacher reads aloud the schedules he has just handed out. He said that he had changed something since last year because it was so difficult and boring to learn the theoretical elements before they knew something more about using a computer. They would also have time to read the pages in the books at the school so they did not have to sit at home reading the difficult book. [. . .] Maria asked whether they would take a test after each element or if they should take all seven tests by the end of the course. The teacher replied that it was a bad idea to take all seven tests at the end, because by then they would have forgotten much of what they had learned. [. . .] Some asked how much it would cost to take the tests and whether they themselves had to pay. It turned out that those with different kinds of benefits would not have to pay themselves. If there was any doubt they should just ask the counsellor at the school who would take care of it and write to the employment offices etc. . . At the end of the session the teacher stressed that it was possible to do something else, of course, and that the schedule could be changed. They could also choose to continue working on one element if they did not think they had a good grasp of it, even though the teaching went on to another element. 'So if you would rather work on your own I will not be mad at you. After all, we are adults'."*

The constant assurances of help and plenty of time just make the uncertain participants even more uncertain about their ability to learn. The teacher tries to protect them against demands that are too tough but in doing so he also puts them in the position of very weak and dependent persons who have to be taken great care of. Various phrases emphasising that the participants are adults were frequently heard at all the schools. But such phrases are ambiguous because it is only relevant to stress that they are adults if they might actually not be treated as such – and this is very typical of the contradictory positions set up for the participants. On the one hand they are viewed as responsible persons and on the other hand as children who have to be constantly supervised and taken care of.

The teacher leaves it pretty much up to the participants to do things in the way they find best. But as they do not know anything about computers, they cannot suggest any alternatives. Even though there is a large degree of openness and sensitivity in the way the teacher phrases his sentences, there are very limited possibilities to affect the schedule fundamentally. The 18 week course consists almost entirely of participants working on assignments from books on computer programmes. Even though most of the participants find it rather boring, they do not suggest working with the computers in a different way, e.g. on projects of their own. Their suggestions remain within the horizon of what they have experienced at the course so far, and this means that the only thing they really influence is how much time they spend on each of the elements. In this sense the classroom sets a firm framework for what the participants can do, even though the school is highly oriented towards an ideology of personal sensitivity and development.

Also at the vocational school the participants tried to influence the content of the course. This was made very difficult because of the lack of information about the course. The participants were constantly surprised about what they were going to be taught, e.g. economics and computers. Some participants tried to suggest that they should learn more about practical skills but this was turned down by the teacher because these activities were included in later modules. This was a clear source of frustration for the participants and they complained much about the course being boring.

The educational strategies

In order to deal with the contradictions both within the classroom and in the participants' approaches and the lack of a clear objective of the courses, the participants develop different strategies to get through the programmes. These are not always conscious strategies which the participants and teachers are aware of as mechanisms for coping. They derive from our interpretations of the interactions in the classrooms in combination with our awareness of the ambivalence that characterises the participants' approaches to adult education.

Complaints and passivity as a strategy

The obvious grumbling and complaining about different things in the schools is a very visible form of reaction to an unsatisfactory situation. The participants complain about a lot of things – e.g. that the teacher is too authoritarian or not authoritarian enough that the other participants are disruptive or just not good enough, that the rooms or the facilities are old-fashioned etc. While on the one hand these complaints have very precise grounds, on the other hand they also reflect the participants' uncertainty as to whether they can learn what they are taught and what the purpose of the whole project really is. At the vocational school, for example, the participants try to influence the content of the course in the direction of something to which they can immediately relate. When this does not happen they first complain a lot, but during the course they develop a strategy of resignation and only passively attend the courses because they have to stay in order to get their certificate. They then take part in the trips outside but without interest, just to pass the time. As some participants say, they assume that the purpose of the trips is to create breaks and pass the time.

Humour and irony as a strategy

The use of humour and irony is another strategy the participants apply to get through the long school days. While complaining overtly reflects displeasure, humour is a more indirect means of expressing frustration, irritation, uncertainty and a feeling of inadequacy. Humour may often be used to express pent-up emotions that it may be difficult to formulate directly. In a psychoanalytical understanding, humour is regarded as a means of expressing repressed libidinal or aggressive feelings in an acceptable way. At the vocational school most participants feel bored and in the interviews they openly admit that they make jokes and witty remarks to break the monotony of the teaching, but at the same time this compounds and reinforces the experience of wasting time. At the day high school humour and disruptive remarks also occur, but here the irony is often turned against the participant him or herself. The underlying message is that the participants feel too silly or incompetent to pick up the computer qualifications while simultaneously being seriously in doubt whether they will ever have a possibility to use what they learn in a job situation – or as a participant put it one day:

"We might as well stay here – we won't get further anyway."

Dynamism as a strategy

For many of the participants in adult education, the aim of their efforts is so vague and far away that their participation appears meaningless when they come to think about it more deeply, as often happens during the interviews. One way of handling such uncertainty in everyday life is to make the activities dynamic by ascribing to them a meaning and importance that can support and legitimise engagement. The reason why the examinations at the compensatory schools are held in such high esteem – in contrast to the ordinary secondary school where examinations are usually hated – is that they offer legitimisation for the activities which the content itself does not always provide. At the day high school the social community spirit may have the same effect, for instance when it becomes possible to use the computers as a means of communicating by e-mail both inside and outside the institution.

Perfectionism as a strategy

Another way of getting through is to commit oneself to selected elements of the content and try to become perfect in limited areas or functions. This strategy is very easy to adopt in the computer courses, the computers offering lots of possibilities where a certain type of task can be repeated again and again until one feels absolutely competent. It is remarkable that participants clearly prefer to spend the ample time that is available in this way and not in throwing themselves into the endless new possibilities that the computers also offer. Another way of practising this strategy is to note down carefully and conscientiously everything the teacher says.

Usefulness as a strategy

Whereas the above mentioned strategies are directed inwards and concentrated on how to get through the long and sometimes boring days in the institutions, some other strategies are of a broader and outward-directed kind focusing on the question: How can I get the most out of this situation? On this level there seem to be two main strategies which are somewhat contradictory in their ways but not more so than that it is possible to use both strategies at the same time. The positive strategy is for the single participant to find out what may be personally useful in a course and concentrate on that in order to maximise the personal outcome; the negative is to find out how one can get through the course and get the formal recognition with a minimum of personal effort. As to the strategy of usefulness, it is obvious that the vocational school and the day high school computer courses offer elements of practical qualification which are generally useful in daily life – and also in working life if one should be so lucky as to get a job. In the compensatory school programmes, such elements may immediately be found in foreign language courses and to some extent in other subjects such as cultural and social studies, but the feeling that the content of the subjects is useful primarily in relation to examinations, and only to a very limited extent in relation to life outside school is very widespread and dominant.

Instrumentalism as a strategy

As to the instrumental strategy of getting through as easily as possible, its application is fundamentally dependent on the formal sanctions. In the vocational courses where presence is the main criterion and only two days of absence are allowed, the strategy will just be to be there. But actually most people cannot stand not to be active in some way, and therefore the (sub)strategies of complaints and humour are very widespread here. In the day high school some of the participants are very focused on passing the computer tests. Others just have to complete the course in a satisfactory way which means that they have to be well-reputed by the staff and management in order to be recommended for another course, and this reputation is primarily gained by being socially active and obliging. In the compensatory courses everything is concentrated on passing the examinations, but in order to go to examination in what is called a "limited syllabus" – which is for most participants a definite condition – one may not exceed 15 per cent absence from the lessons. Thus, this criterion becomes very important and creates much dissatisfaction because it is experienced as being contradictory to relying on the participants to be adult and self-governing.

Adult education: Storage and control, job preparation or emancipation?

We have tried to illustrate above how adults are ambivalent in their attitudes to adult education, how adult education has become a part of labour market policy, how it affects the vulnerable identities of adults in uncertain life situations, and how adults react by developing various strategies to cope with the concrete situations but also to protect themselves and maintain their self respect.

We started the paper by questioning the emancipatory power of adult education, especially in relation to the broad layers of adults with brief schooling who today comprise the majority of adult education participants, and we have further described the background to this questioning. What, then, are the necessary conditions that would make it possible for the participants to learn something of importance and develop themselves in a direction which could be termed emancipatory?

The first and fundamental condition is no doubt that the problematic situations and ambivalence of the adults in question are recognised and taken seriously. They are certainly not showing up in the schools just to improve and develop themselves and to realise old dreams of knowledge and understanding. They are fundamentally sceptical – school is not a positively valued word to them – but almost always there is also a vague element of hope in their attitudes, hope for some sort of help and support to get out of the problematic and unsatisfactory situation that has forced them to go back to school again.

Any emancipatory endeavour must necessarily try to satisfy and link up with such elements of hope. And at the core of these elements is nearly always a burning, but hardly expressible wish to get some work, maybe only part-time, maybe not very enriching, but just about any meaningful job that makes it possible to feel like an acceptable member of society once more. (Again we must stress that the situation is quite different for the youngest adults who do not feel it degrading and humiliating to live on public benefits to the same extent).

Whether one likes it or not adult education has become an integrated part of labour market policy, and the participants clearly also regard it as such. So any emancipatory notion must be combined with serious endeavours to procure realistic job possibilities for the adult students. However, this is not a question of pedagogics or educational strategies; it is a political issue of very high priority in today's welfare societies.

Therefore educators, and especially educators with emancipatory notions and orientations, cannot hope to pursue their goals solely by good and progressive educational activities. They will have to inform and to agitate about the everyday conditions of adult education and the situations and attitudes of the students; they will have to seek alliances with progressive politicians and labour market agents; they will have to accept compromises; and they will constantly have to find out how to optimise their endeavours in relation to changing conditions that are always insufficient.

What is really needed is for as many adult education participants as possible to be guaranteed a meaningful job after successfully completed courses, and that the criteria for this are clear and reasonable viewed from the perspective of the students. This is the main conclusion of the Adult Education Research Project. It has the character of a strong political demand, but it is not unrealistic as unemployment rates are falling in Denmark and many other Western European countries.

Today vast resources are invested in adult educational measures and compulsion which are the result of highly prioritised political effort, but to a great extent this effort fails because the ambivalence of the students and the ambiguities of endeavours are not taken into account. Only a job guarantee would be able to cope with these conditions efficiently.

And for those who cannot obtain such a guarantee it would be better to make it straightforward and allow the freedom to spend the resources on any activity that the persons in question prefer, regardless of whether the activity provides job qualifications or not. This would be more honest and pave the way for more activities that would provide more engagement. It would probably also be more qualifying for the participants and maybe even create more flexible qualifications than the rigid strategies produced by today's compulsion.

References

Ahrenkiel, Annegrethe – Eriksen, Trine (1995): *Med familien på samvittigheden. Kvinders møde med voksenuddannelse set i et hverdagslivsperspektiv.* (With the family on the conscience. Women's encounter with adult education, seen from a perspective of everyday life.) Roskilde: Roskilde University, dissertation.

Ahrenkiel, Annegrethe – Illeris, Knud – Sederberg, Marie-Louise – Simonsen, Birgitte (1998): *Voksenuddannelse og deltagermotivation.* (Adult education and the motives of the participants.) Copenhagen: Roskilde University Press.

Ahrenkiel, Annegrethe – Illeris, Knud – Nielsen, Lizzie Mærsk – Simonsen, Birgitte (1999): *Voksenuddannelse mellem trang og tvang.* (Adult education between desire and compulsion.) Copenhagen: Roskilde University Press.

Alheit, Peter (1995): Biographical Learning. In Peter Alheit et al: *The Biographical Approach in European Adult Education.* Wien: ESREA/Verband Wiener Volksbildung.

Brookfield, Stephen D. (ed) – (1985): *Self-Directed Learning: From Theory to Practice.* San Francisco: Jossey-Bass.

Brookfield, Stephen D. (1986): *Understanding and Facilitating Adult Learning.* Milton Keynes: Open University Press.

Brookfield, Stephen D. (1987): *Developing Critical Thinkers.* Milton Keynes: Open University Press.

Dausien, Betina (1998): Education as Biographical Construction? In Peter Alheit and Eva Kammler (eds): *Lifelong Learning and the Impact on Social and Regional Development.* Bremen: Donat Verlag.

Illeris, Knud (ed.) – (1998): *Adult Education in a Transforming Society.* Copenhagen: Roskilde University Press.

Illeris, Knud – Simonsen, Birgitte – Ahrenkiel, Annegrethe (1998): *Udspil om læring og didaktik.* (Proposals about learning and education). Copenhagen: Roskilde University Press.

Knowles, Malcolm S. (1975): *Self-directed learning.* Englewood Cliffs: Prentice Hall.

Mezirow, Jack (1991): *Transformative Dimensions of Adult Learning.* San Francisco: Jossey-Bass.

Mezirow, Jack – et al (1990): *Fostering Critical Reflection in Adulthood.* San Francisco: Jossey-Bass.

Simonsen, Birgitte (in this book): *New young people, new forms of consciousness, new educational methods.*

Tennant, Mark (1997): *Psychology and Adult Learning.* London: Routledge.

Wildemeersch, Danny – Finger, Matthias – Jansen, Theo (eds) – (1998): *Adult Education and Social Responsibility.* Frankfurt a.M.: Peter Lang.

CHAPTER 12

MISLEARNING, DEFENCE AND RESISTANCE

When learning fails

Most literature of learning deals with what happens when one learns something. However, it is equally important, not least in connection with education, to look at what happens in all the situations where one could learn something but does not, or perhaps learns something completely other than what was intended.

It actually happens very often, perhaps more often than the opposite, that possible or intended learning is not realised. When for example, one watches the news on TV, as a rule one retains very little of it, and correspondingly in many other daily situations. We only pay attention to something of significance to us, i.e. we select on the basis of our own criteria what means something to us personally. Furthermore, what we remember or learn in no way has to be "correct" or "objective". Very frequently we acquire the influences we receive in a form that fits in with our own presumptions and interests, and others who receive the same influences get something else out of them.

These matters are widespread in formalised education also. If everybody learned what was intended, then, for example, we would have no need to give grades because then everyone would only have to be awarded the highest grades in everything. In addition, here one sometimes also learns something quite different from what was intended. For many people, the most significant benefit from nine years of teaching in arithmetic and mathematics can be: "I don't understand maths", just to take one single, well-known and actually rather dramatic example.

Traditional learning psychology has not dealt with these matters to any great extent. But they have partly been studied in other contexts where, as a rule, the approach has not been one of learning theory, but has, for example, had to do with forgetting, mental deviations, brain damage, or societal perspectives such as the sorting function of the school, social heritage etc.

In the following, by relating to the learning theory considerations in the above and to contributions from other disciplines, I shall try to achieve some clearer categories and perceptions in this important area.

Non-learning

One of the few learning theorists who have dealt more closely with these matters is the British educator, Peter Jarvis (Jarvis 1992, Jarvis et al. 1998). He uses the concept of non-learning for all situations where possible learning does not take place, and defines three categories of this: *presumption* implies that one already has an understanding of something and therefore does not notice new learning possibilities; *non-consideration* implies that while one may register new possibilities, one does not relate to them, for example because one is too busy or may be unsure about what they can lead to; *rejection* means that one more consciously does not want to learn anything new in a certain context.

Jarvis' categories thus cover three degrees or levels of consciousness in connection with non-learning, but it can be difficult to distinguish between them because they are defined by means of brief, general descriptions without any clear criteria. However, it is clear that in a very large number of cases, we simply do not relate to possible learning, that we let something go in one ear and out the other, and that this most often takes place more or less unconsciously or automatically.

To achieve a more specific understanding of why this is the case, it is, however, necessary to dig more deeply into how learning takes place and why. A distinction must also be made between when nothing at all happens, so that it really is a case of non-learning, and when some trace is nevertheless left which also is a kind of learning, just not the learning that was intended or which the situation offered, perhaps learning in a completely different dimension – for example, a small contribution to the above-mentioned learning: "I don't understand maths" – or perhaps a simple misunderstanding or mislearning.

"Pure" non-learning may not be as widespread as one would think. On the basis of Jarvis' categories, it could be that in the area of "presumption" a strengthening or nuancing of the existing presumption takes place, that in connection with non-consideration a trace is left of the fact that one has bypassed something, or that when a more conscious rejection takes place that which lies at the basis of the rejection is cemented. Such traces are also a form of learning that perhaps when repeated can gradually be strengthened and built up into something important and meaningful – as precisely in the mathematics example above.

There are thus innumerable degrees and nuances in this field, and when one learns something and when one does not may not be so haphazard at all. In the following I shall try to examine more closely some important areas where it is not just a matter of non-learning, but that learning in some way or other does not just take place in an uncomplicated and direct manner.

Mislearning

In a great number of cases where possible or intended learning does not take place, it is a case of simple *mislearning*, i.e. that in some way or other what happens is what we in ordinary everyday language would call a misunderstanding or failure of concentration occurs, so that the individual does not really understand or catch what is going on, or, in an educational situation, what should be learned. From the point of view of learning, it is most frequently a matter of an assimilation that is characterised by the fact that what is assimilated is in one way or other incorrect.

Everybody has the results of such mislearning embedded in their "knowledge", "perception", or "memory", and as long as this has no serious consequences, it does not matter very much. I have found an everyday example in the work of the American psychologist, Robert F. Mager, who has worked with programmed learning. He was to develop a programmed course in elementary electronics, and during prior testing of the students he found out that even though they all claimed that they did not know anything about electronics, nonetheless they all had a great deal of knowledge and understanding of the area, some of which was misknowledge and misperceptions (Mager 1961). All of them, without it being a matter of education or training, had still learned something about electronics. Although some of what they had learned was wrong, it was only when they were to apply it in a more goal-directed context that they discovered this, and then the mistakes were, of course, corrected. One can thus very well live with one's mislearning, but if it has serious consequences in a new context, one does something about it. From the point of view of learning, this can take place through an accommodation, and this is where one typically gets an "A-ha! ..." experience: "A-ha, that's the way it works!"

But it can also be the case that mislearning is built on, and as learning takes place through a combination of the new and what has already been learned, more extensive misperceptions can thus develop. For example, it could be imagined that one had gathered the impression that $2 + 2 = 5$, and if one were to further develop one's arithmetical skills on this basis, something would have to go wrong at one point or another. But as it would then be discovered and corrected, this type of mislearning does not normally have any great consequences.

In many other cases, however, what is right and what is wrong is not always so obvious. For instance, a teacher may have a quite decided and well-founded perception of how a fairy tale should be interpreted, but if one of the participants experiences it in a different way, it cannot simply be said that this is a case of mislearning. In fact, something similar probably also applies to most everyday matters and to everything that has to do with emotions and interpersonal relations. It can be difficult to draw the borderline between what can be termed mislearning and what is rather disagreement. At one time it was definitely a case of mislearning if one believed that the world was round.

In an educational perspective, mislearning is thus easiest to understand in relation to content areas where right and wrong can be clearly established. Clearly established mislearning can be corrected relatively easily – that is, if it is discovered. Mislearning must, naturally, be avoided as far as possible in education programmes, but a clear distinction between mistakes and non-mistakes can only be drawn in limited areas. If the participants always get to know what is right and what is wrong, what one may do and what one may not do, etc., they do not develop their judgement, independence and responsibility – and in a way this is a type of mislearning, or at any rate contrary to the official objective of the education programmes.

In areas where there can be no doubt that mistakes have been made, an effort must naturally be made to avoid them and to correct them when they nevertheless occur. But, apart from this, it is quite important to hold on to the fact that *different* learnings always take place, because, as emphasised earlier, learning is always a matter of something new being linked to what is there in advance, and what is there in advance is always different. Sensitivity, dialogue and tolerance are necessary. Both for the individual and in general terms, progress may be something that takes place when something is understood in a different way than it usually is.

Defence and everyday consciousness

In many cases – probably mostly where adults are concerned – when non-learning and mislearning occur, the background is one form or another of *mental defence*. We do not learn what we can or what we should because, more or less consciously, we do not want to or cannot manage to learn it.

The concept of mental defence mechanisms is closely linked to Freud and appeared very early on as a key concept in the development of psychoanalytical theory. The classic example is "repression" as a defence against unacceptable instinctive impulses, mental conflicts and acknowledgement of traumatic experiences, but by degrees Freud also referred to many other defence mechanisms, and in the classic book on the area his daughter, Anna Freud, lists a great number of different types of defence mechanisms (Freud 1942).

Such defence mechanisms are, naturally, also active to a high degree in learning contexts, and can lead to blocks against learning and distortion of what is learned. However, the classic defence mechanisms are only of limited interest for a general perception of learning because they are closely linked to the personality of the individual. But in late modern society a type of general defence mechanism has developed which we all share and which is directed precisely at our learning.

The background to this is that all adults in our complex modern society are constantly exposed to such an overwhelming volume of information and impacts that psychologically it is impossible to absorb it all. Sorting must take place and this happens by us building up a defence that we insert between the influences and our acquisition of them, i.e. between influences and learning: we do not immediately learn the content of the influences. We are forced to defend ourselves against both the number of the impacts and often against their nature also. Just think of all the terrible events with which we are presented in a TV news programme that lasts for 30 minutes. If we were to relate in an open and receptive way to it all, the result would quickly be a mental breakdown.

This is why people in modern society develop not only personal defence mechanisms that are triggered in certain contexts, as Freud describes the concept. We also have to develop a larger, coherent defence system, or what the German social psychologist, Thomas Leithäuser, has termed an *everyday consciousness* (Leithäuser 1976, 1992, cf. Illeris 2002, 2003a, 2004).

Everyday consciousness works in the way that we develop some so-called "theme-horizon-schemes", i.e. that within a certain subjectively defined theme or field of perception we adopt a certain impression or mode of perceiving the way things function and are connected. When we then encounter an influence which we attribute to the theme in question, in principle we can deal with it in one of three ways. We can completely reject it, i.e. avoid any kind of acquisition – which can possibly have other consequences for learning as outlined above. There can be a mental distortion so that we perceive the influence in accordance with our theme-horizon – i.e. a "distorted assimilation". Or we can "let it go straight in", thereby accomodatively altering the scheme in question in accordance with the new influence. The latter requires, as a rule, "thematisation", i.e. more goal-directed processing, because special mental effort is required to transgress and reconstruct the schemes that were developed.

In this way everyday consciousness functions both as a necessary defence and as a kind of broad and general form of what we in more acute forms term prejudices. In this way, too, adults' learning potential is less flexible than that of children and young people: the more cemented the theme-horizon-schemes are, the more frequently we have utilised them and thus reinforced them, the more difficult they are to transgress. With another expression from another psychological tradition one can also say that with everyday consciousness we can avoid the experience of "cognitive dissonance" (Festinger 1957), i.e. of contradictory perceptions.

Within adult education the question of everyday consciousness is quite central in that if the participants are to learn anything other than knowledge and skills that are an extension of what they already know and can do, as a rule a thematisation or transgression is necessary. This is intellectually and emotionally demanding and therefore presupposes both strong motivation and a situation or context that contains such a degree of social security that one dares to "lower one's defences". It is obvious that the school culture in general, the form of teaching and not least the teacher as a person are of great importance in this connection.

Identity defence

Identity defence is another type of defence that has been more generally developed in late modern society. As a general psychological phenomenon, the development of personal identity is linked to the individualisation that in earlier centuries, accompanied the transition from the old feudal society to the more modern industrialised and capitalist society. It has to do with experiencing oneself as a unique individual and the experience of how one is experienced by others. Identity is typically formed in the years of youth, and the "classic" perception of the concept was developed by the American psychologist and psychoanalyst, Erik H. Erikson, in connection with his analysis of the psychology of the phases of youth (Erikson 1968). However, it is a characteristic of late modernity that identity development to a lesser extent finishes with a fixed identity formation. The consciousness of the swift pace of change in late modernity and the demand for readiness for change bring with them tendencies for the development of so-called "multiple" identities, or perhaps rather the creation of a limited "core identity", supplemented by a layer of flexibility (cf. Illeris 2003b).

However, it is still characteristic of most adults in our society that their "adulthood" psychologically is precisely linked to a fixed and stable identity embedded in vocation and education, in familial relations and, perhaps, also in e.g. political or religious convictions. Such an identity, developed in the course of many years, usually implies that an identity defence has also been established, i.e. that one has developed mental barriers that can catch influences that could threaten the established identity. Such identity defence precisely finds expression in adults in learning and educational situations aimed at change, retraining or personal development.

For example, if for 10–15 years or more one has had a certain job and has experienced oneself as well-functioning and well-qualified in that context, and one suddenly finds that one is unemployed – not because one is not good enough, but because the company is cutting down, production is moved to another country, or the work is automatised – then one enters a situation where, against one's will, one must break down the existing identity and build up a new one, i.e. one is faced with a demand for a transformative learning process.

This is the background today, in many different forms, of a great number of the participants in adult education, and to the extent that they do not fully acknowledge and accept the situation, it will be a case of identity defence which not infrequently – and for the slightly older and in particular male participants – can prove an enormous obstacle to the intended learning processes.

But it is also the case, to a less pronounced degree, for many other participants in adult education who have not completely accepted that the education in which they find themselves is appropriate or necessary for them.

Active and passive resistance

Although it is not always so easy to distinguish in practice, there is a fundamental difference between mental defence and *mental resistance*. While defence is something that is built up or developed and lies ready to deal with certain types of influence, resistance is something with which one reacts when one encounters influences or situations that seem objectionable or threatening or which in some other way are so unacceptable that one neither can nor is willing to put up with them. One could also say that while defence is typically aimed at the mental acquisition processes of learning, resistance is to a higher degree aimed at the social and societal interaction process of learning.

For this reason, defence is also something that generally gets in the way of relevant learning, while to a high degree resistance in itself can imply or promote learning, and can even be the motive force in extremely far-reaching and transgressing learning processes (cf. Illeris 2002). In some cases there may be both defence and resistance at the same time that can make the situation more complicated, not least for the learner.

Active resistance to learning as a mental way of functioning is usually already established in early childhood in situations where one of necessity must learn to limit and control one's behaviour and activities, but it probably is most markedly something that belongs to the period of youth and can typically play a very important role in the identity formation described in the above. By means of resistance, for example, decisive development and acknowledgement of one's own viewpoints, possibilities and limitations can take place.

In adult education, active resistance is probably less frequent, but on the other hand it is typically less tentative and clearer, sometimes almost unshakeable, in form. Maybe precisely through some challenging learning processes during the years of youth, the adult has landed on some viewpoints, convictions and patterns of reaction that form elements of a more consistent identity. The borderline between resistance and defence can, in this way, become even subtler, but in general the starting point of resistance is more conscious and deliberate in nature, while to a greater extent defence functions on automatic pilot. Therefore, in principle new learning can also indirectly form part of resistance while defence must be broken down or transgressed if significant new learning is to take place.

On the other hand, *passive resistance* is more widespread in adult education and can be expressed in very many different ways that can be irritating and inappropriate in a learning context. The Danish psychologists, Peter Berliner and Jens Berthelsen, have termed the phenomenon, *passive aggression*, and have pointed out that it contains "a protest and an energy to want something else" (Berliner & Berthelsen 1989) – which again is different from defence which precisely does not want anything else. But in some cases active resistance is withheld. The challenge is not found sufficiently important to throw oneself into active protest. Perhaps one feels disempowered in advance, which causes the resistance to find expression in various indirect ways. The consistent reaction is, naturally, that one stops and drops out of the education programme. But in many cases this will lead to some totally unacceptable and insurmountable consequences and then instead one simply mentally steps back and becomes indifferent. Nonetheless one can often not resist making irritated and irritating remarks or in other ways creating a disturbance, more or less demonstratively.

It is important here to maintain that passive resistance actually also contains an important learning potential, and that it can help to resolve the situation and contribute to important learning processes if the resistance can be brought out into the open. On the other hand this often presupposes that the teachers or other participants can see through and identify the situation as a type of passive resistance, and have the courage and the energy to possibly confront it.

References

Erikson, Erik H. (1968): *Identity, Youth and Crises*. New York: Norton.
Freud, Anna (1942 [1936]): *The Ego and the Mechanisms of Defence*. London: Hogarth Press.
Illeris, Knud (2002): *The Three Dimensions of Learning: Contemporary learning theory in the tension field between the cognitive, the emotional and the social*. Leicester, UK: NIACE. (2004 also Malabar, Florida: Krieger Publishing Company).
Illeris, Knud (2003a): Towards a Contemporary and Comprehensive Theory of Learning. *International Journal of Lifelong Education*, 22 (4), 411–421.
Illeris, Knud (2003b): Learning, Identity and Self-Orientation in Youth. *Young – Nordic Journal of Youth Research*, 11 (4), 357–376.
Illeris, Knud (2004): Transformative Learning in the Perspective of a Comprehensive Learning Theory. *Journal of Transformative Education*, 2, 79–89.
Jarvis, Peter (1992): *Paradoxes of Learning: On Becoming an Individual in Society*. San Francisco: Jossey-Bass.
Jarvis, Peter – Holford, John – Griffin, Colin (1998): *The Theory and Practice of Learning*. London: Kogan Page.
Leithäuser, Thomas (1976): *Formen des Alltagsbewusstseins*. Frankfurt a.M.: Campus. [The forms of everyday consciousness].
Leithäuser, Thomas (1992): Teorien om hverdagsbevidstheden i dag. *Unge Pædagoger*, 7–8, 45–56. [The theory of everyday consciousness today].
Mager, Robert F. (1961): On the Sequencing of Instructional Content. Southern University Press: *Psychological Reports*, 9, 405–413.

PART IV

VARIOUS LEARNING APPROACHES TO EDUCATION

CHAPTER 13

THE ORGANISATION OF STUDIES AT ROSKILDE UNIVERSITY

The concept, practice and problems of project organisation

Ever since the start in 1972, it has been a significant part of the image and practice of Roskilde University that studies are primarily carried out by participation in projects. Traditional academic activities such as courses, lectures, and seminars are regarded only as supplementary.

When curricula are being designed, this fundamental idea has usually been applied so that a minimum of 50% of the students' time should be spent on project work. Students themselves generally say that they spend some 70–80% of their active study time on projects, as they usually regard project work as more important and profitable than other study activities.

Roskilde University and the Danish tradition of project education

When the university was being planned in the early 1970s, the concept of project work was rather a catchword of the students' movement and a small group of educational theorists. In practice only a few provisional experiments had been carried out with this form of study. However, during the first stormy years of the university's existence a more coherent design and a set of methodological guidelines were worked out in theory and practice.

Today it is possible to distinguish a significant Danish tradition of project work in education which, with Roskilde University as a central point of reference, has now spread to almost all sections of the Danish educational system from elementary school to university level, and from basic courses for unskilled workers to advanced academic educational activities.

There are many reasons for this development, and many conflicts along the way, but without doubt an important factor has been the underlying development in the demand for what are termed "soft" qualifications, such as flexibility, independence, responsibility, the ability to cooperate and the ability to think analytically. Although it can be difficult to prove, it is broadly accepted that project work is superior to more traditional educational activities for promoting qualifications of this kind. And it is by now a well-established fact that, despite all difficulties, graduates from Roskilde University are doing at least as well on the labour market as graduates from other universities.

The concepts of project work and experiential learning

In an international context it is, however, important to emphasise that the Danish concept of project work cannot be identified either as just an extended kind of group work or as a special sort of exercise. The concept is closely related to a line of educational thinking and philosophy, in Danish identified as "experiential learning", which although similar to, is not the same as, learning by doing, or learning by experience. "Experiential learning" deals with learning processes as integrated aspects of the individual's total development, influenced by personal history, life conditions, situation, interests, motivation, etc. A central issue in project work is, thus, the student's participation in and responsibility for all important decisions in the qualification process.

Methodologically, project work is based on three fundamental theoretical principles.

Problem orientation – in contrast to traditional subject or discipline orientation – indicates that the starting point for the work is a problem or a set of problems. The content of the studies will be whatever material, investigation or theory that can contribute to understanding, illuminating or solving the problem. This principle also implies that effective, valid and durable learning is established by dealing with problems. Furthermore, all problems, also of a social and personal nature, are taken seriously.

Participant direction indicates that the studies should be directed jointly by students, tutors and other relevant participants. While all participants are equal, they have different functions and responsibilities. This makes the role of the tutor particularly demanding. He or she has a specific professional responsibility, but must act in agreement with the students and has no means of forcing them to accept his or her suggestions or standpoints.

Exemplarity indicates that the problems and content of the material chosen should be representative of a larger and essential area of reality. Through deep and serious work on a genuine problem of personal interest, the underlying structures of the problem area are uncovered enabling students to generalise their insight into new contexts.

The phases of a typical project

The course of a typical project can be broken down into a series of phases, but it must be understood that this implies an analytic reduction. It should also be realised that all phases will not in fact occur in all projects, that the order may be changed, and that it is possible to be in two or more phases at the same time or to return to past phases. With these reservations, we usually distinguish the following eight phases.

The introduction, which includes an introduction to the project method, to regulations and practical conditions. It is also an introduction to the subject area in question (which should be appealing and provocative) and, if necessary, a social introduction. Sometimes these functions can be united in a pilot project, which is a short, well-supervised and well-prepared project that should raise more problems than it resolves. By the end of the introductory phase the framework and conditions of the following project process should be clear to all participants.

The choice of theme or subject of the project which is, as a rule, also the phase where project groups are formed. The theme should be chosen in accordance with the principle of exemplarity so that it involves the commitment of the students and a relevant content area at the same time. Groups are usually formed on the basis of interest in content. But simultaneously, and quite justifiably, social preferences and aversions also play an important role.

Problem formulation. In this phase the specific problems that the project is to deal with should be formulated precisely – a process that will also uncover a lot of bias and differences in the project group, forcing the group to make a series of fundamental decisions. Problem formulation is a very significant issue in the project method, and it is important that both students and tutor pay the utmost attention to all details in the formulation so that it can function as a common statement of what precisely the group has agreed on.

Practical planning, which includes planning time, delegation of tasks, internal and external appointments, etc. In this connection the planning of fixed and regular internal evaluations has proved to be of great importance.

The investigation phase: the lengthy central phase during which, in order to probe the problem area selected, an attempt is made to establish ever-increasing understanding, to relate it to relevant theory, etc. In this phase it is particularly important to have a high degree of internal coordination, to write down all agreements, decisions, references, extracts of relevant literature, ideas, drafts, etc.

Another important feature is communication between the project group and the tutor. The tutor must find the difficult balance of providing professional guidance without forcing the group to accept his or her own interests or points of view.

The product phase, in which a report is produced, in writing or any other suitable medium. In this phase time will usually be of the essence, and the group must find out how to dispose, coordinate and produce the report in the most expedient and effective way possible, which is often a hard but very useful learning process.

Product evaluation, which always includes an internal evaluation by other students and tutors and, in most cases, an external examination also. The internal evaluation is important both as feedback to the group and as preparation for the external examination – and it is also important to learn how to evaluate and give feedback to other groups. The external examination is quite different from the usual kind of inquiry, because its starting point is the students' report and not a randomly chosen topic from the curriculum. It usually takes the form of a group examination with individual grading.

Post-evaluation, which is a final internal statement of the benefit and consequences of the project for every single member of the group. Although this phase takes place after the official termination of the project, it is important to carry it through seriously as, especially from the point of view of what the students learn and gain by participation in the project, it is a very profitable phase.

The crucial points in the project process are the problem formulation at the outset and making a manifest product as a conclusion.

Between these two requirements, the central content work is carried out and has its meaning and motivation. This is why the participation in and commitment of the students to decisions made in these phases are so important.

It is also important to mention that the first four phases, which deal with preparing and establishing a basis for the investigation, are equally important and necessary for the process. For beginners at least, this may very well take up one third or even half of the project period – which is often a problem for an inexperienced and impatient tutor. But in project work a considerable part of the transcending learning processes, which are so decisive for the development of the "soft" qualifications, take place in the phases where the group jointly find out what to investigate together, how to do it, and why.

Projects, problem orientation, and interdisciplinarity

The fundamental principle of problem orientation indicates that projects very often must be interdisciplinary, as the problems of reality do not accept any boundaries of disciplines. Therefore it is quite obvious that Roskilde University also has interdisciplinarity as one of its fundamentals, especially in the two years of Basic Studies, but also to a great extent in the study programmes for higher degrees and in various research prográmmes. Interdisciplinarity is, like project studies, an integrated part of our image, and a trademark of our graduates on the labour market.

But although the concepts of problem orientation and interdisciplinarity are closely connected, they are not the same. While problem orientation refers to the process of studies, interdisciplinarity refers to their content, and it is quite possible to conduct problem-oriented studies within the boundaries of a discipline, or to accomplish interdisciplinarity without problem orientation.

Historically, scientific knowledge has been organised systematically within the framework, theories and methods of established disciplines, and if students are not very professional and well-guided in their studies, a fully interdisciplinary approach could easily lead to lack of orientation. Without a command of essential areas of disciplines, it is difficult to develop a reasonable academic standard.

So the issue is not a choice between problem orientation and knowledge of disciplines, but rather how to combine them, which is also the logical basis of interdisciplinarity. And this has without doubt been the central structural challenge at Roskilde University ever since the idea of having no disciplines at all was abandoned during the first years of our existence.

As we maintain project work and problem orientation as the fundamental and principal elements of curriculum for reasons of motivation and adequate qualification, the ideal solution would be to place the disciplines exactly when maximally motivated by the course of the projects. However, many years of practice have taught us that this ideal can be realised only in a few and very fortunate situations.

The solution, then, is generally a compromise, where discipline-oriented courses are placed when they are expected to be most relevant for the students, and at the same time students are encouraged to direct their choice of projects in accordance with the succession of courses. As a supplement it may be possible to organise ad hoc courses on selected topics, but shortage of resources has very much reduced this possibility.

On the whole it must be admitted that it has not been possible within the existing resource framework to find satisfactory solutions to the combination of project work and discipline-oriented studies – and failure to do so can be regarded as the most pressing structural problem of the Roskilde University curriculum design at present.

A higher degree of flexibility and familiarity with students' needs by the teaching staff might be another way to deal with the problem, and some small steps have been taken in this direction.

However, even with this problem more or less unsolved, it is a fact that our curriculum has proved fully competitive with regard to attracting students to the university, the development of a favourable environment, and the demand for our graduates.

CHAPTER 14

PROJECT WORK IN UNIVERSITY STUDIES
Background and current issues

First of all, it is important for me to tell you that it is *great* to be standing here today as the first keynote speaker at the 25th anniversary conference of the university which has been an important part of my life and my very identity for these 25 years.

In the rather short time I have at my disposal, I hope not only to be able to make an interesting contribution to understanding the ideas and dilemmas of the concept of project work, but also to communicate to you some of my enthusiasm about this concept and my pride in this university, the first in the world to launch and develop project work as the primary activity of studies at university level.

My speech will be an introduction to the concept of project education and the way it has been practised at Roskilde University during these 25 years. It will also be an introduction to the present situation and some issues and problems which seem to be of special interest today. For those of you who are staff or students at the university, much of this will be well-known, but I think it is important that everybody, in particular our many foreign visitors, shares this common knowledge when we discuss and perhaps develop the concept of project work through all the sessions of the conference.

I should like to

1. briefly outline the *background* of Roskilde University,
2. explain and briefly discuss the *main features of our concept and practice of project work,*
3. identify some important *challenges* in the present situation, and
4. discuss *how we best can meet these challenges.*

As I have had to prepare a manuscript, but on the other hand hate to hold a speech or lecture by just reading aloud, I shall try to practice a sort of compromise, sticking to the manuscript for the more substantial parts of the content, and talking freely when it comes to examples or more personal comments.

Background

The background to the concept of project work being adopted in 1972 was closely connected with the establishment of the new university, and both were due to what might be called a happy convergence of a number of societal factors and forces.

The immediate cause was an explosion in numbers of university students. In the course of a very few years, student numbers at Copenhagen University had doubled, creating an urgent demand for another university to be established in the region. At the same time, however, a few years after the 1968 student revolution, the need for renewal and an alternative was felt in many circles involved in higher education policy. Five different forces can be identified in this process:

The Social Democratic Party represented, without doubt, the strongest of these forces. The party was then in government and the central theme of its educational policy was equality of opportunity: working class children should have the same opportunities for university education as children of the middle and upper classes. If this was to be possible, it would be necessary to break down exclusive academic traditions and to find new ways.

But there were also quite a few people of influence in *trade and industry* who were of the opinion that the way university studies were organised was old-fashioned and inefficient, not at all geared to mass education. This opinion was shared by important figures in *the central administration* of the Ministry of Education.

The most dynamic force, however, was *the student movement*, which at that time was very strong and radical and extremely self and politically conscious. The movement established a kind of cooperation with a handful of progressive *educational researchers* who referred to the theories of John Dewey, Jean Piaget, and also Oskar Negt (who is now to become an Honorary Doctor of Roskilde University).

It was the students and the educational researchers who launched and developed the concept of project work as the appropriate answer to the challenges I have outlined, and I don't think that this could have been done at that time in any country other than Denmark. It may surprise some of you, but as I see it there is no doubt that the deeply-rooted tradition of the educational thinking of Grundtvig – who some of our foreign guests may not even know by name – constituted the extraordinary background for this.

However, the decisive arguments were of quite another nature. They concerned up-to-date qualification of university graduates, which included the ability to perform independent analysis and problem-solving, training in cooperation involving complex issues, critical attitudes, political awareness and responsibility, professional commitment and overview, or, to put it briefly: a modern profile and the ability to continue to meet the current demands of academic endeavour.

So, the new university was built, 25 kilometres from the centre of Copenhagen and close to the historical town of Roskilde, the site of Denmark's first capital some 800 years ago.

It was decided that the dominant features of the new university would be *project work* as the major form of study and, during the first two years of study, *interdisciplinary basic education* in one of the broad areas of either the humanities, the social sciences or the natural sciences. Physically, the university would be arranged in what we call "*houses*", the small buildings you see on campus, each consisting of offices for 6 teachers and 1 secretary, group rooms for 9 groups of 7 students, an AV workshop, and a canteen.

This was a revolution indeed, and the staff and students who came to the university then also regarded themselves as extremely revolutionary. Politically, this led to much controversy and many confrontations with society "outside" as well as with the academic and political establishment. On one occasion, in 1976, the very survival of the university was secured by a majority of only one vote in the Danish Parliament, while 20,000 students from all over the country were demonstrating outside.

The concept and practice of project work

But throughout these chaotic years, the practice and theory of project work was established and steadily developed.

The basic principles of project work, in my interpretation, are those of *problem orientation, exemplarity* and what we call *participant direction*; the secondary principles are those of *interdisciplinarity* and *group work*.

The main process features are the *introduction*, the phase of *forming student groups around self-selected topics, choosing and formulating problems* within these topics at the outset of the project, *planning* the process, *investigating* the problems selected empirically and theoretically by employing correct scholarly methods, *producing a written report* as output and a basis for *internal evaluation*, and the final *examination*.

In actual fact, during the first two years of Roskilde University's existence, we worked out how to implement projects in practice, the theoretical framework comprising societal background and necessity, and psychological arguments concerning learning and motivation.

It may be somewhat surprising to observe that the fundamental principles, understanding and forms of practice established during the early years have survived all attacks and reorganisation and still function as the foundation on which our activities build.

Quite naturally, there has been ongoing discussion of many issues such as the status of problem orientation versus interdisciplinarity, the question of whether interdisciplinarity presupposes knowledge of the disciplines involved or can be approached directly. Practical problems have also been the subject of continuous discussion. These include the role of the teacher as consultant, instructor, adviser or something in-between, and whether it is possible to function as a teacher in relation to projects that are more or less outside one's own academic field.

However, as both concept and practice, in my opinion the main features of project work at university level have not undergone any essential changes since they were drawn up during the first years of Roskilde University's existence.

Some important challenges

But many other things around us have undergone significant change and today, on our twenty-fifth anniversary, we are facing new situations in some important contexts which challenge the established practice and understanding of the concept of project work. I should like to outline three such changes and briefly discuss how to meet their challenges.

1. The first and most substantial change is the *change in our resources*. Over the last 25 years our resources have been cut many times and in many different ways. The most telling illustration of this is the present teacher-student ratio. When we started in 1972, there was one teacher for every 10.5 students. Today in the humanities and the social sciences, this ratio is 1 to 27 and in some cases as high as 1 to 30! In the 'houses' that I mentioned the original allocation was 63 students and 6 teachers, but today there are usually more than 100 students, 3–4 teachers, and a booking system for the group rooms.

    It is evident that we cannot continue in this way without substantial changes. For students it has resulted in severe cut-downs in project supervision, which many staff find quite unacceptable. For teachers it has meant that in order to continue to provide the students with the supervision they should have, very many of us spend most of the time when we should be doing research in teaching, and conduct our research, more or less sufficiently, outside official working hours.

2. The second challenge has been present all the time, but in some ways it seems to have gathered strength in recent years. It concerns the pressure from *traditional academic attitudes and standards* combined with pressure from a branch of *the political right-wing, back-to-basics movement*.

   In these circles, the project concept has always been regarded with suspicion: do the students really learn what they are supposed to? Behind the question is a quantitative idea of learning related to the ability to reproduce the contents of a fixed syllabus.

   It should be emphasised that when project work at university level was introduced 25 years ago, it was precisely in opposition to this idea of what learning should be. Already then, a quarter of a century ago, this idea had proved inadequate in relation to the qualification demands of contemporary society.

   However, it is obvious that this contrast between project work and traditional teaching does not come down to a question of either/or. A balance must be found between project work and more traditional study activities such as courses and lectures.

   In the original provisions, this balance was formulated in such a way that project work should be the primary activity. Courses and lectures were considered additional. We interpreted this to mean that teacher-directed activities should never exceed 50% of the study time; as students were generally more engaged in projects than in the other, more traditional activities, in reality they spent much more time working on their projects.

   But at present the pendulum is swinging back. Faced with pressure from the rearmament of traditional subjects and disciplines, and being wary of national and international evaluations and ratings which are not by any means based on an understanding of the concept of project-based studies and are thus incapable of measuring their advantages, the Ministry of Education has imposed the opposite measure on us. Now projects may not exceed 50% of the study time.

   Although many students and teachers are doing their best to cope with this totally arbitrary rule, it is damaging in the long term because whenever there is disagreement or discussion, the official rule will function as a standard.

3. The third important challenge has to do with *students' attitudes and consciousness*. In general, young people in the 1990s are very different from the young people of the 70s. In connection with project work, the best illustration of this point is in relation to the kinds of problems students tend to address.

   One of the good old standards always was that for a problem to be suitable, it should be an objective problem that exists and has significance in the real world. It should simultaneously be subjective or personal, engaging the student and providing the drive and motivation to cope with and, eventually, solve the problem.

   It was usually not difficult to formulate such problems. There was a multitude of them and important societal problems were very often also regarded and experienced as personal problems.

   To some extent this seems to have changed: personal experience has come increasingly into focus. Students of today tend to be more personal in their interests, and this is an important source of motivation, creativity, and authenticity in the projects. But sometimes it also implies that it is difficult for the students to explain the general significance of the problems with which they choose to deal. When this occurs, the principle of exemplarity is invalidated. The problem chosen does not function psychologically as an example of a field of reality and, therefore, what is learned is limited to the example itself and cannot be generalised into a broader area.

If this is the case, the traditionalists I mentioned before are – suddenly – right in their assertion that the studies are too narrow, and the authorities are right in limiting the time spent on projects.

How to meet the challenges

Now, if we take these three challenges together, we can perceive the outlines of a situation where students are becoming more uncertain in choosing appropriate problems for their project work, teacher resources are too limited to provide the necessary support, and we are slowly moving towards the unfortunate and unacceptable picture that our critics have been drawing and have issued warnings against for so many years.

But we have certainly not arrived at this point yet. In general, projects function as well as they ever did, and the problems I have outlined are counter-balanced by other developments. For example, many of the problems of the first years have now been overcome and many useful routines have been developed. So there is no reason to give way to the challenges I have described. On the contrary, we must face them and use an opportunity such as the present one provided by our anniversary and this conference to examine our situation carefully and honestly to find ways of coping with the challenges and achieving better conditions for our ideas to be realised.

In my opinion, we must refine the concept of project work in step with the challenges we face. For instance, we must return to the principle of exemplarity and analyse its appropriate understanding today and how to ensure its application in practice without limiting student influence. We must also discover how we can qualify both ourselves and new teachers to be good project supervisors within the time limits we can obtain and in relation to the students of today. And, of course, we must struggle continuously for better resources and at least try to achieve the same levels and ratios as the other Danish universities.

It is my impression that a movement to take up these challenges has already begun. During the last years, quite a number of books about project work at universities have been published, many of them written by authors with experience from Roskilde University itself, as teachers or as students. In our University Quality project (in Danish called the UNIPÆD project), which deals with a broad range of our educational problems and issues, a number of booklets have been published (some of them also in English) concerning specific problems of our practice, and more are to appear in the coming months. I certainly also hope that this conference will contribute to increased attention, at national and international level, to the concept of project work and its continuous development.

As long as we are convinced that this concept is not only competitive but that it also develops more up-to-date qualifications better suited to meeting the demands of today's world and to transcending its limits while contributing to building up a better, more sustainable society, as long as we have reason to believe this, we are part of an important experiment. We also have a mission: to disseminate our ideas and our experience and work together with institutions that are trying in many different ways to break through the ineffective and oppressive sides of academic life and education.

Therefore, we are eager to use this conference to discuss and to learn from the exchange of ideas and experiences of all participants. We welcome you and wish you all a good and inspiring conference.

CHAPTER 15

LEARNING, EXPERIENCE AND PERSONAL DEVELOPMENT

'From experience you shall learn' goes an old Danish folk expression, and there is no doubt that in everyday language, in both Danish and English, experience is reckoned to be better and more profound than 'ordinary learning', having another dimension of personal significance and involving personal commitment. But experience is also a central concept in learning theory, and in the following I will set out how and with which criteria this concept can be used as a common framework for understanding learning, which, in an important way, both covers and brings together the three dimensions I have discussed in detail in the preceding chapters.

I must immediately emphasise – as in section 5.2 – that I use the word 'experience' in a more demanding and qualified sense than it is given in everyday English, more so even than as used by Kolb in his book *Experiential Learning* (Kolb 1984) and many other researchers and debaters in this field. My use of the concepts 'experience' and 'experiential learning' goes beyond distinguishing between the immediate perception and the elaborated comprehension; it implies also that the process does not relate only to cognitive learning (as is, for example, the case in Kolb's work), but covers all three dimensions of learning.

It is this book's contention that all learning includes these dimensions to some degree, although the weighting can be rather unbalanced in some contexts. When I claim that experience is immediately understood as something other, and something more, than ordinary learning, I am, however, referring to a qualitative difference. On the other hand, it is not possible and not in accordance with the nature of learning, to make a sharp distinction between what is experience and what is 'ordinary' learning.

The concept of experience I am setting out here does not, therefore, solely concern the notion that all three dimensions are involved, for they are all in principle always involved, but all three dimensions must also be of subjective significance for the learner in the context. Experience has important elements of content and knowledge, i.e. we acquire or understand something that we perceive to be important for ourselves. Experience also has a considerable incentive element, i.e. we are committed motivationally and emotionally to the learning taking place. And finally, experience has an important social and societal element, i.e. we learn something that is not only of significance to us personally, but is something that also concerns the relationship between ourselves and the world we live in. Thus experience is set out as the central concept in the learning conception of this presentation: experience is characterised by incorporating the three dimensions spanned by the learning conception presented here in an important way.

It is, however, important to further qualify the experience concept, which I do in the following by referring to the two most important approaches that form the basis for the perception of the concept of experience as it is used in Danish pedagogy: first, the progressive approach developed in the USA in the early 1900s, particularly by the previously mentioned philosopher and pedagogue John Dewey. And, second, the approach of German sociologist Oskar Negt, also mentioned previously, who works in extension of the Critical Theory of the Frankfurt School and has played a large role as a theoretical reference for the development of experiential pedagogy in Denmark (see Webb and Nielsen 1996).

While the majority of Dewey's development of pedagogical practice and theory took place in the first decades of the twentieth century, he dealt with the concept of experience later in a short work entitled *Experience and Education* (Dewey 1965 [1938]) based on a series of summarised lectures. Dewey has a broad definition of the concept of experience in accordance with its everyday meaning. We experience things all the time, but what is important in pedagogical terms is – as I have also stated before – the quality of the experiences:

> to discriminate between experiences that are worthwhile educationally and those that are not.. . . . Does not the principle of regard for individual freedom and for decency and kindliness of human relations come back in the end to the conviction that these things are tributary to a higher quality of experience on the part of a greater number than are methods of repression and coercion or force? . . . An experience arouses curiosity, strengthens initiative, and sets up desires and purposes that are sufficiently intense to carry a person over dead places in the future . . . (and not) operate so as to leave a person arrested on a low plane of development, in a way which limits capacity for growth.
> (Dewey 1965 [1938], pp. 33, 34, 38 and 37–38)

Thus, for Dewey, the criteria for what constitutes experiences are based in general humanism and a somewhat unclear growth concept and are thus on a more general level, although perhaps, nonetheless, not so different from my reference to the three learning dimensions. More concretely, Dewey, however, also stresses two integrated principles or dimensions as being central to upbringing, namely the principles of continuity and interaction.

> The principle of continuity of experience means that every experience both takes up something from those which have gone before and modifies in some way the quality of those which come after. . . . Interaction means [that] a transaction [is] taking place between an individual and what, at the same time, constitutes his environment.
> (Dewey 1965 [1938], pp. 35 and 43)

Despite the reference to interaction, however, Dewey's concept of experience has often been criticised as individualistic and lacking a societal dimension. And it is precisely in the societal area that Negt's concept of experience exceeds Dewey's in decisive ways.

Negt's concept of experience is mainly dealt with in the book *Public Sphere and Experience* (Negt and Kluge 1993 [1972]), where it appears in a broad civilisation-critical context, which revolves round the question of the opportunities for the working class to experience their own situation and opportunities in our present society. The concept of experience is thus only directly defined through an oft-quoted and fairly intricate statement from the German philosopher Hegel (1770–1831): 'The dialectic process which consciousness executes on itself – on its knowledge as well as on its object – in the sense that out of it the new and true object arises, is precisely, what is termed experience' (Hegel 1967 [1807], p. 142).

With this reference Negt draws on a long philosophical tradition leading from Kant, through Hegel, to the Frankfurt School. But although the approaches are very different, the distance from Dewey is not, in my view, all that great as far as the concept of experience itself is concerned. What Hegel calls the dialectic process which consciousness executes on itself is the same as what Dewey is attempting to capture through his claim of continuity. And what Hegel calls the dialectical process on its knowledge as well as on its object is present in Dewey's claim of interaction.

This can also be seen as that which is dealt with in this book as, respectively, the internal psychological, and the external social and societal partial processes in learning – by which means the central point in Hegel's statement is that both these processes are dialectic in nature, i.e. they take the form of interplay or tension that may lead to a synthesis, an overlapping agreement. In the internal psychological processes, the dialectic lies between the psychological structures developed previously and influences from the environment (see the approaches of Piaget and Ausubel, section 4.2). In the external interaction processes, the dialectic lies in the interaction between the individual and the environment.

However, a general definition of the Negt approach to experience that is both more accessible and more complete can be found in the work of the Danish educational researcher Henning Salling Olesen:

> Experience is the process whereby we as human beings, individually and collectively consciously master reality, and the ever-living understanding of this reality and our relation to it. Experiences in the plural exist, as in everyday language, but they are to be understood as partial products of this process. Experience is thus a subjective process as it is seen from the point of view of the person experiencing. It is also a collective process because when we experience as individuals we also do so through a socially structured consciousness. It is, finally, an active, critical and creative process where we both see and adapt. ... This concept of experiences is inherited from the German sociologist Oskar Negt ...
>
> (Olesen 1989 [1985], p. 8)

It is interesting to note that despite the explicit reference to Negt, this definition could have been written, word for word, by Dewey, for this indirectly shows that the difference between Dewey's and Negt's conceptions of experience does not lie in the actual nature of the experience itself, but in the question of how the current societal structures actually affect the formation of the experience.

To quote Salling Olesen again, in the Negt conception it is all about the fact that 'reality is not immediately apparent' (Olesen 1989, p. 21), i.e. that there are central societal factors that cannot be immediately experienced, such as, for example, the relationship between utility value and exchange value, or the reduction of the workforce from a general human potential to being an item that can be bought and sold on the market. Although the central capitalistic structures are man-made and therefore may also be changed, they are experienced as natural, like a kind of 'second nature', and thus the entire experiential base is displaced.

In general, it is first and foremost important to maintain the totality of the concept of experience in relation to learning. The concept comprises all aspects of learning in principle, including internal psychological acquisition processes and social interactive processes, content-related aspects and incentive aspects, and all forms of learning and forms of interaction. But for learning to be described as experiential in the way this concept has been set up here, various specific qualitative criteria must be fulfilled.

First, the learning must be of considerable subjective significance with regard to the content, incentive and interaction learning dimensions.

Second, the learning must be part of a coherent process – there must be continuity, as Dewey puts it. Even if we focus exclusively on single experiences, it only makes sense to use the expression experiential learning when the single event can be understood in the context of earlier experiences and future opportunities for experience, for only through this can the single experience gain its significance. Any form of 'building block thinking' that fails to take this into consideration can be said to have misunderstood what the concept of experience is basically about. (Thus, we also encounter a difference in relation to the concept of learning as such, for in some cases it can be possible and meaningful to talk of learning as a more isolated phenomenon.)

Third, the interaction process between the individual and the surroundings must be of such a nature that the individual can be said to be a subject in the situation, i.e. that he or she is present and is self-aware. Whether that person behaves as such in that particular situation can obviously be hard to determine in practice. But in principle it is important to draw the line at situations in which the learner only plays a passive role and is uncommitted. It is not impossible to learn something in such a situation – there are plenty of examples in ordinary school teaching; but this kind of learning cannot be called experiential, for if you are not involved as a subject there will not actually be any mutual interaction process, but instead what is typically called a filling process – or 'banking' as Paulo Freire (1970) calls it.

Fourth, it is important that the formation of experience is always socially mediated. It does not occur in individual isolation, but of necessity requires a social context. Naturally this should not be understood as meaning that there cannot be occasions in which people gain their experiences alone, but for the very reason that it is a continuing process, the isolation is only momentary, and the context in which it takes place will always be socially marked.

Fifth, and finally, in Negt's conception at any rate, the influences from the environment that the interaction is concerned with must be such that they reflect or exemplify relevant societal, material and/or social structures. This is what lies in Negt's conception of 'the principle of exemplarity' or 'exemplary learning' (Negt 1971 [1968]; Christiansen 1999, pp. 60f.). Here, too, there can, in practice, naturally occur a limitation problem – a subject that I will not go into in more detail here, but will instead refer to fuller treatments of the form of project work (Illeris 1999).

In Denmark the concept of experience has come to play a central part in educational thinking since 'experiential pedagogy' crystallised after about 1980 as a kind of common term for a number of pedagogical endeavours and patterns of work that emphasise the formation of experience of the participants, understood as a total learning based on the requirements, problems and interests of the participants (see Webb and Nielsen 1996).

Throughout the 1970s there was a sparkling optimism and faith that new pedagogical creations would not only give pleasure to the participants and help them develop, giving them better qualifications more in tune with the times, but would also help to change society in a more liberating and democratic direction. A common slogan for a large part of these activities was that we should 'use the experiences of the participants as a starting point', and this particular statement was often understood as the maxim of experiential pedagogy. Another and slightly more open statement talked of 'connecting to the experiences of the participants', and in some cases it could be 'contributing to/preparing the formation of experience for the participants'.

In practice, however, the subject proved to be more complex – and on the basis of an analysis of three ambitious experiential pedagogical projects that were carried out around 1980 in primary schools, upper secondary schools, and basic vocational education, respectively, it could be quite clearly concluded that:

> ideal experiential pedagogical processes must be about the pupils' important, subjectively perceived problem areas, that are to be elaborated in a continuing experiential process based on their existing patterns of experience and governed by a forward-pointing action perspective.
>
> (Illeris 1984, p. 32)

Here it is probably the words 'problem areas' and 'action perspective' that are significant. The point was that looking back towards previous experiences is less interesting for pupils than looking forward towards new challenges and experiences. Therefore, the implementation of experiential pedagogy, in practice, had to build on fundamental principles of problem orientation, participant direction, exemplarity and solidarity – and when it was to take place within the framework of institutional education it could typically be done through the application of the pedagogical work pattern developed under the name project work (Illeris 1999).

At international level, since the 1970s the experience concept has been developed in English-speaking countries under the term 'Experiential Learning' and, in particular, Kolb's frequently mentioned book of this title published in 1984 led to widespread interest in the book, not least within the network called 'The International Consortium for Experiential Learning' (ICEL). This consortium was established in 1987 and every second or third year since it has convened large international conferences where at the beginning some of the key names were Australian David Boud, British Susan Weil and the previously mentioned Danny Wildemeersch (section 7.7) and Robin Usher (section 7.8).

Following the first conference, the book *Making Sense of Experiential Learning* (Weil and McGill 1989a) was published, and it quickly came to function as a kind of basic work for the network. In the introductory article, the editors characterise the network as the framework for four 'villages':

> Village One is concerned particularly with assessing and accrediting learning from life and work experience as the basis for creating new routes into higher education, employment and training opportunities, and professional bodies.
>
> Village Two focuses on experiential learning as the basis for bringing about change in the structures, purposes and curricula of post-school education.
>
> Village Three emphasizes experiential learning as the basis for group consciousness raising, community action and social change.
>
> Village Four is concerned with personal growth and development and experiential learning approaches that increase self-awareness and group effectiveness.
>
> (Weil and McGill 1989b, p. 3)

By means of this frame description and the village concept, Weil and McGill succeeded in creating a mode of understanding that could constitute a common platform for the variegated network in which there was room for the great differences, while, at the same time, all could find themselves. Moreover, with its starting point in the different fields of practice, the book clearly underlined the societal embedment of the network.

In another article in the same book David Boud pointed out three dimensions which, to varying degrees, are typical of all activities referring to the term Experiential Learning. These are a dimension concerning 'learner control', a dimension concerning the learner's 'involvement of self', and a dimension concerning 'correspondence of learning environment to real environment' (Boud 1989, p. 39).

Boud, moreover, pointed to four approaches to adult education where Experiential Learning especially has been in the picture as a way of liberating learning from traditional ties: first in connection with teaching technology rationalisations, especially in vocational education, with a view to avoiding superfluous activities – 'freedom from distraction'; second, in connection with self-directed learning processes related to American Malcolm Knowles's concept of 'andragogy' (Knowles 1970, 1973) – 'freedom as learners'; third in connection with student-centred education in the humanistic tradition inspired by Carl Rogers (Rogers 1969; see section 5.6) – 'freedom to learn'; fourth, and last, in connection with critical pedagogics and social action where, in the English-speaking countries, Paulo Freire is the great source of inspiration (Freire 1970; see section 7.7): 'freedom through learning' – (Boud 1989, pp. 40ff.).

Finally, in the same article Boud pointed out three teaching approaches within Experiential Learning, namely 'the individual-centred approach', 'the group-centred approach', and 'the project-centred approach' (Boud 1989, pp. 44ff.).

In so doing Boud placed the concept of Experiential Learning in its academic context and demonstrated its broad field of application. But, as in Weil and McGill, it is the concept and the activity of Experiential Learning which is placed in a societal and pedagogical context, while the understanding itself of what it is to experience, i.e. what lies behind the concept of 'experience', is not elaborated.

A more critical approach was launched by Danny Wildemeersch, who warned against the individualistic tendencies that can lie in the understanding of the concept, and underlined the significance of conversation and dialogue for learning gaining a social perspective (Wildemeersch 1989). British Avtar Brah and Jane Hoy also adopted a societal perspective and drew particular attention to the fact that Experiential Learning can easily become yet another contribution to favouring those who already are privileged at the expense of the less privileged (Brah and Hoy 1989).

Another couple of important collections of articles were published later (Wildemeersch and Jansen 1992; Boud *et al.* 1993), and while the network was moving in the direction of taking up learning conditions in the third world in particular, the concept of Experiential Learning has shifted from being something special to becoming, to a higher degree, an ordinary and generally accepted concept in international educational and learning-oriented literature.

A different and broader concept for holistic learning is 'personal development' or 'personality development'. Unlike experience it cannot be related to a single event or a brief course but concerns the effect of the total learning in a certain context over a certain period of time.

There are many definitions of 'personality', such as 'the person as a whole having different skills, dispositions and qualities, emotions and motives' (Hansen *et al.* 1997, p. 295), and it is typical here that it is about the whole viewed in relation to the qualities, or what we call characteristics, that cut across different divisions such as the learning dimensions. If, for example, one says that a person is 'tolerant', it will normally imply that this tolerance applies across many or all spheres, although perhaps with varying strength. It is thus something that is difficult to specify and measure, but which, on the other hand, plays a major role in life.

In terms of learning there is the particular aspect of personality and personal qualities that they are to some extent anchored in certain individual genetic predispositions – such as what was at one time understood by temperament. These predispositions develop and form through life's influences, however, so some learning is also occurring, but, as mentioned, typically in the form of more general, long-lasting and, as a rule, demanding processes that imply considerable personal efforts and thus presuppose a significant degree of motivation. Put in everyday terms, you only change your personality or substantial parts of it if you perceive that there are good grounds for doing so.

In learning – and particularly institutionalised learning within the educational system and working life – personal development, in general, and the development of specific types of personal qualities, have since the 1960s increasingly become an area of substantial interest and study.

There has been a distinct development in what workplaces require of their staff, where the demand for professional qualifications has gradually been supplemented, and partly overshadowed, by the demand for 'generic' qualifications that precisely have the character of personal qualities. Today this is extremely obvious from job advertisements in the press and is also confirmed by the dominant attitudes of personnel managers.

In connection with a research project on general qualifications I was involved in analysing these matters in greater detail (Andersen *et al.* 1994, 1996), and in the course of this work the current personal qualification requirements were summarised in the following categories:

- Intellectual qualifications, that typically cover definitions such as rational, systematic and analytical thinking, sociological imagination, problem solving, change of perspective and skills in diagnostics, evaluation, planning etc. – centring on the individual's capacity for rational behaviour.
- Perception qualifications, concerning precise sense perception, typically including precision in observation and interpretation – centring on what is defined as sensibility in academic terms.
- Self-control qualifications, covering definitions such as responsibility, reliability, perseverance, accuracy, ability to concentrate, quality and service orientation – centring on the individual's inclinations and capacity to act in accordance with general instructions.
- Individuality qualifications, typically covering definitions such as independence, self-confidence and creativity – centring on the individual's ability to act alone, especially in unforeseen situations.
- Social qualifications, covering definitions such as co-operation and communication abilities, congeniality and sociability – centring on the individual's ability to interact with others.
- Motivational qualifications, covering a range of definitions such as initiative, dynamism, drive, openness, keenness to learn, adaptability etc. – centring on the individual's potential to keep up with and contribute to the 'development'

(the much-used category 'flexibility' is often used as a group description for this sphere, but it also partially includes social qualifications).

(Illeris 1995, pp. 60–61)

What is characteristic of all these categories is that they cover all three learning dimensions but are weighted differently. In the motivational qualifications the incentive dimension is very important, for example, and the same is true of the self-control and individuality qualifications, although to a lesser degree. The main emphasis is on the content dimension in the intellectual qualifications and perception qualifications. The social qualifications clearly draw on the interaction dimension in particular.

With respect to the teaching and learning that can further the development of such personal qualifications, the project concluded that the academic and the general or personality elements in the practical organisation of education may be understood and treated as two aspects of the same thing:

> Briefly, education that is to strengthen general qualifications in a goal-directed way must be neither pure instruction, learning of skills or rote learning, nor pure personal development or therapy. It must on the contrary be organised in such a way that it combines a concrete, typical vocational or academic qualification with opportunities for expanding the participants' motivation to develop understanding, personality and identity.
>
> (Illeris *et al.* 1995, p. 188)

Altogether, development in society's qualification demands thus can be seen to prompt an educational effort for attempting the development of a very broad range of personal qualities by the organisation of teaching to combine a professional and a personality-oriented approach. In practice this typically occurs through problem-oriented and, to some extent, participant-directed projects with a concrete professional content that also involves, recalls and deals with relevant personal function spheres (Illeris *et al.* 1995; Andersen *et al.* 1996).

References

Andersen, Vibeke – Illeris, Knud – Kjærsgaard, Christian – Larsen, Kirsten – Olesen, Henning Salling – Ulriksen, Lars (1994): *Qualifications and Living People*. Roskilde: The Adult Education Research Group, Roskilde University.

Andersen, Vibeke – Illeris, Knud – Kjærsgaard, Christian – Larsen, Kirsten – Olesen, Henning Salling – Ulriksen, Lars (1996): *General Qualification*. The Adult Education Research Group, Roskilde University.

Boud, David (1989): Some Competing Tradition in Experiential Learning. In Susan Warner Weil and Ian McGill (eds): *Making Sense of Experiential Learning: Diversity in Theory and Practice*. Buckingham: Open University Press.

Boud, David – Cohen, Ruth – Walker, David (eds) (1993): *Using Experience for Learning*. Buckingham: Open University Press.

Brah, Avtar – Hoy, Jane (1989): Experiential Learning: A New Ortodoxy. In Susan Warner Weil and Ian McGill (eds): *Making Sense of Experiential Learning: Diversity in Theory and Practice*. Buckingham: Open University Press.

Christiansen, Frederik Voetmann (1999): Exemplarity and Educational Planning. In Henning Salling Olesen and Jens Højgaard Jensen (eds): *Project Studies*. Copenhagen: Roskilde University Press.

Dewey, John (1965 [1938]): *Experience and Education*. New York: Collier Books.

Freire, Paulo (1970): *Pedagogy of the Oppressed*. New York: Seabury.

Hansen, Mogens – Thomsen, Poul – Varming, Ole (1997): *Psykologisk-pædagogisk ordbog*. Copenhagen: Gyldendal, 11th edition, [Psychological-pedagogical dictionary].
Hegel, Georg Wilhelm Friedrich (1967 [1807]): *The Phemenology of Mind*. New York: Harper.
Illeris, Knud (1984): Erfaringer med erfaringspædagogikken. *Unge Pædagoger*, 2, 22–33. [Experiences of experiential pedagogy].
Illeris, Knud (1995): *Læring, udvikling og kvalificering*. Roskilde: The Adult Education Research Group, Roskilde University. [Learning, development and education].
Illeris, Knud (1999): Project Work in University Studies: Background and Current Issues. In Henning Salling Olesen and Jens Højgaard Jensen (eds): *Project Studies*. Copenhagen: Roskilde University Press.
Illeris, Knud – Andersen, Vibeke – Kjærsgaard, Christian – Larsen, Kirsten – Olesen, Henning Salling – Ulriksen, Lars (1995): *Almenkvalificering*. Copenhagen: Roskilde University Press. [General Qualification].
Knowles, Malcolm S. (1970): *The Modern Practice of Adult Education: Andragogy versus Pedagogy*. New York: Associated Press.
Knowles, Malcolm S. (1973): *The Adult Learner: A Neglected Species*. Houston, TX: Gulf Publishing.
Kolb, David A. (1984): *Experiential Learning: Experience as the Source of Learning and Development*. Englewood Cliffs, NJ: Prentice Hall.
Negt, Oskar (1971 [1968]): *Soziologisches Phantasie und exemplarisches Lernen*. Frankfurt a.M.: Europäische verlagsanstalt. [Sociological imagination and exemplary learning].
Negt, Oskar – Kluge, Alexander (1993 [1972]): *Public Sphere and Experience*. Minneapolis, MN: University of Minnesota Press.
Olesen, Henning Salling (1989 [1985]): *Adult Education and Everyday Life*. Roskilde: The Adult Education Research Group, Roskilde University.
Rogers, Carl R. (1969): *Freedom to Learn*. Columbus, OH: Charles E. Merrill.
Webb, Thomas – Nielsen, Jørgen Lerche (1996): Experiential Pedagogy. In Henning Salling Olesen and Palle Rasmussen (eds): *Theoretical Issues in Adult Education*. Copenhagen: Roskilde University Press.
Weil, Susan Warner – McGill, Ian (eds) (1989a): *Making Sense of Experiential Learning: Diversity in Theory and Practice*. Buckingham: Open University Press.
Weil, Susan Warner – McGill, Ian (eds) (1989b): A Framework for Making Sense of Experiential Learning. In Susan Warner Weil and Ian McGill (eds): *Making Sense of Experiential Learning: Diversity in Theory and Practice*. Buckingham: Open University Press.
Wildemeersch, Danny – Jansen, Theo (eds) (1992): *Adult Education, Experiential Learning and Social Change: The Postmodern Challenge*. Haag: VUGA.

CHAPTER 16

TRANSFORMATIVE LEARNING

Transformative and significant learning

The concept of *Transformative Learning* was launched in 1978 by Jack Mezirow, Professor of Adult Education at Teachers College, Columbia University, New York. He defined the term as learning which involves changes in meaning perspectives, frames of reference and habits of mind. The immediate background for this was an investigation of women's learning and liberation processes in community college re-entry programmes, inspired by Paulo Freire's work *Pedagogy of the Oppressed* (1970), about illiterate Brazilian rural workers, Jürgen Habermas's (1971 [1968]) theory of communicative action, and Roger Gould's (1978) psychiatric understanding of *Transformation, Growth and Change in Adult Life*.

It is worth noting that in 1951 the American humanistic psychologist, Carl Rogers (1969), had launched a similar concept of *significant learning*, which supplemented his notions of client-centred therapy and student-centred learning, and which he defined as learning involving change in the organization of the self. Rogers's approach never had the same impact as the later initiative by Mezirow, because social conditions only gradually made it appropriate and attractive to understanding learning in this way. But there are also some fundamental differences between the two approaches, and by comparing them, some important characteristics of Mezirow's thinking can be identified, which may have contributed to the latter's success.

There are two principal areas of difference between the two theorists. First, Rogers refers to the self, which is the psychological core of the person, as a whole, and includes cognitive, emotional and social dimensions, as well as the individual's understanding and experience of themselves; whereas Mezirow refers to individual meaning perspectives, which are principally cognitively-founded attitudes and understandings of the relationship between the person and their surroundings. Second, Rogers's understanding is part of a much broader psychological and theoretical conception of the person, while Mezirow's interest is focused more directly on specific learning processes. Mezirow's more focused approach has been part of the reason for the rapidly growing impact of Transformative Learning during the 1980s and 1990s as it has been reasonably easy to understand and follow for adult educators of all kinds, can be combined with many different types of learning content, and does not directly demand specific psychological qualifications to understand it.

The most comprehensive account of Mezirow's understanding of Transformative

Learning is given in his book *Transformative Dimensions of Adult Learning* (Mezirow, 1991), and also in a series of edited books by Mezirow and Associates (1990, 2000; Mezirow, Taylor and Associates, 2009). Other important milestones in the development and practice of Transformative Learning have been the start of the very ambitious AEGIS (Adult Education Guided Intensive Study) doctoral programme at Teachers College in 1981, the introduction of regular conferences on Transformative Learning since 1998, the publication of the *Journal of Transformative Education* since 2003, and the first Transformative Learning conference in Europe, in Athens, 2012.

A critique of Mezirow's conception

But, as the years have passed, there has emerged a growing dissatisfaction with Mezirow's conception and a desire to frame the concept in a more inclusive way. The most influential critique focuses on Mezirow's cognitive orientation and consequently his insufficient understanding of the emotional dimension of Transformative Learning. When people change their understandings and attitudes it usually involves much more than cognitive insight, and strong emotions are often important incentives. This objection to Mezirow's original programme of understanding has been made by many theorists, most significantly by Patricia Cranton and John Dirkx, who are both important figures in Transformative Learning debates and advocate a Jungian approach (Cranton, 2005 [1994]; Dirkx, 2006, 2012). This has been explicitly recognized by Mezirow (2006, 2009); but he has not since then suggested any other formulation or definition.

Another important critique, originally made by Stephen Brookfield, who was for many years Mezirow's colleague at Teachers College, is that Transformative Learning cannot take place and be understood independently of social and political conditions (e.g. Brookfield, 1987, 2000). Later Edmund O'Sullivan and his collaborators went further in this direction by developing a cosmological approach to Transformative Learning, including issues of sustainability (O'Sullivan et al., 2002; O'Sullivan, 2012). With regards to the relations between Transformative Learning and other kinds of learning, Illeris (2004, 2007, 2014) made a similar point. Transformative Learning is better understood and practised inside and as a part of a comprehensive theoretical framework of learning.

The importance of this insight has latterly and indirectly been confirmed by a growing realization that all learning which in any way goes beyond the remit of traditional classroom teaching can be claimed to be transformative, and thus has come to mean more or less the same as 'good learning' (Newman, 2012, 2014). Another indication that the concept has been weakened is when the organizers of the 11th Transformative Learning Conference in San Francisco, 2012 systematically referred to Transformative Learning not as a specific kind of learning but as a movement, more or less in line with other popular movements such as mindfulness or survival programmes.

There seems to be an obvious risk that the concept of Transformative Learning may be losing its significance and thus its emancipatory power, which have been in the past the source of its importance and popularity. This was precisely what happened to the similar concept of *experiential learning*, which was developed in the 1980s with roots in the path-breaking works of David Kolb (1984) and David Boud et al. (1985), and rapidly gained a central position in the field of adult learning and education (e.g. Weil and McGill, 1989; Wildemeersch and Jansen, 1992). It reached its peak of popularity at the 1996 conference in Cape Town, then gradually declined in importance, and after the 2003 conference in Sydney more or less disappeared, because it became clear, as Kolb had already suggested in 1984, that all learning is in some way experiential.

The need for a new definition

As a consequence, it is therefore important for Transformative Learning to reconfigure itself in new, more precise, and also fundamentally more demanding ways, so that it includes all the dimensions of learning and at the same time also includes a limitation or threshold to exclude trivial and insignificant applications of the concept. In 2000 Robert Kegan raised this problem by asking of Transformative Learning: 'What "Form" Transforms?' in a book chapter called 'A Constructive-Developmental Approach to Transformative Learning' (Kegan, 2000). However, Kegan did not propose a new definition, but rather a specific approach; his contribution was more about the 'how' than about the 'what' of Transformative Learning, and although his critique resulted in much discussion it did not lead to any fundamentally new framing of the concept.

But as the need for change and redirection gradually become more and more urgent, two more explicit and elaborated answers to Kegan's question were recently given. The first of these was provided by Mark Tennant, who is particularly well known for his book, *Psychology of Adult Learning*, which since 1988 has been published in three editions (Tennant, 2005 [1988]). In his later years Tennant has focused on the psychology of the self, mainly inspired by Michel Foucault and other French postmodern philosophers (Tennant, 2009 [1998]). In 2012 he published a book called, *The Learning Self: Understanding the Potential for Transformation* (Tennant, 2012), in which he proposed that Transformative Learning should be defined and understood as learning involving changes in the self; a formulation which certainly resembles Rogers's notion of significant learning, but is in no way related to it. However, Tennant's proposal is an improvement because the idea now includes both cognitive ideas and emotional patterns, and at the same time excludes what is subjectively trivial and insignificant.

The second answer to Kegan's question is provided by Illeris (2014), and given on the basis of a thorough examination of a broad range of terms and concepts, which might be relevant in this context. Illeris (2014) suggested that *identity* is the most appropriate term for what is transformed by Transformative Learning as it is a concept that is close to a notion of the core self, but also explicitly includes the individual's social attitudes and relationships. So Illeris (2014: 40) argued that Transformative Learning should be defined as 'all learning that implies change in the identity of the learner', both because it is comprehensive, and because it has become central in the last three decades to contemporary personality psychology, social psychology and sociology, and therefore has been closely analysed and positioned in relation to current developments in the organization and practice of late modern societies. This needs to be substantiated in the following way.

Identity as the target of transformative learning

There is an agreement that the modern understanding of the concept of identity was developed by the German-American psychoanalyst Erik Erikson, principally in his two books, *Childhood and Society* (1950) and *Identity, Youth and Crisis* (1968). Erikson constructed a model of eight life-stages, which he called *epigenic*, meaning that development passes through intervening, crisis-like transformations so that later stages are indirectly present in earlier stages and are subsequently passed on to the next stage. Central to this process is the crisis leading from youth into early adulthood, which, if it is successfully achieved, results in the development of a personal identity, or if it is not successfully achieved, leads to identity confusion.

Identity was understood by Erikson as a psycho-social mental phenomenon, covering both the persistent experience of being the same in all the different situations and phases of the life-course, and the totality of how the person relates to and wishes to be perceived by others. Thus, according to Erikson, identity is developed during the life stage of youth, at that time estimated to last some 4–5 years between the ages of 14 and 18, finally coming to fruition during the youth crisis at the age of about 18–20, and from then retained and further consolidated throughout adulthood. In this framework Erikson was in agreement with contemporary humanist psychologists such as Gordon Allport (1961) who wrote about 'the mature personality', and Carl Rogers (1961) who used the expression 'the fully functioning person'.

However, very soon, the stability of adult identity began to be questioned as leading psychotherapists reported rapidly growing changes among their clients from classic neurotic symptoms to a new and more diffuse kind of personality problem, termed 'narcissist disorder', which included experiences of emptiness, absurdity, meaninglessness, lack of self-perception, initiative and job-satisfaction, and a tendency to engage in routine behaviour (e.g. Kohut, 1971, 1977). This led to the narcissism debate in which the American historian Christopher Lasch identified a state of decay in cultural values (Lasch, 1979). In contrast, Thomas Ziehe, working in a German university, saw it as a reasonable reaction to contemporary phenomena such as the disintegration of the nuclear family, intensification of work, increasing compensatory consumption, and new possibilities for individual and social emancipation (Ziehe, 1975; Ziehe and Stubenrauch, 1982).

This amounted to radical new understandings of the concept, first in French postmodern philosophy (e.g. Foucault, 1982), then in German and British sociology (e.g. Giddens, 1990, 1991; Beck, 1992 [1986]), followed soon after by the breakthrough in American psychology of social constructionism (e.g. Gergen, 1991, 1994). In different ways, these new understandings led to a new kind of individualized relationship between the individual and society, having important consequences for the condition and importance of identity development.

The source of this was the general detraditionalization in the late 1960s and it persisted with growing intensity through the 1970s. Existing traditions, norms, rules and ways of behaviour were gradually phased out and replaced by more free and casual modes, and, especially among young people, a revolt against social structures, which gradually led to an extensive individualization of social and societal structures. People could and should choose their own lives through personal choices of consumerism, life style, relationships, education, job, sexuality and general behaviour. At the formal level, society, legislation and administration also gradually treated people more and more as individuals with individual rights and duties, and all this made it increasingly necessary for everybody to develop a persona or identity which could guide and co-ordinate the rapidly growing number of individual choices, understandings, meaning perspectives, ways of living, behaviour patterns and the like that the individual was required to make and have. In this way a person's identity changed from a lifelong, well established, and, only in very urgent cases, changeable, centre of consciousness, into an organ for maintaining a *balance* between stability and flexibility, between 'ontological security' and 'existential anxiety', as Giddens expressed it (1991).

It is in line with this gradual and profound change in the individual's life condition that Transformative Learning has today become a central issue; in contrast to Rogers' similar concept of significant learning, which was launched too early to fit with the prevailing zeitgeist. Transformative Learning can in this perspective be defined, described and understood precisely as the process by which we are able to change and develop our identity, not on a daily level, but stepwise through adult life. Whilst identity is the structural answer to the individual's handling of contemporary life conditions, Transformative Learning is the corresponding practical tool by which that identity is kept up-to-date. If we do not, more or less regularly, change important elements of our identity we cannot accommodate and cope with the ever-changing surroundings and life conditions we all experience. These changes are made through learning processes, which take on the character of transformations.

New developments in transformative learning

Having come to the conclusion that the concept of Transformative Learning today needs to be reframed, and that this should be related to identity development as the central and co-ordinating process, combining meaning perspectives with a much wider range of psychological and social processes, and managing and controlling the relationship and interaction between the individual and her or his surroundings, it becomes possible to contemplate a range of new kinds of conditions, connections and fields in which Transformative Learning may be activated, and new kinds of ways in which it may be applied. Precisely because identity today is a part of all our thoughts, understandings, actions and relationships, changes in identity are also possible and relevant in very many different situations. In Illeris (2014) I have made a more comprehensive examination of the most important of these new possibilities. Here I summarize some of these ideas.

Transformative learning in youth

The first of these is that linking Transformative Learning to identity makes it possible to solve what has always been an open question: when can, and how does, Transformative Learning come to fruition? Transformative Learning has always, in theory as well as in practice, been related to adulthood. But where does it come from? It cannot only be a gift from heaven or a public right assigned at the age of majority. However, by connecting it to identity, the ability to engage in Transformative Learning is developed as part of identity development, which has been studied and discussed in psychology ever since the work of Erikson (1950, 1968).

Some basic identity elements are originally developed in early childhood, such as gender identity, family identity, and, later perhaps, religious and national identity, but in Erikson's worldview these are what he called identifications, because they are transferred from parents or others and in no way chosen by the child. Genuine identity development takes place during the period of youth, which today is no longer just a period of some 4–5 years between the ages of 14 and 19, but must be seen as starting at early puberty, at the age of 11–13, and lasting until a reasonably coherent and stable identity is achieved, usually in the middle or last half of the 20s.

However, in relation to Transformative Learning, it is important that transformations cannot take place before there is something to transform, i.e. before there are some well-established identity elements and at least also a kind of early identity pattern or structure. As described by Thomas Ziehe (and Stubenrauch, 1982) the identity process starts with trial-and-error activities, which he calls search movements. Youngsters experiment with more or less provocative ideas, standpoints or ways of behaving, in order to see what reactions they provoke, and in this way get an idea of whether they are worth going on with, or whether they should be changed or discarded, but all of this is not so much planned and controlled as it may seem. On the contrary, in school these search movements are often quite disturbing and derailing in relation to teaching and learning activities.

But gradually, through the early teenage years, experiences form the outlines of a pattern, which can be a foundation for an identity formation; and when this begins to have the character of a coherent structure, at least in certain areas, the possibility of transformations appears. So from about the age of 16–18 Transformative Learning may take place, first on a limited scale, and probably not in full until some time during the late 20s.

Different kinds of transformative learning

The recognition that identity is the target of Transformative Learning also made it possible to differentiate between different kinds of Transformative Learning, because development and transformation of identity may assume many forms in the light of the multitude of changes the individual and groups of individuals are subjected to. Clearly Mezirow identified the kinds of transformations he found most important and wanted them to be as emancipating and progressive as possible. In line with this, it is striking that all the cases and examples, which have been collected together and published in books such as *Transformative Learning in Practice* (Mezirow et al., 2009), are about progressive Transformative Learning in a very wide range of different contexts. But sometimes changes in identity have to be regressive rather than progressive, for example, when life conditions deteriorate, as in cases of unemployment, divorce or other crisis situations. In Illeris (2014) I give examples of different kinds of adult courses and education, which can be characterized as regressive Transformative Learning, and I suggest that this is possibly the most pressing challenge to Transformative Learning today and how to deal with it in practice.

In connection with this there will also be situations that can lead to what is logically the next step, which is to try to realize and practice what I have termed restorative Transformative Learning. This is achieved by turning regressive Transformative Learning practices into new, progressive and more realistic transformations. This is possible precisely because the learner is in a situation of change, and, if not too depressed by the regression, will be eager to try out other ways (an example of this can be found in Illeris 2014: 98).

Collective or communal transformative learning

As identity as a mental construct also includes personal attitudes to relationships between the individual and other individuals or groups, and how one wishes to be experienced by others, Transformative Learning when defined in relation to identity can also be practised as a collective or communal activity and learning. This is in principle the case as soon as two or more individuals in a common process make more or less parallel transformations. These transformations will never be quite the same between two or more learners because learning as a mental process of acquisition is always individual and influenced by the results of subjectively relevant prior learning. But nevertheless, the learning situation and objective may be so alike in a group of people with similar backgrounds that they can identify enough to be able to work together, or take a course together, and on mainly equal terms. Seen from the point of view of learning, this is a very favourable situation because the participants then have the possibility both to help and support each other and also to create an atmosphere of security and goal-directedness, which may qualify the activities and strengthen the learning outcomes.

Transformative Learning activities, as practised by Freire and observed by Mezirow, have to a great extent profited by such collectivity. But the very extensive individualization which has taken place since then has made such collective learning more difficult to establish in practice, and, if the differences between the participants are too big and the solidarity too weak, intended collective Transformative Learning activities may end up in conflicts and disagreement. This may harm the collectivity and result in a range of heterogeneous transformations.

Transformative learning, defence and resistance

Learning research and learning theory have mainly been preoccupied with what happens when somebody learns something, and this is certainly the case in relation to Transformative Learning. But it is even as important to also consider what happens when people do not learn what they intend to learn or what they should or are supposed to learn, or when they only learn in insufficient or distorted ways. Nevertheless, this area of non-learning and mis-learning has only been taken up by very few researchers or peripherally in relation to other considerations. Apart from my own work (Illeris, 2007, 2014) I can only refer to Peter Jarvis (2012) and his references to David Hay (2007) and Ian Kinchin et al. (2008) for serious attempts of this kind. And these sources do not go very deeply into the psychological aspects of non-learners and non-learning.

However, to find the roots of non-learning, insufficient learning and distorted learning as mass phenomena, which they certainly are today, and not only occasional occurrences, it seems necessary to go back to the middle of the twentieth century, when a situation arose in which ordinary people in their daily lives began to cope with a bigger amount of information and impressions than they had capacity to take in as learning, and therefore had to develop what the French philosopher, Henri Lefebvre (1947), and later the German social psychologist, Thomas Leithäuser (1976, 2000) called 'everyday consciousness' as a psychological barrier or defence to avoid being overloaded.

Today this has become the situation for all of us all the time – just think of how the TV news constantly provides us with new information and impressions, or the many changes in our life conditions provoked by happenings and decisions all over the world, which influence our situation and understanding. This implies that we all have to develop a psychological defence system towards learning which reaches much further and may include all kinds of input; and unlimited openness to all the input we receive would inevitably lead to a mental breakdown. But this also leaves us with a very intrusive task of selection, what to take in and what not to take in, which we deal with in two different ways: a lot of information and impressions we simply reject (after half an hour of TV news, five minutes later we only have the ability to recall very limited parts of the content), and quite a lot of what we do take in we will distort so that it is in accordance with what we already know, think and mean, and therefore it will not result in learning. These are psychological processes with which we all have to deal today. Seen from the point of view of learning this means that we accidentally and unconsciously miss learning possibilities which could have been useful and desirable, and this inevitably also happens in educational situations (the immediate pedagogical answer being that important points and conclusions should be emphasized several times and from different perspectives).

The strongest of these defence mechanisms is no doubt identity defence; the closer an input is to the core of our identity, the more we are inclined to reject or distort it. And this sets the scene for very many possible situations of Transformative Learning, which is actually quite sensible because the essential challenge is to keep a subjectively defined balance between the stability and flexibility of our identities. So the conclusion in relation to Transformative Learning, understood as a change of identity elements, is that such learning has to do with balance; and therefore the task of a teacher, instructor, guide or coach is to lead the learner to relevant situations in which this balance is challenged in a clear and well substantiated way, leave decisions and consequences to the learner, and be ready with any mental or practical support if the learner takes up the challenge and tries to come through with some kind of Transformative Learning.

Finally, I will here mention that in addition to learning defence there are also situations in which it would be relevant to talk about learning resistance, the main difference being that defence is there in advance of the given learning situation, whereas resistance is directly provoked by the situation. This occurs when what could be learned is so unacceptable to the learner that she or he cannot or will not take it in, but on the contrary reacts by showing strong opposition, and it may be a difficult and uncomfortable situation for a teacher and other learners. But nevertheless it can be very important to try, eventually later and in a one-on-one conversation, to take up the situation and reaction with the learner, because there is so much mental energy invested in a reaction of this kind that allows Transformative Learning to be the outcome. For many years I started my courses on learning theory with university students by asking them to think of some event in their lives by which they had learned something which they regarded as really epoch-making for them, and far more than half of the answers always referred to situations of learning resistance.

Transformative learning and competence development

Today educational learning is usually formally targeted at the development of competencies. This term has taken over from earlier concepts like knowledge and skills or qualifications and is basically a more appropriate formulation, because competencies are about what a learner actually can do and manage in practice. The transition to this term was strongly promoted by international educational agents, primarily the OECD, and there was a long process to reach an appropriate definition and specification of what should exactly be the content and understanding of the term. Finally the most authoritative formulation became as follows:

> A competence is defined as the ability to successfully meet complex demands in a particular context of work and in everyday life through the mobilization of psychosocial requisites (including both cognitive and non-cognitive aspects). This represents a demand-oriented or functional approach to defining

competencies. The primary focus is on the results the individual achieves through an action, choice, or way of behaving, with respect to the demands, for instance, related to a particular professional position, social role, or personal project. (Rychen and Salganik, 2003: 43)

This definition is at the same time very ambitious, very open and broad, and yet precise in some important parts, signified by the terms 'complex demands', 'psychosocial requisites' and 'cognitive and non-cognitive aspects'. It is certainly about the applications of the competencies in relation to the complex and ever-changing challenges of today's working and everyday life.

But it also operates at the supernational level, in this case mainly the European Union, where this ambitious understanding has been fundamentally betrayed in many ways, most powerfully by having the member states prepare lists of the competencies acquired in each of their publicly acknowledged school and educational programmes, in order that employers cross-nationally can judge the actual suitability of applicants for specific jobs and tasks. These lists for each country include thousands of 'competencies', the great majority of which are certainly far from satisfying the definition above and with absolutely no guarantee that everyone who has been through the education or course in question actually commands each of them, but only that they have probably been through a process which should formally include some acquaintance with this or that competency.

However, if taking the quoted or some other of the many ambitious definitions seriously, it is in the present connection clear that competencies living up to these definitions must be complex in their scope, psychosocial in their practice, and cover both cognitive and non-cognitive dimensions; or, to express the essence of this more directly, must cover both relevant insight, skills and personal qualities, or both relevant professional qualifications and a sustainable personal identity.

So there is a close and mutual connection between competence and identity: a person cannot be competent in an area if the relationship to this area is not an integrated part of her or his identity, and that identity cannot include a commitment to a certain area or job or function without somehow being competent in relation to it. And obviously this implies that the acquisition and development of competencies to some extent must employ Transformative Learning.

It is precisely this connection which right from the start has made Mezirow's AEGIS doctoral programme so very significant and esteemed, because it intentionally includes challenges and demands which encourage and promote Transformative Learning. And this is also in addition to more general and humanistic arguments and interests concerning why the connection between Transformative Learning and identity development is so important to realize, maintain and understand.

REFERENCES

Allport, G.W. (1961) *Patterns and Growth of Personality*, New York: Holt, Rinehart and Winston.
Beck, U. (1992 [1986]) *Risk Society: Towards a New Modernity*, London: Sage.
Boud, D., Keogh, R. and Walker, D. (eds) (1985) *Reflection: Turning Experience into Learning*, London: Kogan Page.
Brookfield, S. (1987) *Developing Critical Thinkers: Challenging Adults to Explore Alternative Ways of Thinking and Acting*, Milton Keynes: Open University Press.
Brookfield, S. (2000) 'Transformative Learning as Ideology Critique', in J. Mezirow and

Associates (eds) *Learning as Transformation: Critical Perspectives on a Theory in Progress*, San Francisco, CA: Jossey-Bass.
Cranton, P. (2005 [1994]) *Understanding and Promoting Transformative Learning*, San Francisco, CA: Jossey-Bass.
Dirkx, J. (2006) 'Engaging Emotions in Adult Learning: A Jungian Perspective on Emotion and Transformative Learning', in E.W. Taylor (ed.) *Teaching for Change. New Directions in Adult and Continuing Education*. No. 109, San Francisco: Jossey-Bass.
Dirkx, J. (2012) 'Nurturing Soul Work: A Jungian Approach to Transformative Learning', in E.W. Taylor and P. Cranton (eds) *The Handbook of Transformative Learning: Theory, Research, and Practice*, San Francisco, CA: Jossey-Bass.
Erikson, E.H. (1950) *Childhood and Society*, New York: Norton.
Erikson, E.H. (1968) *Identity, Youth, and Crisis*, New York: Norton.
Foucault, M. (1982) 'Technologies of the Self', in L.H. Martin, H. Gutman and P.H. Hutton (eds) *Technologies of the Self: A Seminar with Michel Foucault*, Amhurst, MA: University of Massachusetts Press.
Freire, P. (1970) *Pedagogy of the Oppressed*, New York: Seabury.
Gergen, K.J. (1991) *The Saturated Self: Dilemmas of Identity in Contemporary Life*, New York: Basic Books.
Gergen, K.J. (1994) *Realities and Relationships*, Cambridge, MA: Harvard University Press.
Giddens, A. (1990) *The Consequences of Modernity*, Stanford, CA: Stanford University Press.
Giddens, A. (1991) *Modernity and Self-Identity*, Cambridge, UK: Polity Press.
Gould, R. (1978) *Transformation, Growth and Change in Adult Life*, New York: Simon and Schuster.
Habermas, J. (1971 [1968]) *Knowledge and Human Interests*, Boston, MA: Beacon Press.
Hay, D. (2007) 'Using Concept Mapping to Measure Deep, Surface and Non-learning Outcomes', *Studies in Higher Education*, 32(1): 39–57.
Illeris, K. (2004) 'Transformative Learning in the Perspective of a Comprehensive Learning Theory', *Journal of Transformative Education*, 2(2): 79–89.
Illeris, K. (2007) *How We Learn. Learning and Non-learning in School and Beyond*, London: Routledge.
Illeris, K. (2014) *Transformative Learning and Identity*, London: Routledge.
Jarvis, P. (2012) 'Non-Learning', in P. Jarvis and M. Watts (eds) *The Routledge International Handbook of Learning*, London: Routledge.
Kegan, R. (2000) 'What "Form" Transforms? A Constructive-Developmental Approach to Transformative Learning', in J. Mezirow and Associates (eds) *Learning as Transformation: Critical Perspectives on a Theory in Progress*, San Francisco, CA: Jossey-Bass.
Kinchin, I., Lygo-Baker, S. and Hay, D. (2008) 'Universities as Centres of Non-Learning', *Studies in Higher Education*, 33(1): 89–103.
Kohut, H. (1971) *The Analysis of the Self: A Systematic Approach to the Psychoanalytic Treatment of Narcissistic Personality Disorders*, New York: International Universities Press.
Kohut, H. (1977) *The Restoration of the Self*, New York: International Universities Press.
Kolb, D.A. (1984) *Experiential Learning: Experience as the Source of Learning and Development*, Englewood Cliffs, NJ: Prentice-Hall.
Lasch, C. (1979) *The Culture of Narcissism: American Life in an Age of Dimishing Expectations*, New York: Norton.
Lefebvre, H. (1947) *The Critique of Everyday Life*, London: Verso.
Leithäuser, T. (1976) *Formen des Alltagsbewusstseins*, Frankfurt A.M.: Campus [The Forms of Everyday Consciousness].
Leithäuser, T. (2000) 'Subjectivity, Lifeworld and Organization', in K. Illeris (ed.) *Adult Education in the Perspective of the Learners*, Copenhagen: Roskilde University Press.
Mezirow, J. (1978) *Education for Perspective Transformation: Women's Re-entry Programs in Community College*, New York: Teachers College, Columbia University.
Mezirow, J. (1991) *Transformative Dimensions of Adult Learning*. San Francisco, CA: Jossey-Bass.
Mezirow, J. (2006) 'An Overview on Transformative Learning', in P. Sutherland and J. Crowther (eds) *Lifelong Learning: Concepts and Contexts*, London: Routledge.
Mezirow, J. (2009): Transformative Learning Theory, in J. Mezirow, E.W. Taylor, and

Associates (eds) (2009) *Transformative Learning in Practice: Insights from Community, Workplace and Higher Education*, San Francisco, CA: Jossey-Bass.
Mezirow, J. and Associates (eds) (1990) *Fostering Critical Reflection in Adulthood: A Guide to Transformative and Emancipatory Learning*, San Francisco, CA: Jossey-Bass.
Mezirow, J. and Associates (eds) (2000) *Learning as Transformation: Critical Perspectives on a Theory in Progress*, San Francisco, CA: Jossey-Bass.
Mezirow, J., Taylor, E. and Associates (eds) (2009) *Transformative Learning in Practice: Insights from Community, Workplace and Higher Education*, San Francisco, CA: Jossey-Bass.
Newman, M. (2012) 'Calling Transformative Learning into Question: Some Mutinous Thoughts', *Adult Education Quarterly*, 62(1): 399–411.
Newman, M. (2014) 'Transformative Learning: Mutinous Thoughts Revisited', *Adult Education Quarterly*, 64(4): 345–355.
O'Sullivan, E. (2012) 'Deep Transformation: Forging a Planetary Worldview', in E.W. Taylor and P. Cranton (eds) *The Handbook of Transformative Learning: Theory, Research, and Practice*, San Francisco, CA: Jossey-Bass.
O'Sullivan, E., Morrell, A. and O'Connor, M.A. (eds) (2002) *Expanding the Boundaries of Transformative Learning*, New York: Palgrave.
Rogers, C.R. (1951) *Client-Centered Therapy*, Boston, MA: Houghton-Mifflin.
Rogers, C.R. (1961) *On Becoming a Person*, Boston, MA: Houghton-Mifflin.
Rogers, C.R. (1969) *Freedom to Learn*, Columbus, OH: Charles E. Merrill.
Rychen, D.S. and Salganik, L.H. (eds) (2003) *Key Competencies for a Successful Life and Well-Functioning Society*, Cambridge, MA: Hogrefe and Huber.
Tennant, M. (2005 [1988]) *Psychology and Adult Learning*, London: Routledge.
Tennant, M. (2009 [1998]) 'Lifelong Learning as a Technology of the Self', in K. Illeris (ed.) *Contemporary Theories of Learning*, London: Routledge.
Tennant, M. (2012) *The Learning Self: Understanding the Potential for Transformation*, San Francisco, CA: Jossey-Bass.
Weil, S.W. and McGill, I. (eds) (1989) *Making Sense of Experiential Learning: Diversity in Theory and Practice*, Buckingham: Open University Press.
Wildemeersch, D. and Jansen, T. (eds) (1992) *Adult Education, Experiential Learning and Social Change: The Postmodern Challenge*, Haag: VUGA.
Ziehe, T. (1975) *Pubertät und Narzissmus*, Frankfurt A.M.: Europäische Verlagsanstalt [Puberty and Narcissism].
Ziehe, T. and Stubenrauch, H. (1982) *Plädoyer für ungewöhnliches Lernen*, Reinbek: Rowohlt [Pleading for Unusual Learning].

CHAPTER 17

TRANSFORMATIVE LEARNING RE-DEFINED

As changes in elements of the identity

The concept and issue of Transformative Learning

When the American professor of adult education Jack Mezirow launched the concept of Transformative Learning (TL) in 1978, his background was a study of women's liberation processes in adult education courses. For many, these had resulted in essential changes in their self perception and life course (Mezirow, 1978). On this basis, and with references mainly to Freire (1970), Habermas (1968/1971) and Gould (1978), Mezirow defined TL as a learning which involves qualitative changes in the learner's 'meaning perspectives', 'frames of reference' and 'habits of mind' (1978, 1991), i.e. the mainly cognitive mental structures which fundamentally organize our understanding of ourselves and our life world. In this connection, critical reflection, open discourse and implementing new understandings in practice, were seen as important elements (see also Mezirow, 1990, 2000).

However, this definition has been criticized many times and from many sides for being too narrow and too cognitively oriented. Thus, just to mention some of the most important objections, Boyd and Myers (1988) pointed to the importance of unconscious processes in relation to TL, Collard and Law (1989) called for more attention to collective social action, Cranton (1994/2005) and Dirkx (1997, 2006, 2012a) have several times recommended taking account of C.G. Jung's theoretical approach, Brookfield (2000) has found the attention to ideology and political power insufficient, I have missed connections to more general and comprehensive theories of learning (Illeris, 2004), and Dirkx (1998), Cranton (1994/2005), Taylor (2008), and Kokkos (2013) have all tried to sum up and evaluate the various critiques as a whole. However, the most fundamental critique was raised rather recently by Michael Newman in his article 'Calling Transformative Learning into Question', in which he claimed that the very concept of TL is untenable, and alternatively proposed a concept of 'good learning' including nine criteria in which such learning must meet (Newman, 2012).

It is not the purpose of this article to go further into these or other critical discussions of TL. Most of the earlier points, and especially the importance of the emotional dimension, have explicitly been accepted and recognized by Mezirow (2006, 2009), while Newman's critique has been answered thoroughly by Cranton and Kasl (2012) and Dirkx (2012b). In general, I am in agreement with these answers, but the intention behind the present article is of a more basic kind, addressing the very status, position and definition of TL today.

On the practical level my concern in relation to TL has for many years been fed by growing tendencies to consider and speak about TL as a movement, in some cases even a spiritual movement. I experienced these tendencies as early as the international TL conference in New York in 2003, and I know from talks with Mezirow then and later that such tendencies also have troubled him. However, today these tendencies seem to be taking a dominant role, and to be becoming generally accepted—for example, at the international TL conference in San Francisco in 2012 the organizers constantly talked about TL as a movement. This is a very precarious development and situation, which may lead to a disorganization or even a decay if it is not taken up and brought to a solution. For example, this seems to be exactly what happened at the same time to the (parallel) experiential learning perspective (Boud, Koegh, & Walker, 1985; Kolb, 1984; Weil & McGill, 1989). Very popular and important in the 1990s and the first years of the new millennium, this has now almost vanished.

In this connection, I find it crucially important to maintain TL as an academic issue and concept; and at this level the most important demand seems to be to come to some kind of agreement on a new and more inclusive definition of the term TL. Currently, the situation seems to be that everybody in the field more or less agrees that Mezirow's original definition of the term as relating to meaning perspectives, frames of reference and habits of mind is insufficient. But no other definition has taken its place, and although there may be some kind of general, but unspoken, agreement on what it is all about, many different and even conflicting understandings are somehow involved underneath the surface.

Therefore, as I see it, what is needed is a more profound re-consideration of the basis of TL, comprising both the question of what is transformed and the question of the character of the learning process which results in TL. I am afraid that if such a re-consideration is not undertaken there is a real risk that the idea and concept of TL will, in the years ahead, experience a fate similar to experiential learning's.

As to the character of the TL process, I have already pointed to the remarkable lack of connection between TL and general learning theory (Illeris, 2004), to how little investigation there has been into how TL is related to other kinds of learning, or to how a distinction can be made between TL and non-TL. I have tried to handle this question by defining four fundamental types of learning: cumulative, assimilative, accommodative and TL (Illeris, 2007, 2009). That proposal was basically a continuation of the Swiss learning theorist and epistemologist Jean Piaget's theory of the development of human learning and intelligence, launched in the 1930s (e.g. Piaget, 1936/1952); the important point in the present connection is the distinction between learning by addition (assimilation) and learning by reconstruction (accommodation). Newman (2012) rejects this view by referring to the fact that addition and change often take place as elements of the same process; however, as Cranton and Kasl (2012) point out, this in no way prevents the possibility, or even the desirability, of such a distinction being made. It is one of the most important characteristics of the structure of human learning that we make use of and command both these types of learning (Illeris, 2007). On the contrary, Newman's observation is in line with the very fundamental feature of accommodation that it always includes two steps: a break down or abandonment of elements of the existing mental structures (cognitive as well as emotional and social), and an establishment of a basis for alternative assimilative rebuilding of a new understanding or new ways of thinking, feeling and behaving.

In connection with TL, Piaget's understanding and concepts have two important consequences. First, TL must be regarded as a kind of accommodation—the very term 'transformation' means a change from something that was there previously into something which is different. Second, it must also be recognized that TL cannot be identical to accommodation, as it is qualitatively different from the rather simple, cognitive accommodations of factual, mathematical and similar understandings to which Piaget predominantly referred. Thus, there is a challenge to establish a boundary or a distinction between TL and more limited kinds of accommodation.

This last consequence points back to the question which, as I see it, is the most basic problem in relation to the concept, understanding and status of TL today, the question which the American developmental psychologist Robert Kegan presented in the short and precise formulation: 'What "Form" Transforms?' (Kegan, 2000, pp. 35–69).

To answer this question—and thereby provide a better definition of TL—is not in itself enough to rectify all the difficulties, but a debate about this may be an important step forward, and a possible agreement on an appropriate formulation may certainly be a crucial improvement. So in the following, I shall take up the question of the definition of TL, make a new and in my opinion more precise and up-to-date proposal, and try to illustrate some new perspectives and possibilities which could be gained by adopting the re-definition I suggest.

A proposal of a re-definition

In attempting to reach a new definition of TL it seems obvious that key to this definition must be a term which includes all mental dimensions (the cognitive, the emotional and the social—Illeris, 2007) and at the same time delimits the target area in such a way that all the small and less important everyday changes, or school learning of ordinary knowledge and skills, are not accepted as TL—transformation means a change or alteration into something qualitatively different. A survey of a representative selection of the principal contemporary literature on human learning, development and social interaction has shown that this mental totality has been described and investigated in various ways and mainly under such labels as self, identity, the person or personality, the soul and what has been termed biographicity (Illeris, 2014).

All of these labels have been used in relevant psychological or/and sociological research in relation to learning and development, and could be appropriate keywords in a definition of TL. For example, the British expert on adult learning and education, Peter Jarvis, has preferred the term 'the person' (e.g. Jarvis, 2006, 2009), which immediately is the broadest of the terms and the most related to everyday life, while the German sociologist Peter Alheit uses the term of biographicity to stress the relationship to the life course as this is perceived and interpreted by the individual (Alheit, 2009). The term 'personality' seems rather disqualified in the current context: it is today closely related to the use of personality tests and profiles which set up specific elements of the mental totality for measurement; it thereby tends to stand for a specific selection of elements (Illeris, 2014). The term 'soul' has been used by Dirkx (1997, 2012a) in connection with his above-mentioned Jungian approach, but is problematic by including unconscious elements, which may certainly be involved in TL processes, but are primarily related to therapy and are not usually included in the general understanding of learning.

However, in the literature related to TL there is no doubt that the terms 'self' and 'identity' are the most generally used to indicate the individual mental totality. They also seem immediately the most adequate terms in the present connection, because they are most often used in academic contexts, and both are very well established in the area in question. The most frequently used term, no doubt, is the self—including a range of more specific connections such as self-awareness, self-consciousness, self-perception, self-direction, self-reflection, etc. Two very different examples in which the term 'the self' has been used can be mentioned as specifically relevant to the definition of TL.

The first is the use of this term by Carl Rogers, one of the central representatives of the 'Humanistic Psychology' approach, which was launched in the 1950s and 1960s as a 'third way' in psychology—in opposition to behaviourism and psychoanalysis. In this connection, Rogers proposed the term 'significant learning' (Rogers, 1951, 1969), which in content and understanding is actually very similar to Mezirow's concept of TL, and which Rogers defined as learning involving changes in the organization of the self. Rogers' proposal did not have the same impact as Mezirow's approach, probably because the time was not yet really ready to understand and accept the importance of this kind of learning—but in the current context it is interesting that the first academic initiative in the field was explicitly defined by the use of 'the self'.

The other example that I shall take up here is the recent book *The Learning Self: Understanding the Potential for Transformation* by the Australian Tennant (2012), an expert on adult learning well known for his widely used work *Psychology and Adult Learning* (Tennant, 1988/2005). In his recent (2012) book, which is very relevant in the present connection, Tennant states that there is a significant overlap between the terms 'identity' and 'self', but with the important difference that whereas the term self is usually used as an entirely psychological concept, 'identity signals a shift toward the social side of the individual-social dichotomy' (Tennant, 2012, p. 9).

For exactly this reason Tennant—who regards his work as a psychological analysis—chooses to refer to the self as the mental instance to which TL is related. And for exactly the same reason I here propose and recommend the term 'identity', because I see the social dimension and sociological insights as very important for the full understanding of TL. (However, this difference in no way denies the considerable parallels between Tennant's approach and my own contribution; Tennant's book can certainly be recommended to readers who want to go deeper into these matters).

From this background, I therefore propose the following new definition of TL:

> The concept of transformative learning comprises all learning which implies changes in the identity of the learner. (Illeris, 2014, p. 40)

On the basis of this definition, I now proceed to explore a range of topics—both well established and new—related to TL, and to discuss why and how they can contribute to a revised approach, understanding and practice about this important concept and issue.

The psycho-social identity

In the above, I have pointed to 'identity' as the keyword in the definition of TL because it combines individuality and sociality. I shall here develop this by a short historical account of the development of the concept of the identity.

Usually, the German-American psychoanalyst Erik. H. Erikson is referred to as the founder of the modern understanding of identity, which he used and elaborated as the key concept of his so-called epigenetic (i.e. related to the evolution of the human species) scheme of human lifelong development in his three most important books, *Childhood and Society, Identity, Youth and Crisis* and *The Life Cycle Completed* (Erikson, 1950, 1968, 1982). In the present context, it is important that Erikson understood identity as a 'psycho-social' concept, covering both the internal personal experience of being the same in all the different situations of life, and the totality of how we relate to, and wish to be perceived by, others. This double-sided identity was according to Erikson mainly developed during youth and maintained as a core of the personality for the rest of life.

Thus, Erikson was in line with the ideal of the stable personality of mature adulthood which was at the same time celebrated in dominating American personality psychology, for example, by scholars such as Allport (1961) and, as mentioned above, Rogers (1961). But already during the 1970s the stability of adult identity began to be questioned, originally because classic neurotic symptoms in psychotherapy gradually seemed to be replaced by a new type of personality problems, including feelings of lack of self-perception, emptiness, lack of job satisfaction and initiative, absurdity, and an increased tendency towards routine behaviour—altogether described as 'narcissist disorders' or 'pathological narcissism' by the American psychoanalysts Kohut (1971, 1977) and Kernberg (1975).

This was the beginning of a rather heated cultural debate, especially in the USA. The historian Christopher Lasch, in his bestseller *The Culture of Narcissism* (Lasch, 1978), argued that a general cultural narcissism had developed. This was opposed by many others, especially in Europe by the German psychologist Thomas Ziehe, who saw the new trends as reasonable reactions to societal tendencies such as the disintegration of the nuclear family, the intensification of work and the explosion of compensating forms of consumption and substitute satisfaction. Ziehe argued that the new tendencies implied possibilities of cultural and social emancipation, which could be realized by changes in education and learning (Ziehe, 1975; Ziehe & Stubenrauch, 1982).

However, in relation to the concept of identity, this development made it clear that the idea and ideal of a stable identity, developed during youth and maintained throughout adulthood, could no longer be sustained. This can be seen as the underlying perspective which opened up the possibility of TL being more than possible exclusively for a very few people under extreme conditions. The full consequences of this were recognized by the psychological approach of social constructionism, which claimed that psychologically the individual is nothing on his or her own, but only by virtue of the social relations in which she or he is involved—as described by the American psychologist Kenneth Gergen in his books on *The Saturated Self* and *Realities and Relationships* (Gergen, 1991, 1994).

Obviously, there is little room for a personal identity in this understanding, because it situates the psychological arena not inside the individual, but externally in the interaction between people. However, at the same time a more positive renewal and updating of the understanding of identity came from a quite different approach, anchored in new trends in sociology. Some of the most important contributors in this connection have been the Germans Beck and Beck-Gernsheim (1986/1992, 1994/2002), the British Giddens (1990, 1991), the American Sennett (1998, 2006), the British-Polish Bauman (2000, 2001), the Canadian Côté and Levine (2002) and the British Jenkins (2004).

The point of departure for this new approach was that in the post-war period, and especially during the 1960s and 1970s, a de-traditionalization, and liberation from a broad range of norms and values, had taken place in Western countries. This implied a strong individualization, both formally and psychologically, involving increased individual possibilities and freedom, but also an endless number of choices for which the individual became responsible, and the consequences of which he or she must bear. As a result, the development of individual identity became extremely important, but at the same time it also implied an unavoidable duty to create one's own life course and a significant personal profile. At the same time, it was a liberation to increased competition in all important areas of life such as work, education, preferences, and to increased consumption of all kinds. And as competition always creates both winners and losers, considerable polarization was an inevitable outcome.

For the generations which grew up during the 1980s and later, the task or duty of creating their own identities became more and more central. Who am I? Who do I want to be? How can I fulfil my dreams? For some, usually those with the more advantaged social backgrounds, possibilities might be great and never-ending. But for others the proliferation of choice became a strain, a continuous demonstration of their insufficient individual capacity to make things function and capture the success and happiness which should be the outcome of all the choices and possibilities.

As emphasized especially by Giddens, this implied a new kind of personal reflexivity, including an 'interconnection between the two "extremes" of extensionality and intentionality: globalising influences on the one hand and personal dispositions on the other' (Giddens, 1991, p. 1). This demand for reflexivity accentuates the fact that individuals today are, and must be, constantly considering and addressing their self-perception and changing it in relation to the new influences and experiences with which they are confronted all the time. Both in our everyday and working lives things happen: we have to relate these to whether we want them or not, and we must constantly keep up with these developments and adjust or change our self-perceptions in relation to our environment, local as well as global.

In this way, the identity has more than ever before become the core of life—and it makes sense to see TL as the processes by which we deal with the constant possibility, urge and necessity to change and transform elements of our identities. The psycho-social identity has become the central connection between the individual and the social, and it is constantly challenged. TL is an important way of dealing with this.

Connections to general learning theory

A striking feature of the literature on TL is that it contains very few connections to general learning theory. Right from the start, Mezirow referred to, among others, Freire (1970) and Gould (1990), who certainly deal with learning, but in both cases very specific kinds of learning in very specific contexts. Others, such as Kegan (2000) and Dirkx (1997, 2006, 2012a), as already mentioned, refer to general developmental approaches, but not to general learning theory. However, if TL is to be more than a rather isolated concept and practice and, for example, to relate to learning in schools and institutions for further education, where it must be combined with the acquisition of prescribed knowledge and skills, the concept must be discussed and related to a more comprehensive understanding of learning in general. This is a rather obvious point, which I have made several times before

(Illeris, 2002, 2004, 2007); a connection to the concept of identity makes it rather easy to meet.

In general, learning theory it is fundamental, as already mentioned, to distinguish between learning as the addition of new knowledge, skills and other possibilities, and learning as change or restructuring of already acquired content or structures. This makes it easy to see that TL must be a kind of accommodative learning. This recognition directly leads to two important conclusions: first, that there must exist at least two basically different kinds of accommodation—'ordinary' accommodation (e.g. when the learner understands something in a new way, such as why some people in some situations react in certain ways) and transformative accommodations (e.g. when the learner changes her or his meaning perspectives or ways of behaviour in certain situations). Second, and accordingly, that the last mentioned of these two kinds of accommodation is precisely the same as TL, defined as changes in elements of the learner's identity.

At first sight, this may appear a rather unimportant theoretical recognition. In fact, however, it is clearly an advantage to be able to see TL in relation to other kinds of human learning. In connection with the planning and practice of educational learning on all levels, especially, it is important to be able to operate with different categories of learning. Many adult education courses which have been presented as TL do not deserve this designation, no matter how important and innovative they have been (this is the core of Newman's [2012] critique). The proposed definition of TL in relation to identity makes it easier to see what TL is, and what it is not, in practice—and to see what is needed in order to increase the likelihood that TL actually takes place.

TL at different life ages

Right from the start, in 1978, Mezirow connected the new concept of TL exclusively to adult learning. He regarded himself as an adult educator, and his aim was to further understand adult learning, especially in a liberating, emancipating and empowering direction—and ever since then the concept has been used solely in relation to adults. But where does the ability to make such transformations come from, how and when does it start, and at which age can we be regarded as adults?

Of course the possibility of TL in adulthood must somehow be developed, and finding out how this takes place would be an important contribution to the understanding and practice of TL. In this connection the linking of TL to identity opens up significant new possibilities, because ever since the work of Erikson the topic of identity development has been elaborated to a great extent in both psychological and sociological perspectives.

Erikson focused on how the identity was built up during youth, and especially during the difficult transition from youth into adulthood which, he argued, was decisive for developing a stable identity—rather than lifelong identity confusion (Erikson, 1968). But a generation later the American developmental psychologist and psychoanalyst Daniel Stern broke new ground with his intensive studies of how the core self or core identity is gradually built up right from the first months of life (Stern, 1985). Many other psychologists and sociologists have dealt with various aspects of, and various approaches to, identity development in youth (e.g. Bandura, 1997; Beck & Beck-Gernsheim, 1994/2002; Côté & Levine, 2002; Jenkins, 2004; Taylor, 1989)—and in relation to learning in youth the German psychologist Thomas Ziehes has pointed to the so-called 'search movements', i.e. the drafts of ideas, understandings and identity elements which, especially during the first period of youth identity development, are tried out and tested in order to see what reactions they provoke—and thereby whether they will be worth building on (Illeris, 2014; Ziehe, 2009; Ziehe & Stubenrauch, 1982). This may be regarded as the first steps in a more self-directed identity formation through processes that may be carried further into TL.

In general it seems evident that the connection of TL to identity and its development and formation can be strongly conducive to how, when and why TL starts and is developed through childhood and youth.

Competence development

During the last two decades the issue of competence has been central in educational politics and administration, not least as promoted by international organizations such as the OECD and the EU, and in connection with what has been termed 'new public management' (e.g. Illeris, 2009; OECD, 2003, 2005; Rychen & Salganik, 2003).

There has been much discussion, especially in relation to problems about the definition and measurement of competencies. In contrast to TL, many definitions of 'competence' have been proposed (see e.g. Gnahs, 2011; Illeris, 2009, 2012). These can generally be divided up into two groups: those which are in principle not much different from the concept of qualification, i.e. the outcomes of what has been more or less directly learnt or is required for specific tasks, and those which also include a more general capacity to deal with new, unknown and unforeseeable situations.

The most authoritative definition of the modern concept of competence, proposed by the Swiss researchers Dominique Rychen and Laura Salganik (who were the coordinators of OECD's very ambitious so-called DeSeCo Project: Definition and Selection of Competencies), tried to span the two types of understanding by the following formulation:

> A competence is defined as the ability to successfully meet complex demands in a particular context of work and in everyday life through the mobilization of psychosocial requisites (including both cognitive and noncognitive aspects). This represents a demand-oriented or functional approach to defining competencies. The primary focus is on the results the individual achieves through an action, choice, or way of behaving, with respect to the demands, for instance, related to a particular professional position, social role, or personal project.
> (Rychen & Salganik, 2003, p. 43)

It is clear that if the concept of competence is to be something different from, and more demanding and extensive than, qualifications it must imply a kind of learning which goes beyond the traditional understanding and relates to learning in schools, education, everyday life, etc. It must encompass a kind of learning which strengthens the learner's ability to function appropriately in new situations that arise all the time, and which could not be foreseen at the time when the competence was developed.

Seen in relation to what was necessary and required just a generation ago, the important new demand is to handle a constant stream of new situations, which cannot be foreseen, and which are often of decisive importance. In addition to all the necessary qualifications, this directly involves the identity, the question of which one is as a whole. This includes such capacities as creativity, imagination, faculty of combination, flexibility, empathy, intuition and in some situations also critical sense and even resistance (see Illeris, 2012). So this is what competencies fundamentally are about. They involve the whole capacity of the learner and must—if they are to be genuine and more than accidental—be rooted in the learner's identity.

So by linking TL to changes in elements of the identity it becomes evident that genuine competence development involves TL. This is a crucial understanding which goes well beyond the administrative enumeration of required competencies in the official educational statements of the various OECD countries under the new public management approach.

If the idea of competence is to be taken seriously, it must involve TL. But this reaches far beyond what can be obtained by the top-down approaches of modern educational policies.

Regressive and restoring transformations

Connecting TL to the concept of identity and seeing it from the perspective of a comprehensive understanding of learning also draws attention to the fact that not all transformations are progressive. In line with a range of other mental functions—such as thinking, feeling and sociality—TL can be progressive or offensive, regressive or defensive. Of course, the aim and idea of TL has essentially been to overcome personal limitations and difficulties and develop qualitatively new possibilities. But sometimes it becomes important and necessary to realize that progressive transformation can be too demanding and challenging for the learner, so that the outcome rather becomes withdrawal or regression—which can actually also be a kind of transformation. Regressive TL usually happens in situations when the learner does not have the strength or qualifications to get through with something new and then must resign and accept things as they are and find a more secure position (Illeris, 2014). The notion that TL can be both progressive and regressive seems, however, to be almost wholly absent from the existing literature, or at most only dealt with accidentally.

Quite often regressive TL can also lead to what could be called restoring transformations, including situations where the learner has to give up or refuse something but at the same time is able to replace it by something else which is functionable and acceptable instead of what proved, in reality, not to be practicable.

In a world which is constantly changing—in liquid modernity, as Bauman (2000) has called it—many cases of these or similar kinds occur, in which self-inflicted or undeserved circumstances can force people into situations of TL which do not—or at least not immediately—imply transformations into something which is better and experienced as an improvement. But nevertheless, something of importance has happened, things are not as they were before, there is a new feeling, a difference which cannot be neglected. A withdrawal has been unavoidable, some regressive (and perhaps also some restorative) TL has taken place. I cannot here go further into all of these possibilities, but elsewhere I have referred to the same phenomenon, and discussed some examples of regressive and restoring TL more in detail (Illeris, 2014).

Collective learning and action

As already mentioned, Mezirow has been criticized for not paying sufficient attention to collectivity in relation to TL (e.g. Collard & Law, 1989), even though his original inspiration was strongly influenced by Freire (1970) who regarded collectivity as very central in theory, as well as in practice. In fact, Mezirow has never opposed a social or collective dimension in TL, but seems to regard it as contingent, since the transformations themselves are located within single individuals (cf. Kokkos, 2013).

However, by defining TL in relation to identity, the individuality of TL is maintained at the same time as the social and collective influences on identity are taken into account: they are strongly emphasized, described and discussed in contemporary sociological approaches to the development and understanding of identity. So this proposed definition of TL certainly opens the path to a deeper understanding of today's interaction between the individual and the social and collective.

As stressed by Kokkos (2013) there is a tendency for European contributions to the understanding of TL to include the social dimension, influence and dependence, and to involve current sociological understandings of identity, more than the dominant American approaches. This suggests that they may provide the basis for deeper understanding of the role of TL in relation to interaction between the individual and the social.

Learning psychology, motivation and defence

Finally, it must also be noted that there is a wide range of psychological conditions involved in all kinds of learning. These are also relevant to TL, and will be easier to deal with if the proposed broader and more inclusive definition of TL in relation to the identity is accepted. As examples of this, I shall here briefly refer to the topics of motivation and defence as two central areas of general learning psychology (Illeris, 2007).

The question of motivation is very important in any learning, and in relation to more profound or TL the nature and strength of the motivation involved is crucial—people do not transform elements of themselves or their identities if they do not have serious reasons to do so. These reasons may be internal, external or both—but analytically the important thing is that transformations need strong motivation and cannot be expected to occur without this. As most teachers, instructors, managers and supervisors are aware of this, consciously or unconsciously, they try to motivate their students, employees or clients. But in doing so they often make the mistake of trying to create motivation, rather than finding it—not realizing that motivation which is strong enough to trigger TL must be deeply rooted in the person and cannot just be created or imposed (cf. Illeris, 2007). A central challenge in promoting TL is to find and connect to the psychological or practical potentials in learners' existence and life world which are so strong that they can justify the exertion required for transformation.

It is also important to be aware that all learning, and especially more demanding processes of learning, very often involve overcoming barriers to learning in the form of defence or resistance. In liquid modernity we are all confronted with so many new situations and learning possibilities that we have to protect ourselves against being overwhelmed and destabilized by constant change. We therefore develop a learning defence system which is partly unconscious and automatic. We cannot take in all learning possibilities, nor even consciously decide which to take in and which to refuse (cf. Illeris, 2007). A very strong part of this defensive system is the identity defence, which actually protects us against too much TL that could result in some kind of instability. This must be accepted, understood and respected. The way to deal with it is not through ingenious methods, activities or subterfuges, but rather to try to detect whether the learners actually have any interest in involving themselves in transformations—and, if so, where these interests are rooted subjectively and how they can be addressed.

Conclusion

In the contemporary liquid and individualized world there is no doubt that TL will be increasingly important to individuals, as well as to various communities and movements, private and public enterprises, nations and even to the future of the world, which we all share, in order to cope with the constant conditions of change at all levels.

It is therefore also essential that the possibilities and qualities of TL are further developed. This implies a demand for the concept and theory of TL to be updated in accordance with contemporary needs. Thus, a definition which is comprehensive, as well as simple and clear must be developed, and generally accepted. In the above, I have argued why this definition can and should be related to the concept of identity—essentially because this concept, as discussed in Illeris (2014), is a keyword that includes all dimensions of mental activity, excludes less important learning, and has a central and well-elaborated position in contemporary psychology and sociology.

References

Alheit, P. (2009). Biographical learning—Within the new lifelong learning discourse. In K. Illeris (Ed.), *Contemporary theories of learning* (pp. 116–128). London: Routledge.
Allport, G. W. (1961). *Pattern and growth of personality*. New York, NY: Holt, Rineholt and Winston.
Bandura, A. (1997). *Self-efficacy: The exercise of control*. New York, NY: W.H. Freeman and Company.
Bauman, Z. (2000). *Liquid modernity*. Cambridge: Polity Press.
Bauman, Z. (2001). *The individualized society*. Cambridge: Polity Press.
Beck, U. (1986/1992). *Risk society: Towards a new modernity*. London: Sage.
Beck, U., & Beck-Gernsheim, E. (1994/2002). *Individualization: Institutionalized individualism and its social and political consequences*. London: Sage.
Boud, D., Koegh, R., & Walker, D. (Eds.). (1985). *Reflection: Turning experience into learning*. London: Kogan Page.
Boyd, R. D., & Myers, G. J. (1988). Transformative education. *International Journal of Lifelong Education, 7*, 261–284.
Brookfield, S. (2000). Transformative learning as ideology critique. In J. Mezirow, et al. (Eds.), *Learning as transformation: Critical perspectives on a theory in progress* (pp. 125–148). San Francisco, CA: Jossey-Bass.
Collard, S., & Law, M. (1989). The limits of perspective transformation: A critique of Mezirow's theory. *Adult Education Quarterly, 39*, 99–107.
Côté, J. E., & Levine, C. G. (2002). *Identity formation, agency and culture: A social psychological synthesis*. Mahmah, NJ: Lawrence Erlbaum Associates.
Cranton, P. (1994/2005). *Understanding and promoting transformative learning*. San Francisco, CA: Jossey-Bass.
Cranton, P., & Kasl, E. (2012). A response to Michael Newman's 'calling transformative learning into question: Some mutinous thoughts'. *Adult Education Quarterly, 62*, 293–398.
Dirkx, J. (1997). Nurturing soul in adult learning. In P. Cranton (Ed.), *Transformative learning in action* (pp. 79–88). San Francisco, CA: Jossey-Bass.
Dirkx, J. (1998). Transformative learning theory in the practice of adult education: An overview. *Journal of Lifelong Learning, 7*, 1–14.
Dirkx, J. (2006). Engaging emotions in adult learning: A Jungian perspective on emotion and

transformative learning. In E. W. Taylor (Ed.), *Teaching for change. New directions in adult and continuing education* (pp. 15–26). San Francisco: Jossey-Bass.

Dirkx, J. (2012a). Nurturing soul work: A Jungian approach to transformative learning. In E. W. Taylor & P. Cranton (Eds.), *The handbook of transformative learning: Theory, research, and practice* (pp. 116–130). San Francisco, CA: Jossey-Bass.

Dirkx, J. (2012b). Self-formation and transformative learning: A response to 'calling transformative learning into question: Some mutinous thoughts,' by Michael Newman. *Adult Education Quarterly, 62,* 399–405.

Erikson, E. H. (1950). *Childhood and society.* New York, NY: Norton.

Erikson, E. H. (1968). *Identity, youth and crisis.* New York, NY: Norton.

Erikson, E. H. (1982). *The life cycle completed.* New York, NY: Norton.

Freire, P. (1970). *Pedagogy of the oppressed.* New York, NY: Seabury.

Gergen, K. J. (1991). *The saturated self: Dilemmas of identity in contemporary life.* New York, NY: Basic Books.

Gergen, K. J. (1994). *Realities and relationships.* Cambridge, MA: Harvard University Press.

Giddens, A. (1990). *The consequences of modernity.* Stanford, CA: Stanford University Press.

Giddens, A. (1991). *Modernity and self-identity.* Cambridge: Polity Press.

Gnahs, D. (2011). *Competencies: How they are acquired and measured.* Opladen: Barbara Budrich Publishers.

Gould, R. (1978). *Transformation, growth and change in adult life.* New York, NY: Simon & Schuster.

Gould, R. (1990). The therapeutic learning program. In J. Mezirow, et al. (Eds.), *Fostering critical reflection in adulthood: A guide to transformative and emancipatory learning.* San Francisco, CA: Jossey-Bass.

Habermas, J. (1968/1971). *Knowledge and human interests.* Boston, MA: Beacon Press.

Illeris, K. (2002). *The three dimensions of learning.* Leicester: NIACE (American issue 2004. Malabar, FL: Krieger Publishing).

Illeris, K. (2004). Transformative learning in the perspective of a comprehensive learning theory. *Journal of Transformative Education, 2,* 79–89.

Illeris, K. (2007). *How we learn: Learning and non-learning in school and beyond.* London: Routledge.

Illeris, K. (2009). Competence, learning and education: How can competencies be learned, and how can they be developed in formal education. In K. Illeris (Ed.), *International perspectives on competence development* (pp. 7–20). London: Routledge.

Illeris, K. (2012). *Kompetence: hvad, hvordan, hvorfor?* [Competence: What, why, how?] Copenhagen: Samfundslitteratur.

Illeris, K. (2014). *Transformative learning and identity.* London: Routledge.

Jarvis, P. (2006). *Towards a comprehensive theory of human learning.* London: Routledge.

Jarvis, P. (2009). Learning to be a person in society: Learning to be me. In K. Illeris (Ed.), *Contemporary theories of learning* (pp. 21–34). London: Routledge.

Jenkins, R. (2004). *Social identity.* London: Routledge.

Kegan, R. (2000). What 'form' transforms? A constructive-developmental approach to transformative learning. In J. Mezirow, et al. (Eds.), *Learning as transformation: Critical perspectives on a theory in progress* (pp. 35–69). San Francisco, CA: Jossey-Bass.

Kernberg, O. (1975). *Borderline conditions and pathological narcissism.* New York, NY: Jason Arouson.

Kohut, H. (1971). *The analysis of the self: A systematic approach to the psychoanalytic treatment of narcissistic personality disorders.* New York, NY: International Universities Press.

Kohut, H. (1977). *The restoration of the self.* New York, NY: International Universities Press.

Kokkos, A. (2013). Could transformative learning be appreciated in Europe? In *Paper for the 7th European Research Conference,* ESREA, Berlin, September 4–7.

Kolb, D. A. (1984). *Experiential learning: Experience as the source of learning and development.* Englewood Cliffs, NJ: Prentice-Hall.

Lasch, C. (1978). *The culture of narcissism: American life in an age of diminishing expectations.* New York, NY: Norton.

Mezirow, J. (1978). *Education for perspective transformation: Women's re-entry programs in community college.* New York, NY: Teachers College, Columbia University.
Mezirow, J. (1990). How critical reflection triggers transformative learning. In J. Mezirow, et al. (Eds.), *Fostering critical reflection in adulthood.* San Francisco, CA: Jossey-Bass.
Mezirow, J. (1991). *Transformative dimensions of adult learning.* San Francisco, CA: Jossey-Bass.
Mezirow, J. (2000). Learning to think like an adult. Core conceptions of tranformation theory. In J. Mezirow, et al. (Eds.), *Learning as transformation: Critical perspectives on a theory in progress* (pp. 3–33). San Francisco, CA: Jossey-Bass.
Mezirow, J. (2006). An overview on transformative learning. In P. Sutherland & J. Crowther (Eds.), *Lifelong learning: Concepts and contexts* (pp. 24–38). London: Routledge (also in Illeris, K. [Ed.]. [2009]. *Contemporary theories of learning.* London: Routledge).
Mezirow, J. (2009). Transformative learning theory. In J. Mezirow, E. W. Taylor, & Associates (Eds.), *Transformative learning in practice: Insights from community, workplace and higher education* (pp. 18–32). San Francisco, CA: Jossey-Bass.
Newman, M. (2012). Calling transformative learning into question: Some mutinous thoughts. *Adult Education Quarterly, 62,* 399–411.
OECD. (2003). *Definition and selection of competencies: Theoretical and conceptual foundations (DeSeCo).* Paris: Author.
OECD. (2005). *The definition and selection of key competencies: Executive summary.* Paris: Author.
Piaget, J. (1936/1952). *The origin of intelligence in children.* New York, NY: International Universities Press.
Rogers, C. R. (1951). *Client-centered therapy.* Boston, MA: Houghton-Mifflin.
Rogers, C. R. (1961). *On becoming a person.* Boston, MA: Houghton-Mifflin.
Rogers, C. R. (1969). *Freedom to learn.* Columbus, OH: Charles E. Merrill.
Rychen, D. S., & Salganik, L. H. (Eds.). (2003). *Key competencies for a successful life and a well-functioning society.* Cambridge, MA: Hogrefe & Huber.
Sennett, R. (1998). *The corrosion of character.* New York, NY: Norton.
Sennett, R. (2006). *The culture of the new capitalism.* New Haven, CT: Yale University Press.
Stern, D. N. (1985). *The interpersonal world of the infant: A view from psychoanalysis and developmental psychology.* New York, NY: Basic Books.
Taylor, C. (1989). *Sources of the self: The making of modern identity.* Cambridge, MA: Harvard University Press.
Taylor, E. W. (2008). Transformative learning theory. In S. Merriam (Ed.), *Third update on adult learning theory* (pp. 5–16). San Francisco, CA: Jossey-Bass.
Tennant, M. (1988/2005). *Psychology and adult learning.* London: Routledge.
Tennant, M. (2012). *The learning self: Understanding the potential for transformation.* San Francisco, CA: Jossey-Bass.
Weil, S. W., & McGill, I. (Eds.). (1989). *Making sense of experiential learning: Diversity in theory and practice.* Buckingham: Open University Press.
Ziehe, T. (1975). *Pubertät und Narzissmus* [Puberty and narcissism]. Frankfurt a.M: Europäische Verlagsanstalt.
Ziehe, T. (2009). 'Normal learning problems' in youth: In the context of underlying cultural convictions. In K. Illeris (Ed.), *Contemporary theories of learning* (pp. 184–199). London: Routledge.
Ziehe, T., & Stubenrauch, H. (1982). *Plädoyer für ungewöhnlisches Lernen* [Pleading for unusual learning]. Reinbek: Rowohlt.

PART V

LEARNING IN WORKING LIFE

CHAPTER 18

WORKPLACES AND LEARNING

Why learning at work?

During the 1990s 'workplace learning', 'work-based learning' and the like became popular slogans in the context of vocationally oriented education and personnel development. Considerable interest has arisen on many sides – in practice, in theory, in politics, locally, nationally and internationally – for placing rising emphasis on the vocationally oriented learning and development that take place directly at the workplace, because such learning and development meet a number of current challenges to the qualification of the staff perhaps better than learning at courses and in educational institutions.

This situation is fundamentally paradoxical, because as a point of departure workplace learning has precisely been the general and obvious form of vocationally oriented learning and qualification ever since a distinction began to be made between working life and the rest of life. Historically there has been a clear tendency for increasingly larger parts of qualification being transferred from the workplaces to formalized types of school, education and course activity, as working life and the rest of society gradually have become more and more complex. And there have, of course, been important reasons for this. Expensive school and educational systems are not established and developed if they would make no difference.

This development got under way first and foremost with the breakthrough and spread of industrialization and capitalism up through the nineteenth century, and it has been proved time and again that the decisive dynamism in this development lay in the need for fundamental and gradually more and more differentiated socialization and qualification for the requirements of wage labour (cf. e.g. Masuch, 1972). On a basic level, this requires a certain attitude that is not inborn: selling oneself as labour and loyally performing work determined by others within certain time frames.

Ever since wage labour became the general type of work relation, the requirements concerning wage labourers' qualifications, practical as well as personal, have grown and grown. They have become increasingly differentiated and it has become increasingly more difficult for workplaces to undertake up-to-date training.

Originally, apprenticeships in Denmark lasted for seven years and periods at school were not included. In time, the apprenticeship was cut to three to four years and evening schools provided a supplement. Starting in 1956, one weekly school day was introduced, and since 1972 lengthy periods of schooling have been built into all types of apprenticeships, while the time at the workplace has been reduced.

In other European countries there has been a similar development. Today we must reckon with the need for both vocational basic training courses and workplace training having to be brought up to date to a considerable extent with supplementary training or direct retraining outside the workplace.

The trend in this has been absolutely clear: more and more schooling and less and less educational training at the workplaces. How can it be then that it is precisely now that a significant counter trend has arisen that wishes to 'return' as much learning as possible to working life?

The cause of all of this should primarily be sought in the extensive and profound developments and changes in the structures of society that have been described as the transition to late modernity, post modernity, cultural liberation, the knowledge society, the information society and the like, and which encompass the breakthrough of market management, globalization and the new technologies (cf. e.g. Giddens, 1990; Beck, 1992; Bauman, 1998).

This process of change has included two key development trends in the area of learning and education. In the first place, there has been a shift away from the notion that education and qualification were something that essentially belonged to childhood and youth, something that could be finished when a certain vocational competence had been acquired upon which one could base one's activity for a forty to fifty year career, if necessary with occasional updating. This notion was well matched by a school and educational system that could deliver such vocational competences and could be expanded and differentiated in step with developments. But it is clear that this situation no longer prevails. Everyone must be prepared for their working functions changing constantly and radically during the whole of their working lives. Therefore, what is needed today is what is typically called 'lifelong', 'lifewide' and 'lifedeep' learning (cf. e.g. EU Commission, 2000; Illeris, 2004), and the extent and the way it best takes place and the role the school and the educational system can play in this context are open questions.

Secondly, 'what is to be learned' has changed in nature. At one time the learning targets of the school and education programmes were referred to in categories such as knowledge, skills, attitudes, or more generally, qualifications. All of this is, naturally, still necessary. But at the same time it must necessarily be updated, developed, reorganized and recreated constantly to fit new situations, so that it quickly and flexibly can be used in changed contexts that are not known at present but which we know with certainty will come. This is the essence of the current concepts of competences and competence development (cf. e.g. Beckett and Hager, 2002; Illeris, 2004, 2009a). And it is obviously a huge challenge to the school and education system to supply competences for the solution of problems and situations that are unknown at time of learning. How is this to be done?

It is first and foremost on the basis of these matters that the new ideas about workplace learning have emerged and have gained ground. Would it not be easier, less expensive and more efficient if such development and constant adaptation of competences were to take place where the competences are to be utilized and where there is always first-hand knowledge of what is new? In the case of vocationally oriented competences, this would, after all, be directly in the workplaces, or in networks and organizations where the workplaces are partners that can ensure that the processes are always up-to-date.

And would this not also be more democratic? After all, in this way those who are directly affected can always know what is going on and play a part in deciding what is to take place and how. And is there not also a broad interest on the part of society at one and the same time to ensure in this way an up-to-date competence development and co-decision for ordinary people, which can be far more wide-ranging and direct than when learning takes place in schools and institutions that have their own agenda and modes of functioning?

There would seem to be many good arguments for the idea of workplace learning from the point of view of learning theory, efficiency and democracy. This is why it also has obtained many strong adherents. Interest has not least been expressed in the supranational expert organizations such as the OECD, the EU and the World Bank as a key element in the lifelong learning that at one and the same time can lead to economic growth, personal development for the individual and increased social balance, nationally and internationally (cf. e.g. OECD, 2000, 2001). But other interests are also at stake that cannot be disregarded if a full perception of the new trend is to be obtained.

In the first place, it is clear that the steadily growing education requirements are expensive, and the state has, therefore, an obvious interest in some of the burden being moved out of the institutions – but not all of it, because the state also has overall responsibility for the level of education and training of the workforce as an important prerequisite for economic growth and global competitiveness. If vocationally oriented training is left completely to the labour market, the qualification could easily become too short-sighted and narrow. Therefore the state will quite generally aim for interaction between institutionalized vocationally oriented education and workplace learning and seek to get the business sector and the participants to undertake as great a part of the financing as possible.

The enterprises/employers will naturally be reluctant to undertake this. They are basically interested in education being publicly financed unless it is significantly personal or enterprise specific in nature. But on the other hand, workplace learning would give the enterprises more influence over what is learned and how, and a lot of general education in which the individual enterprise can see no direct interest could be reduced in step with learning taking place directly in the workplace. Here also the attitude would in principle be dual, but would very largely tend to welcome more workplace learning, especially if it were linked with some or other type of financial compensation.

The workers and their organizations would also be largely positive. It would be necessary, to a lesser degree, for the workers to 'go back to school': on the individual level the great majority think that they learn better in informal contexts and at their work than in institutionalized education (cf. e.g. CEDEFOP, 2003). And the trade unions would also find it easier to influence the way in which it takes place. On the other hand, it is obvious that formalized education is in general better at ensuring the workforce a good, well-documented level of education, and the unions can perhaps exert more influence when the representatives of the state play a part in decision making than they can achieve in direct interaction with the employers.

Finally, it should not be forgotten that the institutions and the teachers have a strong self-interest in maintenance of the formalized study programmes. Even though there are at present some experiments involving teachers coming out to the enterprises and taking part in organizing interactively oriented courses, this can hardly make up for the safe incomes ensured by permanent courses at the schools.

There are thus many and very different interests at play when it comes to learning in working life, and it is also part of late modern market society that one should not believe all one hears. Today goods, ideas and attitudes are marketed professionally on the basis of interests that are not always immediately visible.

But there are also some quite fundamental problems in connection with workplace learning that are not very much in focus right now. First and foremost, the overall aim of the workplaces is to produce goods and services and not to produce learning. And even though in many cases it would make good economic sense to invest in upgrading the employees' qualifications, there is an unmistakable tendency that when a pressed situation arises – and this seems frequently to be the case in late modern market society – learning measures will often be downgraded in prioritization in relation to current short-term needs.

This is why there is so much focus on the learning that can take place more or less 'by chance' in direct connection with the performance of the work and which thus in principle neither costs anything nor must be prioritized – the learning that in a manner of speaking comes 'by itself' (cf. Marsick and Watkins, 1990; Garrick, 1998). The problem is, however, that precisely this kind of learning, to a far greater extent than learning in working life that is structured and planned, tends to be narrow and lacking in theory. When it takes place in direct connection with the work, one can easily focus on what can create improvements here and now, while the broad lines and the wider contexts are omitted and with them the possibility of the learning having a wider application value in new situations and in connection with a more general understanding and an overview, which is decisive for what we call competence (cf. Billett, 2001; Beckett and Hager, 2002; Illeris et al., 2004 for a broader discussion of these matters).

The great current interest in workplace learning is thus not as unambiguous as it often purports to be. But on the other hand there are clearly also some current matters pulling the picture in this direction, and there is good reason to expect workplace learning to play a greater role in the educational scene in the future. I shall therefore in the following sections first try to develop a more structured conception of the main features of such learning. Next, I shall discuss workplace learning in relation to different theoretical approaches and point out some basic features that must be considered. Finally, I shall relate learning in working life to the concept of competence development, which seems to be the kind of learning that is especially intended or hoped for in this connection.

Some basic issues and concepts on learning

The most fundamental condition of human learning is that all learning includes two essentially different types of process: an external interaction process between the learner and his or her social, cultural and material environment, and an internal psychological process of elaboration and acquisition in which new impulses are connected with the results of prior learning.

The criteria of the interaction process are of a social and societal character, i.e. they are determined by time and place. The individual is in interaction with an environment that includes other people, a specific culture, technology and so on, which are characterized by their time and society. In the late modern globalized world, this is all mixed up in a giant and rapidly changing hotchpotch that offers unlimited, and to a great extent also unstructured, possibilities for learning. Hence, the often formulated need for learning to learn, i.e. creating a personal structure or a value system to sort out what is worth learning from what is not. This is also the background for understandings such as those of the social constructionists, focusing on the needs, difficulties and prevalence of this interaction process in late modernity (e.g. Gergen, 1994).

But no matter how dominant and imperative the interaction process has become, in learning there is also always a process of individual acquisition in which the impulses from the interaction are incorporated. As discussed by such scholars as Piaget (e.g. 1952) and Ausubel (1968), the core of this process is that the new impressions are connected with the results of prior learning in a way that influences both. Thus, the outcome of the individual acquisition process is always dependent on what has already been acquired, and ultimately the criteria of this process are of a biological nature and determined by the extensive, but not infinite, possibilities of the human brain and central nervous system to cope with, structure, retain and create meaning out of impressions as perceived by our senses.

However, learning, thinking, remembering, understanding and similar functions are not just cognitive or content matters, although they have generally been conceived of as such by traditional learning psychology. Whether the frame of reference is common sense, Freudian psychology, modern management, or brand new results of brain research, there is lots of imperative evidence that all such functions are also inseparably connected with emotions and motivation. The Austrian-American psychologist Hans Furth (1987), by combining the findings and theories of Piaget and Freud, has unravelled how cognition and emotions during the pre-school years gradually separate as distinctive but never isolated functions; and the Portuguese-American neurologist Antonio Damasio (1994) has explained how this works in our brain and what disastrous consequences it has when the connections between the two are cut by damage to the brain, even when neither of the functions in themselves has been affected. Thus the acquisition process also necessarily always has both a cognitive and an emotional side, or more broadly spoken: a *content* and an *incentive* side.

Consequently, all learning always includes three dimensions which must always be considered if an understanding or analysis of a learning situation is to be adequate: the content dimension of knowledge, understandings, skills, abilities, attitudes and the like; the incentive dimension of emotion, feelings, motivation and volition; and the social dimension of interaction, communication and cooperation – all of which are embedded in a societally situated context. The learning processes and dimensions may be illustrated by Figure 18.1.

A model of workplace learning

When it comes to the issue of workplace learning the point of departure should be taken in what characterizes workplaces and working life as a space for learning. If this is seen in relation to the learning triangle, it is obvious that it has mainly to do with the interaction dimension. The workplace also includes management, colleagues, the organization and its relations and role in society. From this point of view a triangle depicting the workplace as a learning space and matching the learning triangle can be drawn as shown in Figure 18.2 (Jørgensen and Warring, 2003; Illeris et al., 2004):

Parallel to the division of the acquisition process of learning the workplace environment also contains two fundamentally different elements which can be termed the technical-organizational learning environment and the social-cultural learning environment. The technical-organizational learning environment is about matters such as work content and division of labour, the opportunities for autonomy and using qualifications, the possibilities of social interaction, and the extent to which the work is a strain on the employees. The social-cultural learning environment concerns social groupings and processes at the workplace and matters such as traditions, norms and values and covers communities of work, cultural communities and political communities.

The third dimension of the learning environment is about the interaction between the environment as a whole and the learners. It is, so to say, the same interaction process as the one which is involved in the learning triangle, but seen as part of the learning life and not as part of the learners as individuals. It involves in general such elements as the workers' or employees' social and cultural backgrounds, their actual life situations, and their future perspectives, and specifically in relation to the single learner such elements as their family background and school and work experience.

In the book entitled *Learning in Working Life* (Illeris et al., 2004), these dimensions were merged with the learning triangle into what was termed 'a double perspective on learning in working life' in the 'holistic model' shown in Figure 18.2.

It should be noted that in addition to the dimensions of the two triangles each of them here also includes a central focus area round the meeting point of the double arrows. In the learning triangle this focus area is the learner's personal *identity*, which psychologically is where all that is learnt sums up into the individual experience of 'who I am' and 'how I am experienced by others' (Illeris, 2003, 2007) and especially the parts of the identity which comprise the personal relations to working life and therefore constitute the 'work identity' (Andersen et al., 1994). In the workplace environment triangle the central focus area is the *workplace practice*, which comprises the work activities including all the tools and artefacts, the work patterns and personal and social relations, positions, power conditions, etc.

In this way the model shows that the essential general workplace learning takes place in the interaction between workplace practice and the learner's work identity – and it is also this learning that takes on the character of competence development (to which I shall return later). But there is also in the model space for less essential learning processes that more or less circumvent these core fields, such as the acquisition of certain technical skills that can take place in a more limited interaction anchored between the workplace's technical-organizational learning environment and mainly the content dimension of the learner's acquisition, but naturally also can be related to the model's other elements to a greater or lesser extent.

Different approaches to workplace learning

On the more concrete level, there are a number of approaches to what is central in connection with the understanding of workplace learning. In line with a classic learning understanding, most of these approaches place the main emphasis on the individual acquisition process, corresponding to the horizontal double arrow at the top of the model in Figure 18.2.

This applies, in the first place, to the so-called industrial sociological approach, which in particular has interested itself in the qualification requirements the work has of the employees and how the qualifications are developed, now also including to a high degree what has been termed the 'process independent' or later the 'generic qualifications'.

Next, it applies as point of reference to the management-anchored approach also, which is termed 'organizational learning'. Americans Chris Argyris and Donald Schön have been key figures here for a generation, and they have emphasized, *inter alia*, that the employees' learning is crucial to the development of the enterprises and that a distinction must be made between single-loop learning, which remains within, and double-loop learning, which exceeds the existing frames of understanding (cf. Argyris and Schön, 1978, 1996; Argyris, 1992).

Finally, it also refers to the approach that has roots in general adult education,

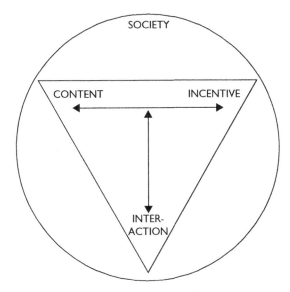

Figure 18.1 The basic processes and dimensions of learning

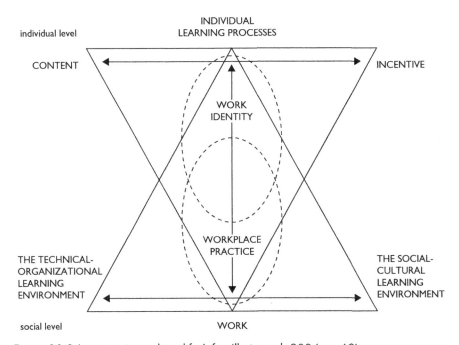

Figure 18.2 Learning in working life (after Illeris et al. 2004, p. 69)

mostly to individual learning when it, typically on a humanistic basis, interests itself in the employees' experience and interest in learning (cf. e.g. Weil and McGill, 1989; Marsick and Watkins, 1990; Boud and Garrick, 1999; Billett, 2001; Ellström, 2001; Evans et al., 2002; Rainbird et al., 2004).

In contrast are the approaches that very largely focus on the workplace as learning environment and the development or 'learning' of the workplace, i.e. on the bottom horizontal double arrow in Figure 18.2. This primarily concerns the approach that goes under the name of 'the learning organisation'. This is originally a branching out of the organizational understanding of learning, but with the decisive difference that here the focus is on what is understood as the organization's 'learning' that is made independent as something different and more than the sum of the employees' learning. A key work here is Peter Senge's book about 'the fifth discipline' (Senge, 1990). It must be clear, however, that with the learning concept which has been introduced here one cannot say that the organization can learn – and much of what is marketed under the term 'the learning organization' in my opinion has more to do with management and sometimes smart formulations than with learning.

Also the approach that was launched with the book by Jean Lave and Etienne Wenger on *Situated Learning* (Lave & Wenger, 1991) and later continued by Wenger in *Communities of Practice* (Wenger, 1998), must be said to be mainly oriented towards the workplace as the focal point of learning. This is the case despite the fact that to a large extent it has its roots in the Russian cultural-historical tradition and Vygotsky's understanding of learning, which is quite classically oriented towards the individual acquisition process. In Lave and Wenger it seems almost to be the case that when the individual has first entered a community of practice, by means of a learning process he or she will automatically move from 'legitimate peripheral participation' towards a more central and competent position. A more individual oriented formulation of Vygotsky's approach can, however, be found in Finnish Yrjö Engeström, who, though he may work with learning in organizations, does so with a high degree of focus on the individuals (cf. e.g. Engeström, 2009).

I am thus on the way towards the third major approach to workplace learning, namely the approach that primarily focuses on the interaction between the social and the individual level, i.e. on the vertical double arrow in the middle of the model in Figure 18.3. Here there is reason to note the approach that has its roots in the 'critical theory' of the German-American so-called Frankfurt School. The best-known representative of this school is the German sociologist and philosopher Jürgen Habermas (1984–87) – but in relation to workplace learning other names are more important (although they have generally published only in German). They have focused mainly on the social conditions and their significance for the consciousness formation of the individual, in particular with Oskar Negt's work concerning 'Sociological Imagination and Exemplary Learning' (Negt, 1968, cf. Illeris, 2007). But an important contribution is also to be found in the work of Ute Volmerg concerning the significance of the employees' opportunities for organizing their own work, for communication with others at work and for applying the qualifications they have acquired as the three decisive focal points for their learning possibilities in working life (Volmerg, 1976). Finally there should be mention of Birgit Volmerg et al.'s study of 'The Life World of Private Enterprises', i.e. the way in which the employees seek and utilize the possibilities of the workplace for a free space to set their own agenda (Volmerg et al., 1986; Leithäuser, 2000).

It is basically also this type of approach I have followed in my work although I simultaneously include the individual acquisition process to a high degree (Andersen et al., 1994, 1996; Illeris et al., 2004; Illeris, 2005, 2007, 2009b).

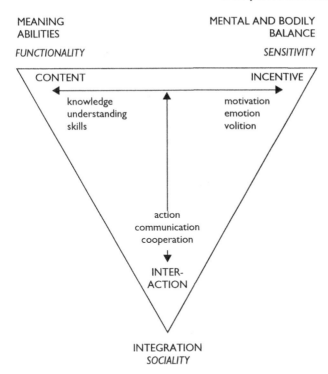

Figure 18.3 Learning as competence development

General features of workplace learning

If one tries to cut across all these approaches, it is possible in general to extract a number of possibilities and problems that especially characterize workplace learning. Quite fundamentally, a huge amount of learning takes place in direct connection with the performance of the work, and as mentioned earlier, the employees typically experience that this learning is of greater importance for them than learning in institutionalized education (CEDEFOP, 2003). Viewed from the outside it must, however, be maintained that fundamentally this learning is accidental in nature and that it is usually narrow and without theoretical foundation.

However, by systematically building up a learning-oriented environment this learning can be strengthened considerably – this is the main idea behind the approaches called 'organizational learning' and 'the learning organization', although they do not agree when it comes to the relation between the individual and the organization. Nonetheless the risk will still remain of the learning obtaining a certain accidental flavour and an inadequate structure and systematics. Moreover, there is a tendency for the employees who are already best qualified to profit more from this procedure. But it is also possible to try to counteract this by introducing such types of activities as self-directed groups, projects or action learning programmes for all employees (cf. Illeris et al., 2004).

Another possibility – which can very well be combined with organizational learning – is to aim at targeted learning measures in close connection with the work. This can take place by means of personal backing for the individual employee in the form of instruction, pedagogic mentoring, partner guidance, mentor schemes or coaching, through broadly based support from so-called 'ambassadors', 'super users' or 'gardeners', who are especially used in the ICT field, or through access to consultant assistance, and it can take place through teaching activities in close connection with the work. All of this can be backed up by means of regular staff development interviews or the like (cf. Illeris et al., 2004).

Finally, there can be emphasis on more general measures, such as internal or external networks and experience groups or job exchange and job rotation schemes, where there is also a possibility for involving all staff organizationally (cf. Illeris et al., 2004).

Under all circumstances there are three important issues that exist to one extent or another. The first is that workplace learning, to an even higher degree than learning by means of institutionalized education, has a tendency to especially favour those who already have the best education (the so-called 'Matthew effect': "For whoever has to him shall be given and he shall be caused to be in abundance", Matthew 13:12). The second is that the necessary work will always receive higher priority than learning-oriented measures. The third is that learning measures can have a disturbing effect on the targeted work which is the purpose of the workplace.

These issues can be dealt with to a certain degree by workplace learning being combined with courses and education programmes, for example such as those that take place in the so-called alternating education programmes in the apprentice and professional fields where there is alternation between school and work experience periods.

Learning as competence development

In relation to workplace it is today also important to discuss how such learning in theory and practice can obtain the qualities of what is termed 'competence development' as this to a great extent seems to be what could be a main advantage of learning in more or less direct connection to the workplace. I shall start this discussion by examining, in slightly more detail, some general matters to do with each of the three learning dimensions, namely what we generally – consciously or unconsciously – aim at achieving within each of the three dimensions when we learn something, and what the overall result could be.

As already mentioned, the content dimension is about what we learn. In this dimension the learner's *knowledge, understanding, skills* and generally his/her ways of dealing with life are developed and through this we attempt to generate *meaning*, i.e. a coherent understanding of the different matters in existence (cf. e.g. Bruner, 1990; Mezirow, 1990, 1991; Wenger, 1998), and also to develop *abilities* that enable us to tackle the practical challenges of life. To the extent that we succeed in this endeavour, we develop out *functionality* as a whole, i.e. our capacity to function appropriately in the various contexts in which we are involved. This appropriateness is directly linked to our placing and interests in the current situation in relation to our qualifications and future perspectives, but as such quite general, just as learning as a whole is related to the survival possibilities of the individual and the species.

As mentioned before, it is very largely the content dimension that learning research traditionally has concerned itself with, and it is also this dimension that is in direct focus when one speaks about learning in everyday language. But the learning triangle points to other matters being at stake in connection with learning.

Acquisition has also an incentive dimension covering the motivational, the emotional and the volitional – or what can be summed up as the motive forces or engagement of learning. This dimension is concerned with mobilization of the mental energy required by learning, and we fundamentally engage ourselves in this mobilization in order to constantly maintain our *mental and bodily balance*. In so doing, through this dimension we simultaneously develop our *sensitivity* in relation to ourselves and our environment.

These two dimensions are activated simultaneously and in an integrated fashion by impulses from the interactive process between the individual and the environment. The content that is learned is therefore, as previously mentioned, always marked or 'obsessed' by the nature of the mental engagement that has mobilized the mental energy necessary for the learning process to take place. On the other hand, the incentive basis is also always influenced by the content with which the learning is concerned. For instance, a new understanding or an improved skill alters our emotional and motivational and also perhaps our volitional patterns.

Learning psychology has traditionally studied the acquisition of content independent of the incentive dimension – but there have also been learning researchers who have strongly emphasized the connection, for example Lev Vygotsky (1986 [1934]) and Hans Furth (1987), and this has later been conclusively supported by brain research, e.g. Antonio Damasio (1994).

Finally, there is the interaction dimension of learning, which is concerned with the individual's interaction with his/her social and material environment on two levels: on the one hand the close, social level in which the interactive situation is placed, for example in a classroom or a working group, and on the other hand the general societal level that establishes the premises for the interaction.

This dimension promotes the individual's *integration* in relevant social contexts and communities and by this contributes to the development of the learner's *sociality*, i.e. ability to become engaged and function appropriately in various forms of social interaction between people. The development itself of sociality, however, takes place through the two dimensions of the acquisition process and is thereby marked by what concerns the interactive process and the nature of our relationship to it.

It is now possible to elaborate the learning triangle in Figure 18.1 into a new triangle as shown in Figure 18.3 by entering the signal words used to qualify the nature of each of the three dimensions, and outside each of the angles to place the key words for what we aim at (upright) and what we generate (italics). What then emerges is that in our learning as a whole we attempt to develop meaning, skills, mental and bodily balance and social and societal integration, and in this way we simultaneously develop our functionality, sensitivity and sociality.

Such a general characterization means that learning as a whole can promote the development of what in modern parlance is called the learner's *competence*. Or the other way around: that if learning is to be in the nature of competence development, it must contribute to the generation of relevant functionality, sensitivity and sociality which are the main general characteristics of competences. The widespread popularity of this concept is precisely due to its embracing the total scope of the learning dimensions – in contrast to the more limited focus on the content dimension of traditional educational thinking.

Workplace learning and competence development

It is not so very many years ago that competence was mainly a formal and legal matter, something that gave a person a legal right to make decisions in a certain area, especially in the public administration. However, over the last two decades the use of the word has permeated the educational area, working life, management and politics as a modern expression for what a person is actually able to do or achieve.

Thus, in recent years the concept of competences has taken a central position and more or less displaced the concept of qualifications – and this is not merely a chance or indifferent linguistic innovation. On the contrary, it could be said that this linguistic change has pointed to some features which are significant for contemporary learning demand. A very useful definition of the concept, which draws attention precisely to how it surpasses terms as abilities, skills and qualifications, has been given by a Danish social psychologist and member of the former 'Danish Competence Council':

> The concept of competence refers [...] to a person's being qualified in a broader sense. It is not merely that a person masters a professional area, but also that the person can apply this professional knowledge – and more than that, apply it in relation to the requirements inherent in a situation which perhaps in addition is uncertain and unpredictable. Thus competence also includes the person's assessments and attitudes, and ability to draw on a considerable part of his/her more personal qualifications (Jørgensen 1999: 4).

Competence is thus a unifying concept that integrates everything it takes in order to perform in a given situation or context. The concrete qualifications are incorporated in the competence rooted in the personality – or to be more accurate, the work identity – and one may generally also talk of the competence of organizations and nations, including the pattern of personal competences and how they work together.

Where the concept of qualifications historically has its point of departure in requirements for specific knowledge and skills, and to an increasing degree has been used for pointing out that this knowledge and these skills have underlying links and roots in personality, the perception in the concept of competence has, so to speak, been turned upside down. In this concept, the point of departure lies at the personal level in relation to certain contexts, and the more specific qualifications are something that can be drawn in and contribute to realization of the competence. So the concept of qualifications took its point of departure in the individual elements, the individual qualifications, and gradually developed towards a more unified perception, whereas the concept of competence starts with a unity, e.g. the type of person or organization it takes to solve a task or fulfil a job, and on the basis of this points out any possible different qualifications necessary.

It is characteristic that the concept of competence does not, like the concept of qualifications, have its roots in industrial sociology (cf. Braverman, 1974), but in organizational psychology and modern management thinking. This has made it more adequate in relation to modern working life, but it has also given it a dimension of 'smartness' which makes it easier to 'sell' politically and tend toward a superficiality which in this context seems to characterize large parts of the management orientation (cf. Argyris, 2000). Some problems have also developed because a number of national and supranational bodies have taken over the concept and sought to implement it as a tool to govern educational institutions. Wide-ranging work has been initiated to define a number of competences that the various education programmes should aim at and to make these measurable in order to make it possible to judge whether the efforts succeed (cf. Illeris, 2004, 2009b).

However, at the same time it is difficult to deny that the concept of competence captures something central in the current situation of learning and qualification. It is ultimately concerned with how a person, an organization or a nation is able to handle a relevant, but often unforeseen and unpredictable problematic situation, because we know with certainty that late modern development constantly generates new and unknown problems, and the ability to respond openly and in an appropriate way to new problematic situations is crucial in determining who will manage in the globalized market society.

So I find it very important to maintain a broad and holistic understanding of competence both on the general level and *vis-à-vis* a technocratic understanding which is rapidly becoming the horse dragging a carriage of narrow economically oriented control interests that empty the concept of the liberating potential springing from the place of the competences as relevant contemporary mediators between the societal challenges and individual ways of managing them.

The concept of competence can thus be used as a point of departure for a more nuanced understanding of what learning efforts today are about – with a view of reaching a theoretically based and practically tested proposal concerning how up-to-date competence development can be realized for different people in accordance with their possibilities and needs, both within and outside of institutionalized education programmes. Such an approach has, in my opinion, far better and more well-founded possibilities for contributing to real competence development, at the individual level as well as the societal level, than the measuring and comparing approach that has been mentioned above. However, it will to a much higher degree be oriented towards experiments and initiatives at practice level than the top-down control approach inherent in the measuring models.

Quite concretely competence development may be promoted in environments in which it is habitual to re-actualize experience and contexts which lie behind present situations and problems, to interpret ongoing activities in a theoretical conceptual framework, and to deal with topical learning possibilities in relation to the participants' biographies and future perspectives. In such environments there will be room for a meaning and conception-oriented reflection and a steady alternation between the individual and the social levels within the framework of a community (cf. Illeris, 2004).

It is precisely these qualities that make competences so important and attractive in the modern ever-changing world, and at the same time constitutes an immense challenge to education and training of any kind. How can people be educated or trained to function appropriately in situations that are unknown at the time of the acquisition?

This is actually a question that undermines a lot of traditional educational thinking which starts by formulating precise objectives and then tries to deduce educational measures from this. Fundamentally, it must be realized that competences are not something that can be produced like commodities, but precisely something that must be *developed* in and by the person, hence the concept of 'competence development'.

In general it is obvious that the concept of competences captures something that is essential in relation to education and training today, precisely because it relates to how a person, an organization or a nation is able to manage in the constantly changing globalized market society. Thus, the societal changes that fostered this concept and other linked concepts such as 'the learning society', 'the learning organization' and 'lifelong learning' imply a new conception of the relation between learning and education/training with increased focus on informal learning possibilities outside the educational institutions in daily life and in working life especially.

But to capture the impact of this change of perspective it is not enough just to refer to 'practice learning' or 'workplace learning' as has often been the case. It is obvious that the school and education system will still be the 'State Apparatus' which is constructed to be the fundamental public means of providing the competences demanded. Moreover, it will inevitably – also in the future – be in the practical and economic interests of both the private and the public sector that as many competences as possible should be developed outside the workplace and without placing a strain on the economy and daily work conditions of companies and organizations.

Therefore competence development cannot be a means of ensuring savings on public education budgets, which some politicians seem to imagine. On the contrary, it is a challenge demanding increased cooperation between education and training institutions and private as well as public workplaces. In all likelihood this will lead to increased costs for both parties if the promises of adequate and up-to-date competence development are to be met – which is regarded as a key factor in future competitiveness.

Finally, it must also be stressed that a decisive factor in all this will be that competence development programmes are set up in accordance and cooperation with the persons and groupings that are to implement the competences. Whereas qualifications to some extent could be understood and dealt with as "objective" qualities, it is inherent in competences that they include personal and collective motivations, emotions and engagement, and their practical value to a great extent is dependent on a positive interest and attitude. From this point of view competence development could be an important democratizing factor in working life and society in general. But this is by no means always the case.

So, it is a persistent question whether the great commitment to the idea of competence development will be able to meet the positive prospects that it most certainly implies. Like other keywords from the same vocabulary, the concept of competence development seems to have a double impact and to demonstrate tension between a very promising and useful interpretation of significant demands of modern societies and a buzzword, which, behind the tempting surface, hides new smart means of human and economic exploitation of labour (Illeris, 2009a).

References

Andersen, Vibeke, Illeris, Knud, Kjærsgaard, Christian, Larsen, Kirsten, Olesen, Henning Salling, and Ulriksen, Lars (1994) *Qualifications and Living People*. Roskilde: The Adult Education Research Group, Roskilde University.

Andersen, Vibeke, Illeris, Knud, Kjærsgaard, Christian, Larsen, Kirsten, Olesen, Henning Salling, and Ulriksen, Lars (1996) *General Qualification*. Roskilde: The Adult Education Research Group, Roskilde University.

Argyris, Chris (1992) *On Organizational Learning*. Cambridge, MA: Blackwell.

Argyris, Chris (2000) *The Next Challenge in Organizational Learning: Leadership and Change*. Paper presented at the Learning Lab Denmark Opening Conference, Copenhagen, 6 November.

Argyris, Chris and Schön, Donald (1978) *Organizational Learning: A Theory of Action Perspective*. Reading, MA: Addison-Wesley.

Argyris, Chris and Schön, Donald (1996) *Organizational learning II – Theory, Method, Practice*. Reading, MA: Addison-Wesley.

Ausubel, David P. (1968) *Educational Psychology: A Cognitive View*. New York: Holt, Rinehart and Winston.
Bauman, Zygmunt (1998) *Globalization: The Human Consequences*. Cambridge, UK: Polity Press.
Beck, Ulrich (1992 [1986]) *Risk Society: Towards a New Modernity*. London: Sage.
Beckett, David and Hager, Paul (2002) *Life, Work and Learning: Practice in Postmodernity*. London: Routledge.
Billett, Stephen (2001) *Learning in the Workplace: Strategies for Effective Practice*. Crows Nest, NSW: Allen & Unwin.
Boud, David and Garrick, John (eds) (1999) *Understanding Learning at Work*. London: Routledge.
Braverman, Harry (1974) *Labor and Monopoly Capital*. New York: Monthly Review Press.
Bruner, Jerome (1990) *Acts of Meaning*. Cambridge, MA: Harvard University Press.
CEDEFOP (European Centre for the Development of Vocational Training) (2003) *Lifelong Learning: Citizens' Views*. Luxembourg: Office for Official Publications of the EU.
Damasio, Antonio R. (1994) *Descartes' Error: Emotion, Reason and the Human Brain*. New York: Grosset/Putnam.
Ellström, Per-Erik (2001) Integrating Learning and Work: Conceptual Issues and Critical Conditions. *Human Resource Development Quarterly*, 4, pp. 421–436.
Engeström, Yrjö (2009) Expansive Learning: Toward an Activity-Theoretical Reconceptualization. In Knud Illeris (ed.), *Contemporary Theories of Learning*. London: Routledge.
EU Commission (2000) *Memorandum on Lifelong Learning*. Brussels: EU.
Evans, Karen, Hodkinson, Phil and Unwin, Lorna (eds) (2002) *Working to Learn – Transforming Learning in the Workplace*. London: Kogan Page.
Furth, Hans G. (1987) *Knowledge As Desire*. New York: Columbia University Press.
Garrick, John (1998) *Informal Learning in the Workplace: Unmasking Human Resource Development*. London: Routledge.
Gergen, Kenneth, J. (1994) *Realities and Relationships*. Cambridge, MA: Howard University Press.
Giddens, Anthony (1990) *The Consequences of Modernity*. Stanford, CA: Stanford University Press.
Habermas, Jürgen (1984–87 [1981]) *The Theory of Communicative Action*. Cambridge, UK: Polity Press.
Illeris, Knud (2003) Learning, Identity and Self Orientation in Youth. *Young – Nordic Journal of Youth Research*, 4(11), pp. 357–376.
Illeris, Knud (2004) *Adult Education and Adult Learning*. Copenhagen: Roskilde University Press/Malabar, FL: Krieger Publishing.
Illeris, Knud (2005) A Model for Learning in Working Life. *Journal of Workplace Learning*, 8(16), pp. 431–441.
Illeris, Knud (2007) *How We Learn: Learning and Non-Learning in School and Beyond*. London: Routledge.
Illeris, Knud (ed.) (2009a) *International Perspectives on Competence Development*. London: Routledge.
Illeris, Knud (2009b) From Learning to Competence Development. In Knud Illeris (ed.), *International Perspectives on Competence Development*. London: Routledge.
Illeris, Knud and Associates (2004) *Learning in Working Life*. Copenhagen: Roskilde University Press.
Jørgensen, Christian Helms and Warring, Niels (2003) Learning in the Workplace: The Interplay Between Learning Environments and Biographical learning Trajectories. In Christian Helms Jørgensen and Niels Warring (eds), *Adult Education and the Labour Market VII B*. Copenhagen: Roskilde University Press.
Jørgensen, Per Schultz (1999) Hvad er Kompetence? *Uddannelse*, 9, pp. 4–13. [What is Competence?].
Leithäuser, Thomas (2000) Subjectivity, Life World and Work Organization. In Knud Illeris (ed.), *Adult Education in the Perspective of the Learners*. Copenhagen: Roskilde University Press.

Marsick, Victoria J. and Watkins, Karen E. (1990) *Informal and Incidental Learning in the Workplace*. London: Routledge.

Masuch, Michael (1972) *Politische Ökonomie der Ausbildung*. Reinbek: Rowohlt. [The Political Economy of Education].

Mezirow, Jack (1990) How Critical Reflection Triggers Transformative Learning. In Jack Mezirow and Associates (eds), *Fostering Critical Reflection in Adulthood*. San Francisco, CA: Jossey-Bass.

Mezirow, Jack (1991) *Transformative Dimensions of Adult Learning*. San Francisco, CA: Jossey-Bass.

Negt, Oskar (1968) *Soziologisches Phantasie und exemplarisches Lernen*. Frankfurt a.M.: Europäische Verlagsanstalt. [Sociological Imagination and Exemplary Learning].

OECD (2000) *Knowledge Management in the Learning Society*. Paris: OECD. Centre for Educational Research and Innovation.

OECD (2001) *Cities and Regions in the New Learning Economy*. Paris: OECD. Centre for Educational Research and Innovation.

Piaget, Jean (1952 [1936]) *The Origin of Intelligence in Children*. New York: International Universities Press.

Rainbird, Helen, Fuller, Alison and Munro, Anne (eds) (2004) *Workplace Learning in Context*. London: Routledge.

Senge, Peter (1990) *The Fifth Discipline: The Art and Practice of the Learning Organization*. New York: Doubleday.

Volmerg, Birgit, Senghaas-Knobloch, Eva and Leithäuser, Thomas (1986) *Betriebliche Lebenswelt: Einer Sozialpsychologie industrieller Arbeitsverhältnisse*. Opladen: Westdeutscher Verlag. [Life World at Work: A Social Psychology of Work Conditions in Industry].

Volmerg, Ute (1976) Zur Verhältnis von Produktion und Sozialisation am Beispiel industrieller Lohnarbeit. In Thomas Leithäuser and Walter Heinz (eds), *Produktion, Arbeit, Sozialisation*. Frankfurt a.M.: Suhrkamp. [Conditions of Production and Socialization in Industrial Wage Labour].

Vygotsky, Lev (1986 [1934]) *Thought and Language*. Cambridge, MA: MIT Press.

Weil, Susan Warner and McGill, Ian (eds) (1989) *Making Sense of Experiential Learning: Diversity in Theory and Practice*. Buckingham: Open University Press.

Wenger, Etienne (1998) *Communities of Practice: Learning, Meaning and Identity*. Cambridge MA: Cambridge University Press.

CHAPTER 19

WORKPLACE LEARNING AND LEARNING THEORY

Introduction

Within the field of the education system and education research that traditionally has dealt with vocational training and labour market education, radical changes and development have taken place in recent years, and they have also found linguistic expression. On the one hand, the focus has shifted from education and teaching to learning and/or competence development. On the other hand, the interest in vocational training has moved in the direction of workplace learning or work-based learning, including also work-related learning activities outside the workplace.

The background of these changes is to be found broadly in the international and societal development expressed in terms such as "late modernity", "globalisation" and "the knowledge society". It is part of this development that human competence is becoming an increasingly decisive resource and parameter of competition. Additionally, the competence that is needed cannot be established and acquired through education in the more traditional sense – because there is a constant need for change and renewal and because its usability depends on its being linked to a number of personal characteristics such as flexibility, creativity, independence, the ability to cooperate, responsibility, service orientation, etc. For this reason learning and competence development are more interesting focal points than education and teaching, and it has become vital to discover the extent to which this learning and competence development can take place directly in working life in close association with the ongoing change and renewal, or when it would be preferable to put them at some distance by means of more course- and education-like activities.

This whole development can, of course, be viewed from many angles, but it is important to be aware of the fact that this is a unity which always spans such diverse questions as:

1. What are the personal prerequisites for the intended learning/competence development to take place (motivation and perspectives)?
2. What types of activity can further the intended learning/competence development (education, practice learning, participation, assessment, supervision, approval)?
3. Where is it most appropriate for these activities to take place (in or outside the workplaces or in a process of interaction between them)?
4. In the final analysis, also, what are the intention and yardstick for it all (for

example, acquisition of practical skills, insight and understanding, retraining and/or general personal competence development)?

However, the urgent necessity of adult vocational education, the radically increasing costs and the unpredictable market have played a part in starting up some decisive new developments which, as mentioned, are centred on upgrading workplace learning and growing scepticism about more traditional forms of education, and in some cases great and sometimes naïve interest in how ICT can be utilised in this connection.

A development in this direction seems to have great appeal for the business sector and among the agents in labour-market policy. For employers it implies that the resources are used on activities that are of immediate relevance for the individual enterprise, and a great deal of general and theoretical material of, in the best case, indirect importance for the work processes is avoided. Employees find it tempting not to have to "go to school" again and many of them are also rather sceptical about general and theoretical "school knowledge" in contrast with the practical skills of their work. Moreover, in many cases education also implies a drop in income.

At the same time there is a great deal of confusion and uncertainty concerning the more general qualifications and personal competencies which are regarded as increasingly central and vital. But how can more targeted orientation of these competencies be created? Is this best done directly on or in association with the workplace, or should there be courses and training? How are these measures then to be designed in practice? How should the results be measured? A great deal of fine words and high-flown intentions can very easily remain in the air while in reality the concentration is on the traditional qualifications developed in the schools through ordinary teaching or at the workplaces by means of instruction or learning from colleagues, both in ways that hinder rather than promote general and personal competence development.

For this reason there has been a growing interest in different ideas and theories about what characterises work-related education and learning and how to conduct this most suitably in different contexts, the barriers that exist, the general qualifications that are necessary etc. There are many offers, very different in character and substance. They frequently have catchy terms such as human resource management, organisational learning, the learning organisation, transformative learning, experiential learning, learning by expanding, neuro-linguistic programming, spirituality at work, team building, situated learning, communities of practice, and technologically-related e-learning, computer-based learning, distance learning etc. – to name but a few of the options that are most often utilised within a haphazardly selected range.

Even professionals find it difficult to negotiate these areas, not to speak of small companies with no particular educational function, nor of the employees whom they ultimately concern. What is tenable and what is just words? What options are suitable and in what contexts? Can one really be sure of achieving everything that is offered? The well-known Harvard professor, Chris Argyris, who himself is a central figure in the field of organisational learning, has assessed that the great majority of courses offered on the European and US consultant markets within this field cannot create any significant improvements (Argyris, 2000). It would thus seem eminently possible to make the wrong choice at the same time as both companies and employees will increasingly find themselves in situations where some or other type of organisational and competence development seems to be a must.

Learning as an individual and social process

In this paper, the basic viewpoint is that the issue of workplace learning cannot fully be understood or handled unilaterally or mainly as a question of management as in many of the approaches mentioned. Learning is, after all, something that happens within the individual and involves specific biological qualities which the human species has acquired over thousands of years. The expression, "the learning organisation", is thus a misnomer, a kind of verbal theft, as organisations do not have and cannot develop such qualities. (The correct expression for what is meant should be something like either "the effectively and qualitatively developing organisation" or "the organisation in which learning is promoted".) But it is not only a misnomer. It is also an inadequate approach, because the questions of how human beings learn and why they so often fail to learn what is intended by the management are not addressed as basic psychological issues. Understanding learning simultaneously implies understanding the human psychological mechanisms involved and the external conditions and their adequacy.

Historically, this double issue has been mainly addressed by three very different approaches, all of them reaching back into the inter-war period:

1. in Russia by the so-called cultural historical approach developed primarily by Lev Vygotsky (1978, 1986) and Aleksei Leontyev (1981);
2. in Germany by the approach of critical theory (or the so-called Frankfurt School), combining a Freudian understanding of the individual with a Marxist understanding of society (e.g. Negt, 1971; Lorenzer, 1972; Leithäuser, 1976; Ziehe and Stubenrauch, 1982); and
3. in the USA by the tradition of humanist adult education as started by Eduard Lindeman (Anderson and Lindeman, 1927) and later carried further by adult educators such as Malcolm Knowles (1970, 1973), Stephen Brookfield (1987) and Jack Mezirow (1991).

In the area of workplace learning, two current trends seem to be related to these approaches. One of these has as its keywords "situated learning" and "communities of practice" and its most important representatives are Jean Lave and Etienne Wenger (Lave and Wenger, 1991; Wenger, 1998). However, although Wenger relates to such concepts as meaning and identity in his 1998 book, and the concept of individual trajectories has also come to play an important role, this approach does not include what I would accept as a genuine learning conception, because assumptions about how and why the individual learns are not really included. In fact, it sometimes seems that the relevant learning simply takes place only if a person is part of a community of practice. In this way the Lave and Wenger conception resembles other social learning and social constructionist approaches which more or less explicitly deny or exclude the individual dimension of learning (e.g. Gergen, 1994).

The other trend may be characterized by such key concepts as critical learning, transformative learning and learning by expansion, launched by Stephen Brookfield, Jack Mezirow and Finnish Yrjö Engeström, respectively (Engeström, 1987). These concepts have in common that they refer to the kind of learning which implies that the learner in some way transcends his or her existing limits or self. In this respect they resemble the concept of significant learning as developed by the psychotherapist Carl Rogers in the 1960s (Rogers, 1969). This resemblance is interesting because it indicates what was expressed clearly by Rogers, namely that only learning of this far-reaching kind is worth dealing with. In today's fast-moving and ever-changing risk society such learning has certainly grown in importance, outside the therapeutic area also. Actually, this is often what is demanded by ordinary people in order to keep up with changes in their environment or situation, whether it be inside or outside the workplace. But, on the other hand, it leaves out all the necessary and less dramatic demands which also always form part of the learning pattern.

Thus, what is needed as a grounding, in relation to workplace learning as well as learning in other settings, seems to be a contemporary and comprehensive learning theory in which learning is understood as both an individual and a social process, comprising both ordinary everyday learning and more complex personal development and, not least, also deals with what happens when intended learning does not take place. In other words, a theory is needed which relates to the learner as a human being in general, as a member of the present late modern globalised market and risk society, and as a specific individual with a personal life history, situation and future perspective.

This is, of course, a very ambitious request. Nevertheless, in the following I shall attempt to outline some main points for such a theory, as developed in my book, *The Three Dimensions of Learning* (Illeris, 2002), on a background of many years' theoretical studies with reference to all three historical approaches mentioned above and other relevant understandings ranging from Piaget's epistemology (e.g. Piaget, 1952) to Giddens' interpretation of late modernity (Giddens, 1990, 1991).

Finally, I shall briefly illustrate how this approach may be used in relation to a central issue in workplace learning today. In this part I draw, in addition to the theoretical basis, on practical developmental work in the Danish vocational training system over three decades and a recent cross-sector study of adults' learning in the Danish adult education systems, the results of which I have summarised in the article: "Adult education as experienced by the learners" (Illeris, 2003a).

The processes, dimensions and levels of learning

The point of departure for my concept of learning is that learning must be understood as all processes leading to permanent capacity change – whether they be physical, cognitive, emotional or social in nature – that do not exclusively have to do with biological maturation or ageing. This means that the learning concept also extends to such functions as personal development, socialisation, qualification and competence development, as the difference between these terms is mainly a matter of the point of view towards learning that is adopted.

Simultaneously, the concept also implies that all learning is part of a certain structure that includes two very diverse types of processes and three dimensions. The two types of process are closely integrated and both must be active before learning can take place. On the one hand, there are interaction processes between the learner and the surroundings and, on the other hand, there are the inner mental acquisition and elaboration processes, by means of which impulses from the interaction are linked to results of earlier learning. The interaction processes are social and cultural in nature and in general follow a historical-societal logic, i.e. they are fundamentally dependent on how and when they take place, as the interactive possibilities are different in different societies and different historical epochs. Conversely, the acquisition processes are psychological in nature and in general follow a biological-structural logic, i.e. they follow the patterns that have

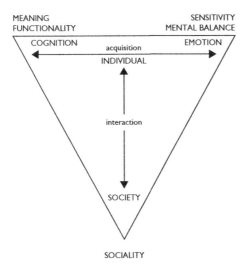

Figure 19.1 The processes and dimensions of learning

been genetically developed through the ages as part of the phylogenetic development process of the species.

In addition, the acquisition processes always include two integrated sides: the cognitive or rational, knowledge and skills side, and the emotional side, covering also other psychodynamic areas such as motivations and attitudes. During the pre-school years the two sides of the acquisition processes gradually split away from each other, but they are never totally separated (Furth, 1987). All cognitive learning always has an emotional component which is marked or "obsessed" by the emotional situation that was prevalent during learning, for example, whether it was motivated by desire, necessity or compulsion. All emotional learning also contains rational elements, knowledge or understanding of the matters at which the emotions are directed.

In this manner learning will always include three integrated dimensions, which may be termed the cognitive, the emotional, and the social-societal dimensions. Through the cognitive dimension knowledge, skills, understandings and, in the last analysis, meaning and functionality are developed. Through the emotional dimension patterns of emotion and motivation, attitudes and, in the last analysis, sensitivity and mental balance are developed. Through the social-societal dimension potentials for empathy, communication and cooperation and, in the last analysis, sociality are developed. Figure 19.1 illustrates the connection between the two types of process and the three dimensions that enter into and mark learning and which must always be included if one wishes to form a complete picture of a learning situation or process.

The results of learning are stored in the central nervous system as formations that can be described as schemes or mental patterns. When it is a matter of the cognitive dimension of learning, one typically speaks of schemes or, more popularly, of memory. In the emotional and the social-societal dimensions, one would employ terms such as patterns or inclinations. Under all circumstances, it is decisive that the results of learning are structured before they can be retained. This structuring can be established in various ways, and on this basis it is possible to distinguish between four different levels of learning which are activated in different contexts, imply different types of learning results, and require more or less energy. (This is an elaboration of the concept of learning originally developed by Jean Piaget cf. Illeris, 2002).

When a new scheme or pattern is established, it is a case of cumulative or mechanical learning. This form of learning is characterised by being an isolated formation, something new that is not a part of anything else. Therefore, cumulative learning is most frequent during the first years of life, but later occurs only in special situations where one must learn something with no context of meaning, for example, a telephone or pin code number. The learning result is characterised by automation that means that it can only be recalled and applied in situations mentally similar to the learning context.

By far the most common form of learning is termed assimilative or additive, meaning that the new element is linked as an addition to a scheme or pattern that is already established. One typical example could be learning in school subjects that is precisely built up by means of constant additions to what has already been learned, but assimilative learning also takes place in all contexts where one gradually develops one's capacities. The results of learning are linked to the scheme or pattern in question in such a manner that it is relatively easy to recall and apply them when one is mentally-oriented towards the field in question, for example, a school subject, while they may be hard to access in other contexts.

However, in some cases, situations occur where something takes place that is difficult to fit into any existing scheme or pattern, something one cannot really understand or to which one can not really relate. But if it seems important or interesting, if it is something one is determined to acquire, this can take place by means of accommodative or "exceeding" learning, which implies that one breaks down (parts of) an existing scheme and transforms it so that the new situation can be linked in. Thus one both relinquishes and reconstructs something and this is a task that can be experienced as hard and energy-demanding. One must cross former limitations and understand or accept something that is significantly new or different. The result of the learning is very resistant to oblivion and it can be recalled and applied in many different, relevant contexts. It is typically experienced as having got hold of something which one really has internalised.

Finally, in special situations there is also a far-reaching type of learning that has, *inter alia*, been described as transformative learning (Mezirow, 1991) or expansive learning (Engeström, 1987). This learning implies real personality changes and is characterised by simultaneous restructuring in the cognitive, the emotional and the social-societal dimensions, a break of orientation that typically occurs as the result of a crisis-like situation caused by urgent and unavoidable challenges, making it necessary to change oneself in order to get any further. Transformative learning is thus both profound and extensive and can often be directly physically noticed, typically as a feeling of relief or relaxation.

To sum up: what has been outlined is a concept of learning which basically is constructivist in nature, i.e. it is assumed that the learner him or herself actively builds up or construes his/her learning as mental structures that can be termed, for example, meaning, functionality, sensitivity, mental balance and sociality. This more complex concept of learning is of great importance when one specifically wishes to deal with certain learning processes, for example, those that mark workplace learning. It establishes, namely, that there are different types of learning that are widely different in scope and that the whole field must always be in the picture, and that one, for example, cannot understand cognitive-professional content learning without also considering what happens in the emotional and social-societal dimensions. In this way this learning concept corresponds to the modern concept of competence development.

Defence and everyday consciousness

However, it is also important to be aware of the fact that both the learning concept in the above and the concept of competence development are about what happens when somebody actually learns something. But it is just as important to think about what takes place in all the situations where somebody could learn something but does not, or perhaps learns something quite different from what had been intended. This concerns matters such as mislearning, distortion, mental defence or resistance, which naturally can be due to misunderstandings, miscommunication and the like, but which in our complex late modern society must necessarily also be generalised and take more systematised forms because nobody can remain open to the gigantic volumes of influences with which we are faced.

This is why today people develop a kind of automatic sorting mechanism *vis-à-vis* the many influences or what the German social psychologist Thomas Leithäuser has described as an "everyday consciousness" (Leithäuser, 1976 [cf. Illeris, 2002]). This functions in the way that one develops some general pre-understandings within certain thematic areas and, when one meets with influences within such an area, these pre-understandings are activated so that, if elements in the influences do not correspond with the pre-understandings, they are either rejected or distorted to make them agree. In both cases, this results in no new learning but, on the contrary, often in the cementing of the already-existing understanding. Thus, through everyday consciousness we control our own learning and non-learning in a manner that seldom involves any direct positioning while simultaneously involving a massive defence of the already acquired understandings and, in the final analysis, our very identity. There are, of course, also areas and situations where our positioning takes place in a more target-oriented manner, consciously and flexibly.

Therefore, in practice the issue of learning very often becomes a question of what can penetrate the individual, semi-automatic defence mechanisms and under what conditions. These defence mechanisms are the most common reason for the gulf between the impulses being communicated, for example, in an everyday situation, a work situation or a teaching situation, and what is actually learned.

Adult learning

The central fact in relation to adult learning is that adults, in contrast with children, are no longer minors and are capable and willing of taking responsibility for their behaviour, actions and opinions and thus also for their learning. At any rate this definition is at the core of society's definition of adulthood. One has formally attained the age of majority when one reaches the age of 18 and, even though teachers, for example, may often feel that this is not the case, as a point of departure we would all very strongly claim the right to make our own decisions. This is, *inter alia*, fundamental to what we regard as freedom and democracy.

Viewed in this perspective, for example, the well-known tendency for adults in an educational situation to apparently leave the responsibility up to the teacher comes to seem that it is the teacher, the syllabus, the curriculum, the authorities or society that take the responsibility which is actually the students' own. But they can only take responsibility for the teaching. Each individual student is still responsible for the learning and it is the participant him or herself who, consciously or unconsciously in the actual situation, with respect to all three dimensions of learning, decides whether the result is to be learning, distortion or non-learning – or perhaps a little of each.

Fundamentally, learning is a desire-based function (Furth, 1987). It is a part of human beings' phylogenetically developed potential that they can learn far more and much more complex matters than all other creatures, and this learning potential is the strongest and most crucial element in the species' struggle for survival.

Just like all other innate potentials for the survival of the individual and the species, the practice of learning is also basically desire-based. This can be seen most clearly during the first years of life when the child acquires a number of basic skills and concepts, but as a point of departure it also applies to adults. The difference consists of the fact that one has gradually had a number of experiences to the effect that learning can also be difficult and unpleasant, for example, when one has to learn about the limits to one's fulfilment, and in general when one must learn something that one has not decided oneself and of which one cannot see the point. This is, naturally, inevitable, as soon as a social formation is involved, in which case a balance must be found between individual interests and common considerations, and modern, complex society involves huge amounts of learning more or less determined by others.

This is why adults are rather sceptical about everything that others want them to learn and which they themselves do not feel an urge to learn. Consciously, or unconsciously, they want to decide for themselves. For this reason, in the case of adult learning, as a point of departure it is important to be aware of the following:

- adults learn what they want to learn and what is meaningful for them to learn;
- adults draw on the resources they already have in their learning;
- adults take as much responsibility for their learning as they want to take (if they are allowed) (Illeris, 2002, p. 219); and
- it is equally important to acknowledge that adults are not very inclined to learn something in which they are not interested, or in which they cannot see the meaning or importance. At any rate, typically they only learn partially, in a distorted way or with a lack of motivation that makes what is learned extremely vulnerable to oblivion or application in situations which are not subjectively related to the learning context.

Thus adults undertake a very stringent process of selection in connection with their learning and the premises for this selection are to be found in their experience and interests. This can be a matter of very superficial, short-term interests, something that challenges their curiosity, or which is topical and perhaps provocative. But more fundamentally, adults usually have some life projects that are relatively stable and long-term, for example, a family project that concerns creating and being part of a family, a work project that concerns a personal and financially satisfying job and even perhaps pursuing a more or less certain career, perhaps a leisure-time project concerning a hobby, a life project about fulfilment in certain ways, or a conviction project that is religious, political etc. in nature (cf. Giddens' concept of "life policy" [1991]).

These life projects are embedded in the life history, present situation and possible future perspectives of the individual and closely related to what we call identity. It is on this basis that we design our defences so that we usually let what is important for our projects come through and reject the rest. It is also on this basis, as the central core of our defences, that we develop our defence mechanisms to be able to counter influences that could threaten the experience of who we are and would like to be.

Adult education, motivation and learning

In relation to adult school-based education, the result of this starting-point for learning is usually a situation that is well-known from courses and study programmes: if the adult participants are not very motivated from the beginning, they usually start by leaning back and waiting for the teacher to start up something, after which they can decide if they want to engage themselves. If then the individual feels that something exciting, challenging or meaningful begins to take place, he or she begins to mobilise mental energy. But if everything is simply experienced as "being at school again" (the expression most often used by the participants about the situation), then it is just like the news on TV: it rolls over the screen and is looked at if it is found interesting. And if something occurs that the individual experiences as a defeat, humiliation or other negative experience from when they really were at school, very swiftly a thick wall of defence can be mobilised, which will take strong impulses to break through.

These matters typically comprise the fundamental premises for school-based adult education seen from the perspective of the participants. They make the participants' initial motivation quite crucial, i.e. the way in which they regard the study programme or course in question in relation to their life projects.

In some cases, adult education can lead to extensive, enriching development for the participants if they come with positive motivation and the study programmes live up to their expectations, and perhaps a little more. But the previously mentioned study in the broad Danish adult education programmes showed that a quite considerable proportion of the participants only become positively engaged in adult education if they meet a challenge that "turns them on" at the beginning or along the way. In too many cases the actual situation is that the participants only engage themselves superficially and do not learn very much, leading to the waste of a great number of human and financial resources (Illeris, 2003a).

The conditions concerning adults' relationship to school-based learning that are outlined here quite obviously form some of the reasons why, in step with the large-scale expansion in adult education of recent years, a certain degree of uncertainty has developed in relation to when and on what conditions it can actually live up to the great expectations about the vocationally-oriented competence development of adults, which is an important justification for the many resources expended on the area. But then the question is the way in which these subjective conditions apply if the learning is more directly linked to working life practice.

Therefore, as a proposal for coming further, in the following I shall attempt to view learning in working life from the learner's perspective in the same way as I took part in the adoption of this perspective in the project referred to above. This leads initially to the fact that this perspective is quite different for different groups with a fundamentally different relationship with working life. In general, three main groups can be identified:

1. adults with a more or less secure position in working life, but who need to continue developing their competencies to keep up with "development" (further qualification);
2. adults who have been "cut out", perhaps because their field of work has become out-dated or overtaken by "development", perhaps because they

themselves have not had the resources to keep up, or perhaps because they have simply been so unlucky as to have been employed by one of the losers in the stepped-up global competition (re-qualification); and
3. young people or young adults who are on their way into working life and thus need more general professional and personal qualifications (basic qualification).

In the following I will examine these three groups more closely and independently.

Adults needing further qualification

Adults who have a relatively safe position on the labour market usually have a positive attitude to supplementary training or upgrading training. For example, following through investigation of the attitude of general industrial workers to training activities, my colleague Christian Kjærsgaard concluded that:

- to a high degree the workers are conscious and formulated with respect to their own training needs;
- the workers' qualification needs are also determined by individual experiences and collective norms in relation to their work situation and expectations of development possibilities; and
- subjective strategies form the starting-point of the individual worker's training motivation (quoted from Illeris, 2002, p. 196).

This conclusion points not only to the fundamentally positive attitude to supplementary training and upgrading training but also to the fact that a number of conditions are linked to it.

First and foremost, the activities must be regarded as immediately relevant in relation to the current job or development possibilities in the work lying within the subjective horizon, i.e. typically changes in work content or organisation or personal re-deployment, of which one already is aware or for which one personally wishes to qualify. It must be possible to immediately see for what the learning can be used on the basis of one's current situation and future perspectives. In addition, there usually are a number of matters to do with, for example, time and payment that must be in order.

During the learning activities themselves, it is also typical that the adults in this group are narrowly interested in their currently experienced needs and are not very inclined to engage themselves in general perspectives in which they cannot see any meaning. It could also be said that their immediate orientation is towards assimilative learning and that special impulses must be present before they mobilise themselves for the more demanding accommodative processes.

In practice these conditions mean that, for this group, if the need for upgrading activities is not experienced directly in connection with work, as a rule they will only become engaged to the extent that they previously, or in connection with the activities, have come to understand and accept the purpose of the upgrading and, in addition, that subsequently they will actually be able to make use of the qualifications they have acquired. A great deal of experience and research in adult vocational training shows that these preconditions are not very often in order, and that many of the resources used on vocationally-oriented upgrading therefore do not produce the intended learning results (cf. Andersen et al., 1996).

On the other hand there may be results with respect to personnel policy or network creation, for example, the importance of which should not be underestimated.

It should also be noted that a large part of the identity of permanent staff is usually linked to their job and their workplace and they can thus be open to ongoing and more general competence and personality development in relation to work, or to collegially embedded learning processes connected to what Thomas Leithäuser describes as the hidden niche that staff at all enterprises must necessarily create for themselves (Volmerg et al., 1986; Leithäuser, 2000).

Adults needing re-qualification

The situation is quite different for adults who for one reason or another have been "cut out" of the position they have had in working life. Already in an earlier empirical study I registered that participants in short adult vocational training courses were in this situation engaged in the general and personally-oriented parts of the course content to a considerably higher degree than participants holding permanent jobs. As a rule they understood and accepted that general and personal upgrading was of central importance for their possibilities of obtaining new, satisfying work (Illeris et al., 1994).

Later I have deepened this type of investigation leading to a more subtle understanding that certain adults are thrown into a process of readjustment covering not only specific professional qualifications but also a necessary and very demanding change of identity. These are typically people who have developed and cemented a working identity over a number of years, linked to a certain profession and/or certain functions, something they experienced, of which they were capable and by means of which they could support themselves and achieve self-respect and social status. This is now gone and has in reality become worthless. Even though they still have a number of qualifications, often specialised, these now have no genuine economic importance or status (Ahrenkiel and Illeris, 2000).

This situation is extremely demanding from the point of view of learning because it implies that the existing identity must be phased out while a new identity is developed, and usually on the basis of some very uncertain, in some cases almost hopeless, premises. It is an external demand that makes such an extremely difficult and sensitive process of mental readjustment necessary, defined as transformative learning in the above, and it must be dealt with in a situation in which one's self-respect and status are hard hit and one has practically and financially been degraded to the most vulnerable third of society.

Thus there is a need for understanding, loyal guidance and types of qualification which to the highest possible degree respect the situation and preconditions of the individual, and in most cases these needs are only met to an inadequate extent in present day adult education programmes (Illeris, 2003a).

Young adults needing a basic qualification

With respect to the third main group, young adults on their way into the labour market, it is also the case that learning must include both professional qualification and identity development, but both elements are far easier to approach when unlearning and readjustment do not have to take place simultaneously.

It is with specific reference to this group that the idea of a return to the apprenticeship system has been brought forward once more, to a high degree with reference to Lave and Wenger's books about "situated learning" and "communities of practice" (Lave and Wenger, 1991; Wenger, 1998; Nielsen and Kvale, 1997). However, in Denmark there have also been many objections referring in part to the severe criticism formerly levelled at apprenticeship with respect to, for example, power relations and insufficient breadth and theory, on the one hand, and, on the other hand, to the fact that already in the present schemes it is impossible to obtain a sufficient number of qualified trainee places. Complete rehabilitation of the apprenticeship system would seem to be both a romantic dream and a practical impossibility, at the same time as a great deal of doubt has arisen about the degree to which qualification in communities of practice actually works and its solidity in relation to the needs of late modern society.

To this may be added a number of conditions to do with young adults' forms of learning and identity development today. In our present choice and market society, so many options and impulses exist that, in their vocational choice and the identity development linked to this, young people cannot as a matter of course draw on the family and the societal norms with which they have met at home to the same extent as previously. In this way, what earlier was in the nature of an almost automatic sorting mechanism comes to function as difficult choices and a far more demanding and unsure identity process (Illeris, 2003b).

Today young adults must often undergo a lot of testing and "search movements" in connection with their qualification and identity development, leading to change and drop-out from study programmes, training programmes and apprenticeships. This points in the direction of the need to make the qualification possibilities very flexible, which is also the main trend in the modernisation of vocational training systems in many countries (Simonsen, 2000).

The need for a differentiated concept

The previous sections point to three main groups of adults with very different backgrounds for and attitudes to vocationally-oriented learning and competence development, and within each of the groups there, naturally, exists extensive differentiation, right down to the individual differences which, in the final analysis, determine the learning and development that actually take place. Similarly, one could point to the fact that the conditions for workplace learning are very different in different types of enterprises. One main point is therefore obvious: firm formulas for the right type of qualification and education organisation will, in the best case, only be applicable to some limited group – perhaps the group in focus when the formula was developed – but the only general solution must necessarily be far-ranging variation.

This variation must be based on the needs of society, the enterprises and the participants, all of which are very differentiated today. While there must be room for differences, a certain degree of structure and clarity is also necessary. The right mixture will never be found because even under ideal conditions it will have changed while it was in the process of being designed.

It is clear that the possibilities for learning and competence development at workplaces, in direct relation with the workplaces, and at very different courses at schools and educational institutions, should be included. It is also becoming increasingly clear that there is a need for comprehensive expansion of impartial and loyal guidance options far different from what usually takes place today.

Apart from this, nothing seems to be particularly clear because there are too many options and strong opinions on the scene and, as mentioned in the introduction, it is not easy to separate what is effective from what cannot be used. At the same time, many of the options and discussions are disqualified by lacking any idea of the subjective sides of learning, i.e. for the importance of the learners' understanding of and attitude to what is taking place, and by regarding the learners as mechanisms and learning as a production process, thus actually cutting themselves off from understanding what is at stake.

It is against this background that the Danish National Labour Market Authority (at present the part of the Authority that is now integrated in the Ministry of Education), in cooperation with the new Learning Lab Denmark, has taken the initiative to set up a "consortium" to work with research and development in the field of workplace learning and competence development, both directly in working life and at vocationally-oriented educational institutions, and in this connection with how different types of computer-supported activities can and cannot be used. There is certainly enough to do.

References

Ahrenkiel, A. and Illeris, K. (2000), "Adult education between emancipation and control", in Illeris, K. (Ed.), *Adult Education in the Perspective of the Learners*, Roskilde University Press, Copenhagen.

Andersen, V., Illeris, K., Kjærsgaard, C., Larsen, K., Olesen, H.S. and Ulriksen, L. (1996), *General Qualification*, Adult Education Research Group, Roskilde University Press, Copenhagen.

Anderson, M.L. and Lindeman, E.C. (1927), *Education through Experience*, Workers' Education Bureau, New York, NY.

Argyris, C. (2000), "The next challenge in organizational learning, leadership and change", lecture at the Opening Conference of Learning Lab Denmark, Copenhagen, 6 November.

Brookfield, S.D. (1987), *Developing Critical Thinkers*, Open University Press, Milton Keynes.

Engeström, Y. (1987), *Learning by Expanding: An Activity-theoretic Approach to Developmental Research*, Orienta-Kunsultit, Helsinki.

Furth, H.G. (1987), *Knowledge as Desire*, Columbia University Press, New York, NY.

Gergen, K.J. (1994), *Realities and Relationships*, Harvard University Press, Cambridge, MA.

Giddens, A. (1990), *The Consequences of Modernity*, Stanford University Press, Stanford, CT.

Giddens, A. (1991), *Modernity and Self-Identity*, Polity Press, Cambridge, MA.

Illeris, K. (2002), *The Three Dimensions of Learning*, Roskilde University Press, Copenhagen/ NIACE, Leicester.

Illeris, K. (2003a), "Adult education as experienced by the learners", *International Journal of Lifelong Education*, Vol. 22 No. 1.

Illeris, K. (2003b), "Learning, identity and self-orientation in youth", forthcoming.

Illeris, K., Ulriksen, L. and Warring, N. (1994), *Almenkvalificering påKorte Kurser (General Qualification in Short Courses)*, Adult Education Research Group, Roskilde University Press, Copenhagen.

Knowles, M. (1970), *The Modern Practice of Adult Education: Andragogy versus Pedagogy*, Association Press, New York, NY.

Knowles, M. (1973), *The Adult Learner: A Neglected Species*, Gulf Publishing Company, Houston, TX.

Lave, J. and Wenger, E. (1991), *Situated Learning: Legitimate Peripheral Participation*, Cambridge University Press, New York, NY.

Leithäuser, T. (1976), *Formen des Alltagsbewusstseins, (Forms of Everyday Consciousness)*, Campus, Frankfurt am Main.

Leithäuser, T. (2000), "Subjectivity, lifeworld and work organization", in Illeris, K. (Ed.), *Adult Education in the Perspective of the Learners*, Roskilde University Press, Copenhagen.

Leontyev, A.N. (1981 [1959]), *Problems of the Development of the Mind* (collected manuscripts from the 1930s), Progress, Moscow.

Lorenzer, A. (1972), *Zur Begründung einer materialistischen Sozialisationstheorie (Reasons for a Materialist Theory of Socialisation)*, Suhrkamp, Frankfurt am Main.

Mezirow, J. (1991), *Transformative Dimensions of Adult Learning*, Jossey-Bass, San Francisco, CA.

Negt, O. (1971), *Soziologische Phantasie und exemplarisches Lernen (Sociological Imagination and Exemplary Learning)*, Europäische Verlagsanstalt, Frankfurt am Main.

Nielsen, K. and Kvale, S. (Eds) (1997), "Apprenticeship: learning as social practice", *Nordisk Pedagogik/Journal of Nordic Educational Research*, Vol. 17 No. 3, special issue.

Piaget, J. (1952), *The Origins of Intelligence in Children*, International Universities Press, New York, NY.

Rogers, C.R. (1969), *Freedom to Learn*, Charles E. Merrill, Columbus, OH.

Simonsen, B. (2000), "New young people, new forms of consciousness, new educational methods", in Illeris, K. (Ed.), *Adult Education in the Perspective of the Learners*, Roskilde University Press, Copenhagen.

Volmerg, B., Senghaas-Knoblauch, E. and Leithäuser, T. (1986), *Betriebliche Lebenwelt: eine Sozialpsychologie industrieller Arbeitsverhältnisse (Workplace Lifeworld: A Social Psychology of Industrial Work Conditions)*, Westdeutscher Verlag, Opladen.

Vygotsky, L.S. (1978), *Mind in Society: The Development of Higher Psychological Processes*, Harvard University Press, Cambridge, MA.

Vygotsky, L.S. (1986 [1934]), *Thought and Language*, MIT Press, Cambridge, MA.

Wenger, E. (1998), *Communities of Practice: Learning, Meaning, and Identity*, Cambridge University Press, Cambridge, MA.

Ziehe, T. and Stubenrauch, H. (1982), *Plädoyer für ungewöhnliches Lernen (Argumentation for Unusual Learning)*, Rowohlt, Reinbek.

CHAPTER 20

THE WORKPLACE AS A FRAMEWORK FOR LEARNING

Learning as a secondary matter

In contrast to all other learning, learning in the workplace is specifically characterised by its special situatedness (cf. Lave & Wenger 1991, Illeris 2002). Learning is always influenced by the context in which it takes place, and learning in the workplace is fundamentally influenced by the fact that the workplace constitutes a learning environment that is subject to special conditions.

First and foremost, it is important that the workplaces have certain specific purposes and conditions of existence that are not primarily related to a learning perspective, but nonetheless inevitably are of importance for the learning that can take place. We are looking at some specific framework conditions, and these framework conditions are not primarily directed towards learning in the way they are in schools and educational institutions, but towards the production of goods and/or services which the workplace in question supplies, and ultimately, for private sector organisations, towards the maximisation of profits, while the corresponding public sector goal is ultimately that of maximising politically formulated goals within a given financial budget framework. It is inherent in this that submission to quantifiable efficiency and effectiveness parameters is a fundamental condition for learning in working life.

In addition to this, there are in workplaces (with some few exceptions) certain power structures that may be managed in many ways, but which fundamentally mean that there is a management who makes decisions and possesses the right to supervise and distribute tasks, to hire and fire employees, and ultimately to discontinue operations, move, merge, restructure and generally decide all issues pertaining to the existence and conditions of the workplace.

No matter how employee and learning oriented a workplace may be defined by management, it is always these fundamental conditions, the efforts to achieve efficiency and effectiveness and the privilege of management, which constitute the fundamental conditions for learning. The learning that is the objective of more or less focused efforts must of necessity directly or indirectly serve the interests of the workplace as defined by management, and the incidental learning which also always takes place among the employees outside, and in some cases contrary to, the interests of management, is also of necessity influenced by the fact that it takes place under these conditions (cf. e.g. Volmerg et al. 1986, Leithäuser 2000).

Learning in the workplace thus encompasses both a large volume of learning that is in accordance with the intended functions of the workplace, and which ranges from acquisition of the necessary skills and insights in connection with mastering the various work processes to a personal and identity-related development in accordance with the aim and practice of the workplace, and at the same time learning concerned with ways in which employees individually and collectively are able to handle their own situation in the workplace in a way that is manageable and satisfying to themselves.

The latter part of workplace learning may in some cases be in direct opposition to the interests of management. There is, however, also a more adaptation oriented form of "counter-learning", concerned with developing routines and modes of perception directed towards ways in which employees may satisfy their own needs and attitudes while at the same time they discharge their work duties in an acceptable manner. This is the way in which employees develop what e.g. Argyris & Schön, in their books on organisational learning, call "defensive routines", and which they consider to be the most significant obstacle to the development of appropriate learning in accordance with the need of the workplace. Therefore organisational learning is, among other things, much concerned with breaking down the defensive routines and developing some modes of functioning that may be more appropriate seen both from the perspectives of management and employees (cf. Argyris & Schön 1996).

As we continue in the following sections with considering various initiatives that may be relevant in connection with learning in the workplace, it is therefore of key significance on the one hand to maintain that this learning is always related to the primary purpose and power structures of the workplace, and on the other hand to be aware that employees themselves contribute with their own perspectives and interests, which may both be in accordance with, and more or less in opposition to, the primary purposes and power structures.

It is the same fundamental tension between the workplace-rational perspective and the subjective perspective of learning that is central to the model for learning in working life that was described in the first part of the book. We find it essential in connection with learning in the workplace that the parties involved recognise, accept and acknowledge this tension, something which is in clear opposition to the view of a major part of the management-oriented literature in the area, which more or less exclusively considers workplace learning on the basis of the workplace-rational management perspective.

At the same time, it is important to emphasise that the outlined double perspective is not just assumed on the basis of ethical and democratic viewpoints, but that it is also better in accordance with reality and therefore better suited as the basis for rational reflection.

Incidental learning in the workplace

One very important form of learning in the workplace, and presumably also the most widespread, is the learning that takes place without anybody planning it in connection with and as part of the discharge of the daily duties and daily contact.

The understanding and significance of this was brought to the centre of the stage with the book "Informal and Incidental Learning in the Workplace", which was published in the USA by Victoria Marsick & Karen Watkins in 1990. The book defined "incidental learning" as

"... a by-product of some other activity, such as task accomplishment, interpersonal interaction, sensing the organizational culture, or trial-and-error experimentation." (Marsick & Watkins 1990, p. 6–7).

Incidental learning thus involves at the same time the more professionally oriented learning of work methods and procedures for implementing the various activities specific to the work of that particular workplace, and at least in equal measure the input of perceptions and attitudes – or workplace socialisation – that takes place if not automatically then at least without any consciously planned aim.

The fact that this learning is not intentional or planned also of course makes it difficult to direct it towards a specific goal. Once it is realised and acknowledged that incidental learning is of great significance and therefore important to consider, the workplace must either make direct attempts at modifying it, in which case it is no longer incidental, or else there must be a general effort to change the learning environment of the workplace so that other and more desirable forms of incidental learning obtain better conditions and thereby also become more probable (which actually was the essence of Marsick & Watkins's book).

However, the concept of incidental learning itself is not without problems. This is partly because the character of the learning environment can have a significant impact on the relative likelihood of various types of incidental learning, and partly because the background and preferences of the individual employee also have a major impact on what this individual takes note of and thereby learns. Incidental learning is thus not as random as a cursory glance might suggest, but is generally dependent on both the learning environment and who the employees are.

It is also on this background that the Australian John Garrick has raised serious objections to this concept (Garrick 1998, p. 11), and later suggested that "incidental learning" should be viewed as informal learning (a concept which we shall consider in the next section), but that we might in special cases talk of "accidental learning" when for some reason an entirely fortuitous event takes place, an unpredictable coincidence or an episode from which someone may learn a lesson (Garrick 1999, p. 219).

In summary, we shall here first and foremost maintain that in any workplace there is much incidental learning taking place without planning or explicit request, but which may nonetheless have great impact on both the function of the workplace and on the individual employee. This type of learning can, however, only be influenced indirectly and at a general level, and thus it overlaps to a great extent with informal learning, which we shall consider in the following section.

Informal learning in the workplace

Informal learning encompasses everything that is not formalised, e.g. in the form of teaching, instruction, debate meetings or similar, but it may well be intentional, e.g. if an employee asks advice from another employee, where employees discuss approaches for dealing with a situation that has arisen, or similar. More extensive forms may involve self-directed or group-directed learning, where the learner or learners without any formal framework orientate themselves in various ways towards learning something they need or in which they are in some other way interested.

In recent years it has become common to distinguish between informal learning and non-formal learning (e.g. the EU Commission 2000, p. 8), for instance in connection with the interest in "lifelong learning", where the latter typically takes place in associations, projects, movements, or through specific initiatives in work places that do no make use of institutionalised training, while informal learning proper may take place in all sorts of contexts that do not involve any organised endeavour.

However, the terminological practice for reference to informal, non-formal and formal learning has been made the subject of research in England and published as a report by Helen Colley, Phil Hodkinson and Janice Malcolm. The authors conclude that while it is possible to a certain extent to distinguish between formal learning on the one hand and informal and non-formal learning on the other hand, it is virtually impossible to maintain an even somewhat clear distinction between informal and non-formal learning. It may thus make a certain measure of sense to use the terms formal and informal learning if it is kept in mind that there may well be formal elements in informal learning, and that there are almost always informal elements in formal learning, while non-formal learning is a category so vague that it is hardly expedient to use it generally (cf. Colley et al., 2003).

These questions are not merely of academic and linguistic interest, because behind the use of these concepts lies, as a rule, an assumption that informal learning in a number of contexts is better than formal learning, and, in addition to this, there are also in political circles efforts to implement the assumption that transferring much of the learning which in our society predominantly takes place in the institutionalised school and educational system to other contexts, including not least working life, might be done with success. Lave & Wenger's work on situated learning (Lave & Wenger 1991) and communities of practice (Wenger 1998) has provided an important contribution in connection with these efforts. Significant matters that have formed part of the argumentation have partly been concerned with the motivational basis assumed generally to be better in informal contexts, partly with the so-called transfer problem, i.e. that there may be great difficulties involved in applying what a person has learned in one context, e.g. in an education programme, in another context, e.g. in a work place (cf. e.g. Tennant 1999).

It is hardly subject to serious doubts that these arguments have substance and that there are great qualities involved in learning through practice, learning through experience, learning in the work place, self-directed learning, and whatever else has been mentioned in these contexts. However, there are also considerable arguments pulling in the opposite direction. It is especially important that institutionalised learning usually possesses better possibilities for going into depth, not least when the subject matter examined consists of complex and theoretical perceptions, while informal learning has a tendency to focus exclusively on the immediately apparent and more superficial level, and there is often lack of time, space and qualified input in the informal contexts. Especially in workplaces, learning-oriented initiatives may in many contexts have a disturbing effect, and neither public nor private organisations seem generally to be interested in taking on interns and apprentices to an extent commensurate with the need in the areas in question. At the same time, it should not be overlooked that the discussion on where learning may best take place may also involve underlying financial issues concerned with who is to pay for which part of the qualification and competence development of the work force.

It is thus on the one hand clear that the argument placing more emphasis on informal learning is both important and justified. However, on the other hand there is at the same time a need for a realistic weighting of the pros and cons, and not least for a qualification of informal as well as formalised learning and the interaction between the two. This weighting and qualification will be a key issue in the rest of this book.

The significance of the learning environment

Under all circumstances, the learning environment is of altogether fundamental significance for both the extent and character of the learning that takes place in the workplace. In chapter 2, we offered an account of the intricate character and most important elements of learning environments. Here we shall take a closer look at the significance of learning environments for learning.

It has been pointed out in many contexts that different types of workplaces offer very different learning environments with very different learning opportunities. David Beckett & Paul Hager have pointed out that the most significant general factor affecting the quality of a workplace as learning environment is *the variation* in the opportunities and situations it offers the employees (Beckett & Hager 2000, 2002). This may be compared with an earlier and very basic sociology of consciousness analysis by the German Ute Volmerg, who demonstrates that the central dimensions of such variation are concerned with, respectively, the employees' possibilities for disposition (i.e. the possibilities for themselves to make decisions concerning their work), their possibilities for interaction (i.e. the possibilities for being part of interaction and communication with others), and their possibilities for applying their acquired qualifications (Volmerg 1977, s. 21f).

Another important contribution to the understanding of these matters was made by the Swede Per-Erik Ellström, who points out both the significance of external factors such as stronger competition, higher quality demands and the fluctuations of the macro-economic environment, which have an impact on the learning environment, and a number of internal factors, including the combination of individual-oriented and company-oriented learning strategies, the employees' involvement in initiation, planning and implementation of learning initiatives, time schedules, management's motives and commitment in connection with learning initiatives, and management's pressure and support in connection with learning in the workplace (Ellström 2004).

These three contributions are adequate for illustrating both the breadth and complexity of the factors that have an impact on the character and quality of a workplace as a learning environment. It also makes it clear that both management's attitude to these matters and the employees' own attitudes play a crucial role, while at the same time external factors may also have a decisive impact.

It is part of modern management endeavours that many workplaces make extensive and determined efforts to live up to all these challenges in ways which, especially from management's point of view, appear expedient in relation to the learning environment. However, in practice it is not always so straightforward. On the basis of a survey carried out by a well-known Danish organisation which is in the vanguard in this area, Mette Morsing found that in an open learning environment it is especially competition and conflict that drive development and learning forward, and the important issue is

> "to get competition and co-operation to coexist, to balance between change and stability [. . .] it is the fractured surface between different 'types of reason' which in practice holds the potential for innovation."
> (Morsing 1995, s. 22 and 26).

It is of course correct that both competition and conflict may generate much learning, but it will then also have an impact on the character of this learning, and it may even go so far that the learning efforts revert to their opposite. In Denmark Jesper

Tynell has recently documented this very strongly. For some time, he observed the work in a modern Danish IT enterprise with super-modern Human Resources Management strategies, where the employees' very extensive independence and responsibility seems to lead to such a degree of exploitation of their labour and responsibility that it leads to extensive colonisation, there is not room for much else in their life, and at the same time to mental decomposition and illness (Tynell 2001). In a corresponding study, psychologist Nadja Prætorius points out how modern management strategies, including also those applied in the public sector, cause an increasing number of employees to seek help from psychologists to relieve stress and burnout (Prætorius 2004).

Tynell's example may be extreme, but Prætorius' observations nonetheless point to the way in which it fits into a significant trend, which may also be seen as a reminder that the questions concerning the learning environment and learning in working life are not a simple, one-dimensional area in which more and more also means better and better. Like all inter-human matters, the learning environment holds many facets and contains both great development potential and risks.

ICT as a constituent part of the learning environment

One element in the learning environment of the workplace that there is every reason to pay attention to these days is the deployment of modern information and communication technology (ICT).

Lone Dirckinck-Holmfeld (2004) has described how ICT as a learning tool to a very great extent is gaining a strong position in European workplaces, and there are thoughts of e-learning as a form of mass education, which is to reach all categories of employees on a large scale and more or less replace other forms of work-related learning:

> "We see many different examples of how ICT is involved and how ICT is able to contribute to the learning processes. From more traditional courses, in which ICT is primarily used for training the employees in relatively limited skills, to new forms of collaborative and project-oriented courses, in which ICT is used as a communicative and collaborative infrastructure for building bridges between the need for learning in the workplace and theories and methods from the institutions, to radical forms of virtual learning environments that are operated by self-directed learners, and which build on motivation structures and dynamics imported from informal learning environments." (Dirckinck-Holmfeld 2004, p. 28).

In one of our projects we have, among other things, seen how a global company with employees in most of the world has been able to implement a running upgrade of skills via e-learning, with great benefits, both in financial and learning terms. The audiovisual communication possibilities offer advantages including reduced travel costs, courses that may be extended over longer periods of time, the simultaneous development of digital competences of both instructors and students, and the ability to develop co-operation and other "soft" competences through collaborative and project-oriented courses (Danfoss 2004).

However, Dirckinck-Holmfeld does point out "that there is still most focus on design of the technical tools", while, if the learning is to be up to date, "the learning processes and the situation and motivation of the learners must constitute

The workplace as a framework for learning 237

the point of departure" (p. 28). Bente Elkjær, in a Danish survey, has found that e-learning in working life is predominantly practised as individual self-studies, in which "the IT supported learning processes close around the individual's 'interaction' with PCs and education programme" (Elkjær 2002, p. 116).

Current literature on the topic provides many examples that can illustrate this. A Swedish survey of two major initiatives of this character that aimed to serve employees who are early school leavers within, respectively, the automotive industry and the timber industry found that the function of e-learning was inexpedient and that the results produced were disappointing (Thång & Wärvik 2004). The evaluation of a major Norwegian project within the graphic industry concluded that "in summary, we can say that the project made obvious the chasm that separates the expectations attached to net-based learning in the workplace and the outcome which is actually realisable today" (Lahn 2004).

There seems to be broad agreement that there are great possibilities in using ICT as an important aid in connection with learning in the workplace. However, it is not enough just to introduce PCs and learning programmes that the employees may use. Like all other learning, e-learning forms part of a complicated interaction which encompasses both the conditions in the workplace in the broadest sense, the learners' prior qualifications and motivation, the character of the programmes used (including possibilities for being together when learning is taking place and not being isolated as individual PC users), as well as the possibilities for using the tools in accordance with the employees' working rhythms and needs.

More generally, it might be said that the main issue involved is that of making ICT learning an integrated part of the daily learning environment. The Swedes Carina Åberg and Lennart Svensson (2004) have, on the basis of a number of broadly conceived projects, formulated a model of what will be required (Figure 20.1).

The figure focuses on the many different matters that have an influence on the learning that takes place in the direct interaction between the individual employee and the computer, and the article offers a detailed account of these different matters. However, it does not show what in this context is probably the most important issue, which is that if e-learning is to deliver the learning possibilities necessary for it to become a significant and active element in workplace learning, the interaction between the individual and the computer can only be one element in the learning environment of the workplace as a whole. The point of departure

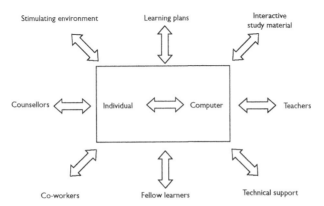

Figure 20.1 E-learning in the workplace (Aberg & Svensson 2004, p. 80).

for the development of this environment should not be computers and programmes but employees and the learning they need and are motivated for.

It is easy enough to see the great potential learning possibilities that e-learning provides. However, much experience is today unanimous in its testimony to the fact that if this potential is to be realised, it must be supported by a learning environment and a culture of education that incorporates technology as an integrated element and not just a fascination with technology or the wish to achieve savings, even though the latter factor will, as a rule, provide some of the impetus.

This requires partly up-to-date technology with interactive programmes that incorporate interaction options between the learners and their instructors and mutually among the learners, partly easy access to specialists able to solve the technical problems that unavoidably arise, and this also demands a management that puts a whole-hearted effort into the development of such an environment, makes the necessary financial and technological resources, as well as the necessary time, available, and who understands that technology must be developed and offered on the basis of the needs of the employees. If these conditions are not met, e-learning will continue to have very limited functional scope for professional instruction, and there will be many frustrations and conflicts attached to more extensive use of ICT in workplace learning.

Organisational learning and "the learning organisation"

More generally, the discipline and study of education encompasses a field called "organisational learning", which lies in the twilight zone between management and work and organisation psychology and is much concerned with development of the learning environment and the learning possibilities in organisations and in the workplace, and the concept of the development of "the learning organisation" has become a powerful and penetrating brand for these endeavours (cf. e.g. Elkjær 1999).

Two key names in this connection include the Americans Chris Argyris and Donald Schön, who have already been mentioned several times. They have worked in this field for many years, and in 1996 they published the book "Organizational Learning II", which has assumed a dominating position in the field (Argyris & Schön 1996). In the book, the authors explain organisational learning as follows:

> "Organizational learning occurs when individuals within an organization experience a problematic situation and enquire into it on the organization's behalf. They experience a surprising mismatch between expected and actual results of action and respond to that mismatch through a process of thought and further action that leads them to modify their images of organization or their understandings of organizational phenomena and to restructure their activities so as to bring outcomes and expectations into line, thereby changing organizational theory-in-use. In order to become organizational, the learning that results from organizational inquiry must become embedded in the images of organization held in its members' minds and/or in the epistemological artifacts (the maps, memories, and programs) embedded in the organizational environment." (Argyris & Schön 1996, p. 16)

The quotation pinpoints a key issue concerning organisational learning. Argyris & Schön maintain, as we maintain it in chapter three, that actually individuals do learn but learning can only be called organisational if it leads to development in the organisation. Furthermore, even though the work of Argyris & Schön contains some significant and fundamental learning psychology reflections, it is clearly enough, in their work and more generally in connection with organisational learning, the organisation and its development that take centre stage, while individuals act and learn "on behalf of the organisation" (cf. e.g. Illeris 2002).

At the psychological level, Argyris & Schön are occupied by the difference that they very often have encountered in practice between the theories of the organisation expressed by employees and management ("espoused theories") and the rationales that provide the basis for practical action ("theories-in-use"). If such a difference is to be overcome so as to make actions rational given the intended aim, there must be so-called "double-loop learning", which, as opposed to the ordinary "single-loop learning", not only leads to changes of "strategies of action or assumptions underlying strategies in ways that leave the values of a theory of action unchanged" (Argyris & Schön 1996, p. 20), but also "results in a change in the values of theory-in-use, as well as in its strategies and assumptions" (Argyris & Schön 1996, p. 21). This requires a preparedness to transcend the established "defensive routines". The learning concepts used are highly similar to the learning types accommodation and assimilation, as mentioned in section 3.3, but there is the significant difference that Argyris & Schön's concepts explicitly are related solely to organisational learning, which means that the modes of definition underlying their work is constantly related to the organisation.

It is also worth noticing that these fundamental psychological reflections only occupy a minor part of Argyris & Schön's work. As in the other literature on organisational learning, the main emphasis is placed on the organisation and the development of the learning possibilities it offers. Therefore there is no clear distinction between the field of organisational learning and the concept of "the learning organisation" (cf. Elkjær 1999), except for the discussion on what exactly it means that an organisation learns.

The account of the concern of "the learning organisation" generally considered the most qualified is that of the American Peter Senge, in his book "The Fifth Discipline" (Senge 1999). His approach probably involves the generally most comprehensive and extensive attempt to describe and understand the development of work-places as learning environments, but it lies at the same time on the periphery of the field of interest of this book, specifically because it is not primarily concerned with the employees' learning and development. They tend to be viewed as agents acting "on behalf of the organisation", i.e. they are of interest merely to the extent that they are bearers of learning in the organisation in question.

There is generally a colossal field of interest surrounding organisational development, which in many ways overlaps with our present field of interest, learning in working life, but which it would take us too far afield to examine in detail in this context. We shall therefore limit the consideration of it to what has been provided above, which deals with the most immediate field of overlap, and otherwise refer the reader to a number of important recent contributions in the borderland between organisational development and organisational learning: Harvard Business Review 2001, Wenger et al 2002, Easterby-Smith & Lyles 2003, Nicolini et al. 2003.

Conclusion and perspectives

This chapter has focused on the general prerequisites for learning in the workplace. It has been pointed out that the workplace is a special learning space with certain specific qualities, including first and foremost that learning is not the primary aim of the workplace, but takes place in relation to certain rationales and power structures anchored in other intentions. At the same time, the workplace is undoubtedly an arena for extensive and significant learning processes of both work-oriented and general character.

Much learning in the workplace is of informal and partially incidental character, but is nonetheless influenced by being subjected to the conditions of workplace learning. At the general level, workplace learning that is not related to specific learning-oriented initiatives can only be influenced by a development of the learning environment of the workplace, which is a very complicated and multi-faceted matter that may lead to considerable gains for both society, the organisation and its employees, but which in extreme cases may also lead to critical "overload".

Generally there are considerable interests and perspectives attached to a development of workplaces as a learning environment, an endeavour that in a professional context has especially been the focus within the field called "organisational learning", and which currently especially relates to the notion of "the learning organisation". However, this endeavour shows a tendency to be predominantly disposed to viewing learning and learning possibilities from the perspective and interests of the organisations.

For employees, and for the quality and versatility of the learning, it is important that these matters are also being worked on on the basis of an understanding of the interaction between the organisation-related and the employee- or individual-related rationales. Especially from the perspective of early school leavers there is an obvious risk that attempts to strengthen workplace learning solely through a general development of the learning environment of the workplaces, without special learning-directed initiatives, will mean that it will also here be especially employees with better educational qualifications that will be able to benefit from the endeavours.

In what follows we shall therefore proceed with considering different forms of special learning-oriented initiatives at the workplaces, first some more traditional initiatives in the direction of instruction, tutorials, exchange of experience, and similar, then subsequently different counselling-oriented initiatives, and last in this part of the book, initiatives building on the transcending of employees' current job situation.

References

Åberg, Carina – Svensson, Lennart (2004): Arbejdspladsen – en arena for uddannelse og læring? In Anne Marie Kanstrup (ed): *E-læring på arbejde*. Copenhagen: Roskilde University Press. [The Workplace: An Arena for Education and Learning?].

Argyris, Chris – Schön, Donald A. (1996): *Organizational Learning II – Theory, Method, Practice*. Reading, Mass.: Addison-Wesley.

Beckett, David – Hager, Paul (2000): Making Judgments as the Basis for Workplace Learning: towards an epistemology of practice. *International Journal of Lifelong Education*, 4, 300–311.

Beckett, David – Hager, Paul (2002): *Life, Work and Learning: practice in postmodernity*. London: Routledge.

Colley, Helen – Hodkinson, Phil – Malcolm, Janice (2003): *Informality and Formality in Learning.* London: Learning and Skills Research Centre.
Danfoss (2004): *Futurecom* – see http://www.futurecom-group.com/Media/Danfoss/index.asp
Dirckinck-Holmfeld, Lone (2004): Et europæisk perspektiv på eLæring. In Anne Marie kanstrup (ed): *E-læring på arbejde.* Copenhagen: Roskilde University Press. [A European Perspective on E-Learning at Work].
Easterby-Smith, Mark – Lyles, Majorie A. (eds) (2003): *Handbook of Organizational Learning and Knowledge Management.* Oxford: Blackwell.
Elkjær, Bente (1999): In Search of a Social Learning Theory. In Mark Easterby-Smith, John Burgoyne & Luis Araujo (eds): *Organizational Learning and the Learning Organization.* London: SAGE.
Elkjær, Bente (2002): E-læring på arbejdspladsen. In Knud Illeris (ed): *Udspil om læring i arbejdslivet.* Copenhagen: Roskilde University Press. [E-Learning at the Workplace].
Ellström, Per-Erik (2004): Kompetenceudvikling på arbejdspladsen: Forudsætninger, processer, resultater. In Vibeke Andersen, Bruno Clematide & Steen Høyrup (eds): *Lærings på arbejdspladsen – udfordringer til læreprocesser på arbejdet.* Copenhagen: Roskilde University Press. [Competence Development at the Workplace: Conditions, Processes, Results].
EU Commission (2000): *Memorandum on Lifelong Learning.* Bruxelles: EU.
Garrick, John (1998): *Informal Learning in the Workplace: Unmasking human resource development.* London: Routledge.
Garrick, John (1999): The Dominant Discourses of Learning at Work. In Davis Boud & John Garrick (eds): *Understanding Learning at Work.* London: Routledge.
Harvard Business Review (2001): *On Organizational Learning.* Harvard: Harvard Business School Publishing Corporation.
Illeris, Knud (2002): *The Three Dimensions of Learning: Contemporary learning theory in the tension field between the cognitive, the emotional and the social.* Leicester, UK: NIACE. (2004 also Malabar, Florida: Krieger Publishing Company).
Lahn, Leif Chr. (2004): Udvikling af net-baserede læringsomgivelser i arbejdslivet. In Anne Marie Kanstrup (ed): *E-læring på arbejde.* Copenhagen: Roskilde University Press. [The Development of Net-Based Learning Environments in Working Life].
Lave, Jean – Wenger, Etienne (1991): *Situated Learning: Legitimate peripheral participation.* Cambridge, Mass.: Cambridge University Press.
Leithäuser, Thomas (2000): Subjectivity, Lifeworld and Life Organization. In Knud Illeris (ed): *Adult Education in the Perspective of the Learners.* Copenhagen: Roskilde University Press.
Marsick, Victoria J. – Watkins, Karen E. (1990): *Informal and Incidental Learning in the Workplace.* London: Routledge.
Morsing, Mette (1995): Organisatorisk læring af anden orden – fra en struktur- til en procorienteret teori om læring. *Virksomhedens strategi og ledelse,* 5, 1–28. [Organizational Learning of Second Order: From a Structure-Oriented to a Process-Oriented Theory of Learning].
Nicolini, David – Ghwerardi, Silvia – Yanow, Dvora (eds) (2003): *Knowing in Organizations.* New York: M.E. Sharpe.
Prætorius, Nadja U. (2004): Livet som undtagelsestilstand. *FOFU-NYT,* 1, 13–26. [Life as a State of Emergency].
Tennant, Mark (1999): Is Learning Transferable? In David Boud & John Gerrick (eds): *Understanding Learning at Work.* London: Routledge.
Thång, Per-Olof – Wärvik, Gun-Britt (2004): Pruktionsnær uddannelse med IT-støtte for erhvervsaktive i den svenske industri. In Anne Marie Kanstrup (ed): *E-læring på arbejde.* Copenhagen: Roskilde University Press. [IT-Supported Production-Based Education of Employees in Swedish Industry].
Tynell, Jesper (2001): *Da medarbejderne blev en ressource. Magtrelationer i en virksomhed, der profilerer sig på at pleje og udvikle medarbejdernes menneskelige ressourcer.* Roskilde: Roskilde University. [When the Employees Became a Resource: Power Relation in an Enterprise Raising its Profile by Supporting and Developing the Human Resources of the Employees].
Volmerg, Birgit – Senghaas-Knobloch, Eva – Leithäuser, Thomas (1986): *Betriebliche*

Lebenswelt. Eine Socialpsychologie industrieller Arbeitsverhältnisse. Opladen: Westdeutscher Verlag. [Life World at Work: A Social Psychology of Work Conditions in Industry.

Volmerg, Ute (1977): Zur Verhältnis von Produktion und Sozialisation am Beispiel industrieller Lohnarbeit. In Thomas Leithäser & Walter Heinz (eds): *Produktion, Arbeit, Sozialisation.* Frankfurt a.M.: Suhrkamp. [Conditions of Production and Socialisation in Industrial Wage Labour].

Wenger, Etienne (1998): *Communities of Practice: Learning, meaning and identity.* Cambridge, Mass.: Cambridge University Press.

Wenger, Etienne – McDermott, Richard – Snyder, William M. (2002): *Cultivating Communities of Practice.* Boston: Harvard Business School Press.

CHAPTER 21

WORKPLACE LEARNING AS COMPETENCE DEVELOPMENT

The need for competence development

In the previous chapters I have dealt with the basic structures and elements of workplace learning. However, before going on to consider learning at a more concrete and practical level, it is necessary to address the general question of the kind and quality of workplace learning that is needed today. As a central concept for this discussion I shall take up the issue of 'competence development'. This is an important concept, and one currently much in vogue, because, when used correctly, it encompasses the most important qualities that workplace learning needs to include to be up-to-date not only in working life, but in modern life in general.

It is not so very many years ago that the concept of competence was mainly a formal and legal matter, something that gave a person a legal right to make decisions in a certain area, especially in terms of public administration. However, over the last two decades, the use of the word has permeated the areas of education, working life, management and politics as a modern expression for what a person should be able to do or achieve.

During the 1990s, this led to a pronounced change in language usage in relation to the intended results of education and the human resource demands of the labour market, implying that the concept of competences to a great extent was being substituted for that of qualifcations. Moreover, this was not just an incidental or trivial language renovation. It should rather be understood as an attempt to recognise the full consequences of the change in the types of abilities that were demanded.

The concept of qualifications has its roots in industrial sociology and fundamentally relates to labour demands for concrete knowledge and skills. Most significantly, it was used in relation to the so-called de-qualification of labour demands as a result of industrialisation (see Braverman 1974). However, this was gradually accompanied by a trend towards an increase in demand for a range of personal or generic qualifications such as flexibility, reliability, responsibility, creativity and independence.

Conversely, the concept of competences was first taken up in organisational psychology and modern management. Here, the point of departure is on the personal level, particularly an individual's ability and readiness to meet the changing challenges of a job. Precisely such competences as the above-mentioned personal and generic qualities are needed for this purpose, while the more formal qualifications become something that can be called upon to contribute to implementing the competences in specific situations.

This could also be expressed by saying that the concept of competences attempts to include different types of qualifications in an understanding which spans a person's potential and practical abilities, i.e. a holistic concept integrating all that is necessary to manage a given situation or challenge: concrete qualifications are integrated into the personal competence in relation to a specific task. Whereas the qualification approach started with single elements and gradually developed in the direction of a more coherent understanding, the competence approach starts with the whole – such as the type of person who will be able to manage a certain task – and, from this position, eventually identifies different qualifications that must be available or acquired.

Definition and important qualities of competences

When dealing with the concept of competence, however, it soon becomes very apparent that there is great uncertainty about and great variety in interpretations of what precisely is meant. Very many different definitions have been proposed, and none of them can be said to be authoritative or generally accepted. A typical and generally accepted definition is the following, which was formulated by the Swiss Dominique Rychen and Laura Salganik as a result of their intensive work for the OECD (Organization for Economic Co-operation and Development) on the topic:

> A competence is defined as the ability to successfully meet complex demands in a particular context through the mobilization of psychological prerequisites (including both cognitive and noncognitive aspects). This represents a demand-oriented or functional approach to defining competencies.
> (Rychen and Salganik 2003, p. 43)

However, I shall also mention another definition – proposed by Per Schultz Jørgensen, a Danish Professor of Social Psychology and leading member of the Danish National Competence Council – because this definition explicitly includes the central condition that competences involve the potential to deal appropriately with future and unforeseen situations:

> The concept of competence refers [...] to a person's being qualified in a broader sense. It is not merely that a person masters a professional area, but also that the person can apply this professional knowledge – and more than that, apply it in relation to the requirements inherent in a situation which, in addition, may be uncertain and unpredictable. Thus competence also includes the person's assessments and attitudes, and ability to draw on a considerable part of his/her personal qualifications.
> (Jørgensen 1999, p. 4)

As an extension of these definitions, I shall here draw attention to some of the most important qualities of competences that make this concept more comprehensive and up to date than, for example, qualifications, knowledge, skills, attitudes and other concepts that deal with the outcome of learning and education.

Competences relate to the application in specific situations

As mentioned in Jørgensen's definition, competences can be applied in relation to the requirements inherent in specific situations. It is not sufficient that a person commands a professional area. To be competent the person must also be able to apply his or her professional knowledge and other attributes, such as insights, techniques and methods, in practice.

The competent person is able to act appropriately in specific areas or in specific kinds of situations, and this must be emphasised because it is a demand that clearly exceeds prevailing understandings of knowledge as the central aim of learning and education and to some extent also the concept of qualifications, which does not always include the dimension of application. In contrast, it is an integral feature of the concept of competence that specific knowledge and professional qualifications are necessary but not sufficient for competence: it does not automatically follow that knowledge and qualifications can be applied in all the many situations of practice. For example, in learning psychology the well-known concept of transfer of knowledge implies precisely that students and learners are often unable to activate what they have learned in relevant situations that are different from the learning situation (see, for example, Illeris 2006 2007).

Competences are situation related in the sense that they clearly include the ability to handle specific kinds of situations, which can be defined with respect to, for instance, a job or certain groups of people. So competences are not expressed themselves and do not achieve their concrete form until they are applied in appropriated situations. And competences are also related to action, i.e. they express themselves through the relevant and appropriate actions they release when required.

In this way competence is a concept which, more than other concepts in the field, is in line with today's dynamic and changeable society, in which new challenges and situations are constantly arising.

Competences have the nature of potentials

Jørgensen's definition of competences also explicitly states that the competent person is able to use his or her competences in future situations, which 'may be uncertain and unpredictable'. This is, as I see it, one of the most important qualities of competences in comparison with qualifications. Competences have the potential to be further developed or deployed in future unknown situations. Another Danish definition pays special attention to this:

> A competent person [. . .] is a person, who is in possession of certain qualifications and also commands the exercise of these qualifications in a specific situation which may be unknown to him or her. [. . .] Competence is something which is practiced in situations when the results are not known in advance. This implies that it is possible to be well qualified, but not competent.
> (Jensen 2000, pp. 126 and 136)

To be competent in a certain area implies that the person has acquired the prerequisites or potentials to handle both well-established situations and new situations, something that in our late modern society happens regularly and demands understanding, attitudes, handling, taking a stand and solving problems.

The fact that potentials are central to competences is probably the most decisive quality that makes the concept of competence so important today. We live in a world and at a time in which the conditions are constantly changing and nobody knows in advance exactly what the changes will be, only that they will occur frequently. Change ranges from small changes in everyday matters to fundamental changes in conditions, and it can take place from one day to the next.

Thus, 'flexibility' and readiness to change have become key capabilities, and which potentials are at one's disposal when a new situation or challenge occurs is of decisive importance.

This is also why the greatest and most important challenge to schooling and education today is to help develop students' potentials, i.e. to prepare them to handle problems and situations that are not yet known and cannot be predicted. In working life, the potentials that workers and employees possess and are able to draw on when needed are clearly crucial. At the same time, both in education and in working life, this implies abilities which fundamentally cannot be described or measured fully, because they include reactions to challenges which are partly or totally unknown and unpredictable.

Competences include insight, empathy and structural understanding

An important aspect of potentials is that they include insight into how an area is structured and related to other areas, which incentives, balances and power conditions are at stake, which criteria are decisive in determining what is good and bad practice, why things are as they are and, not least, a familiarity with the subject, meaning not only an intellectual but also an emotional and social engagement, including well-substantiated opinions, preferences and a conscious attitude as to one's own position and views.

All these qualities must be so well established that they work together as a whole so that they function even when conditions are changing or strained. Competences should be acquired and developed so that they allow changes, flexibility and remodelling. It is not enough just to know and understand the principal structures and criteria in the area, it is also necessary to adopt a personal, conscious and deliberate attitude and to have the ability to react frankly and at the same time critically to new trends and changes that constantly arise and demand a reaction and often well-founded support or opposition.

Thus, taken seriously the concept of competence implies quite extensive demands for flexible insight and empathy in relation to the reality in which it is to be displayed.

Judgements and decisions are central elements of competence

Another essential and crucial element of competences – one which again is more than just qualifications – is that they, when used in practice, to a great extent imply the ability to make qualified judgements and appropriate decisions in relation to the area in question. When applying one's competences one must, especially in relation to the continuous stream of new situations, be able to decode what is at stake, judge its impact and make relevant and workable decisions about what to do, and all of this often has to be done immediately and under time pressure.

These special conditions and qualities of competences have primarily been pointed out and emphasised by the Australian educational researchers Paul Hager and David Beckett (Hager and Beckett 1995; Beckett and Hager 2000, 2002; Beckett 2004, 2009). As stated by Beckett:

> judgements-in-contexts are at the heart [. . .] of competence. [. . .] By this I mean that in these postmodern times, those who can 'read the moment' (or the situation in general) for its particularities and opportunities, are probably those most likely to identify a niche, a hybridity, or an innovation which serves

and may even extend prevailing circumstances, thereby reaching new understandings of workplace practices.
(Beckett 2009, p. 71)

Beckett and Hager strongly emphasise the importance of what they term 'the inferential understanding' in connection with judgements and decisions:

> the reflective action of making a 'judgement' is central. Workers do this all day, every day, and I have claimed [. . .] that these adult education experiences are central to a new concept of holistic competence. Frequently, what humans find themselves doing [. . .] is making decisions (judgements) about what to do next. Workplace learning is increasingly shaped by this sort of fluid experience ('knowing how' to go on), but it needs to be made explicit. [. . .] The 'making explicit' is what the best adult teachers and trainers can do, in facilitating, even revealing, adults' experiences for educational purposes.
> (Beckett 2009, p. 76)

Although many writers share this largely rational and cognitive approach to the concept of competence, there are also other voices attaching more importance to empathy and intuition, as, for example, the American Dreyfus brothers in their five-step model of 'human intuition and expertise', which claims that human intelligence will always be superior to any computer in certain vital areas (Dreyfus and Dreyfus 1986). The relationship between the cognitive and the emotional is altogether a psychological topic, and one which for quite some time has been very much in focus (see, for example, Damasio 1994; Goleman 1995; Illeris 2007); it also has a gender dimension (Baron-Cohen 2003), but I shall not explore that further here. I shall only draw attention to the fact that, not least in connection with judgements and decisions that have to be made immediately in an unexpected situation, it is very difficult or almost impossible to distinguish between what is due to cognitive reasoning and what must be referred to empathy and intuition. Both elements will nearly always be involved in a combination that cannot be unravelled in any way.

What is essential, and what is also the central message for Beckett and Hager, is that judgements and decisions are central matters in connection with the application of competences in practice.

Competences exist and can be displayed at all levels

A last general point about competences to mention here is that they in a sense have a certain democratic quality, because it is possible to have and display competences in all possible connections at all levels. For instance, in the Scandinavian countries we use the expression 'real' or 'de facto' competences for anything people have learned informally outside the school and educational systems and we have, like in many other countries, formal systems to validate such competences (see, for example, Skule 2004; Lucio *et al.* 2007; Parker and Walters 2009).

Competence is found everywhere and is relevant and necessary in all activities at all levels. Thus, everybody possesses some competences, because we have all been involved in some activities which we have learned to handle. One of the most popular Danish books on developmental psychology, which has been translated into several languages, has the title *Your Competent Child* (Juul 2001), and another is called *Children's Competences* (Cecchin 2000). We also talk, in general, about, for instance, social competences, personal competences, professional competences and even key competences (Rychen and Salganik 2003; Rychen and Tiana 2004).

Competence is not necessarily elitist, i.e. limited to a few specialists in the same way as, for instance, expertise (see, for example, Dreyfus and Dreyfus 1986; Herling 2001; Jarvis 2009). We all develop competences in relation to what we deal with and in particular to what we are absorbed in or committed to. There are many television programmes in which members of the public compete against each other to test their competence in a particular area – this can be seen as a contrast to the many television experts who are constantly explaining and commenting on everything.

Of course, competences are also concerned with learning, developing and improving, but always starting at the level and position one has already reached. Thus, competence, like learning and development, is something common and general – and only when somebody wants something from us might it take on an elitist aspect.

Problematic ways of using the concept of competence

In the above I have highlighted and discussed five specific and important qualities of the concept of competence, and I hope that this has made it visible and understandable why I find this concept an appropriate and agreeable term to use in relation to the qualitative side of workplace learning. I do believe that this concept is well qualified and quite precise in relation to what is needed for the individual to function appropriately and be well integrated in today's complicated and ever-changing society and working life. It seems to cover the whole range and complexity of the very comprehensive challenges we face both individually and as a society. It reaches far beyond both what public education has traditionally aimed at and to a great extent also what industrial and organisational psychology have taken up. And, finally, it should be able to maintain that what is at stake are human capacities in their totality and mutual connectedness, and not just some more limited qualifications.

Nevertheless, there are also important reasons to be cautious about using the competence concept, because it has been greatly misused and involved in tendencies leading to an overload and sometimes even impoverishment of human resources. Competence has been and is still one of several buzzwords that have contributed to press human labour and capacity to the edge, and sometimes even over the edge of what human beings can endure. The concept has been an integrated element in some tendencies, which for many have led to stress, burnout, mental breakdown and other symptoms of a serious overexertion. Two tendencies, in particular, in their different ways, have played a part in this.

First, the concept of competence in the current sense was launched by the trend that in general is known as human resource management, or HRM (see, for example, Tyson 2006; Boxall *et al.* 2008). This is a way of managing, leading or directing human resources, i.e. other people, a kind of modern management that fundamentally regards workers and employees as resources to be treated in ways that make them function as effectively as possible, ultimately with regard to the earnings and profit of the company – or, as more directly expressed by the South Korean Professor of Lifelong Learning, Soonghee Han, as a 'commodification of human ability' (Han 2009). But it is a modern trend, and it tries to achieve its goal not, as in the early days of industrialisation, by compulsion or coercion, but rather by positive incentives, self-direction and responsibility.

However, there are very many and very different practices that could be called or understood as HRM, but which do not necessarily lead to radical exploitation – and many people today prefer to speak about human resource development (HRD), to stress the developmental element and not so much the management (see, for example, Swanson and Holton 2001). In any case, in relation to competences, there obviously is a risk that HRM and also HRD in practice will encourage or lead to an uncritical ability to direct oneself to do what is expected by the management without being able to set any limits. And this is often encouraged by an unmistakable tendency of HRM and HRD to stand for everything that is regarded as trendy and modern – it may be more important to follow the newest trend than to know where it will take you.

Second, the most far-reaching misuse of the concept of competence is actually taking place in the public sector, related to the approach which has been named 'new public management' (see, for example, Lane 2000; Horton 2006; Hjort 2009). This approach was introduced in the 1980s in the USA and the UK in the time of Ronald Reagan and Margaret Thatcher and later spread to many other countries, mainly in the West, strongly supported by supranational organisations such as the EU, the OECD and the World Bank. In general new public management is about strict economic government and regulation, especially through detailed objectives, budgets, rules, measurements and incentives and strong autocratic leaders of large organisations created by merging existing institutions.

As to competence, the extensive and uncritical use of this concept in the legislation and administration, particularly of educational systems, has in many respects made it unclear what is actually meant and referred to. There does not seem to be any limits as to the number of competences that should be developed, and at the same time it can be quite unclear what is actually required. For instance, in the official regulations of the education of nurses in Denmark (Danish Ministry of Education 2008), the word 'competence' appears 51 times, and the interminable enumeration of competences that the nurses are supposed to acquire includes everything that they might possibly come across. Among many other competences, nurses are expected to be able to:

- practise independent, responsible and well-founded, patient-directed nursing;
- observe and document patients' health conditions, health risks, disease symptoms and treatment results;
- describe the chemical and anatomical composition of humans and human development through the course of life in the interaction with the environment and micro-organisms; and
- act professionally in an interdisciplinary, societal, cultural and organisational context.

The reader is inevitably left wondering what all these high-faluting demands really mean in practice.

Perhaps this is part of the reason why the Ministry has also been very eager to join the OECD project, which was originally launched in the late 1990s, and has the aim of establishing so-called national competence accounts. Later, in the early 2000s, the focus was changed to measuring and comparing so-called key competences in a broad range of areas including, for example, literacy, numeracy, social competences, learning competence, communication competences, self-management, political competence, ecological competence, cultural competences and health competence (Trier 2001). And gradually the ambitions have then been downscaled to the current so-called PIAAC project (Programme for the International Assessment of Adult Competencies), which, as a parallel to the highly discussed PISA project (also an OECD project), shall include adult competences in the more measurable areas of (OECD 2010, p. 6)

- problem-solving in technology-rich environments;
- literacy;
- numeracy;
- assessment of reading components.

After some delay the first results of this are now scheduled to be published in 2013.

It is obvious that the extensive and unclear use of the concept of competence and the somewhat doubtful measuring and comparing of key competences have resulted in a devaluation and blurring of the concept and totally disregard the special qualities that I have dealt with above. The reason for talking about competences rather than qualifications disappears to the same extent that its content is treated precisely as what Soonghee Han (2009) has critically termed the 'commodification of human abilities', i.e. as goods which can be produced, weighed, measured, declared, quantified, priced and bought and sold on the (labour) market. This is exactly the opposite of what I regard as the most fundamental strength of the idea of competences: that they refer to human qualities which cannot be produced but only developed, which cannot be regarded quantitatively but only qualitatively, which cannot be described as mechanical functions but only as potentials, and which cannot be declared precisely but only in relation to certain challenges and tasks.

I have in my own practice heard many nursing teachers and teachers in other areas with similar kinds of regulations question the meaning and implications of these lists of competences. And when the results of the PIAAC are published, there will, no doubt, be a renewed discussion about what has been measured and how this defects attention and effort from all other areas to those narrow functions which are measured – just as we have seen in relation to the PISA outcomes.

If the competence concept is to be taken seriously it must be understood that it fundamentally refers to the application of potentials, the ability to deal with unknown future situations, challenges and problems – and this cannot be measured. To try to measure the least complicated of many relevant competences and draw some far-reaching conclusions is to devalue the very concept of competence, which is distinguished precisely by its relevance to the present realities in all their multitude and complexity.

In addition, it is worth mentioning that one outcome of the application of new public management has been that some of the most negative aspects of HRM have been transferred to the public sector in a very unfortunate way, such that stress and burnout have been joined by a strong demotivation as a result of the constant changes and reorganisations forced on the workers and employees by autocratic leaders, very often in direct opposition to the professional norms and attitudes in the area. The mixture of stress and demotivation causes extreme mental strain, and the consequence tends to be a personal depression that may result in being both worn out and unemployed. In Denmark there has been, during the 2000s, a large increase in this kind of syndrome among public servants (Prætorius 2007).

Competence development in practice

In this last section of Part I of this book some general features of competence development in relation to workplace learning shall be lined up – before the more specific discussions of different kinds of workplace learning are taken up in Part II.

Competence development, school and education

First, I believe that it is important to state that the development of work competence cannot be achieved by schools, courses or educational programmes unless they are in some way combined with work practice, for example in the form of apprenticeship, trainee service, alternating school and practice periods or school practice projects. This is because competences, as stated previously, are closely related to application in specific situations, and if the kinds of specific situations in question are work situations the competence development must at least to some extent include such situations.

However, this certainly does not mean that schooling and education are not relevant for competence development in general or for work competence development in particular. On the contrary, it is only in very special cases that school or educational learning is not relevant or necessary for work competence development, either as an indispensable precondition or as an integral or parallel part.

When the nature and quality of competences are taken seriously, it is a huge challenge to schools and educational institutions to take part in goal-directed competence development. In a nutshell, it could be asked how it is possible for a school or other educational institution to develop potentials to cope appropriately with situations and problems that take place elsewhere and are not known and cannot even be foreseen. This is actually a question that undermines a great deal of traditional educational thinking that takes as its starting point the formulation of precise objectives and then tries to deduce educational measures from these.

On the other hand, in principle, the role of schooling and education has always been to prepare students for something which is placed outside in time and space. And in today's society it is hardly possible to think that the highly qualitative work competences that are demanded at almost all workplaces can be developed without comprehensive contributions from the school and educational system. It is obvious that the school and education system will also in the future be the 'state apparatus', which is constructed to be the fundamental public means of providing the major contributions to the competences demanded. Moreover, it will inevitably – even in the future – be in the practical and economic interest of both the private and the public sector that as much competence development as possible takes place outside the workplace so that it does not strain the economy and daily working conditions of companies and organisations.

So the proper question to ask is, rather: how can schools and educational institutions be geared to optimally develop competences which are relevant for further competence development at workplaces and elsewhere outside the educational system? And the answer obviously must meet demands in the areas of both content and ability to perform activities.

As to content, schooling and education must still include essential general skills such as literacy, numeracy, information technology and foreign languages, a basic grounding in subjects such as biology, health, history, natural sciences, social studies and the arts, as well as the general prerequisites for further competence development in one or more professional areas. All this must be thought through from the perspective of what is relevant and necessary today, but it is unlikely to be much different from what we are already used to.

The more important changes needed to strengthen schooling and education in the direction of competence development will be related to the organisation and practice of school and educational activities: traditional teaching must be supplemented by, and there must be much more emphasis on, participation in decision-making, social relations, responsibility, planning of processes and projects, interdisciplinarity, individual and social reflection and the like. It is obvious when looking back on the important qualities of competences described earlier in this chapter that achieving such qualities will require something like a revolution in schooling and education that is carried through right down to the roots of how it is practised. This again will require a good deal of serious experimentation and research and, probably the most important, difficult and decisive point, an open-minded and dedicated attitude by all the many politicians, professionals, students, parents and people from working life who need to be involved. (In this connection a good piece of advice could be to consult some literature presenting a comprehensive and up-to-date understanding of human learning such as, for example, Illeris 2007.)

Conditions for competence development programmes at work

Competence development at work is different from educational competence development, not least because it is to a greater or lesser extent integrated into the very activities in which it can be utilised, so the borderline between competence development and competence application is often hardly visible. This is probably also part of the reason why the conditions for competence development at work is a topic which in itself and systematically has not been researched very much. However, recently, the Swedes Per-Erik Ellström and Henrik Kock have attempted to survey the literature in the area and give a systematic overview of 'What characterizes successful strategies for competence development in organizations?' (Ellström and Kock 2009, p. 48ff.). Their main conclusion is that the effects of competence development depend on an interplay between four kinds of factors.

The first group of factors concern the prior experiences of the participants, i.e. previous experience of education, self-confidence, motivation and already developed competences. Ellström and Kock, in this connection, primarily refer to the well-known condition that the higher an individual's social background and the educational level, the more likely it is that he or she will participate in further educational activities, and this also seems to be the case in relation to programmes and activities that aim at competence development at work. From this can also be drawn the conclusion that, if such programmes or activities are to involve workers or employees with a lower educational level and social background, special measures and considerations should be taken (Illeris 2005, 2006d; see also Chapter 12).

The second group of factors comprise the planning, content, design and implementation of programmes and activities. Here Ellström and Kock emphasise that the motives for engagement should be problem oriented, i.e. that the competence development should be viewed as part of a specific strategy or activity in which the company is involved, for instance a new work organisation or a new production, and that the staff should be involved directly, or indirectly through representatives, in the planning and direction.

The next group of factors have to do with the relationship between programmes or activities and internal organisation and company culture, for example recruitment, counselling, design, job extension, proportions of time and personnel involved and supervision. In all such dimensions it is important that there is an agreement and relation to the internal norms and understanding and if possible that deviances, extensions or changes are made open, substantiated and discussed – so that there are no grounds for suspecting that managers are trying to follow some hidden agenda.

Finally, there are factors related to the external environment, such as the competitive situation, the labour market and the rate of technological development in the field. According to Ellström and Kock these conditions can be assumed to be related mainly indirectly to the effect of investments in competence development. However, as shown by the world developments that have occurred since 2009, it is difficult to accept that they can be ignored. Rather, a situation of stability in the external context must be regarded as out of reach so that the risks and changes must be openly faced and taken into account.

However, overall, Ellström and Kock seem to draw a very useful and reliable picture of the general conditions in which important and sustainable competence development in the workplace needs to take place.

Guidelines for the process of competence development at work

As to how the competence developmental processes can be thought of and arranged as learning courses on the social and individual levels, some guidelines can be drawn from the special qualities of competences as described above in combination with learning theoretical and educational considerations.

As competence development implies important and demanding learning processes, a first requirement must be that the participants are personally committed to the idea and the process which are set up. *Commitment*, engagement and motivation are needed to mobilise the mental energy which can make learning a deeper process than just the acquisition of new knowledge (Illeris 2007). Another prerequisite on the personal level is, of course, that participants have a reasonable level of professional knowledge, skills, insight and understanding in relation to the area(s) in which the competence development is supposed to take place. These requirements can be seen as a practical utilisation of the first group of factors concerning the prior experiences of the participants in Ellström and Kock's overview, and in relation to their special concern about the low-skilled it should be observed that any competence development programme that includes this group must be effected in ways that meet the positive motivations and also the concerns they may have (see Chapter 12). It is a waste of energy and resources to offer competence development opportunities and programmes that do not correspond with and respect the motivational conditions and prerequisites of the participants. Thus, representatives of the participants should also be involved at an early stage.

Next, competence development activities in workplaces must to some extent be integrated with or involve the daily work *practice*, and in most cases also intended future practice. This is well in line with what Ellström and Kock have observed. Seen from the participants' point of view this is because work practice – as shown in Figure 21.1 – is the area that overlaps with work identity, and serious competence development must be anchored in and influence participants' work identities. In effect, this means that serious competence development processes cannot exclusively be activities that do not involve participants' work practice.

They cannot involve only teaching, exercises, discussions, explanations, demonstrations, excursions or the like. All such activities have a part to play, and can be very important elements, but practice cannot be left out and must in general play the principal part and must always be referenced in other kinds of activities.

Finally, and I think my advice here goes beyond the points of Ellström and Kock, it is of fundamental importance that competence development activities include *reflection*. It is through reflection that experience can be turned into potentials for the future, and this is also the deeper reason why the concept of reflection has gained a very central position in contemporary learning theories, especially in relation to adult and workplace learning. There are many slightly different interpretations and understandings of this concept, but they can be summed up in two main categories. One category is what the American psychologist Donald Schön has called reflection-in-action (Schön 1983, 1987), indicating that such reflection takes place as an integrated part of action – actors reflect, individually or in groups, on what they are doing when they are doing it in order to make the best out of their actions. This is certainly very important in relation to competence development, but it refers to what can and should always be part of the nature of goal-directed activities, and so it is rather a general requirement of the work culture and not something that can be specifically planned. If it is planned and scheduled as a special element of competence development arrangements it is no longer reflection-inaction, but reflection-on-action, and this is what most researchers have pointed to – not least the American adult educator Jack Mezirow in relation to his concept of 'transformative learning' (Mezirow 1990, 1991, 2009) and the British-American adult educator Stephen Brookfield in relation to his concept of 'critical reflection' (Brookfield 1987, 1996) – and what is essential for the planning and practice of competence development programmes. Systematically including and practising individual and shared reflection activities as a kind of evaluation and adjustment of programmes leads to a high probability of genuine competence development.

So as a sort of general formula for the planning and practice of workplace learning as competence development I can recommend the simple triad of

commitment–practice–reflection

This is, of course, an oversimplification of a very complex topic, but I have found that it is a handy rule of thumb to keep the arrangements on the right track. Commitment is a necessary point of departure for all who are involved. Including practice ensures that activities do not lose relevance. And reflection is the way in which experience can be turned into potentials – which is the same as turning more ordinary learning into competence development.

Competence development and the learning triangle

As a last point in relation to competence development I shall return to the learning triangle to point out the theoretical basis of the qualities that learning should possess in order to obtain the nature of competence development. I shall do this by referring to the three learning dimensions:

1. The content dimension concerns what is learned. This is usually described as knowledge and skills, but many other elements, such as opinions, insight, meaning, attitudes, values, ways of behaviour, methods and strategies, may also be considered learning content. The endeavour of the learner is to construct *meaning* and the *ability* to deal with the challenges of practical life. An overall personal *functionality* can thereby be developed.

2. The incentive dimension provides and directs the mental energy that is necessary for the learning process to take place. It comprises such elements as feelings, emotions, motivation and volition. Its ultimate function is to secure the continuous *mental balance* of the learner and thereby it simultaneously develops a personal *sensitivity*.

   These two dimensions are always initiated by impulses from the interaction processes and integrated in the internal process of elaboration and acquisition. Therefore, the learning content is, so to speak, always 'obsessed' with the incentives at stake, e.g. whether the learning is driven by desire, interest, necessity or compulsion. Correspondingly, the incentives are always influenced by the content, e.g. new information can change the incentive condition.
3. The interaction dimension provides the impulses that initiate the learning process. This may take place as perception, transmission, experience, imitation, activity, participation, etc. It serves the personal *integration* in communities and society and thereby also builds up the *sociality* of the learner. However, this building up necessarily takes place through the other two dimensions.

In Figure 21.1 the signal words from the above have been placed outside each of the learning triangle angles which show the three learning dimensions. The words that signify what the learner is aiming at are written in regular type and the words that signify the general outcome are written in italics. Thus by accentuating in italics the qualities of the learning outcomes in each of the three dimensions this figure highlights what are also the three necessary and crucial components of all competences.

It should be noted that these qualities are in principle the qualities of all learning, but in relation to competence development it is particularly important to emphasise that precisely these three qualities – functionality, sensitivity and sociality – are the basic building blocks, and it is the strength of these three qualities that is decisive for the extent to which learning takes on the nature of competence development. The holistic demand that this concept implies can adequately be specified into a

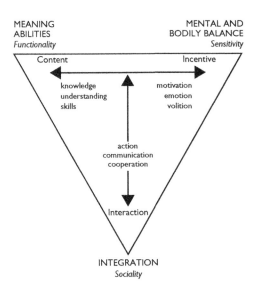

Figure 21.1 Learning as competence development (after Illeris 2007, p. 28).

claim that functionality, sensitivity and sociality must be involved with considerable weight in relation to the area in question. Therefore, for learning to have the quality of competence development it must include all three learning dimensions in ways that are important and relevant in relation to the required competence.

References

Baron-Cohen, S. (2003) *The Essential Difference*. London: Penguin.
Beckett, D. (2004) Embodied competence and generic skill: the emergence of inferential understanding. *Educational Philosophy and Theory* 36, 497–508.
Beckett, D. (2009) Holistic competence: putting judgements first. In Illeris, K. (ed.) *International Perspectives on Competence Development*. London: Routledge.
Beckett, D. and Hager, P. (2000) Making judgements as the basis for workplace learning: towards an epistemology of practice. *International Journal of Lifelong Education* 19, 300–311.
Beckett, D. and Hager, P. (2002) *Life, Work and Learning: Practice in Postmodernity*. London: Routledge.
Boxall, P., Purcell, J. and Wright, P. (eds.) (2008) *The Oxford Handbook of Human Resource Management*. Oxford: Oxford University Press.
Braverman, H. (1974) *Labour and Monopoly Capital*. New York: Monthly Review Press.
Brookfield, S.D. (1987) *Developing Critical Thinkers: Challenging Adults to Explore Alternative Ways of Thinking and Acting*. Milton Keynes: Open University Press.
Brookfield, S.D. (1996) *Understanding and Facilitating Adult Learning*. Buckingham: Open University Press.
Cecchin, D. (ed.) (2000) *Børns kompetencer [Children's Competences]*. Copenhagen: BUPL.
Damasio, A.R. (1994) *Descartes' Error: Emotion, Reason, and the Human Brain*. New York: Grosset/Putnam.
Danish Ministry of Education (2008) *Bekendtgørelse om uddannelse til professionsbachelor i sygepleje [Departmental order on the education of bachelors of nursing]*. 24 January 2008. Copenhagen: Undervisningsministeriet.
Dreyfus, H. and Dreyfus, S. (1986) *Mind over Machine*. New York: Free Press.
Ellström, P.-E. and Kock, H. (2009) Competence development in the workplace: Concepts, strategies and effects. In Illeris, K. (ed.) *International Perspectives on Competence Development*. London: Routledge.
Goleman, D. (1995) *Emotional Intelligence: Why it can Matter More than IQ*. London: Bloomsbury.
Hager, P. and Beckett, D. (1995) Philosophical underpinnings of the integrated conception of competence. *Educational Philosophy and Theory* 21, 1–24.
Han, S. (2009) Commodification of human ability. In Illeris, K. (ed.) *International Perspectives on Competence Development*. London: Routledge.
Herling, R.W. (2001) Operational definitions of expertise and competence. In Swanson, RA. and Holton, E.F. (eds.) *Foundations of Human Resourse Development*. San Francisco: Berrett-Koehler Publishers.
Hjort, K.(2009) Competence development in the public sector: development, or dismantling of professionalism? In Illeris, K. (ed.) *International Perspectives on Competence Development*. London: Routledge.
Horton, S. (ed.) (2006) New public management: its impact on public servants' identity. *International Journal of Public Sector Management*, 19 (special issue).
Illeris, K. (2005) Low-skilled workers learn at the workplace. *Lifelong Learning in Europe* 10.
Illeris, K. (2006) Lifelong learning and the low-skilled. *International Journal of Lifelong Education* 25, 15–28.
Illeris, K. (2007) *How We Learn: Learning and Non-learning in School and Beyond*. London: Routledge.
Jarvis, P. (2009) Learning to be an expert: competence development and expertise. In Illeris, K. (ed.) *International Perspectives on Competence Development*. London: Routledge.
Jensen, P.E. (2000) Kapabiliteter og kompetencer som ledelsesværktøj [Capabilities and

competences as a tool of management]. In Andersen, T., Jensen, I. and Prahl, A. (eds.) *Kompetence i et organisatorisk perspektiv*. Copenhagen: Roskilde University Press.

Jørgensen, Per Schultz (1999) Hvad er kompetence? [What is competence?]. *Uddannelse* 9.

Juul, J. (2001) *Your Competent Child*. New York: Farrar Strauss & Giroux.

Lane, J.-E. (2000) *New Public Management*. London: Routledge.

Lucio, M.M., Skule, S., Kruse, W. and Trappmann, V. (2007) Regulating skill formation in Europe. *European Journal of Industrial Relations* 13, 323–340.

Mezirow, J. (1990) How critical reflection triggers transformative learning. In Jack Mezirow et al. (eds.) *Fostering Critical Refection in Adulthood*. San Francisco: Jossey-Bass.

Mezirow, J. (1991) *Transformative Dimensions of Adult Learning*. San Francisco: Jossey-Bass.

Mezirow, J. (2009) An overview on transformative learning. In Illeris, K. (ed.) *Contemporary Theories of Learning*. London: Routledge.

OECD (2010) *The OECD Programme for the International Assessment of Adult Competencies (PIAAC)*. Paris: OECD Publication No. 88999.

Parker, B. and Walters, S. (2009) Competence-based training and National Qualifications Frameworks in South Africa. In Illeris, K. (ed.) *International Perspectives on Competence Development*. London: Routledge.

Prætorius, N.U. (2007) *Stress – det moderne traume* [Stress – the Modern Trauma]. Copenhagen: Dansk Psykologisk Forlag.

Rychen, D.S. and Salganik, L.H. (eds.) (2003) *Key Competencies: For a Successful Life and a Wellfunctioning Society*. Cambridge, MA: Hogrefe & Huber.

Rychen, D.S. and Tiana, A. (2004) *Developing Key Competencies in Education*. Paris: Unesco International Bureau of Education.

Schön, D.A. (1983) *The Reflective Practitioner: How Professionals Think in Action*. New York: Basic Books.

Schön, D.A. (1987) *Educating the Reflective Practitioner*. San Francisco: Jossey-Bass.

Skule, S. (2004) Learning conditions at work: a framework to understand and assess informal learning in the workplace. *International Journal of Training and Development* 1, 8–20.

Swanson, R.A. and Holton, E.F. (2001) *Foundations of Human Resource Development*. San Francisco: Barrett Koehler.

Trier, U.P. (2001) *12 Countries Contributing to DeSeCo – A Summary Report*. Neuchâtel: University of Neuchâtel on behalf of the Swiss Federal Statistical Office.

Tyson, S. (2006) *Essentials of Human Resource Management*, 5th edn. Oxford: Butterworth-Heinemann.

INDEX

Note: Page numbers in *italic* refer to figures.

Åberg, Carina 237
abilities 210, 254
accommodation 21, 23–4, 107–8, 116–19, 187
acquisition 106, 205, 210, 221; processes 10, 21, 47, 58
action: collective 193–4; perspective 169
activity theory 119
Adorno, Theodor 105
adult education 143–5, 225–6; ambivalence in 136–7; between emancipation and control 135–45; challenge from everyday life 124–5; institutional practices 139–41; responsibility in 128–30; strategies for 136–7
Adult Education Guided Intensive Study (AEGIS): 175, 182
adult identity 177
adulthood: definition of 49; learning in 52–4, 61–2, 74–83, 124–34, 191, 223–5, *see also* mature adulthood
adults: attitudes to learning 77; compared with children 75–7; current learning theory 80–1; education *see* adult education; further qualification of 226–7; identity of 137–8; learning possibilities 78–9; re-qualification of 227; young *see* youth
age: and learning 29, 75–7; and transformative learning 191–2
Alheit, Peter 81, 108
Allport, Gordon 177, 189
ambivalence 16; approaches 138–9; subjective feeling of 86–7
andragogy 75, 124, 170
application 117
apprenticeship model 121, 227–8
Argyris, Chris 15, 81, 104, 206, 218, 232, 238–9

assimilation 21, 23–4, 107–8, 116, 118–19
assimilative (additive) learning 14–15, 48, 59, 107–8, 116, 118–19, 222
association 118
attendance monitoring 94
attention deficit/hyperactivity disorder (ADHD): 37
Australia: Project for Enhancing Effective Learning (PEEL): 132–3
Ausubel, David 22, 103, 205

balance: mental–bodily 211
Bandura, Albert 105
barriers to learning 1, 3, 15–17, 22, 29, 79, 108–9, 194, *see also* defence; resistance
Bauman, Zygmunt 80
Beck, Ulrich 80
Beckett, David 235, 246–7
behaviourism 23; and early learning research 101–2
Berliner, Peter 151
Berthelsen, Jens 151
biographical approach 81, 105
biographicity 187
Blair, Tony 34
Bloom, Benjamin S.: 42–3
Boud, David 169–70, 175
Brah, Avtar 170
Brookfield, Stephen 62, 78, 175, 219, 254
Broudy, Harry S.: 117
Brückner, Peter 105, 124
Bruner, Jerome 103
burnout 35, 38, 236, 248, 250

catharsis 104
childhood: definition of 48; learning in 49–50, 61, 76

Index

children: compared with adults 75–7
choice: and identity 63–4
class: and adult learning 54
cognition: and learning 101–11; and learning dimension 106–7
cognitive capacity 49, 51
cognitive development 62
cognitive dimension 27, 58, 221
cognitive dissonance 150
cognitive science 103
cognitive theory 58, 78
Cole, Michael 103
collective learning 193–4
Colley, Helen 234
commitment 253–4
commodification of human abilities 248, 250
communities of practice 219
competence 30, 211–12; and the competitive state 34, 41; concept of 212–14; definition of 192, 212; development *see* competence development; problematic use of concept 248–50; to choose 126, 132, *see also* competencies
competence development 12, 96, 192–3, 202–3, 209, 210–11, 217; and company culture 252–3; and environmental factors 253; guidelines for 253–4; learning as 255; and learning triangle 254–6; need for 243–4; in practice 251–6; programme implementation factors 252; in schooling and education 251–2; and transformative learning 181–2; at work 252–3; and workplace learning 211–14
competencies 24, 30, 212, 243–4; definition of 244; display of 247–8; essential elements of 246–7; key 249; as potentials 245–6; qualities of 244–8; situation-specific application of 244–5; targeting of 218
competition state 30–1; learning in 33–44; untenability of 38–9
complaining: as a strategy 141–2
compulsion 89, 127
conditioning 14
confusion 66
consensus 131
contacts 88–9
content 21, 47–8, 205; dimension 11–12, 28–9, 210–11, 254
continuation schools 36
control: and adult education 135–45
Copenhagen University 160
core identity 68, 72, 191
counselling: supportive 89–90
counter-learning 232

counter-qualification: pedagogy of 24–5
Cranton, Patricia 175, 185–6
critical reflection 254
critical theory 105, 166, 208
cumulation 21, 23, 107–8, 116, 118–19
cumulative (mechanical) learning 14–15, 59, 107–8, 116, 118–19, 222

Damasio, Antonio 205, 211
death drive 26
decision making 130–1, 246–7
defence 17–18, 22, 25, 27, 48, 79, 108–9; and everyday consciousness 149–50, 223; mechanisms 16, 22, 67; and transformative learning 180–1, 194–5
defensive routines 232, 239
Definition and Selection of Competencies (DeSeCo) Project 192
Denmark 24, 34–8, 84, 124, 144, 236; Adult Education Centres (VUC): 136; adult education programmes 89, 94, 113, 136, 220, 225; Adult Education Research Project 3, 84, 113, 135–6, 144; Adult Vocational Training (AMU) system 135; age of majority in 128–9; apprenticeships in 201, 227–8; concept of experience in 168–9; Day High Schools 136; e-learning in 237; education of nurses 249; educational researchers 160; General Qualification Project 113; Learning Lab 4, 84, 229; Ministry of Education 160, 162, 249; National Competence Council 244; National Labour Market Authority 229; project work in 120, 130, 155, 160; Research Consortium on Workplace Learning 84–5; school system 126, 166, 168; Social Democratic Party 160; stress syndrome in 250; student movement in 160; teaching programmes 92, 127; UNIPÆD project 163; vocational training 92, 120, *see also* Roskilde University
Descartes, René 101
detraditionalisation 177, 190
Dewey, John 23, 28, 104, 120, 160, 166–8
Dirckinck-Holmfeld, Lone 236–7
direction 126–8
Dirkx, John 175, 185, 187, 190
disabilities 36–8
disciplines: combining in project work 158
division of responsibility 90–1, 93
double-qualification 25
dream crushing 88
Dreyfus, Hubert 247
Dreyfus, Stuart 247

dropout 35–6
dynamism: as a strategy 142

early school leavers 85
Ebbinghaus, Hermann 102
education: adult 53, 225–6; changing yardsticks for 71; and competence development 251–2; and the competitive state 33–4; consumer choice in 71; economic standardisation of 41; funding of 203; and identity development 70–2; institutionalised 62; and learning 3–4, 34, 41; problems in 34–5; reactionary attitudes in 162; responsibility in 128–30; return to 135; strategies 137; sustainability of 40; time, place and context of 91–2; vocational 35, 37, 41, 169–70, 218; youth 18–19, 36–7
effectiveness 231–2
efficiency 126; quantifiable 231–2
elaboration: internal process of 10
Elkjær, Bente 237
Ellström, Per-Erik 15, 235, 252–4
emancipation: and adult education 135–45
emotional dimension 26–8, 58–9, 105–6, 221
empathy 30, 59, 192, 221, 246–7
employees 36, 88, 92, 206, 218, 232, 239; as company resource 248; exploitation and colonisation of 236; learning by 206–9, 233–5, 237–40; low-skilled 85, 252; motivation of 194; qualifications of 204, 206, 209; self-organisation 208, 232, 235; stress and burnout 205, 236, 250
employers 36, 120, 182, 203; demands of 51, 139; perspectives of 232; and workplace learning 218
encounter groups 104
Engeström, Yrjö 81, 103, 108, 208, 219
engrams 13
enthusiasm 71–2; lack of 88
environments: and competence development 253; correspondence of 170; ICT in 236–8; significance of 235–6; workplace 205
Eraut, Michael 117
Erikson, Erik H.: 50, 65–6, 69, 74, 80, 104–5, 150, 176–7, 189, 191
espoused theories 239
European Union (EU): 38–9, 41, 77, 249; competencies in 182, 192; and workplace learning 203
evaluation 93–4
everyday consciousness 16, 61, 79, 109, 180; and defence 149–50, 223
everyday learning 114
exemplarity 120, 156, 161

exemplary learning 75
expansive learning 108
experience 165–73
experiential learning 156, 169, 175, 186; village concept of 169–70

field theory 102
financial effectivity 30
Foucault, Michel 176
Frankfurt School 24, 105, 124, 166–7, 208
freedom: from traditional ties 170
Freire, Paulo 75, 168, 174, 180, 185, 190, 193
Freud, Anna 149
Freud, Sigmund 26, 104, 205
fully functioning person 74
functionality 210, 254
funding: of workplace learning 214
Furth, Hans 26, 205, 211
further qualification 225–7

Garrick, John 233
gender 17, 29, 50–2, 64, 178, 247; and youth 51
general learning theory: and transformative learning 190–1
generative themes 75
Gergen, Kenneth 67, 189
Germany 102, 219
Gestalt psychology 23, 102, 119
Giddens, Anthony 68, 80, 178, 190, 220
Goleman, Daniel 106
Gould, Roger 174, 185, 190
group work 120, 156, 161
Grundtvig, N.F.S.: 160

Habermas, Jürgen 105, 174, 185, 208
Hager, Paul 235, 246–7
Han, Soonghee 248, 250
Hannover University 24
Hay, David 180
Hegel, Georg W. F.: 167
Heron, John 105
Hodkinson, Phil 234
Horkheimer, Max 105
Hoy, Jane 170
human learning: basic features of 47–8
human resource development (HRD): 74, 81, 249
human resource management (HRM): 248–50
humanistic psychology 188
humour: as a strategy 142–3

identity 63–4, 79–80, 187–8, 206; in adults 137–8; concept of 41, 64–6, 80; defence 16, 150–1, 181; development 37, 52, 69–72, 228;

dissolution trends in 67–9; and learning problems 35–6; preoccupation with 57; problems 66–7; psycho-social 188–90; and transformative learning 176–8, 185–98; at work *see* work identity; in youth 57–73, 137–8, 178–9
implementation 93–4
incentive 21, 47–8, 205; dimension 11–13, 28, 210–11, 255
inclinations 59, 221
individuality 43, 65, 188, 194; qualifications 171–2
individuation 55
inflexibility 65
influence 126–8
information and communication technology (ICT): 210, 218, 236–8
insight 11, 31, 42, 48, 84–5, 92, 254; and competencies 182, 218, 246, 253; generalisation of 156; learning as 102, 107, 175
institutional practices: in adult education 139–41
instrumentalism: as a strategy 143
integration 211, 255
intellectual qualifications 171
intelligence 17, 29, 102; development of 186; superiority of 247
interaction 21; dimension 12, 28, 211; environment–learners 206; processes 10–11, 47, 58, 106
interdisciplinarity 158, 161
interest-based learning 114
International Consortium for Experiential Learning (ICEL): 169
interpretation 117–18
interpretive professional 95
introduction: to project work 156
intuition 192, 247
investigation phase: of projects 157
irony: as a strategy 142
irresponsibility 127

Jarvis, Peter 81, 106, 147, 180, 187
Jørgensen, Per Schultz 244–5
Judd, Charles 112
judgements 246–7

Kant, Immanuel 104, 167
Kasl, Elizabeth 185–6
Kegan, Robert 30, 81, 106, 176, 187, 190
Kernberg, Otto 66, 189
Kilpatrick, William 120
Kinchin, Ian 180
Kjærsgaard, Christian 226
knowledge 210; and transfer 118–19, 245; types of use 117–18
Knowles, Malcolm 75, 124, 170, 219

Kock, Henrik 252–4
Kohut, Heinz 66, 189
Kolb, David 25, 28, 104, 165, 169, 175–6

Langager, Søren 37
language of publication 1
Lasch, Christopher 177, 189
Lash, Scott 72
Lave, Jean 105, 121, 208, 219, 227, 234
law-of-effect 102
learner control 170
learning 165–73, 225–6; accidental 233; accommodative *see* accommodative learning; activity theory 119; adaptation-oriented 15; additive *see* assimilative learning; in adulthood 52–4, 61–2, 74–83, 124–34, 223–5; and age 29; approaches to education 3–4; assimilative *see* assimilative learning; barriers to *see* barriers to learning; basic issues on 204–16; Bloom's taxonomy of 42–3; in childhood 49–50, 61, 75–7; cognitive 7, 58, 101–18; collective 193–4; as competence development 210–11, 217, 255; in the competition state 33–44; comprehensive understanding of 9–20, *10*; concepts of 58–60, 204–16, 220; conditioned 102; content 92–3; control of 31; counter *see* counter-learning; critical 219; cumulative *see* cumulative learning; current adult theory 80–1; defence *see* defence; definition of 9, 75, 101; desire-based 224; development-oriented 15; dimensions of 10–*12*, 22, 27–8, 59, 106–7, 205, *207*, 210–11, 220–3, *221*, *see also* content dimension; emotional dimension; incentive dimension; interaction dimension; double loop 15, 104, 206, 239; and education 34, 41; electronic (e-): 236–8; emotional 58, *see also* emotional dimension; environment 235–6; everyday 114; exemplary 75; by expansion 108, 219; expansive *see* transformative learning; experiential 169, 175, 186; exploitation of 33; failure of 146–7; formal 234; four types of 13–15; goal-oriented 52–4; human 47–8; identity in 65, *see also* identity; incidental 233–4; as individual process 219–20; informal 233–5; institutionalised 62; interest-based 114; internal and external conditions 17–18, 204; jumps 28; and knowledge 118–19; levels of 220–3; and life course/phases 2, 48–50, 60–3; lifelong (lifedeep;

learning (*cont.*)
 lifewide) 47–56, 75, 202, 234; in mature adulthood 54–5; and measurement 31; mechanical *see* cumulative learning; methods of 28–9, 92–3; net-based 115; non-formal 234; organisational *see* organisational learning; participant responsibility for 90–1; practice 119–20; preconditions to 29; problems 35–6; processes of 10–12, *11*, *59*, *207*, 220–3, *221*; psychology 194–5, 211; quality 40–3; resistance *see* resistance; restructuring 48; school and educational 12–13, 114, 225; as a secondary matter 231–3; selective 76; self-directed 76; significant *see* transformative learning; single loop 15, 104, 206, 239; situated 105, 219; social dimension of 105, 219–20; society 112–23; spaces 28–9, 114–15; special issues 2–3; structure of 21, 29; styles 17; and sustainability 39–40; targeted 209–10; tension field of 12; theory of *see* learning theory; transcendent *see* transformative learning; transfer of 3, 18, 112–23; transformative *see* transformative learning; transitional *see* transformative learning; transitory 108; triangle 21, 27–8, 106, 205, 210–11, 254–6; types of 29, 48, 107–8, 115–17; understanding of 35; visible 42; in the workplace *see* workplace; workplace learning; in youth 50–2, 57–73
learning organisation 208–9, 213, 219; and organisational learning 238–40
learning society 213
learning theory 1–2, *10*, 21–32, 119–20; and workplace learning 217–30
Lefebvre, Henri 25, 180
Leithäuser, Thomas 24–5, 61, 67, 105, 109, 124, 149, 180, 223
Leontjev, Aleksei 81, 219
Lewin, Kurt 102, 104
liberation 55; from traditional ties 170
life course/phases: learning through 48–50, 60–3
life policy 224
life projects 79–80, 224
life-span theory 60
life story 67–8
life turn 54
lifelong learning 47–56, 75, 136, 213; lines of development in 55
Lindeman, Eduard 219
liquid modernity 80
location: of education 91–2
Lorenzer, Alfred 105

low-skilled learners: ambivalence of 86–7; identification of 85–6; investment in 96; problem of 84–5

McGill, Ian 169–70
Mager, Robert F.: 148
Malcolm, Janice 234
management: interests of 232, 235–6
Marcuse, Herbert 105
Marsick, Victoria 233
mass media 180; role in childhood 49–50
Matthew effect 74, 210
mature adulthood: definition of 49; inflexibility in 65; learning in 54–5
mature personality 74
meaning 103, 210, 254
measurement: and learning 31; and regulation 43
memory 59
mental–bodily balance 211, 255
mental defence 149, 151, *see also* defence
mental patterns 14, 221
mental resistance 17, 151, *see also* resistance
mental schemes 13, 116
mental strain 36–8, 250
Mezirow, Jack 28, 30, 75, 80–1, 104, 108, 174–5, 179–80, 182, 185–6, 188, 190–1, 193–4, 219, 254
mislearning 22, 25, 147–9
monitoring 93–4
Morsing, Mette 236
motivation 107, 137, 194–5, 225–6
motivational qualifications 171–2

Næss, Arne 101
narcissism 66–7, 177, 189
negativity: problem of 89
Negt, Oskar 24, 75, 105, 124, 160, 166–8, 208
net-based learning 115
new public management 192, 249
New Zealand, Early Childhood Education and Primary School Curriculum Framework 132
Newman, Michael 185–6
Nissen, Thomas 23–4, 107
non-consideration 147
non-learning 147

Olesen, Henning Salling 167
opportunities: need for 87–8; variation in 235
organisational learning 206, 209; and the learning organisation 238–40; theory 104
organisations: competence development in 252–3; promoting learning 219

Organization for Economic Cooperation and Development (OECD): 41, 77, 181, 192–3, 244, 249–50; and workplace learning 203
O'Sullivan, Edmund 175
outreach: by co-worker 88–9; need for 87–8
overloading 16

participants: direction 24, 120, 130, 156, 161; enabling responsibility of 90–1; prior experiences of 252; strategies by 141–3
passive aggression 151
passivity: as a strategy 141–2
patterns 59, 221
Pavlov, Ivan 102
pedagogy 75, 126; critical 124; and responsibility 128
perception qualifications 171
perfectionism: as a strategy 142–3
'the person': 187
personal development 58, 104–5, 165–73
personal qualities 26, 93; responsibility as 125–6
personality 187; development 170–1
Piaget, Jean 14–15, 23–4, 26, 62, 78, 81, 102–5, 107–8, 116, 119–20, 160, 186, 205, 220
placement 89–90
post-evaluation: of projects 157
postmodernism: and responsibility 131–2
potentials 245–6
power 94; distribution of 126–8; surrender of 90–1
practical planning: of projects 157
practice 253–4
Prætorius, Nadja 236
presumption 147
problem areas 169
problem formulation 157
problem orientation 24, 120, 156, 158, 161
product evaluation 157
professionalism 37
Programme for the International Assessment of Adult Competencies (PIAAC): 250
Programme for International Student Assessment (PISA): 42, 250
project work 120, 130–1, 158; challenges 161–4; concept of 156, 161; phases of 156–7; practice of 161; reactionary attitudes to 162; in university studies 159–64
proximal development zone 103
psycho-dynamic dimension 27
psycho-social identity 188–90
psychological problems 66–7

psychology: internal process of 10–11; learning 194–5; of lifelong learning 47–56
puberty 62–3, 66, 78, 178

qualification theory 24, 26, 125
qualifications 58, 243–4; basic 93, 226; categories of 171–2; concept of 212; further 225–7; generic 206; process independent 206; responsibility as 125–6

Rasmussen, Poul Nyrup 34
Reagan, Ronald 249
rebellion 62, 66
reflection 29, 104, 254
reflection-in-action 254
reflexive losers 72
reflexivity 190
rejection 147
remedial instruction 35, 37
replication 117
re-qualification 225–7
resistance 17, 22, 25, 27, 48–9, 62, 66, 79, 109; active and passive 151–2; and transformative learning 180–1
responsibility 55, 63–4, 125–8; in adult education 128–30; division of 90–1, 93; and postmodernism 131–2; as a qualification/personal quality 125–6; radical 126; social 126
retraining: and unemployment 19
Rogers, Alan 75
Rogers, Carl 23–4, 28, 104, 108, 119, 174, 177, 188–9, 219
Roskilde University: background of 155, 159–60; challenges 161–4; organisation of studies at 155–8; reactionary voices against 162; resources of 161–2; student attitudes and consciousness 162–3
Russia 219
Rychen, Dominique 192, 244

Salganik, Laura 192, 244
saturated self 67
Scandinavia 3, 114; competencies in 247; e-learning in 237; project work in 120
schemes 59, 221
Schön, Donald 15, 25, 81, 104, 206, 232, 238–9, 254
schools: and competence development 251–2; and educational learning 114; learning model in 12–13; returning to 77
school–workplace interaction 121–2
science-centred curriculum 103
search movements 179, 191
search processes 69–70

selection 61, 79
self 174, 187–8; involvement of 170
self-control qualifications 171
self-directed groups 209
self-identity 68
self-orientation 69–72; in youth 57–73
self-respect 87
Senge, Peter 208, 239
sensitivity 211, 255
separation 36–8
Shotter, John 67
significant learning 28, 104, 108, 119, 174–5, 188
skills 210; not in demand 86
Skinner, B.F. 102
social constructionism 67, 105
social learning 105
social qualifications 171
social-cultural learning environment 205
social-societal dimension 27, 58–9, 221
socialisation 58; sociological theories of 105
sociality 211, 255
society: changes in 202
soul 187
spaces: concept of 28–9, 114–15
Stern, Daniel 68, 191
stress 35, 38, 55; and competence 248, 250; and learning environment 236
structural understanding 246
structural unemployment 86–7
students: accepting responsibility by 129; attitudes and consciousness 162–3
subjective anchorage 95–6
sustainability: and learning 39–40
Svensson, Lennart 237

T-groups 102, 104
teachers: and adult learners 53–4; exercise of responsibility by 127, 129–30; self-interest of 203; task of 95
teaching: best practice 41–2; experiential learning approaches to 170
technical-organisational learning environment 205
Tennant, Mark 176, 188
Thatcher, Margaret 249
theme-horizon-schemes 149–50
themes 149; choice of 156–7; generative 75
theories-in-use 239
theory: development of 21–32
thinking: capacity development 63, 78
Thorndike, Edward Lee 102, 112
trade unions 26, 203
training: time, place and context of 91–2
transfer 112–23; four levels of 118

transformation 21, 108, 117–19
transformative (expansive; significant; transitional) learning 4, 15, 28, 30, 60, 75, 79–80, 104, 108, 117–19, 174–5, 219, 222; and age 191–2; collective or communal 179–80, 193–4; and competence development 181–2; concept and issue of 185–7; critique of 175–6; and defence 180–1; development of 195; and general learning theory 190–1; and identity 176–8, 185–98; kinds of 179; as a movement 186; new definition of 176; new developments in 178; re-definition of 187–8; regressive and restoring 193; and resistance 180–1; in youth 178–9
transitory learning 108
Tynell, Jesper 236

understanding 210
unemployed workers: links to workplace 93
unemployment: and retraining 19
United States of America (USA): 75, 103, 166, 189, 219, 249
university studies: project work in 159–64
unlived lives 135
usefulness: as a strategy 143
Usher, Robin 169

village concept 169–70
vocational training 26
Volmerg, Birgit 208
Volmerg, Ute 208, 235
Vygotsky, Lev 15, 81, 102–3, 105, 119, 208, 211, 219

wage labour 201
Watkins, Karen 233
Watson, John 102
Weil, Susan 169–70
welfare state 33
Wenger, Etienne 105, 121, 208, 219, 227, 234
Wildemeersch, Danny 126, 131, 169–70
Woodworth, Robert 112
work identity 206, 212
workers: retraining of 19; short-term 86; unmarketable 86–7; vulnerable 85–6
workplace: competence development in 252–3; e-learning in 237–8; incidental learning in 233–4; informal learning in 234–5; interaction with school 121–2, 201; as a learning framework 231–42, *see also* workplace learning; power structures of 232; practice 206

workplace learning 4–5, 114, *207*; approaches to 206–9; as competence development 243–57; double perspective on 206; funding of 214; general features 209–10; industrial sociological approach 206; learning organisation approach 208; and learning theory 217–30; management-anchored approach 206; model of 205–6; need for differentiated concept 228–9; reasons for 201–4; short-term narrowness of 204, 209; situated learning approach 208; situatedness of 231; social–individual interaction approach 208; targeted 209–10

World Bank 77, 249; and workplace learning 203

youth 63–4; basic qualification of 227–8; definition of 48–9; education of 18–19; identity and self-orientation in 57–73; learning in 50–2, 57–73, 178–9, 191–2

Ziehe, Thomas 24, 66, 69, 105, 124, 177, 179, 189, 191